MASTERING THE PUBLIC OPINION CHALLENGE

MASTERING THE PUBLIC OPINION CHALLENGE

Sherry Devereaux Ferguson

IRWIN
Professional Publishing
Burr Ridge, Illinois
New York, New York

Patrimoine canadien / Canadian Heritage

© RICHARD D. IRWIN INC., 1994

Sponsoring editor: Cynthia A. Zigmund
Project editor: Denise V. Santor
Production manager: Irene H. Sotiroff
Art manager: Kim Meriwether
Compositor: TCSystems, Inc.
Typeface: 10/12 Times Roman
Printer: Book Press, Inc.

Library of Congress Cataloging-in-Publication Data

Ferguson, Sherry Devereaux.
    Mastering the public opinion challenge   /   Sherry Devereaux
  Ferguson.
        p.   cm.
    Includes bibliographical references and index.
    ISBN 1-55623-811-8
    1. Communication in organizations.   2. Public relations-
  Corporations.   I. Title.
  HD30.3.F47   1994
  659.2'85—dc20   93–1269

Printed in the United States of America
1   2   3   4   5   6   7   8   9   0   BP   0   9   8   7   6   5   4   3

Dedicated to Eric, Alexandra, and Cameron

PREFACE

Mastering the Public Opinion Challenge looks at how companies and governments have been trying to take control of their issue environments, to meet the needs of their publics, and to survive and prosper in an information-rich environment.

Chapter 1 lays a foundation by discussing why organizations seek to control their information environments. The chapter explores the relationship among power, influence, and control of information. It further argues that relatively recent changes in the nature of information, in the media, in publics, and in organizational structures have placed increasing demands on organizations, threatening the old operational paradigms and creating new criteria for interaction between organizations and their constituencies. In an environment where information is portable, leaky, and diffusive; where communication reaches all levels of society at the same time; where the organization's publics expect to be consulted and informed; and where trends toward globalization and partnerships characterize all sectors of society (public, private, and voluntary), the old patterns of interaction are dysfunctional. It is not only inappropriate but also counterproductive for organizations to cling to outdated operating modes (e.g., seeking to contain and conceal information, engaging in unilateral decision making, and ignoring the potential for adversaries to become partners). As long as a significant number of governments and companies seek to sustain the belief that they can stand alone on a stage where a million strings make us all marionettes, none will realize the potential that exists in group scriptwriting.

Acquiring a sophisticated understanding of the public opinion environment, both domestic and global, means that organizations must engage in continuous learning. Chapter 2 explores some of the scanning, monitoring, and forecasting activities that characterize 20th-century organizations. The book describes intelligence systems that have been set in place in U.S. and Canadian organizations and argues for environmental analysis as the basis for planning for issues management. It also offers specific advice on how to set up systems. Results from recent unpublished surveys of major businesses and government organizations are discussed.

The book attempts to construct, from an eclectic literature, a theoretical basis for analyzing and managing issues. It draws together insights from different fields: business and public administration, communication, policy studies, marketing, and public relations. Chapter 3 follows in the spirit of books such as

James Brown's *This Business of Issues: Coping with the Company's Environments* to describe how organizations prioritize their issues, taking into account issue, stakeholder, and organization variables. Using a decision-tree approach, I propose strategic responses that are appropriate to issues of different priority levels.

Mastering the Public Opinion Challenge offers an expanded vocabulary for discussing issues management concepts, sufficiently broad that the terms and examples can be applied to public, private, and voluntary organizations. The fourth chapter of the book is concerned with framing relevant questions about the media's treatment of issues. Because of extensive experience in tracking issues in the media, I have developed a series of questions to be used as a springboard for engaging in media analysis. Sample analyses illustrate how these questions may be applied in typical situations.

There has been a tendency on the part of some writers in the issues management field to engage in proselytizing—espousing the merits of environmental analysis and planning for issues management—without moving beyond that point to develop guidelines for carrying out the functions. Chapters 5 through 8 offer practical advice to environmental analysts. An extended treatment of content analysis techniques in Chapter 5 demonstrates how this methodology can be adapted to the study of current issues. Chapter 6 describes why and how organizations engage in public opinion surveying, and Chapter 7 identifies some of the pitfalls of surveying. A discussion of focus group testing in Chapter 8 reveals how governments and corporations use this qualitative technique to acquire additional information on the public opinion environment. A large number of tables, charts, graphs, and sample analyses give practical help to those who are attempting to set up and maintain environmental intelligence systems.

Chapters 9 through 12 deal with the planning function in issues management systems. The chapters propose that planning for issues management should be a part of the strategic and operational planning cycles, integrated with the other corporate planning processes, not set apart. Chapter 9 introduces the reader to strategic planning, and Chapter 10 discusses operational planning for issues management. Work planning is discussed as a subset of operational planning. Specific planning formats are described, and sample strategic, operational, and work plans are included. Chapter 11 addresses limited-scope or single-purpose communication plans, the type that are developed to guide an organization through planning for specific events and single issues. Contingency planning for crisis management is discussed in Chapter 12.

The final chapter of the book, Chapter 13, seeks to identify what makes an issue more or less controllable and what governs an organization's decision to invest in controlling the issue. It also suggests criteria that must be met by organizations seeking to use the media for their own ends.

Organizations that set out to establish environmental intelligence and issue-planning systems find a dearth of materials to assist them. At present, only two or three courses in business intelligence are offered by U.S. universities, and no university has a management program devoted to the intelligence area. "Practitioner skills," it is said, are "usually derived from one-day seminars and the few textbooks that are available on the subject."[1] Surveys reveal that a large number of organizations are turning research and analysis functions over to public affairs and public relations units.[2] Yet, few communication managers are trained researchers, and they contract out much of this type of work.[3] Moreover, work on business intelligence in the existing literature either takes a piecemeal approach (e.g., public opinion theories, survey or focus group techniques, strategic planning, content analysis, or trend watching) or, alternatively, speaks in highly propositional terms, with *ex post facto* analysis of case studies. This book attempts to pull together these different areas of study, offering both a theoretical framework for understanding environmental intelligence concepts and practical guidelines for developing systems and practices. It also emphasizes opinion research. Furthermore, the materials have been market-tested and have undergone several revisions; they have been used in workshops taught to more than 500 Canadian government officers and middle and senior managers.

As issues management, both the research and the planning components, continues to develop into the 1990s as a field of study, there will be a heightened concern with integration of knowledge. The eventual merging of the business and public administration literature on environmental analysis and strategic and operational planning and the communication and political science literature on public opinion seems inevitable. Increasing stress on the research function in public relations further justifies the approach taken in this book. Also, development of this field requires serious efforts at organizing current insights. Moreover, these theories must be capable of being extended into practice, of being operationalized. There will be a need for a generic vocabulary to address the issues management function as it is practiced in both public and private sector organizations. This book, which draws heavily on my experiences in the issues management field, aims to contribute to such anticipated needs.

This book will be of interest to corporation and government executives, who want to know both how to establish environmental intelligence and planning systems and how to integrate the research and planning functions; directors of intelligence, research, and analysis and other planning and business units, who want to expand their existing systems and learn how to gain greater credibility with upper management; organization practitioners (public, private, and nonprofit sector), who are responsible for carrying out environmental analysis and planning for issues management; and consultants, who are asked to advise upper management on setting up intelligence and planning systems. Many of the practitioners will be based in public affairs, public relations, communication, marketing, and planning units in business, government, and nonprofit organizations. Because the book was motivated, in the first place, by a need to develop training materials, training consultants will find useful illustrations and approaches to teaching issues management concepts. This book recognizes research and analysis as the foundation for all strategic decisions made by the organization; it argues that those who choose to ignore the products of an information society do so at their own peril. The book will be of equal interest to students of communication and public relations, business administration, and public administration. Those engaged in the study of marketing research practices will find the book a useful complement to their studies.

I would like to express my appreciation to some of the people who made important contributions to this book—sometimes on a professional level and sometimes on a personal level (often a blend of both). I would like to thank my editor Cynthia Zigmund for her patience, support, and encouragement. Her suggestions were invaluable in helping me to achieve a final version of the book. I would also like to thank the other members of the Business One Irwin team, especially project editor Denise Santor and marketing manager Colleen Tuscher for their conscientious efforts.

I would like to acknowledge a number of professional relationships that were responsible for my initial interest in this research area. I am indebted to the Privy Council Office, Government of Canada, particularly those who formerly constituted the Communication Management Review group, for a grant that enabled me to conduct research in the area of environmental analysis and planning. Mary Gusella, Assistant Deputy Secretary of Communications, Privy Council Office of Canada, was the instigator of the research project; and Nicole Henderson suggested my involvement in the project. The Working Group on Public Environment Analysis served as a steering committee, offering useful advice in the early stages of my research. Individuals such as Alan Morgan, Claire Posen, David Davidson and Dawn Nicholson O'Brien contributed useful insights into the functioning of systems in government. Don Rennie, Peter Lantos, and Dennis Orchard deserve special note. Dennis led the Communication Management Review group at the initiation of the project and later Don took over. Peter acted as a liaison between our university project team and government. I learned much from my association with these individuals. My former research assistant and presently a communications officer with Employment and Immigration Canada, Ilona Koszegi, worked long and hard on the 1989 Privy Council project.

Within the university, I have appreciated the cooperation and support of my dean Carlos Bazán, my chairman Denis Bachand, Graduate School research administrators Gilles Morier and Jean Farrell, and my colleagues within the department. Natalie Lam of the Faculty of Business Administration worked with me in developing the sample strategic plan and the operational communication plans that appear in Chapter 9. Emma Cockerill assisted with proofing my original manuscript. Rollande Diotte, Lyse Piché, Diane LeBrun, and Francine Ducourneau (retired but not forgotten) have been generous with their time and friendship, and I have appreciated the many favors.

I want to thank my son Eric for the many hours that he contributed to this book. He is responsible for developing presentation formats for the numerous protocols, charts, and graphs. He generated the table of random numbers and the table to determine sample size; He also edited the more quantitative portions of Chapter 6. Above all else, Eric was always there when I needed help. My husband Stewart was also a valuable ally. In professional terms, he contributed a myth versus fact sheet to Chapter 4 and helped to create the content for the two print media and electronic media protocols in Chapter 4. The formats for operational and work planning that appear in Chapter 10 were inspired by earlier models that Stewart generated while working for the Solicitor General of Canada. On a personal level, I have appreciated his cheerful assumption of many of the day-to-day chores that I had to forfeit when working on the book—not an easy task since he was simultaneously building our new home!

On a strictly personal, but equally important level, I am grateful to my mother Maureen Devereaux; my sisters Barbara Champagne, Claire Smith, and Desirée Devereaux; my niece Ashley Smith; and my two daughters Alexandra and Cameron (as well as their many friends: Serge, Peter, Bruno, Ralna, Allyson, Pascale, Chris, Julic, Ron, Glen, Alexandra, Shawn, Christian, Cam, and others) for helping me to remember that there is more to life than working on books. Their laughter, shared confidences, friendships, and endless ringing of the telephone have relieved the tedium of long hours on the computer. Thanks, Leslie, for understanding why I had so little time when you came to visit.

Sherry Devereaux Ferguson

NOTES

1. Jan P. Herring, "Senior Management Must Champion Business Intelligence Programs," *Journal of Business Strategy*, September/October 1991, pp. 50–51.
2. Surveys conducted by Sherry Devereaux Ferguson in spring 1991 and spring 1992 with Fortune 500 companies, the Canadian government, and Canadian "top performers" in business.
3. David M. Dozier and Fred C. Repper, "Research Firms and Public Relations Practices," *Excellence in Public Relations and Communication Management*, ed. James E. Grunig (Hillsdale, N.J.: Lawrence Erlbaum Associates, Publishers, 1992), p. 185.

TABLE OF CONTENTS

CHAPTER 1

ORGANIZATIONS WITHOUT BOUNDARIES: SHARING AND PARTNERING

Organizations traditionally have sought to maintain tight control over their information environment. In the 1980s and 1990s, this task has become increasingly difficult for private, public, and voluntary sector organizations, largely as a consequence of changes in the nature of information, publics, and organizational structures. In many regards, the concept of control over information has become outdated, as boundaries have disappeared between organizations, their external environments and constituencies, and other organizations.

CHANGES IN THE NATURE OF INFORMATION

Information, the dominant resource in 20th-century society, has certain characteristics that influence its use. More than ever, as a consequence of the new media, it is expandable, portable, leaky, and shareable.[1]

Information expands as you use it; the more you use, the more you have. Whole industries have developed to exploit the potential for information to grow exponentially: publishing, computer software businesses, research, technology transfer, advertising, and public relations.[2]

Information is also highly portable. Contemporary technologies allow us to move information at close to the speed of light. Space and time barriers disappear with computer conferencing and teleconferencing. Laptop computers grow more sophisticated each year. We can store, retrieve, transmit, and take information with us wherever we go. Modems allow us to access information from our home offices and from our workplaces. Information is instantly reproducible on fax machines, photocopiers, and laser printers. Satellite signals carry information between states and countries, and laws to control these signals are unenforceable. Within this lifetime, many people will have witnessed live on television the assassinations of John Kennedy, Lee Harvey Oswald, and Robert Kennedy; public executions in Viet Nam and in China; and a war broadcast live

1

from Kuwait. Third World leaders complain that their task of governing is made increasingly difficult by the rising expectations that come with exposure to the lifestyle and products of industrialized Western societies.

Information is leaky, diffusive; it is difficult to hide, control, monopolize, or own. The grapevine is as active in organizations today as when it was first identified in the early 1950s;[3] efforts to control informal communication channels yield uneven results. A number of recent events have demonstrated the embarrassment that can come to corporate executives when conversations held over cellular telephones become common knowledge. Photocopiers make it possible to duplicate the most secret of documents in a span of seconds. Attempts to set up computer networks are often hampered by concerns that the networks can be accessed by unauthorized individuals or groups. In such an information environment, maintenance of privacy is almost impossible. The average citizen is stored—in bits and pieces, like a dismantled mannequin—in hundreds of data banks. The private lives of celebrities, corporation executives, and public officials are regularly strung out for public viewing. Everything from a hostage taking to the birth of a celebrity's child is exposed to the eye of the television camera. Organizations complain that they are under constant scrutiny.

As a consequence of leaks and freedom to information legislation, the innermost workings of 20th-century organizations have become daily grist for the media mills. In such circumstances, efforts to conduct private business and negotiate agreements have become increasingly difficult. International audiences become privy to acquisition negotiations and free trade deals as they unfold. Wars are conducted live, with step-by-step analysis by CNN reporters operating out of Sarajevo, Beirut, and Palestine. In the case of a terrorist attack on the Turkish Embassy in Ottawa, Canada, both the terrorists and the police watched the actions of the other side on television. Crisis management teams deal daily with the implications of this essentially laissez-faire uncontrolled media environment.

The leakiness of information also makes it difficult to own or monopolize, resulting in what has been termed "the nervous breakdown of copyright protection."[4] Better and faster means of piracy are being invented each day: new kinds of cable systems, satellite dishes, videotape machines, photocopiers, laser printers, and fax machines. Copyright and patent laws are unable to keep up with the new technologies. The situation is analogous to that of attempts to legislate against illicit drugs. As soon as one designer drug is outlawed, another version replaces it. In the case of copyright and patent laws, the situation is aggravated because the concept of ownership is itself obsolescent. The idea of intellectual ownership of ideas is increasingly detached from reality:

> That you or I can "own" a fact or an idea, that a message of any kind "belongs" to a person or a corporation or a government is . . . rather a peculiar notion to begin with. The person from whom you got the message didn't lose it; any right you acquire by receiving it is at best shared with the sender, the carrier, and often a good

many other nosy people who are privy to it. Even if you paid to get the message (if, for example, it was a piece of research you hired someone to do), or if someone paid to get it to you (a friend who sent you a cable, a company that sent you a commercial), it was the assembly or delivery service, not the information contained in the message, that was paid for. The researcher could not "own" the facts and ideas she or he strung together for your use, and neither can you even if you use them as your "own."[5]

Laws to protect books, phonograph records, and broadcasts are becoming ever more difficult to apply. An interesting new twist has also occurred. It is increasingly difficult for countries and corporations to assert ownership over resources of all types, tangible and intangible. For example, who owns the air waves that carry communication signals? Is it the country that generates the air waves or the country into whose space the air waves impinge? The eradication of boundaries crosses many spheres. When salmon swim from Vancouver Island to Washington State, who owns them? Can one country legislate quotas and expect the other country to take their nets out of the water as alien salmon swim by? If one country sets a limit on the number of fish that can be caught, but another country enters nearby waters and harvests the crop of fish, who is in the right?

In the same way, questions of ownership of information and intelligence are littering the court dockets, and recent controversies have erupted when companies have accused employees of taking corporate secrets with them when they transferred jobs. The owner of one U.S. pizza franchise, for example, sued a former executive for theft of corporate secrets. Owners of the pizza franchise alleged that the executive had taken knowledge of marketing techniques acquired during his tenure with the pizza firm and applied the knowledge to marketing his own chicken business, started after he left the pizza company. Another case involved a suit by a firm that lost five employees to a California competitor. The firm claimed that these employees took trade secrets with them when they left to join the new firm. Management claimed the California firm hired the employees because they had acquired certain skills and information in the performance of their previous job. The employees, on the other hand, asserted that they had the right to apply knowledge and skills gained in one job to future employment opportunities. Several former GM employees, now with Volkswagen, are facing similar charges. The question then becomes: Who owns knowledge once it has become an integral part of an individual's storehouse of experience? The question is a difficult one to answer, with philosophical as well as legal dimensions.

Policies based on the idea that knowledge can be owned are in "maximum disarray": "every newly miniaturized recording or micrographic device, and every new satellite launched for communication or photography or remote sensing make it more difficult to sustain the doctrine that national governments [or corporations] can own, or control, their information resources".[6] So it is that we share information, rather than exchange it.

CHANGES IN THE NATURE OF PUBLICS

With the increase in information networking and communication flow within and between organizations and their publics, stakeholders and constituencies are showing new patterns of involvement. In the 1992 U.S. election, voter turnout for the contest between Bush, Clinton, and Perot was unexpectedly large. In Canada, in 1992, unprecedented numbers of people (about 75% of eligible voters) went to the polls to vote down a national referendum issue. The environmental movement has benefited from an expanding percentage of the population who are sensitized to, and ready to speak out on, issues such as the seal hunt, depletion of the ozone layer, and toxic waste disposal. The abortion issue has polarized the U.S. population to an extent never before believed possible, and all levels of government—national, state, and municipal—complain that they are judged on single issues. Corporations have had to get their houses in order, as shareholders mobilize campaigns to capture the organization's agenda;[7] sometimes the corporate response has been to create special business units to deal with these issues.

CHANGES IN ORGANIZATIONAL STRUCTURES

Loss of control of information can also be tied to trends toward globalization. With globalization, transactions of organizations are extended across space and time, resulting in an inability to maintain the same kind of confidentiality that is possible in domestic situations. Different cultural norms may also exert pressure on the organization to focus on collective over individual goals or on cooperation over competition. The European business culture is said to be, for example, more amenable to cooperative ventures than to acquisitions.[8] In such an environment, secrecy systems and "cocooning" practices—the tendency of organizations to create a protective shield around themselves and to be inner rather than outer directed—may be viewed negatively.

Other structural factors that affect the ability of organizations to control their information environments include an increasing emphasis on horizontal networking, partnerships, and alliances. A growing number of organizations are substituting horizontal networks (e.g., technology-sharing networks, ownership networks, and development networks) for vertical hierarchies. Multifunctional work teams and partnerships that involve customers, suppliers, and even competitors are becoming commonplace in leading-edge organizations. A number of firms are finding that alliances with customers are more dependable than open market transactions.[9] Other firms such as McDonald's treat franchisees as alliance partners.[10]

Examples of alliances with competitors can be found in the soft drink, automobile manufacturing, semiconductor, and women's magazine industries.[11] In the workstation business, Digital has paired off with MIPS Computer of Sunnyvale, California, to produce leading-edge microprocessors, and it has worked with Tandy to manufacture personal computers. In the automobile industry, Mitsubishi-Daimler has partnered with Benz. The Big Three U.S. manufacturers have well-established supply alliances with their Japanese counterparts: GM with Isuzu, Ford with Mazda and Nissan, and Chrysler with Mitsubishi.[12] Air France and Lufthansa are cooperating in areas such as cargo handling, pilot training, marketing, and acquisitions; they are also seeking to establish a global network that includes JAL and Global. Other cooperative ventures have involved Westdeutsche Landesbank of Germany and Standard Chartered Bank of Britain. Airbus, one of Boeing's major competitors, is a "consortium of West German, French, British, and Spanish businesses".[13] The most powerful firms in every sector are those who have learned how to use alliances successfully (e.g., Merck and Glaxo in pharmaceuticals and Motorola and Northern Telecom in telecommunications).

Other firms are creating opportunities for extensive vendor involvement.[14] The collaborative relationships that are being forged between customer firms and suppliers often involve extensive social, economic, service, and technical linkages.[15] Firms such as the German automotive parts manufacturer Robert Bosch work to build long-term relationships with key subcontractors. Nippon Telephone and Telegraph has involved dozens of firms in joint research efforts. IBM alliances include Japanese firms commissioned to help complete its product line, Seiko Epson to produce parts for its Proprinter, and Canon to manufacture the color printer that is used in many of IBM's desktop publishing and printing systems.[16] Silicone Valley computer makers are employing the same approach, working with microprocessor makers from the beginning stages of projects. Many major firms see themselves as a "web of subcontractors".[17] At the same time that organizations are building stronger associative relations with suppliers, they are being more selective in their choice of suppliers. Some estimates suggest that U.S. companies have cut back on the number of suppliers they use by as much as 90 percent, demanding higher-quality service and products from those they do select.[18] Motorola has some 320 supply alliances in its communication sector, and it picks suppliers on the basis of corporate values, not on the basis of price, product design, or other attributes.[19] Many firms are seeking longer-term relationships with both suppliers and employees.[20]

At the same time, companies are going, more and more often, outside their organizational boundaries to get specialized expertise, to add people during peak periods, and to obtain fresh viewpoints. Alliance partners, consultants, third-party contractors, and freelance firms complement the internal resources of organizations.[21] All of the above efforts represent a trend toward creating organizations without boundaries. General Electric's CEO Jack Welch wrote in his often quoted *1990 Annual Report*, "Our dream in the 1990s is a boundaryless company . . . where we knock down the walls that separate us from each other on the inside and from our key constituencies on the outside."[22]

One of the best examples to illustrate the concept of the "boundaryless" organization is Galoob Toys, a San Francisco firm that employs 115 people. Its business is one of relationships: "It farms out manufacturing and packaging to a dozen contractors, uses outside distributors without ever taking delivery from the manufacturers, and sells its accounts receivables to a manufacturing company."[23] In much the same way, General Motors is said to have "virtually eliminated" boundaries between itself and its suppliers (although the suppliers remain legal entities). GM's requirement that suppliers link their computers to its own in order to have the minimum of paper transactions has provoked some suppliers to claim that GM is now running the operation. Boundaries become unclear when responsibilities are unclear: For example, in the case of GM, who "owns the transactions" and who has the right to use resulting data and knowledge?

Such transactional processes also alter the concept of "organization." At one time, an organization was defined as the place where communications are most concentrated (e.g., within the confines of a building or a plant).[24] This sort of distinction no longer applies. The travel agent who books hotels, car rentals, insurance policies, and sightseeing tours for customers interacts far more frequently with employees of other organizations and with customers than with his or her own organization. As in the case of GM's suppliers, the travel agency is a "meta-business," a "quasi-firm created by electronic linkages between organizations that so tightly couple participants' operations that it is impossible to say where the boundary of one firm ends and the boundary of another begins."[25] Some companies, by choice, make "nothing"; companies such as MCI are best defined as "networks."[26] Former Berkeley Business School Dean Ray Miles speculated that, if this trend continues, we could soon have switchboards instead of corporations.[27] This concept of organization differs greatly from the traditional idea.

Cross-industry linkages are growing in popularity: "Digital information technologies are consolidating once-disparate industries and making them more related, as computer chips, microprocessors, and fiber optics are now found in consumer electronics, office equipment, cars, and appliances."[28] Hitachi Construction Machineries (HCM) has formed strategic alliances with FiatGeotech and with John Deere and Company. In 1987, Fiat-Hitachi Excavations joined together to manufacture and market a new line of hydraulic excavators targeted for the European market. HCM joined with John Deere to supply the U.S. market with hydraulic excavators. Other strategic alliances have been formed between Hewlett-Packard and Yokogawa Electric Company.[29] General Motors has invited managers and engineers from PPG to oversee its hourly workers at a Buick paint shop.[30]

Investment in technology fusion research will necessitate greater numbers of partnerships and joint ventures. *Technology fusion research* refers to research that builds on present knowledge and combines existing technologies to serve new purposes. Whereas "breakthrough" approaches are linear in nature (e.g., the electric light bulb replaced the oil lamp, and the word processor replaced the typewriter), technology fusion is "nonlinear, complementary, and cooperative."[31] Adding one technology to another enables the researcher to come up with a solution that is greater than the individual parts. Such collective research is becoming increasingly common in Japan; major proponents include Fanuc, Nissan, NEC, Sharp, and Toray. In 1988, for example, there were 27 instances of collective research in the computer manufacturing area; yet each research venture engaged only one of the five major rival computer makers (Toshiba, Fujitsu, Mitsubishi, NEC, or Hitachi). In another 27 cases, research ventures engaged only one of five major steel companies. There were 11 cases of research that involved only one of the three dominant textile companies.[32] Successful technology fusion grows out of long-term cooperative efforts involving a variety of companies across many different industries.

Large numbers of partnerships increasingly are being formed between business and government to deal with concerns that span the public and private sector:[33] for example, drugs in the workplace, housing for seniors, environmental programs, and products and services for disabled individuals. Research partnerships are also being formed that involve business, industry, government, and universities. Three dozen U.S. firms joined to create the Semiconductor Research Corporation; this corporation sponsors more than half of all U.S. university research into computer chips of the future.[34] Environment Canada has cultivated hundreds of partnerships with private sector firms, activist groups, labor, industry, volunteer organizations, and provincial and local governments.[35] For an alliance to work, organizations must have mutual objectives and complementary needs; they must be willing to share risks.[36] Cooperation rather than competition is at the foundation of successful alliances.

CONCLUSIONS

The old approaches to controlling and owning information no longer apply; the best way to compete may be to understand and work with your many constituencies (competitors, clients, customers, suppliers, all levels of government, and other stakeholders). Information increasingly has become a shared commodity, leaky and difficult to contain; organizations that fail to make the adjustment to this new sharing environment face the possibility of extinction, or in the case of government, rejection. The largest number of progressive organizations are deciding that "cocooning" is an inappropriate response to the demands of a global information society.

Terms such as *strategic alliances, joint ventures, partnerships, boundaryless* and *borderless organizations* pepper the current organizational literature. These terms imply new strategic and operational approaches to dealing with a dramatically changed information environment. Whereas organizations once preserved their place among competitors by guarding information and following a policy of containment, many now attain their competitive edge by sharing and partnering with competitors, suppliers, customers, research organizations, universities, and all levels of government. Governments, in the same way, are forming partnerships with business, industry, not-for-profit organizations, and interest groups to tackle the most pressing issues of the century: the environment, drugs, the aging population, and many other concerns. Computer networking and videoconferencing are creating further opportunities for sharing that neither public nor private sector organizations can ignore.

The most forward-looking organizations are making unprecedented efforts to tear down the walls that once separated "insiders" from "outsiders." Customers and vendors are being pulled into the "inner sanctum" of the organization:[37]

> The new fleet-of-foot, opportunistic organization will have no "outsiders"—people (customers, vendors) who aren't allowed to walk the hall without being "badged," . . . without access to the organization's innermost secrets. "Outsiders" must become "insiders" post haste, if we are to achieve the fast-paced innovation aims that are requisite for survival in any industry today. Customers and vendors (and franchisees, reps, etc.) must routinely be "discovered" walking "our" halls, acting as part-time or full-time members on "our" teams and assessing anything from logistics to new products.[38]

There appears to be an emerging political approach to governing organizations and managing organizational issues, a response to a discredited corporate America: "Wall Street for its greed, managers for their sloth, and raiders for what is perceived as a predatory search for assets and callous disregard for the social costs of their transactions."[39] A political approach to governance takes into account the views of all constituencies—shareholders and investors, employees, customers, community activists, and others—and encourages an open debate of alternatives. Through a democratic, decentralized process, a variety of groups can press their point of view and receive a hearing: "It is a political solution to what has become a political problem."[40] It is the means by which the corporate world may be able to regain its credibility and demonstrate accountability to an increasingly diverse group of stakeholders.

The new consultative organizations will be forced to look to many different sources to stay up-to-date on rapidly evolving technologies and to access the fast-amassing knowledge base that characterizes modern information societies. They will also need to establish systems that will allow them to assess the needs, attitudes, and wants of stakeholders who refuse to be excluded from the innermost workings of industry and government. Subsequent chapters in the book will suggest some specific means by which organizations can establish systems to enable them to gather, process, and stockpile, on an ongoing basis, this type of information.

NOTES

1. Harlan Cleveland, "The Twilight of Hierarchy: Speculations on the Global Information Society," *Public Administration Review*, January/February 1985, pp. 185–195.
2. Cleveland, p. 186.
3. Keith Davis, "Management Communication and the Grapevine," *Harvard Business Review*, September/October 1953, pp. 43–49. This article is an *HBR* classic.
4. Cleveland, p. 191.
5. Ibid.
6. Cleveland, p. 192.
7. John Pound, "Beyond Takeovers: Politics Comes to Corporate Control," *Harvard Business Review*, March/April 1992, pp. 83–93.
8. Robert Porter Lynch, "Building Alliances to Penetrate European Markets," *Journal of Business Strategy*, January/February 1990, p. 7.
9. William Copulsky, "Balancing the Needs of Customers and Shareholders," *Journal of Business Strategy*, November/December 1991, p. 46.
10. Jordan D. Lewis, "The New Power of Strategic Alliances," *Planning Review*, September/October 1992, pp. 45–46.
11. Jordan D. Lewis, "Using Alliances to Build Market Power," *Planning Review*, September/October 1990, p. 6.
12. Joel D. Goldhar and David Lei, "The Shape of Twenty-first Century Global Manufacturing," *Journal of Business Strategy*, March/April 1991, p. 39.
13. Lynch, p. 4.
14. Tom Peters, "Part One: Get Innovative or Get Dead," *California Management Review*, Fall 1990, p. 16.
15. James C. Anderson and James A. Narus, "Partnering as a Focused Market Strategy," *California Management Review*, Spring 1991, p. 96. See also Joseph P. Aleo, Jr. "Redefining the Manufacturer-Supplier Relationship," *Business Strategy*, September/October 1992, pp. 10–14.
16. Goldhar and Lei, p. 39.
17. Peters, "Part One," pp. 13 and 16.
18. J. Enshwiler, "Suppliers Struggle to Improve Quality as Big Firms Slash Their Vendor Rolls," *The Wall Street Journal*, August 18, 1991, p. B1.
19. Lewis, "The New Power of Strategic Alliances," p. 46.
20. Copulsky, p. 46.
21. Frank K. Sonnenberg, "Partnering: Entering the Age of Cooperation," *Journal of Business Strategy*, May/June 1992, p. 49.
22. Quoted in Larry Hirschhorn and Thomas Gilmore, "The New Boundaries of the 'Boundaryless' Company," *Harvard Business Review*, May/June 1992, p. 104.
23. Peter G. W. Keen, "Redesigning the Organization through Information Technology," *Planning Review*, May/June 1991, p. 6.

24. Sherry Devereaux Ferguson and Stewart Ferguson, *Organizational Communication,* 2nd ed. (New Brunswick, N.J.: Transaction Books, 1988), p. 45.
25. Ibid.
26. Peters, "Part One," p. 13.
27. Quoted in Keen, p. 6.
28. Goldhar and Lei, p. 37.
29. Peter Lorange and Johan Roos, "Why Some Strategic Alliances Succeed and Others Fail," *Journal of Business Strategy,* January/February 1991, pp. 25–26.
30. Peters, "Part One," p. 14.
31. Fumio Kodama, "Technology, Fusion, and the New R & D," *Harvard Business Review,* July/August 1992, p. 70.
32. Ibid., pp. 70–78.
33. Barry Z. Pozner and Warren H. Schmidt, *California Management Review,* Spring 1992, pp. 84–85.
34. Lewis, "Using Alliances to Build Market Power," p. 6.
35. Transition Team Steering Committee on Consultations and Partnerships, Environment Canada, *Consultations and Partnerships: Working Together with Canadians (EC in Transition),* Ottawa, Ontario, June 12, 1992.
36. Lewis, "The New Power of Strategic Alliances," p. 45.
37. Peters, "Part One," p. 16.
38. Peters, "Part One," p. 25.
39. Pound, p. 92.
40. Ibid.

CHAPTER 2

CREATING ENVIRONMENTAL INTELLIGENCE SYSTEMS: SCANNING, MONITORING, AND FORECASTING

It has been observed that we are moving from a " 'pre-Copernican' business world, where the individual company is at the center of the universe, to a far more fluid 'post-Copernican' business environment, where each company is but one point in an extended network of equals."[1] In a world of equals, the opinions of all groups count, and what happens to one group has an impact on others in the network. In order to function and prosper in such an environment of interdependencies, organizations must acquire a more sophisticated understanding of the other network members (e.g., the driving forces behind their actions, the demands of their constituencies, and the results of other social, economic, political, and technological influences).

Moreover, as North American organizations turn more frequently to cooperative alliances and partnerships with network members, they will need to generate a different kind of organizational culture. This culture will place an increased stress on long-term rather than short-term planning and on continuous learning processes.[2] As group decisions become the norm, strategic planning will assume a new level of importance. Empowered groups expect to participate in decision making, and participation implies the need to articulate shared goals and to establish accepted means for reaching those goals. Well-articulated mission and mandate statements ensure that everyone knows where the organization is going; operational decisions follow logically from these strategic choices.

Environmental analysis is the starting point for strategic planning. A well-informed organization has the best chance of making intelligent strategic and operational decisions and of managing its issues. Industrial globalization potential, for example, depends on factors such as markets, government regulations, and competition, all of which may be monitored and analyzed.[3] Whether private or public sector, profit or not-for-profit, all varieties of organizations are becoming increasingly dependent on forces in their external environment: media, interest groups, governments, and other institutionalized actors. Systems theory tells us that every part of an organization must understand the functioning of its other parts. If suppliers, vendors, customers, and even competitors are to become fully functional partners, the organization must make every effort to understand each perspective and to take it into account in decision-making processes. As organizations become increasingly customer centered or client centered, an emphasis that is now a well-established trend, this understanding becomes critical.

As noted in Chapter 1, some are suggesting that firms should be pulling clients and vendors into the inner sanctums of the organization, involving them in the organization's most important decisions. The businesses that are thriving today are listening closely to their customers, seeking to anticipate their needs. Steve Jobs and Ted Turner are said to be on a "special wave length" with their customers.[4]

One of the 200 best small companies, Paychex, expanded its business into the profitable tax payment area, largely as a consequence of listening to what customers were saying.[5] Globalization increases the range of customer choices, and to compete successfully, companies must move from "thinking like producers to thinking like customers".[6] After all, products are "nothing more than a tangible means for getting a service performed"; they derive their meaning solely from the uses to which customers put them.[7] In a comparative survey of American, German, and Japanese organizations, it was found that 82 percent of the Germans, 65 percent of the Americans, and 42 percent of the Japanese confirmed executive contact with customers.[8] The Japanese, however, are said to be zealots when it comes to involving customers in product conceptualization.[9]

The publics to which organizations must respond become more and more diverse and numerous in an information society. The linkages that connect groups and individuals are extensive. Even in the 1980s, surveys indicated that CEOs of many large companies were spending as much as 40 percent or 50 percent of their time obtaining information from, and interacting with, the external environment.[10] This trend has progressed decidedly since that time. A recognition of the need to become more customer centered (or client centered) and more responsive to the broad range of its constituencies (vendors, competitors, shareholders, employees, customers, and others) is leading organizations to institutionalize opportunities for continuous learning.

WHAT IS THE PURPOSE OF ENVIRONMENTAL INTELLIGENCE SYSTEMS?

Some of the most prestigious financial institutions and real estate developers in North America—Citibank, First Boston, Paine Webber, the Bank of Montreal, Dillon Read, Prudential, Olympia and York, and the DeBartolo Corporation—

invested close to $10 billion between 1986 and 1988 in the ventures of real estate developer Robert Campeau. During this period, Campeau acquired Allied and Federated Stores. A year later, the Campeau empire collapsed, leaving lenders with billions in uncollected debts.[11] Events such as these have given fuel to the argument that a fully dedicated intelligence support system for senior management does not constitute a luxury, but a necessity.[12]

According to the business press, no one should have been surprised by the misfortunes of Campeau. Signs of the problem were present for those who chose to look: the eccentric behavior of Campeau, the objections raised by Allied's CEO in 1988 to acquisition negotiations, and the financial problems of Allied in the postacquisition period. Other sectors also offer examples of such myopia, including classic cases from the U.S. automobile industry. In the 1990s, the U.S. automobile industry not only failed to perceive changing consumer preferences, but it also failed to identify the growing threat posed by foreign manufacturers of small cars. For years, Coca-Cola attached credibility to the Pepsi taste tests, making unnecessary changes to its own product. And the most telling statistic of all is that, since 1979, 40 percent of Fortune 500 companies have been dropped from this list.[13]

Much of what organizations need to know can be readily located by consulting the media, internal stakeholders (employees, managers, boundary spanners), the general public, and other groups and individuals. Businesses study media trends to predict public response to new products and services, to understand customer needs, and to monitor technological developments. Governments, in the same way, commission studies to identify relevant characteristics of the opinion climate into which a new policy will enter or attempt to anticipate responses to new legislation. They analyze correspondence from experts to determine potential problem areas in policies and legislation. Large corporations track shifts in government policies in order to identify threats and opportunities. Once a campaign to inform or persuade is in place, the sponsoring organization may choose to track the extent to which the media picked up and transmitted the organization's preferred messages.

By seeking to understand the background and implications of issues and by projecting scenarios related to their potential development, the organization creates a framework for issues management and crisis management. Through scanning and monitoring, the firm acquires information that will enable it to interact in positive ways with customers, competitors, vendors, and other stakeholders. The continuous-learning organization strives to stay abreast of the latest political, economic, technological, and social developments. On the basis of its acquired intelligence, the corporation or the government department can decide upon the most appropriate partners for joint ventures. Firms can also gather the necessary information to engage successfully in fusion technology research (discussed in more detail in the previous chapter and later in this chapter). They can monitor the health of the organizations on which they depend for critical resources, examining both economic and political risk factors. In a continuous-learning environment, detailed and updated information is made available to everyone in the organization, as well as to external stakeholders.[14] In learning models, change grows out of an exploration of alternatives,[15] resulting in organizations that can "design, produce, and innovate faster than ever before."[16]

Environmental intelligence systems attempt to pick up signals (sometimes "weak" signals) from the larger environment, to analyze the signals' significance for the organization, to track the most relevant of these signals, and to forecast the signals' development.[17] Few changes in the environment occur spontaneously. They start as ideas. These ideas eventually obtain public expression in the press, radio, television, university conferences, and scientific journals. Scanning involves a process of picking up early hints of change from these various media or other sources.[18] The purpose of environmental scanning is "not to foretell accurately the future but to plot the issues which are likely to have an impact on the company and be prepared to cope with them when they arise."[19] For example, many single-issue groups are forming that will be influential several years from now. Divorced fathers, the elderly, euthanasia groups, and societies against reproductive technology have relatively little influence at present. By 1999, these groups may be powerful lobbies. If these groups persist, as is likely, and continue to garner support, their issues may well become national priority items at some future date. Scanning systems center on identifying these issues at an early stage in their development. It is said that had governments recognized the burgeoning of environmental groups 10 years ago, they would be better prepared to answer the demands of these groups today.

Studies indicate that it often takes as much as 8 to 15 years for a need or an idea to become law. Five steps intervene between the seeding of the idea and the passing of legislation: developing membership support, seeking media attention, gaining prominent endorsements, obtaining a government study or investigation, and introducing the idea to the legislative process.[20] Scanning and monitoring teams can aid in tracking ideas from their seeding to their final development. The term *scanning* refers to the picking up of *new* signals from the environment (e.g., identifying emerging trends and shifts in trends). Early identification of issues generates opportunities for organizations to deal with their issues in a proactive way.[21] *Monitoring* refers to tracking previously identified trends. Using the analogy of radar, scanning is said to involve broad sweeps of the early warning radar, whereas monitoring involves a telescopic examination of what has been spotted on radar.[22] Although scanning is more oriented toward the future,[23] monitoring is more oriented toward the present. Scanning and monitoring activities can be carried out in an irregular, periodic, or continuous way.[24]

Irregular systems are reactive; these systems respond to environmentally created crises. Focusing on specific short-term problems, they pay little attention to identifying and evaluating future environmental trends and events. Environmental analyses carried out in irregular systems are often of an ad hoc nature, responding to some immediate situation. These analyses tend to be retrospective in nature, making them most useful for tactical rather than strategic planning. Organizations using these systems often lack strategic planning cultures.

Periodic (or *regular*) systems differ in degree, rather than in kind, from irregular systems. They tend to focus on the current situation and to draw on the past. Participants in these scanning and monitoring systems carry out annual or regular reviews of the environment. They attempt to identify current issues and to delineate alternative choices of action. In this sense, periodic systems do have a proactive element: they anticipate the near future.

Continuous systems differ from both irregular and periodic systems. Their focus is broad. They may shift from identifying possible problem areas in the environment to locating opportunities. Continuous systems draw on experts with eclectic backgrounds. Analysts monitor many different environments, including political, regulatory, and competitive; they do not restrict themselves to monitoring specific events. In other words, the approach is systems oriented. In a continuous system, the time span brought into consideration may vary from long to futuristic. Whereas issue management teams often restrict themselves to issues likely to mature during the next 18 to 36 months, those working in continuous systems may extend this focus to five or more years.[25]

This chapter describes some of the systems currently in place in organizations.

DIFFERENT APPROACHES TO ORGANIZING THE ENVIRONMENTAL INTELLIGENCE FUNCTION

A 1992 survey of Fortune 500 companies found that 5 out of 15 respondents reported the presence of a continuous scanning and monitoring system, 8 reported a periodic system, and 2 said that they had an irregular operation.[26] Other observers also confirm that many Fortune 500 companies have established intelligence departments to gain competitor or marketplace intelligence. "Much of corporate America," they say, "has accepted the concept of competitor or business intelligence."[27] These results suggest a potential change from 1988, when a Conference Board survey found only 3 percent of U.S. corporations had "fully developed competitive intelligence systems; almost two thirds had either no system at all or only very loosely defined operations."[28] Many of the earliest systems that were established ended up as "libraries or information desks for line management and middle management."[29]

Most experts agree that scanning and monitoring systems should be continuous and should not operate in spurts. "Data is like a shooting star: visible one moment, invisible the next. Corporations cannot assume that the competitor is going to reveal his hand during the strategic planning cycle, when an intensive research effort takes place."[30] In organizations without an established intelligence function, the information needs of top management and the governing coalition are the most frequently ignored. In many such organizations, executives convene on an ad hoc basis to consider the company's strategic issues. They are left to collect and analyze the information that is readily available to them on short notice, including personal sources, departmental information, and a limited amount of external data. The quality of the executives' contacts and research and analytical skills ultimately determines the success of the meeting.[31] Yet time is necessary to collect and assimilate information. Specialized skills are required to collect and collate intelligence.[32] Intelligence programs can take three to five years to mature: Networks of contacts must be developed, adequate filing systems and databases must be established, and staff analysts must develop the skills to carry out the function. Those in charge of the operations must have time to build credibility.

Formal intelligence-gathering systems vary greatly from organization to organization and even within the same industry. Some systems include networks of offices around the world that monitor patent applications; others engage in extensive reading of published materials; still others establish tracking systems to identify innovative companies and technologists. Informal intelligence-gathering operations often call on managers, employees, and research assistants to gather and disseminate information. The Japanese rely extensively on the latter approach.[33]

Organizations have taken different approaches to setting up the intelligence function. In some cases, the intelligence function is housed in marketing. In other situations, competitive analysts are attached to public relations units. In more ideal circumstances, organizations have created specialized research units, with staff functions, to support line management in researching and analyzing the company's issues. In such a situation, the research unit may have a standing equal to human resources, marketing, finance, and other support functions. This specialized unit gathers and analyzes environmental intelligence and later uses the information in planning. Analysts produce reports that deal, for example, with "general economics, customer behavior, competitor behavior, the legal and regulatory climate, environmental issues, national and international political developments (to the extent that they provide business opportunities and threats), and technological trends."[34] Some units create libraries to organize and store the products of their research (e.g., survey and focus-group results, trend reports, media analyses, competitor profiles, market data, special studies, and database directories).

In a stable business environment, analysis of the environment is tolerably straightforward. The organization knows its competitors and recognizes who controls what share of the market. In an unstable environment, new competitors appear frequently, old competitors change their behavior, "invisible" enemies materialize as the technology changes, and market share fluctuates. As the research and analysis function becomes more important, managers have less time to carry out the function. In this type of environment, a business unit that is dedicated to research and analysis makes sense.[35] Members of the research staff identify the issues, define strategic options, and evaluate the alternatives available to management.[36] Some organizations have more than one research and analysis unit. In these instances, the unit typically reports to and supports the corporate vice president or the general manager of the business unit. In 1984, for example, the CEO of McDonnell Douglas Corporation directed each of his company's major components to establish an independent competitive intelligence function.[37]

The size of research units will vary, according to the size of the corporation and the scope of the unit's mandate. In many companies, two or three people will carry out the function. In large corporations, a staff of 12 or more analysts may be required. Some functions are contracted out. As Figure 2.1 indicates, Fortune 500 companies said that their scanners are most commonly found in the public affairs or public relations areas, followed by specialized business research units, planning, personnel, legal, executive, finance, policy, service, and clerical/administrative areas.

In 14 out of 15 companies, the public affairs or public relations divisions were responsible for the monitoring function. Research, planning, and personnel units were mentioned by more than half the respondents, and six companies

FIGURE 2.1
Location of Scanners within the Organization

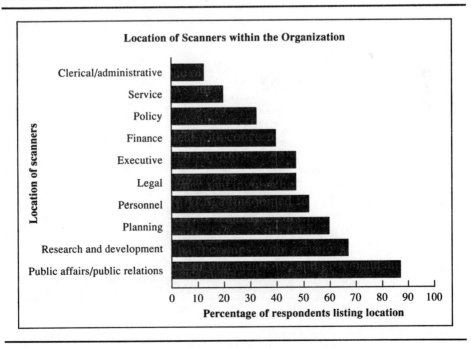

listed sales and marketing areas. Executive, finance, policy, and legal departments came next. Areas that received little mention were service, clerical or
administrative, and programs[38] (see Figure 2.2). In some situations, more than
one unit (e.g., legal, finance, and marketing) cooperated on environmental
analysis tasks.[39] In some government departments, both policy and communication personnel contributed to analyses of organizational issues.

Whether the research function is carried out in a public affairs unit or a
dedicated business unit, most companies agree that the support of upper management is critical to establishing the viability of the unit. Furthermore, experts
agree that there must be broad-based management use and cultural acceptance
of the function.[40] Some research units say that they have an initial credibility
problem of getting decision makers to accept and use their research products.[41]
Part of the problem may be that in a newly established research unit, analysts
tend to summarize rather than analyze their data. As analytical products become more sophisticated, management becomes more dependent on the research and analysis unit.

FIGURE 2.2
Location of Monitoring Function

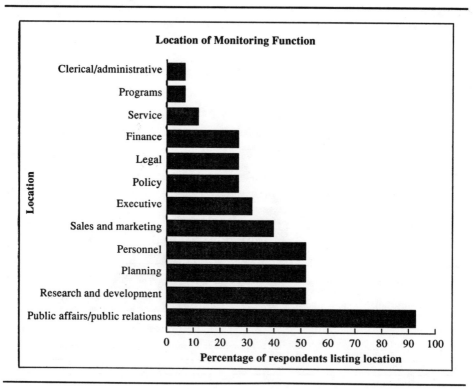

Some organizations use scientific advisory committees (SACs) to advise senior management on the direction of technological change. Academics and/or scientists, who make up the committees, have links to the external scientific community. SACs usually meet on a quarterly or semiannual basis to review the organization's position regarding new technologies. General Motors, for example, set up an SAC in the early 1970s that reports to a GM executive committee. Its membership consists of a rotating group of scientific experts from academic and private institutions. SACs are not widely used. A study of 13 Fortune 500 firms, for example, found that only 2 used an SAC made up of outside consultants. A few multinational firms have adapted the concept and substituted their own organizational members for outsiders on such committees. Some organizations fear that the outsiders may leak information or betray confidences, but companies that employ SACs say that the members of SACs quickly become "insiders" who are loyal to the firm.[42]

Indicators of the degree to which the intelligence function has gained credibility in the organization are:[43]

Institutionalization of the function—the extent to which firms have made specific units responsible for the function (e.g., established a research and analysis unit, created special job categories for people who perform this work, or granted responsibility for the function to a specific unit such as public affairs).

Reporting accountability—whether or not the director of the intelligence unit reports directly to the highest level of management (e.g., the CEO), sits on executive committees, and attends board meetings.

Integration with line management—the extent to which research and analysis specialists consult with line managers and policy experts on an ongoing basis to obtain their views and perspectives, as well as to address managers' concerns in the scanning and monitoring processes.

Integration with corporate planning—the extent to which research and analysis results are taken into account in the corporate planning process or the extent to which research analysts produce an issues component that appears in long-term and short-term plans.

Regularity of committee meetings to discuss scanning and monitoring results—the extent to which the organization schedules regular and frequent meetings to discuss scanning and monitoring results, thus creating opportunities for a proactive rather than reactive response to escalating or emerging issues.

Circulation of research and analysis products—the extent to which the organization circulates trend reports, media analyses, survey results, and other materials generated by the research and analysis units.

Resource allocation—the extent to which business units are given sufficient staff and money to carry out the function.

Recommendations to those setting up an intelligence system include:[44]

1. Assess the information needs of top management and identify strengths and weaknesses to implementing systems to meet these needs.
2. Establish clear goals for the intelligence function.
3. Determine clients to be served and prioritize the list (e.g., CEO, board, top-level executives, policy committees).
4. Institutionalize the interface between top decision makers and intelligence professionals.

Studies have determined that there is a relationship between the extent to which an organization has formalized its intelligence operations and the extent to which it depends on external institutionalized groups (e.g., interest groups). A survey involving 130 issues management specialists in the utilities industry found a significant correlation between interest group pressures on an organization and allocation of human and financial resources to the intelligence-gathering function.[45]

Research and analysis units with the highest credibility are those that "add value" to the original information[46] (i.e., interpret the information, draw implications from the data, and extrapolate trends). Those units with the lowest credibility do no more than provide raw data, abstracts, and summaries of the results of their scanning and monitoring efforts. Data becomes intelligence only after being analyzed. In companies with well-developed intelligence systems (e.g., Adolph Coors and Banc One) a network of people in the field contribute raw data, which the intelligence unit then processes and analyzes. Coors and Banc One downplay the role of technology in deciding the success of intelligence operations. These companies say that although computerized data banks are important, they are not substitutes for expert analysis.[47] My own experience (over the past five years) in training people to carry out research and analysis functions in the Canadian government confirms this observation.

AN IDEAL MODEL

Governments seem to be setting the trend for intelligence system models that work. Both the U.S. government and the Canadian government have well-established intelligence-gathering and processing systems. Motorola's CEO Bob Galvin built a system at Motorola that was based on his experience with the Presidential Foreign Intelligence Advisory Board. He was assisted in his task by a former senior CIA officer. Galvin designed the program to support top management. The intelligence unit director and the CEO jointly designate priority issues. These cooperative efforts are facilitated by the presence of the director at executive committee and board meetings. In an ideal model, the intelligence unit director reports directly to the CEO:

> The history of military intelligence activities has proved that placing layers between the commander-in-chief and the intelligence officer is tantamount to destroying the effectiveness of the function. . . . A good intelligence advisor presents the CEO with more than important facts or intelligence estimates: He or she attempts to increase the decision maker's understanding of how other players think (e.g., competitors, customers, regulators) as well as the pattern of logic behind events in the environment. As an independent observer with no stake in particular strategy options, the DOI [director of intelligence] is probably the only corporate player who can offer the CEO a relatively objective assessment of the consequences of adopted strategies.[48]

Informal sessions present an opportunity for the director of intelligence and the CEO to discuss critical issues for which the CEO requires intelligence input.

In Galvin's system, researchers and analysts work together with internal experts, who are assigned to task forces and project teams. The creation of account manager or account executive positions allows an organization to gain an intimate understanding of its clientele. In such a system, experts are assigned to track specific competitors, technology experts, government officers, particular technologies, and designated agencies. The researchers and analysts draw on the network of internal experts for help in acquiring and analyzing data.

In some public sector organizations, account executives are assigned to different branches of the organization. They have dual reporting obligations. In the Canadian government, for example, account executives at Health and Welfare Canada are deployed throughout the organization. They report to a communication executive who is part of the information services group—their official job classification group. They also report to policy and program managers in their specific unit of the department (equivalent, in business terms, to business units), for example, health promotion, medical services, seniors' secretariat, or fitness and amateur sport. When annual or other planning takes place, the account executives represent the information services group in contributing communication insights to the planning exercise. At the same time, they acquire a sophisticated understanding of the special needs of the group they serve. The account executives are physically housed in the client areas of the department, but they attend meetings of information services personnel as well.

Those who have worked with setting up intelligence systems believe that the essence of any worthwhile system is its ability to coordinate internal expertise.[49] Employees in both line and managerial positions hold a wealth of information, but they are rarely encouraged to share and contribute their knowledge. A later section of this chapter discusses this point in more detail.

WHAT ARE THE FUNCTIONS OF THE ENVIRONMENTAL ANALYST?

Routine services performed by research staff members include:

- Analyzing media (print and electronic media, magazines, etc.).
- Analyzing correspondence.
- Writing monthly trend reports.
- Planning, conducting, and analyzing focus-group sessions.
- Designing questionnaires for surveys.
- Analyzing survey results.
- Researching the views of elite opinion leaders.
- Generating interest-group profiles.
- Writing abstracts of scanning results.
- Generating executive summaries of reports (full reports typically are sent to experts in specific areas; executive summaries typically are sent to upper management, who can request a full report if necessary).
- Creating an environmental analysis component for corporate plans (or, alternately, producing a separate plan for communication that can be used in the corporate plan).
- Producing background material for press kits.
- Briefing upper management.
- Producing issues calendars and issues books.

The first duty of environmental intelligence unit members is to respond to requests from the CEO and other executive officers. Line managers also request specific products and services. Research and analysis specialists consult frequently with line personnel regarding their information needs. Credibility is often related to the way in which research personnel interact with line managers or, in the case of government, to policy and program individuals. The analyses that are generated feed into the strategic planning and operational planning processes.

An increasing number of organizations are making use of electronic mail networks to establish clippings folders. At the end or beginning of each work day, research analysts put items in the clippings folders that are relevant to the expertise or job duties of organizational members. In other cases, analysts flag important or emerging issues. Another option is to set up videoconferencing programs to collect information on issues. Personal networks of analysts and managers are not sufficient, however, on their own to generate an intelligence system. Nor are electronic clippings services. As was previously noted, value-added analysis is required, at some point, to transform a data system into an intelligence system.

Regular meetings of research and analysis members facilitate coordination of the research and analysis effort. At Canadian federal government departments such as Employment and Immigration Canada, there are biweekly meetings to discuss issues that have an impact on the organization. Figure 2.3 illustrates a typical format for reporting issue developments.[50] Six out of 15 Fortune 500 companies indicated that they hold monthly meetings to discuss monitoring results; one of the companies surveyed holds semiannual meetings. Members may include executives, senior managers, middle managers, and staff; the most frequent attendees are middle and senior managers.

SUBJECT AREAS TYPICALLY SCANNED OR MONITORED

Scanning and monitoring processes often tend to center on one aspect of an organization's environment (e.g., technological, financial, competitive, or stakeholder interests). Corporations may study the economic and regulatory environments, including the climate for mergers and acquisitions, but they may fail to broaden their scope to include other relevant environments such as technological and social systems.[51] Governments, on the other hand, tend to concentrate on political variables, often ignoring other dimensions. It is said that the "more strongly a company . . . identifies itself with a single dimension, the greater the risk of being blind-sided over time by the emergence of important issues from other dimensions."[52]

Because there has been a growing research emphasis on technology fusion (as opposed to "breakthrough research"), industries will need to become more attuned to changes in other sectors. They will need to monitor not only "visible" enemies (companies and industries in their own sector), but also "invisible" enemies[53] (companies outside the industry with technological capabilities that could pose a threat if turned to new markets). Such companies may not show up on a company's "industry structural screen."[54] Because technology fusion merges rather than replaces existing technologies, it is necessary to adopt a different mindset in monitoring this area. It is not sufficient for a company that is monitoring threats or opportunities in technology fusion to restrict its focus to the present or to immediate competitors. Furthermore, it must collect information from many different media and channels. The focus must be futuristic to monitor "invisible" competitors. For example, the manufacturers of small, form-factor disk drives face a potential long-term threat from the sellers of storage devices that use flash memory semiconductors. The latter, which were developed initially for the computer market by companies such as Intel, AT&T, Fujitsu, and Mitsubishi, are expected to "migrate" into other segments of the office equipment market such as fax machines and cellular phones.[55]

FIGURE 2.3
Sample Issue Tracking Report Format

Issue:
Priority based on Strategic Objectives:

Trends in Issue Development:	Events Influencing:

Opportunities for Organization:	Threats to Organization:

Action Required:
Responsible Party:

A competitor can be "anything that takes customers' money away":

Movie theaters now compete against home video rental centers and cable TV. The post office now competes against Federal Express, and both compete against electronic mail. Banks compete against Merrill Lynch and Sears Roebuck, all of them offering a variety of competing financial services. Greyhound and Trailways buses now compete against airlines, of all things, offering no-frills fares, and both compete against video games and computer games. Mail-order catalogs compete against shopping. Travel agents compete against direct, desk-top computer reservations systems.[56]

Some of the following points may be indicators of organizations that pose "invisible" threats to companies outside their sector. Such organizations are likely to have:[57]

- Cross-functional organizational structures.
- Clear and empowered employee roles.
- Managerial focus on processes rather than control.
- Long-term profit orientation.
- Relatively unfocused support functions.

Organizations also monitor events and issues that are relevant to other organizations on which they are dependent. The most obvious example is business monitoring the legislative and regulatory agendas of local, state, and national governments. However, a firm may also monitor events and issues that affect suppliers or other firms on which they are dependent for parts, services, or critical resources.[58]

More sophisticated scanning and monitoring systems take many different social forces into account, including social indicators (i.e., noneconomic measures related to the social state of the nation and to its governmental and nongovernmental institutions); these social indicators are closely tied to quality-of-life considerations.[59] For example, at Coors, researchers sort, file, and analyze news coverage on major competitors; they also monitor governmental developments.[60] Strong interdependencies exist between firms and their political environment because many government interventions are aimed at "creating new industries, changing competitive conditions within established industries, and creating or protecting industries seen as vital to defense interests."[61]

Thirteen out of 15 Fortune 500 companies said they scan areas specific to the organization's mandate, business and economics, and politics and government. Eighty percent scan areas related to science and technology, and 53 percent scan social sciences. Figure 2.4 shows these responses.[62]

The following topic areas are potential subjects for scanning and monitoring efforts by business and industry.

- Political implications in a specific event or issue; for example, stakeholder concerns and attitudes (political dimension).

FIGURE 2.4
Areas Scanned

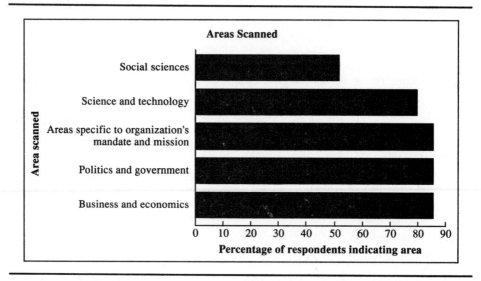

- Regulatory or policy concerns related to an issue (political dimension).
- Technological innovations or scientific advances with potential to affect an organization; also public response to those innovations (technological, economic, social, and political dimensions).
- Technological innovations or scientific advances likely to affect foreign and domestic competitors; also competitor response to potential innovations (technological, economic, social, and political dimensions).
- Profiles of technological innovators (technological, political, and social dimensions).
- Identification of less visible competitors (those in other industry sectors who pose no present threat, but could become competitors at some future date, given the possibilities in technological fusion), alone with profile of these competitors (technological dimension).
- Identification of leading technologists and opportunities for technology fusion (technological dimension).
- Identification of investment opportunities, along with assessment of political risks (economic and political dimensions).
- Macroeconomic and industry-specific trends (economic and technological dimensions).
- Opportunities for strategic alliances and partnerships (economic, political, and technological dimensions).

- Demographic trends—customer or client profiles (social dimension).
- Psychographic trends—customer or client profiles (social dimension).
- Competitor profiles—companies and their leadership (social and economic dimensions).
- Opinion leader profiles—financial analysts, journalists, etc. (political and social dimensions).
- Identification of market opportunities in a state, region, or country (political, economic, and social dimensions).
- Public image of company and its leadership (political and social dimensions).
- Extent to which preferred company messages surface (political dimension).
- Environmental concerns (economic, social, and political dimensions).

Businesses usually find it easier to monitor general business concerns than to monitor the firm's special interests because the media tend to concentrate on more general issues.[63] To compensate for these shortcomings, some organizations hire outside consultants such as Opinion Research Center, Inc.; Louis Harris and Associates; and Yankelovich, Skelly and White to collect information on organizational image.[64] A 1992 survey of Fortune 500 companies found that only 3 out of 15 firms admitted to monitoring reactions to performance of the organization or to individual officers of the firm.[65]

The following exemplify the focus of government monitoring efforts:

- Identification of stakeholders and their concerns (who, what, where, why).
- Public or media reactions to specific policy or program announcements (concerns, arguments and reasoning, tone and intensity of reaction).
- Interest-group reactions to policy or program announcements (concerns, arguments and reasoning, tone and intensity of response).
- Reactions to tabling or debate of legislation by media, general public, interest groups, opposition parties, congressmen, senators, industry, etc. (concerns, arguments and reasoning, tone and intensity of responses).
- Reaction to "trial balloon" floated by government (concerns, arguments and reasoning, tone and intensity of response).
- Public or media evaluation of leadership performance (either on a specific occasion or in general).
- Assignment of blame in specific situations—by media, public, interest groups, lobbyists, or other stakeholders.
- Recommendations for policy or program development.

- Extent to which government is depicted as being in control of its issue environment.
- Extent to which preferred government messages surface.
- Ranking of issue on media or public agenda.
- Identification of opinion leaders (public or private sector, media, etc.).
- Identification of possible partners for joint ventures.

SOURCES OF INFORMATION

External Sources: Looking Outside

A 1992 survey of Fortune 500 companies showed the most frequently scanned external information sources are newspapers, magazines, business and financial reports, television, academic journals, books, and newsletters. Also popular were opinion leader reports, surveys, radio, and "think tank" reports, listed by two out of every three respondents. Trend monitoring reports, demographic statistics, and telephone inquiries fell next in line, and more than half of the respondents said that they refer to futurist journals, conference proceedings, records of House and Senate debates, focus-group reports, lobbyist reports, and correspondence. Court cases, public consultation reports, records of complaints, and interest-group profiles were cited by 40 percent of the respondents. Figure 2.5 illustrates these patterns.[66]

Films and theater ranked relatively low on the list of sources scanned by Fortune 500 respondents, most of whom were public affairs directors or managers (a few were vice presidents or CEOs). This low rating for scanning films and theater products is ironic, because artists are likely to be ahead of their time in perceiving future directions. By definition, an artist is someone who invents new ways of looking at the world. On the other hand, a number of companies listed academic journals, conferences, and books; these also are good predictors of technological, scientific, and social change in society. Theory is often ahead of practice. It has been recommended that researchers should scan sources so diverse as "Nobel-level science"; biographies of Winston Churchill, T. E. Lawrence, Charles De Gaulle, and George Patton; and books such as *Fast Forward* (about the development of VCRs) and *Final Cut* (about making the movie world's "biggest fiasco").[67]

Fortune 500 companies use many of the same sources in monitoring as in scanning their issue environment. All of the organizations, for example, cited reference to newspapers and magazines. Newsletters and business and financial reports came next at 87 percent. Books and television followed, mentioned by 80 percent of the respondents. Academic journals, conference proceedings, radio, trend monitoring reports, and records of House and Senate debates were

FIGURE 2.5
External Sources Scanned

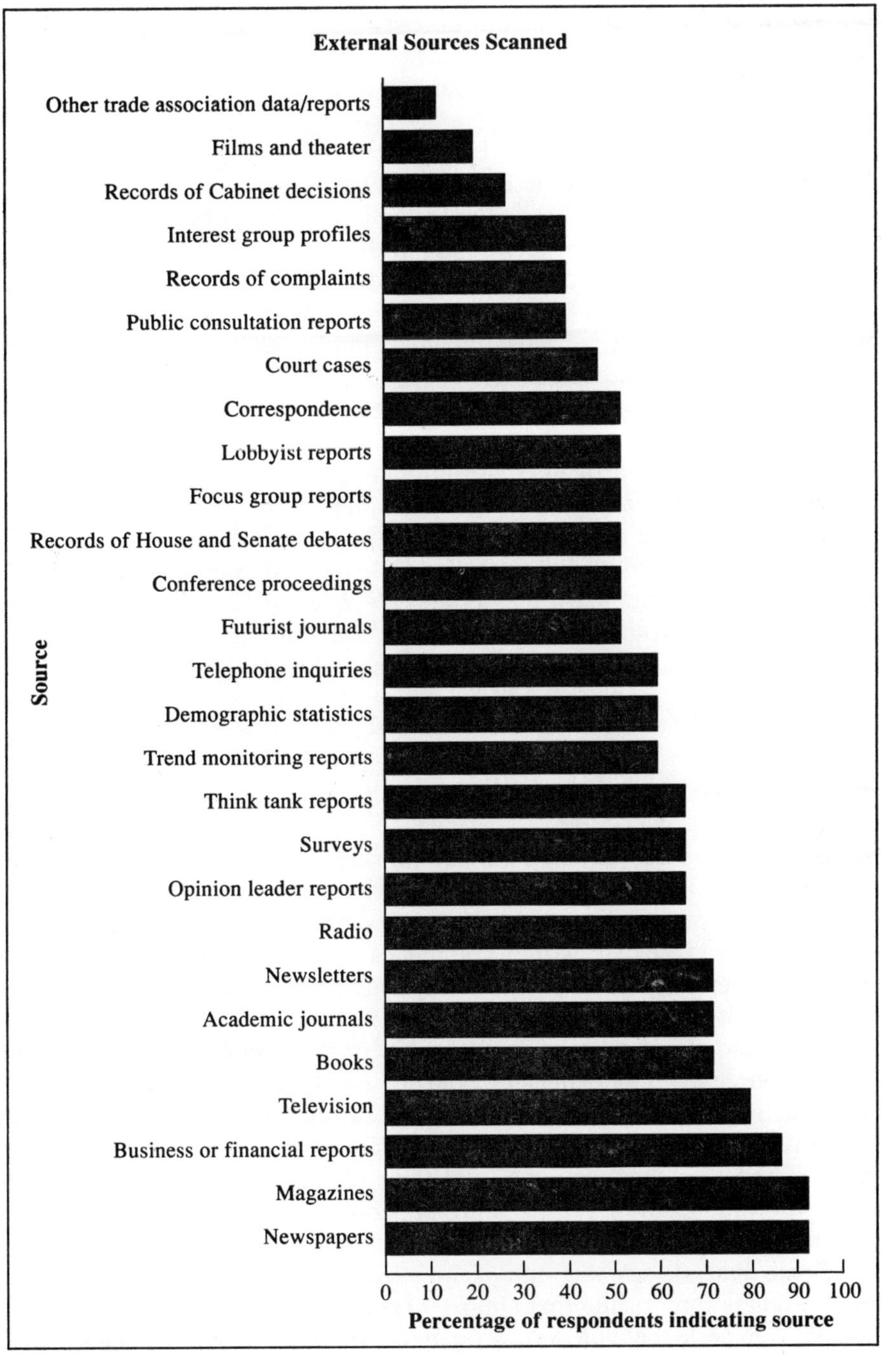
External Sources Scanned
Other trade association data/reports
Films and theater
Records of Cabinet decisions
Interest group profiles
Records of complaints
Public consultation reports
Court cases
Correspondence
Lobbyist reports
Focus group reports
Records of House and Senate debates
Conference proceedings
Futurist journals
Telephone inquiries
Demographic statistics
Trend monitoring reports
Think tank reports
Surveys
Opinion leader reports
Radio
Newsletters
Academic journals
Books
Television
Business or financial reports
Magazines
Newspapers
Source
0 10 20 30 40 50 60 70 80 90 100
Percentage of respondents indicating source

close behind, with responses ranging from 73 percent to 67 percent. Sixty percent of the respondents listed futurist journals, correspondence, and surveys; 53 percent listed telephone inquiries, opinion leader reports, focus group reports, and think tank reports. About half of the group included interest-group profiles, and 40 percent said they refer to records of complaints, court cases, and lobbyist reports. One third of the respondents listed demographic statistics, but few indicated that they refer to films or theatre[68] (see Figure 2.6). At Banc One, the marketing director oversees the collection of brochures and news releases on product launches.[69] Not mentioned in the survey but frequently monitored by corporations are patent applications and sales reports. Many of these same sources were mentioned by public relations executives in a survey of 253 practitioners from Fortune 500 companies, public relations agencies, nonprofit organizations, and academics.[70]

Some research directors complain that budgetary constraints make it necessary for them to choose inexpensive, easily available information (e.g., newspapers and magazine articles) over more costly information (elite opinion surveys, commercial trend monitoring reports, and focus-group testing).

Useful reference books for the corporation research and analysis specialist are Dun and Bradstreet *Million Dollar Directory;* Dun and Bradstreet *Middle Market Directory;* Standard and Poors' *Register of Corporations, Directors, and Executives;* Thomas' *Register of American Manufacturers; Fortune's* "Directory of Largest Corporations"; *Fortune's* "Annual Directory Issues"; and *Black Enterprise's* "The Top 100."[71]

Internal Sources: Looking Within

Some of the sources selected for monitoring, as in these examples, will be external to the organization; others are internal.[72] The president of one research and analysis firm says that over half of the competitive information that companies need already exists within companies. Others say that companies have between 75 percent and 90 percent of the intelligence they need, already inside the organization.[78] Both those employees who have been with the company for a long time and those who have worked with other companies are important internal sources. Senior managers, who are in frequent contact with government and industry leaders, can be excellent sources of information. It can be useful to keep an updated inventory of experts in the company. Consultants recognize the value of these internal sources, and they typically collect information from inside the organization before going outside. After adding some information from outside, consultants sell the package back to the client organization.[74]

Some analysts say that one of the most important sources of unpublished information is rumors and that almost 70 percent of rumors turn out to be true. Corning's experience with setting up an environmental intelligence system has suggested that the accuracy of rumors may be even higher than 70 percent.[75]

FIGURE 2.6
External Sources Monitored

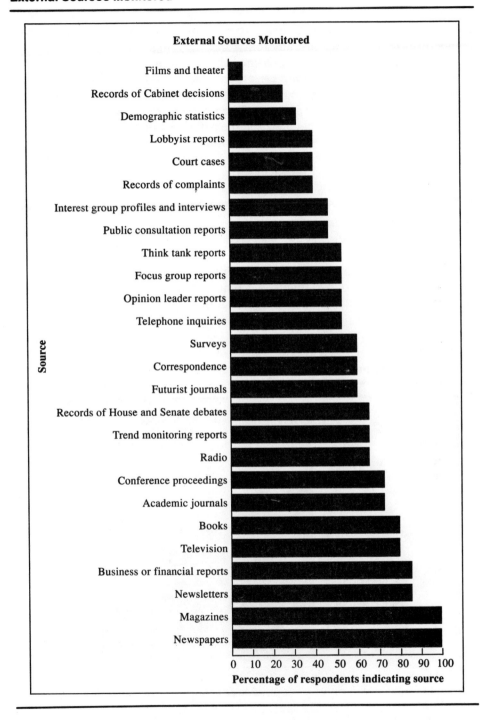

Analysts at Coors also take rumors into account; they evaluate the capacity of competitors to expand against any rumor that they might expand. Other studies in the chemical industry have confirmed that important information can come from unexpected personal sources: a conversation on an airplane, a chance meeting with a friend or neighbor. A benchmark study found that such personal sources can provide up to 70 percent of the strategic information required by an organization. This study concluded that the pattern of strategic information flow in organizations is predominantly bottom-up, suggesting the importance of drawing on people who are lower in the organizational hierarchy.[76] Confirming this last point, a Fortune 500 survey found that almost half of respondents claimed to acquire relevant environmental data from chance meetings with people.[77] Two thirds of those surveyed noted that they received useful information from informal discussions with organization members. These more informal means of acquiring information appeared to be as important as more formal techniques such as surveys, focus groups, and formal interviews. Sixty percent of the respondents said they use surveys and formal interviews, whereas 40 percent used focus group techniques. Computer networking and teleconferencing were less frequently cited (see Figure 2.7).

FIGURE 2.7
Internal Information Gathering Methods

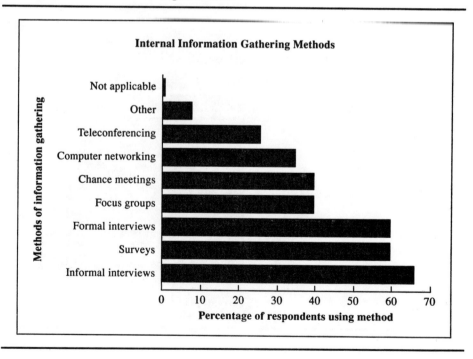

Tapping the knowledge of all employees is critical to an effective scanning and monitoring operation. Interviews with organization executives, program experts, regional representatives, branch company managers, and concerned employees can be useful in contributing to organizational intelligence. Good surveillance goes beyond formal efforts such as monitoring publications; all employees, senior managers and frontline workers, must become part of the environmental surveillance process. Everyone must accept responsibility for becoming active receivers of information. At Frito-Lay, service and sales people are "encouraged to pass information upwards, rather than just be recipients."[78] The Japanese regard such openness to information as just another job duty. Companies like Honda, NEC, Sharp, Sony, and others have "elaborate intelligence-gathering networks, both formal and informal."[79] The marketing director at Banc One supervises an extensive network of employees who regularly scan the marketplace for signals of change.[80] In another system that took four years to construct, one individual in a major plastics manufacturing firm operates at the hub of a 500-member electronic mail network. This person receives up to 30 messages a week, which he summarizes and publishes in a monthly newsletter; he also maintains a databank of responses.[81]

Cosmopolites serve an especially important information-gathering function in organizations. The term *cosmopolites* refers to people in the organization who act as boundary spanners, or boundary-role persons.[82] They are located at the periphery of the organization, in positions that allow them to pass information between internal and external constituencies and to represent the "perceptions, expectations, and ideas of each side to the other."[83] Cosmopolites serve an important function in organizations that require high levels of feedback from their larger environment. Cosmopolites may be found at the top and at the bottom in most organizations. The receptionist in a medical office, a door-to-door salesperson, and the interoffice courier all act as cosmopolites, serving as the "open doors and windows of an organization, allowing for cross-ventilation of new ideas."[84] Because of their boundary-spanning nature, marketing and sales departments are rich information sources.[85] Likewise, the executive who joins a golf club, the politician who speaks at a dinner banquet, and the bureaucrat who attends a convention in a distant city are all acting out cosmopolite roles. Acting as boundary spanners, they not only give information on the organization to the public, but they also obtain feedback from the public on their organization's performance. A consultant is a another kind of cosmopolite whose association with the organization allows the entry of an outside viewpoint.

In organizations where there is little upward communication, vital environmental intelligence gained at lower levels can be lost to the organization. While most organizations recognize the value of the executive or consultant acting as a cosmopolite and attach credibility to information acquired from these high-level employees, organizations rarely attach the same significance or credibility to information derived from lower-level cosmopolites. Yet studies confirm that the

FIGURE 2.8
Sources of Information on Stakeholders

Business/Industry	Special Interest Groups	Elected Representatives
Interviews with clients Interviews with consultants Interviews with competitors Interviews with suppliers Interviews with financial institutions Wall Street trading reports Business and financial journals Trade journals and shows Technical journals and conferences Academic journals and conferences Research reports Annual financial reports Newspapers Television documentaries and news reports Corporate magazines Employee newsletters Press releases and press conferences Hotlines Patent applications Sales reports Speeches Brochures Advertisements	Organizational correspondence Interviews with interest group spokespersons Newsletters originating with interest groups News and feature articles Letters to the editor Group profiles provided by commercial firms Special position papers generated by interest groups Surveys of business and consumer groups by region Presentations to House and Senate committees Access to information requests News releases Consultation with NGOs (nongovernment organizations) Records of lobbyist efforts Interviews with lobby groups, etc. Speeches Reports of conferences and annual meetings Ethnic media	Records of House and Senate debates Interviews Speeches Comments in state legislatures Voting records of Senators and Congressmen Court decisions Administrative decisions Media Household newsletters

Organized Labor
Annual financial reports Interviews with union spokespersons Newsletters Public records of proceedings Media Speeches

General Public	Government	Elite Opinion Leaders
Public opinion surveys and polls Letters to the editor Organizational correspondence Relevant statistics (e.g., demographic information) Focus group testing results Evaluation and audit reports regarding public perception of programs and services Public consultation reports Public inquiry records Complaints Speaker's bureau reports Court cases	State of the Union address Relevant Cabinet records of decision Annual reports of organization Speeches News releases Background papers Briefing notes Interviews with policy or program experts and managers Press conferences Special publications Interdepartmental and intradepartmental surveys Court cases Strategic plan Executive agenda Access to information requests	Interviews Journal articles Articles produced by "think tank" groups Surveys Summaries of public briefs to government committees Newsletters originating with special interest groups Profiles provided by commercial firms Speeches Association meetings (e.g., farmers association)

Media
Print media reports Radio reports Television reports Ethnic media Alternative media

most important strategic information flow in an organization is bottom-up. Some experts warn that intelligence programs should be located where employees can see the uses to which the information is being put; otherwise, they may stop supplying it.[86] Even at higher levels of the organization, information can get lost or withheld. The experience of one health care company illustrates this point. The European parent firm knew about the risks in reformulating a certain medication but did not transmit this intelligence to its American subsidiary. The resulting crisis caught the U.S. subsidiary off-guard. To remedy the situation, the American organization subsequently established part-time liaison positions to connect the two firms.[87] The most customer-centered, or client-centered, organizations such as Japanese companies, pay a great deal of attention to information obtained from boundary-role individuals. Many attribute a large part of their success to this emphasis. Figure 2.8 suggests a relatively comprehensive set of sources to which researchers can go in their study of organizational issues.

SCANNING PROCEDURES

A 1992 survey of Fortune 500 companies found that 10 out of 15 respondents said scanning is a regular organizational function in their companies; 4 said that such activities occur from time to time; and 1 company is planning to expand these activities in the near future[88] (see Figure 2.9). Similar 1991 surveys found that 70 percent of Canadian businesses and 73 percent of federal government departments consider scanning to be a regular organization function.[89]

One of the best-known scanning systems was set up by Weiner, Edrich, and Brown in New York City. This Trend Analysis Program (TAP) was designed for the insurance industry. Another similar program is called TEAM. Both systems depend upon a network of scanners in the organization.[90] These volunteer scanners assume responsibility for reading, on a regular basis, one or more publications. Because of the relative ease of using print sources, scanning typically relies most heavily on these sources. In reading the publications, which may range from *The Wall Street Journal* to *Omni* or the *Futurist,* the scanners look for articles that meet certain criteria. These criteria vary from organization to organization. Sometimes the scanners also will include conference proceedings, academic papers, books, television shows, films, and plays in their selection of materials to examine. Publications chosen for examination include both trade and specialized magazines. Typically, the publications are drawn from four different areas: science and technology, social sciences, business and economics, and politics and government. An organization may scan as many as 100 or more sources.

The scanners prepare abstracts of the articles, conference proceedings, books or other events examined. They also add their personal comments to the

FIGURE 2.9
Scanning Activities within the Organization

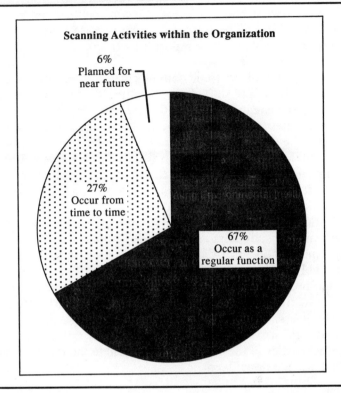

Scanning Activities within the Organization

6% Planned for near future

27% Occur from time to time

67% Occur as a regular function

summaries. They submit these abstracts to an analysis committee, which is headed by a program administrator. This committee, often composed of middle managers, meets monthly to review the abstracts. The committee seeks to integrate the information into a whole, dropping irrelevant points and retaining the most germane. It examines the information in the light of future decisions that will have to be made by the organization; it also prepares and distributes summaries of its findings to the scanners, to other relevant organization members, and to a steering committee of senior managers or executives. These upper-level managers are generally in a position to decide future actions of the organization in regard to specific programs. They can use the information to further their program aims or to benefit the organization as a whole. They can also decide to track some issues, to put other issues on the back burner, or to request in-depth analysis of specific issues.

In the Weiner, Edrich, and Brown trend evaluation and monitoring system, scanners at the consultancy firm provide monthly reports based on information gleaned from a core list of 50 publications. Scanners within the client firm read additional publications that supplement the report provided each month by the consultancy firm. Some of these publications are specific to the needs of the organization, whereas the core publications read by Weiner, Edrich, and Brown are more diverse. In a study of 15 Fortune 500 companies, 3 reported hiring outside firms to report on a standardized core list of publications.

Scanners often look to trend-setting cities and states for early hints of change. Early indicators of shifts in public attitudes, for example, can be found in five bellwether states: California, Oregon, Washington, Connecticut, and Florida. These states were identified by analyzing the content of 200 U.S. daily newspapers.[91] The study of 100 years of historical data also enabled the identification of seven U.S. jurisdictions classified as *early innovators* and harbingers of sociopolitical change. Included in these seven jurisdictions are two cities (New York City and Boston), one county (Dade County, Florida), and three states (New York, Massachusetts, and California).[92] New York City, Boston, and New York State are typically about four years ahead of the next category, *early adopters*. Early adopters include Dade County, Florida; California; Massachusetts; and Illinois. Jurisdiction characteristics include the fact that the areas are highly urban, densely populated, superaffluent, highly educated, youthful, and progressive. *Early and late majorities* include a number of state and local jurisdictions; these jurisdictions follow the early adopters by some four to eight years. Deep South states such as Mississippi, Louisiana, and Alabama and rural areas such as Wyoming typically trail by another two to six years. Characteristics of these jurisdictions include the fact that they are rural, tradition-bound, and nonaffluent.[93]

GOING GLOBAL

Other studies have identified trend-setting countries. Early innovators in the area of sociopolitical change are Sweden, Norway, Denmark, the Netherlands, and Switzerland. Countries such as Germany, Great Britain, the United States, and Canada follow. Sweden is typically about 10 years ahead of countries such as the United Kingdom, the United States, and Canada; and these second-cycle nations are often several decades ahead of certain other Third World countries.[94] Evidence suggests that Canadian family law typically follows Sweden and the Netherlands; constitutional law precedents are typically set by Britain, Germany, and France. Advances in criminal law most often come from the United States. These are leading jurisdictions that are three, five, or even seven years ahead of Canada.[95] By studying what is happening in trend-setting countries, a country can predict options it is likely to be considering a few years from now. Businesses, in the same way, must seek to recognize developing trends.[96]

Some scanning systems are developing a global orientation. Largely because of Europe '92, many current reports, speeches, and articles argue the need for increased international awareness. It has not been very long, however, since a survey by the Society of Competitive Intelligence Professionals demonstrated that, instead of pursuing an international perspective, many U.S. organizations remained committed to domestic data sources and a focus on U.S. competitors.[97] A 1989 management survey, conducted by Korn/Ferry International and the Columbia University Graduate School of Business, suggested that these practices may explain America's "lagging competitiveness." The survey found that business leaders in Japan, Western Europe, and Latin America believe that the major challenge of the 21st century will be coping with international competition; to meet this challenge, CEOs will need to be multilingual. American CEOs, on the other hand, expressed the view that the greatest challenge of the next century will be dealing with the threat posed by government regulations; they believe the challenge to CEOs will be to become more adept at public speaking and at dealing with the media.[98] Some intelligence experts have concluded that (with exceptions such as AT&T, Coors, Kodak, and Motorola) few American organizations are placing a priority on developing competitive intelligence systems.[99] When Corning undertook a review of its intelligence-gathering function, it found that almost half of its competitors were foreign based; yet at that time, it subscribed to a limited number of foreign publications. Upgrading the system implied a need to establish formal scanning procedures with a global perspective and to implement requirements for synthesis of scanning results.[100] In the 1980s, Kodak's CEO Colby Chandler hired the former director of the U.S. Census Bureau, Vince Barabba, to establish an intelligence infrastructure at Kodak.[101]

Scanning and monitoring efforts in the international arena can give organizations a critical edge in both planning and positioning. The challenge for executives is to expand their scanning and monitoring efforts sufficiently to obtain information on global forces, both political and economic. Of great potential impact, for example, are global developments such as the yen/dollar agreement signed by the United States and Japan, cooperative agreements signed by the United States and China, rapid economic growth in Southeastern Asia, restructuring and integration programs in Latin America, and internationalization of the U.S. service sector.[102] A global approach to scanning would also take into account developments in political risk areas[103] and macroeconomic uncertainties such as exchange rates, interest rates, inflation, and relative prices.[104]

Recommendations for moving one's organization in the direction of a global scanning perspective include:

- Tailored reading programs for managers and executives.
- A global component to customized clippings services.
- A substitution of global information sources for some domestic information sources.

- A global component to information packages circulated to managers and executives.
- A global component to business plans.
- Periodic staff reviews of key topic areas to ensure the presence of a global perspective.
- Special studies to give a framework for understanding the structure and dynamics of international events.

WHO ARE THE SCANNERS?

Dividing up the environment for purposes of scanning can increase the likelihood that an organization will pick up and decode signals in the environment. When issues have more than one dimension, specialists from different parts of an organization come together in order to understand the interaction of the different dimensions. For that reason, members of scanning teams typically come from all areas of influence and responsibility in an organization. Scanning creates an opportunity for people to see issues from a broader organizational perspective, to look beyond the limits of his or her authority. It allows the scanner a "momentary entry into the otherwise closed policy circles of the firm, and the opportunity to experience a breadth of perspective denied to all but a few peers."[105] This expanded perspective can motivate participants to put aside the biases that come with identification with a particular business unit or government department.

A scanning unit dedicated to the gathering of environmental intelligence ideally should include economists, business and financial analysts, social scientists, environmental experts, and technologists. Desirable qualities in an analyst include strong methodological skills and knowledge in areas such as "trend analysis and extrapolation, time series estimation, scenario generation, paths and tree construction, portfolio analysis, patent trend analysis, technology assessment, economic and financial analysis, market research methods, interview and group dynamics techniques, content analysis, competitor analysis, and strategy simulation."[106] Energy, flexibility, and openness to change are said to be requirements for effective functioning as a scanning-team member.

In 1988, the Department of Justice Canada set up systematic scanning activities similar to the TEAM and TAP systems. A team of 8 to 10 people were selected to represent all areas of the department. The team members were selected on the basis of having an outward-looking and eclectic perspective. Each person on the team was assigned three to four sources, including futurist publications, to scan on a monthly basis. The scanners reported the results of their research to an executive committee.[107]

Most Fortune 500 survey respondents said scanners come from middle management, and over half listed senior management. Six of the 15 Fortune 500 representatives said their scanners include individuals holding executive-level positions; six also named lower levels of the organization. While many scanning teams are staffed by junior managers, they typically have the support of senior management (see Figure 2.10).

MONITORING PROCEDURES

Monitoring implies tracking an issue over time, through means such as public opinion surveys, media tracking, and focus-group testing. If a researcher tracks an issue over time, each analysis should refer to previous analyses of the public opinion environment and should attempt to extrapolate trends. Media monitoring of an issue implies a reliance on content analysis techniques and in-depth consideration of what is being said on the issue, by whom, and with what frequency; scanning techniques attempt only to identify the issue as a subject of potential interest to the organization, one worth monitoring.

It is said that different skills are involved in scanning and monitoring operations. Whereas scanning stresses intuition and pattern recognition, moni-

FIGURE 2.10
Position of Scanners within Organization

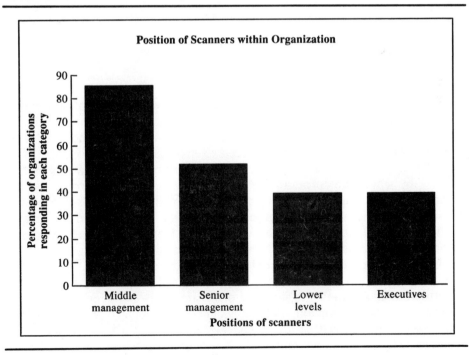

toring requires attention to detail and the ability to synthesize large amounts of material. Monitoring does not require the same breadth of perspective as scanning. Monitors become experts in the specific policy areas that they track on an ongoing basis. Scanners, in contrast, must be able to recognize crossover relevance to developments in many different areas. More organizations have well-developed monitoring capacities than have scanning systems. Because many organizations react on an ad hoc basis to crisis situations, they have set in place units for dealing with those contingencies. Monitoring units are more reactive in nature than are scanning units. All of the Fortune 500 companies surveyed reported in-house issue monitoring functions; 27 percent said they sometimes contract out their monitoring activities.

As demonstrated by Figure 2.11, many situations can activate these monitoring systems. Eighty-seven percent of survey respondents said they may be asked to analyze reactions to some event, policy program announcement, legislation, etc. Organizations sometimes leak information and then monitor reaction to the trial balloon.[108] Two-thirds said they may be called upon to analyze the historical development of an issue, positioning it in the present issue climate. Over half stated that they may be asked to analyze the issue climate prior to some event, policy program announcement, or legislation. In one third of the organizations surveyed, issue monitoring reports sometimes take the form of a monthly trend report. Relatively few said they analyze reactions to the general performance of the company or its officers. Figure 2.11 summarizes these findings.

FORECASTING

Effective environmental surveillance is proactive in nature, anticipating events and decisions likely to influence issue development. The analyst is trying to predict the following: "What will happen if this event takes place?" "What decisions will the organization be forced to make in 1995? Year 2000? Year 2005?" "At what date will this issue reach maturity?" Forecasting is "an exercise by which the corporation projects a scenario of the terrain that lies beyond its monitoring and scanning capacities."[109] In other words, it forecasts the timing of future events. This projection, however, is often based on scanning and monitoring data, which have been used to identify and analyze trends. These trends will have been determined on the basis of changes in demographics, social conditions, regulations, and economic activity. The analyst uses this kind of trend data to forecast the timing of future events. It is perhaps important, in this context, to note the distinction between events and issues. Whereas an *issue* is a fundamental policy question facing an organization,[110] an *event* is a social, political, or technological "happening." Events influence the development of issues. Examples of issue-activating events include the im-

FIGURE 2.11
Purpose of Issue Analysis Report

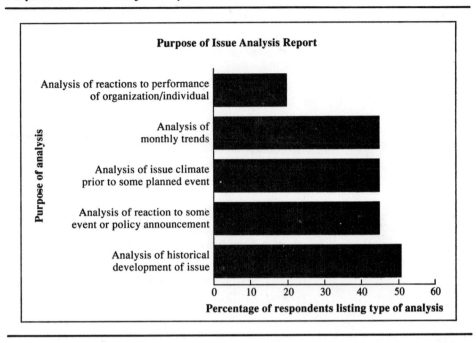

pending takeover of Hong Kong by the People's Republic of China, a corporate takeover, the signing of an agreement related to acid rain, or a technological or scientific breakthrough such as a cure for cancer. *Trends,* in contrast, are the "general tendency or course of events."[111] As a consequence of certain events or trends, the policy issues that an organization confronts may shift, influencing the choices available to the policy maker. For example, Zimbabwe's major problem yesterday was educating as many members of the population as possible; its problem today is finding work for an overeducated population in an underdeveloped country. Israel faced a similar problem a number of years ago; there were too many Ph.D.s and not enough workers. Dealing effectively with the United States' refugee problem in 1993 may mean limiting the numbers of immigrants in order not to overload the country's social and economic systems. The problem in year 2003 may be increasing the numbers of immigrants to alleviate the financial burden of providing social benefits to growing numbers of aging Americans.

Many methods may be used to forecast the timing of events. Two of the most subjective involve intuition and extrapolation. Intuitive insights are often described as "gut feel," with the analyst relying on his or her collective experience and judgment. Extrapolation assumes that you can use the past as a valid guide to the future. Other qualitative techniques include reasoned opinion and speculation. More objective methods, such as quantitative forecasting models, try to reduce the impact of personal judgment and bias. Such models are, however, difficult to apply in areas involving values, human behavior, and new technologies, which respond better to sound judgment (based on highly educated instincts).[112] Multiple techniques that draw both qualitative and quantitative input into the forecasting process are another alternative.

Although forecasting is discussed frequently in the planning literature, only 6 out of 15 Fortune 500 companies reported sometimes using social forecasting or futures research techniques to decide the priority of issues. The remainder responded that they seldom or never rely on these techniques. None indicated that they always, or even often, use the techniques. In the 1970s, many companies experimented with "high-powered econometric models, without gaining much precision in return for their investment".[113] In the 1980s, many firms turned to "least-cost planning" and scenario building.[114] Present disillusionment with forecasting techniques may have resulted from a tendency in the 1950s to oversell these techniques to companies such as Monsanto, Sears, and General Electric: "The resulting emphasis on questionable long-range, pie-in-the-sky projections led the whole field of futures studies, except for a few major think tanks, to fall into disrepute."[115] As a consequence, many managers now concentrate on short- or medium-term (one to five years) social and political trend studies.

CONCLUSIONS

Some companies have expressed the fear that intelligence units could be misunderstood by the public, the media, customers, and even their own employees. Yet such systems contribute to informed decision making and shield organizations from the unexpected. Organizations most in need of intelligence programs are those with large external constituencies and a global focus. The more open the organization, the more uncertain its environment and the greater the need to be alert to change. A buzz word in business and government today is "proactive," which means that rather than waiting for events and circumstances to have an impact upon them, organizations plan ahead for contingencies. They set out scenarios that have some potential for happening; then they design strategies for coping with those contingencies.

For many organizations, scanning and monitoring (and sometimes trend forecasting) are preliminary stages to strategic planning. The situational audit draws upon the information acquired through these techniques. Almost half of the Fortune 500 companies that participated in the survey indicated that they have a formal strategic planning framework into which their scanning and monitoring functions feed. This last point is a good indicator of the extent to which the environmental analysis functions have garnered more than the rhetorical commitment of organizational decision makers. In earlier periods, scanning units were not integrated into the organization, and when their advocates (executives who established the function) left the organization, the scanning units disappeared.[116]

What makes some scanning and monitoring systems better than others will relate to the organization's investment in human resources (knowledge, skills, time), financial resources, support systems (clerical, storage, retrieval), quality of networks in place (face-to-face and mediated), and the long-term commitment of upper management. In setting up intelligence systems, the organization will need to ascertain the existing gap between its information needs and its information resources (people, money, support systems, etc.). Some say that what is required, in a large number of organizations, is not additional people or more resources, but a better organized effort and a new "architecture." This new architecture must be molded to the existing corporate culture and decision-making processes.[117] Others say that organizations must establish systems that are capable of capturing lost or withheld information.[118]

NOTES

1. Tom Peters, "The Boundaries of Business: Partners—The Rhetoric and the Reality," *Harvard Business Review*, September/October 1991, p. 98.

2. George S. Day, "Continuous Learning About Markets," *Planning Review*, September/October 1992, p. 47.

3. George S. Yip and George A. Coundouriotis, "Diagnosing Global Strategy Potential: The World Chocolate Confectionery Industry," *Planning Review*, January/February 1991, p. 5.

4. Tom Peters, "Part One: Get Innovative or Get Dead," *California Management Review*, Fall 1990, pp. 16–26.

5. Fleming Meeks and Jean Sherman Chatzky, "The 200 Best Small Companies: Hear, Watch, and Sell the Customer," *Forbes*, November 11, 1991, p. 220.

6. Rosabeth Moss Kanter, "Think Like the Customer: The Global Business Logic," *Harvard Business Review*, July/August 1992, p. 9.

7. Ibid.

8. Peters, "The Boundaries of Business," p. 98.

9. Fumio Kodamà, "Technology, Fusion, and the New R&D," *Harvard Business Review*, July/August 1992, p. 71.

10. Reported in Rogene A. Buchholz, William D. Evans, and Robert A. Wagley, *Management Response to Public Issues: Concepts and Cases in Strategy Formulation* (Englewood Cliffs, N.J.: Prentice-Hall, Inc., 1985), p. 17.

11. Benjamin Gilad, "U.S. Intelligence System: Model for Corporate Chiefs?" *Journal of Business Strategy*, May/June 1991, p. 20.

12. Ibid.

13. Ibid., pp. 20–21.
14. Tom Peters, "Part Two: Get Innovative or Get Dead," *California Management Review*, Winter 1991, p. 13.
15. Theresa K. Lant and Stephen J. Mezias, "Managing Discontinuous Change: A Simulation Study of Organizational Learning and Entrepreneurship," *Strategic Management Journal*, Summer 1990, p. 150.
16. Joel D. Goldhar and David Lei, "The Shape of Twenty-first Century Global Manufacturing," *Journal of Business Strategy*, March/April 1991, p. 38.
17. H. Igor Ansoff, "Managing Strategic Surprise Through Response to Weak Signals," *California Management Review*, Winter 1975, pp. 21–23.
18. Francis J. Aguilar, *Scanning the Business Environment* (New York: Macmillan, 1967).
19. John Preble, "Corporate Use of Environmental Scanning," *University of Michigan Business Review*, September 1978, p. 14.
20. Harland W. Warner, "Issues Management," *Public Relations Journal*, June 1980, p. 35.
21. Max Meng, "Early Identification Aids Issues Management, *Public Relations Journal*, March 1992, p. 22.
22. Ibid.
23. Paul S. Forbes, "Applying Strategic Management to Public Relations," *Public Relations Journal*, March 1992, p. 32.
24. Liam Fahey and William R. King, "Environmental Scanning for Corporate Planning," *Business Horizons*, August 1977, pp. 62–63.
25. Raymond P. Ewing, "Evaluating Issues Management," *Public Relations Journal*, June 1980, p. 14.
26. Survey conducted by Sherry Ferguson, to which 15 Fortune 500 companies responded, Spring 1992.
27. Leonard Fuld, "A Recipe for Business Intelligence Success," *Journal of Business Strategy*, January/February 1991, p. 12.
28. Jan P. Herring, "Senior Management Must Champion Business Intelligence Programs," *Journal of Business Strategy*, September/October 1991, p. 48.
29. Gilad, p. 22.
30. Fuld, pp. 15–16.
31. Gilad, p. 20.
32. Ibid., p. 21.
33. Kodama, p. 75.
34. Stephen M. Millett and Rolf Leppanen, "The Business Information and Analysis Function: A New Approach to Strategic Thinking and Planning," *Planning Review*, May/June 1991, p. 11.
35. Ibid., p. 11.
36. Andrea L. Simpson, "Ten Rules of Research," *Public Relations Quarterly*, Summer 1992, p. 28.

37. Andre G. Gib and Robert A. Margulies, "Making Competitive Intelligence Relevant to the User," *Planning Review,* May/June 1991, p. 16.
38. Ferguson, Spring 1992.
39. Millett and Leppanen, pp. 11–12.
40. Herring, p. 50.
41. Gary B. Roush, "A Program for Sharing Corporate Intelligence," *Journal of Business Strategy,* January/February 1991, p. 5.
42. Gerald S. Rosenfelder, "How to Stay at the Forefront of Technological Innovations," *Journal of Business Strategy,* May/June 1991, p. 44–45.
43. Several of these points are also discussed in Daniel Greening, "Organizing for Public Issues: Environmental and Organization Predictors of Structure and Process," in *Academy of Management Best Papers Proceedings 1991,* Jerry L. Wall and Lawrence R. Jauch, 51st Annual Meeting, Miami Beach, Florida, August 11–14, 1991, p. 332. Greening drew his indicators from interviews with practitioners at the Annual Meeting of the Center for the Study of Business and Public Issues, Pennsylvania State University. The author's own experiences with the Canadian government confirmed the indicators mentioned by Greening, as well as suggesting additional points.
44. Gilad, p. 25.
45. Greening, p. 334.
46. Roush, p. 5.
47. Fuld, p. 14.
48. Gilad, pp. 24–25.
49. Gilad, p. 24.
50. This chart is a variation on formats developed by Sharon Hanna and the issues management team at Employment and Immigration Canada.
51. Fahey and King, pp. 61–71. See also Fremont Kast, "Scanning the Future Environment: Social Indicators," *California Management Review,* Fall 1980, p. 24.
52. John D. Stoffels, "Environmental Scanning for Future Success," *Managerial Planning,* November/December 1982, p. 7.
53. Kodama, p. 75.
54. Bernard C. Reimann, "The 1992 Strategic Management Conference: The New Agenda for Corporate Leadership," *Planning Review,* July/August 1992, p. 41.
55. Kodama, p. 75.
56. Michael M. Robert, "Managing Your Competitor's Strategy," *Journal of Business Strategy,* March/April 1990, p. 24.
57. Reimann, p. 42.
58. Greening, p. 331.
59. Kast, p. 25. See also Elizabeth Parr-Johnston, "Policy Making in Uncertainty," *Policy Options/Options Politiques,* July 1984, p. 44; and Judith Eleanor Innes, *Knowledge and Public Policy: The Search for Meaningful Indicators* (New Brunswick, N.J.: Transaction Publishers, 1990).

60. Fuld, p. 13.
61. Peter Smith Ring, Stefanie Ann Lenway, and Michele Govekar, "Management of the Political Imperative in International Business," *Strategic Management Journal*, February 1990, pp. 141–51.
62. Ferguson, Spring 1992.
63. Kathleen A. Getz, "Selecting Corporate Political Tactics," in *Academy of Management Best Papers 1991*, eds. Jerry Wall and Lawrence R. Jauch, 51st Annual Meeting, Miami Beach, Florida, August 11–14, 1991, p. 328.
64. Otis Baskin and Craig E. Aronoff, *Public Relations: The Profession and the Practice*, 3rd ed. (Dubuque, Iowa: Wm. C. Brown Publishers, 1992), p. 126.
65. Ferguson, Spring 1992.
66. Ibid.
67. Peters, "Part Two," pp. 17–18.
68. Ferguson, Spring 1992.
69. Fuld, p. 13.
70. Walter K. Lindenmann, "Research, Evaluation and Measurement: A National Perspective," *Public Relations Review*, Summer 1990, p. 10.
71. Baskin and Aronoff, p. 114.
72. Robert, p. 25.
73. Herring, p. 52.
74. Roush, p. 6.
75. Ibid., p. 7.
76. Aguilar, 1967.
77. Ferguson, Spring 1992.
78. Day, p. 47.
79. Kodama, p. 71.
80. Fuld, p. 13.
81. Ibid., p. 17.
82. Sherry Devereaux Ferguson and Stewart Ferguson, *Organizational Communication*, 2nd ed. (New Brunswick, N.J.: Transaction Publishers, 1988), pp. 46–47.
83. Raymond A. Friedmann and Joel Podolny, "Differentiation of Boundary Spanning Roles: Labor Negotiations and Implications for Role Conflict," *Administrative Science Quarterly*, March 1992, p. 29.
84. Everett Rogers and Rekha Agarwala-Rogers, *Communication in Organizations* (New York: Free Press, 1976), p. 140.
85. Frank V. Cespedes, "Agendas, Incubators, and Marketing Organizations," *California Management Review*, Fall 1990, pp. 28–29. Also Fuld, p. 17.
86. Ibid., p. 17.
87. Fuld, p. 14.
88. Ferguson, Spring 1992.

89. Surveys conducted by Sherry Ferguson, Spring 1991, with 24 Canadian businesses and 15 government departments.

90. James K. Brown, *This Business of Issues: Coping with the Company's Environments* (New York: The Conference Board, 1979), pp. 22–28. See also Robert H. Moore, "Planning for Emerging Issues," *Public Relations Journal,* November 1979, p. 45.

91. Ewing, p. 15.

92. Graham T. Molitor, "The Hatching of Public Opinion," in *Corporate Planning Techniques and Applications,* eds. R. J. Allio and M. W. Pennington (New York: American Management Association, 1979).

93. Ibid.

94. Studies by General Mills are discussed in Philip S. Thomas, "Environmental Scanning—The State of the Art," *Long Range Planning,* February 1980, p. 24.

95. Interview with Dawn Nicholson-O'Brien, Director General, Communications Directorate, Department of Justice Canada, Spring 1989.

96. Frank K. Sonnenberg, "Partnering: Entering the Age of Cooperation," *Journal of Business Strategy,* May/June 1992, p. 49.

97. John E. Prescott and Patrick T. Gibbons, "Europe '92 Provides New Impetus for Competitive Intelligence," *Journal of Business Strategy,* November/December 1991, p. 20.

98. Herring, p. 48.

99. Ibid., p. 48.

100. Roush, p. 6.

101. Herring, p. 51.

102. William H. Davidson, "The Role of Global Scanning in Business Planning," *Organizational Dynamics,* Winter 1991, pp. 5–13.

103. William D. Coplin and Michael K. O'Leary, "Annual Analysis: 1991 World Political Risk Forecast," *Planning Review,* January/February 1991, pp. 16–22.

104. Lars Oxelheim and Clas G. Wihlborg, "Corporate Strategies in a Turbulent World Economy," *Management International Review,* 1991, p. 293.

105. Ibid.

106. Millett and Leppanen, p. 13.

107. Nicholson-O'Brien, Spring 1989.

108. Richard B. Kielbowicz, "Leaks to the Press as Communication Within and Between Organizations," in Ferguson and Ferguson, pp. 290–302.

109. Andrew Gollner, *Social Change and Corporate Strategy* (Stamford, Conn.: Issue Action Publications, 1983), p. 128.

110. John M. Bryson, "A Strategic Planning Process for Public and Non-profit Organizations," *Long Range Planning,* February 1988, p. 76.

111. Preble, p. 14.

112. S. Enzer, *INTERAX: An Interactive Model for Studying Future Business Environments,* Center for Futures Research, Graduate School of Business

Administration, University of Southern California, December 1989. See also Gollner, p. 133.

113. "Least-Cost Planning: a Technique with Diverse Applications," *Planning Review,* January/February 1991, p. 26.

114. Ibid.

115. Robert Heath and Alan Nelson, *Issues Management: Corporate Public Policymaking in an Information Society* (Newbury Park, Calif.: Sage Publications, 1986), p. 161.

116. Sharon Russell and Michael J. Prince, "Environmental Scanning for Social Services," *Long Range Planning,* October 1992, p. 106. Also Herring, p. 49.

117. Herring, p. 52.

118. Fuld, p. 14.

CHAPTER 3

PRIORITIZING AND MANAGING THE ORGANIZATION'S ISSUES: DECIDING WHAT'S IMPORTANT AND WHAT TO DO ABOUT IT

The typical organization faces an array of competing issues. Because the resources of organizations are limited, it is necessary to select some of these issues for in-depth monitoring and to disregard others. Out of the relevant environment, the organization seeks to identify its most critical issues—those with potential to affect its bottom line. Some believe that management can deal effectively (i.e., can consider or act upon) no more than a small number of issues at one time. Some say 6, others 8 or 10 issues.[1] While responsibility for identifying issues may take place at different levels of the organization, the final prioritization of issues will usually involve top executives.

WHO DECIDES ISSUE PRIORITY?

Acting on their own initiative, the Chief Executive Officer or top-level organizational executives may identify priority issues. Because these individuals act in a cosmopolite function, with extensive connections to the external environment, they often play an important part in prioritizing issues. In corporations, the CEO and his or her executive constellation may compose the team that makes ultimate decisions on issue priorities. A 1992 survey of Fortune 500 companies showed that 6 out of 15 companies indicated the presence of executive involvement in prioritizing the company's issues.[2] In government, these individuals may be found at the highest levels of the bureaucracy.

In other instances, senior or middle managers may have primary responsibility for identifying priority issues.[3] In a growing number of situations, public affairs departments or specially designated research units engage in an initial ordering of issues. Staff members who are responsible for the issue-monitoring function report to middle or senior managers. Their superiors, in turn, sit on

FIGURE 3.1

Sample Executive Survey for Prioritizing Issues

It has been suggested in previous surveys of company executives that our firm may be faced with making decisions in the following 8 areas, relevant to senior consumers, in the next 10 years. Please indicate which of the areas have the strongest priority for your business unit or department.

Part A. Issues of Current Priority to Your Business Unit/Department

Rate each area according to its current level of priority for your business unit or department.

Issue	Strong Priority	Moderate Priority	Some Priority	No Priority
Product Design				
Transportation for Consumers				
Telemarketing				
Home Delivery Service				
Catalog Order Service				
Senior Discounts & Rebates				
Packaging Options				
Employment Policies				
Employee Pension/Benefit Issues				
Alternative Payment Options				

senior management or executive committees that decide final issue priorities. Fourteen out of 15 Fortune 500 companies that responded to a 1992 survey of U.S. organizations reported senior management involvement in the prioritizing of the company's issues, and 8 out of 15 reported middle management involvement.[4]

In some cases, a task group develops lists of issues for upper management's collective consideration,[5] or, alternatively, such groups summarize information received from managers in order to identify the organization's most important issues.[6] The final results may be presented to either domestic or international division executives at an annual communication conference or a management

FIGURE 3.1 (*continued*)

Part B. Issues of Future Priority to Your Business Unit/Department
Rate each area according to its probable future level of priority for your business unit or department.

Issue	Strong Priority	Moderate Priority	Some Priority	No Priority
Product Design				
Transportation for Consumers				
Telemarketing				
Home Delivery Service				
Catalog Order Service				
Senior Discounts & Rebates				
Packaging Options				
Employment Policies				
Employee Pension/Benefit Issues				
Alternative Payment Options				

workshop. At this point, executive management selects the specific issues to be managed and helps to define the strategic objectives to be achieved. Heinz, for example, has an annual "growth meeting," an opportunity for presidents to meet with marketing directors of affiliates and to brainstorm on critical issues and trends. This meeting supplements more frequent meetings of presidents and the midyear and annual budgetary reviews.[7] Twenty-eight percent of the firms who participated in one survey of U.S. organizations claimed to employ similar issues committees, teams, or task forces to prioritize and track issues.[8] The purpose of these committees is to articulate positions on interdivisional issues.

WHAT INFORMATION COLLECTION METHODS ARE USED?

Business and government use a variety of instruments and techniques to gather information required in making a decision on the priority of an issue. Eight out of 15 Fortune 500 companies that responded to a 1992 survey use survey informa-

FIGURE 3.1 (*continued*)

Part C. Maturity Date for Issues
If not a current priority, please indicate the date at which you feel each of the 8
issue areas previously mentioned could become a moderate or strong priority for
your business unit or department.

Issue	Maturity Date for Your Business Unit
Product Design	
Transportation for Consumers	
Telemarketing	
Home Delivery Service	
Catalog Order Service	
Senior Discounts & Rebates	
Packaging Options	
Employment Policies	
Employee Pension/Benefit Issues	
Alternative Payment Options	

tion to prioritize their issues; 8 use interviews; 8 use focus groups; 7 use
literature reviews; 6 utilize nominal group techniques; and 6 use brainstorming.
Six companies reported the use of social forecasting or futures research techniques.[9] An example of a survey questionnaire that was designed to be administered to corporation executives appears in Figure 3.1. The questionnaire is
concerned with the designation of priority issues.

CRITICAL VERSUS NONCRITICAL ISSUES

Some of an organization's issues fall into the *noncritical* category—questions or
problems that are not critical to the organization's survival or success.[10]
Charges of corruption laid against a corporation official, the revelation that
profits have dropped by 20 percent, or the announcement of a CEO's resignation
may have more or less potential for bringing the credibility of the company into

FIGURE 3.1 (*concluded*)

Part D. Ranking of 9 Possible Scenarios
Please rate each of the following scenarios in terms of their potential
impact on your business unit or department, should they occur sometime
in the next 10 years.

	Critical	Very Important	Somewhat Important	Not Important	Irrelevant
Inadequate numbers of younger persons are replacing older workers who retire					
Increasing numbers of seniors are acting as caretakers to elderly parents and grandchildren					
Large numbers of seniors choose to remain in workforce					
Bus and rail services find it necessary to discontinue senior discounts					
Services for rural seniors decline as cutbacks become necessary					
Seniors become important resource in volunteer sector					
Senior housing cooperatives gain in popularity					
Buying power of seniors declines					
Seniors become an important consumer lobby					

question. Other issues that typically appear in the noncritical category are
foreign policy issues, which tend to fall low on the public's list of priorities: "A
characteristic response to questions of foreign policy is one of indifference. A
foreign policy crisis, short of the immediate threat of war, may transform
indifference to vague apprehension, to fatalism, to anger; but the creation is still
a mood, a superficial and fluctuating response."[11]

Unlike noncritical issues, *critical* issues can rarely be ignored; they have to
be addressed in an open, direct way. A Tylenol poisoning or claims that portable

cellular phones cause brain tumors necessitate the involvement of top-ranking officials. Many critical issues are said to be the product of "punctuational change," a "structural reordering of the environment that threatens an organization with extinction."[12] The "engines" of punctuational change can be technological innovation, scientific discoveries, political upheaval, regulatory changes that impose new operational criteria on the organization, or macroeconomic change. In the case of the doomed Pan Am flight over Lockerbie, Scotland, the failure of Pan Am to disclose an early bomb threat seriously undermined public confidence in the airline. As a result of the *Challenger* explosion, the future of the American space program came into question. How an organization deals with its critical issues determines whether it prospers and, sometimes, whether it survives.[13]

Organizations face hundreds of potential issues, but because of limited resources, they concentrate on issues that have a measurable impact.[14] Many establish criteria for designating issues as having high, medium, or low impact potential. Xerox, for example, reported using the following classification scheme:[15]

High priority—"those issues on which we need to be well-informed in order to provide knowledgeable counsel or take specific action."

Nice to know—"those issues which are interesting but neither critical nor urgent enough to warrant spending a disproportionate amount of time and resources on."

Questionable—"those unidentified or unframed issues that will become important as soon as something happens or somebody elevates them."

Likewise, PPG Industries classifies issues according to their potential impact on the organization:[16]

Priority A—"Issue is of such critical impact on PPG as to warrant executive management action, including periodic review of the issue and personal participation in implementing plans to manage the issue."

Priority B—"Issue is of such critical impact on PPG as to warrant division general manager or staff department executive involvement."

Priority C—"Issue has potential impact so as to warrant government and public affairs department surveillance, assessment, and reporting."

Some analysts assign weights to the impact and probability of occurrence of issues. They rate issues such as A, B, C, D, and E on a scale of 1 to 10 in terms of probable impact on the organization. After attaining an average score for each issue, they rate the likelihood (on a scale of 0.0 to 1.0) that the scenario will materialize. Again, they attain an average score for each issue. They multiply the predicted impact (e.g., on bottom line, image, and internal morale[17]) by the probability of occurrence to obtain an overall ranking for the issue (see the following table as an example):[18]

Issue	Impact (1–10)	Probability of Occurrence	Impact x Probability	Ranking of Issue
A	8.8	0.3	2.64	4
B	6.7	0.7	4.69	1
C	4.4	0.9	3.96	2
D	3.8	0.8	3.04	3
E	2.1	0.5	1.05	5

To add a time factor into these considerations, the analyst adds another column to the tabulation and gives a weight to alternative dates on which issues might have an impact. Earlier dates have a greater weight. Adding a date weighting has the potential to change the rank ordering of the issues.

Formulas such as the preceding can be problematic. For example, criteria for determining impact are not always clearly specified. Moreover, a relatively low-impact issue with a high probability of occurrence could conceivably be weighted the same as a high-impact issue with a low probability of occurrence or a medium-impact issue with a moderate probability of occurrence. Yet the three issues call for quite different strategies. The first issue, no matter how high the likelihood of its occurrence, may be of such limited interest that the organization will choose not to invest precious resources in managing it. The second issue, on the other hand, may have such potentially serious ramifications that the organization cannot ignore the threat. In the same way, some issues relate to an organization's mandate; others do not. Some issues have relevance for the achievement of strategic objectives; others have only peripheral relevance. It is necessary to take these additional variables into account.

The decision tree approach, represented in Figure 3.2, attempts to overcome some of these problems; it also suggests strategies for managing different types of issues.

USING OWNERSHIP QUESTIONS TO IDENTIFY "TYPE 1" ISSUES

The first question on the issue-screening decision tree asks: Does the organization own the issues? Questions of ownership relate to the issue's bearing on the organization's mission or mandate. Strategic issues affect mandate and mission. A *strategic issue* is a "fundamental policy question affecting the organization's mandates; mission and values; product or service level and mix, clients, users or payers, cost, financing, management or organizational design."[19] An organization, in order to survive and prosper, must deal "expeditiously and effectively" with its strategic issues.[20] Because they have limited resources to assign to issues management, organizations would be foolish to prioritize issues without taking mission and mandate into account.

Deciding who owns an issue requires making a judgment on the broad areas

FIGURE 3.2
Issue-Screening Decision Tree

QUESTIONS

A   Does the organization own the issue?

B   Does the issue have characteristics (salience, value potency, maturity, and field of influence) that could make it a potentially high impact issue?

C   Does the issue attract opposition stakeholders with sufficient power capability and credibility to propel its development?

D   Does the organization have the power capability and credibility to defuse the threat?

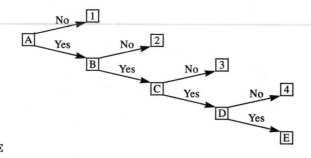

RESPONSE
TYPE

1   Ignore issue, or clarify matter of ownership.

2   Continue scanning efforts to detect future changes in character of issue.

3   Initiate monitoring efforts to determine when/if opposition grows stronger among stakeholders with power capability and credibility.

4   Continue monitoring efforts. Initiate low-cost, low-profile public relations strategies (e.g., consulting with elite opinion leaders, conducting focus groups, etc.) to lower threat potential. Respond as required, with greater allocation of resources, to specific threat situations (e.g., a crisis).

5   Continue monitoring efforts. Invest in high-cost, high-profile strategies (e.g., advertising and lobbying campaigns, conducting extensive public consultations, commissioning surveys, etc.).

of social or public concern into which the issue fits. In other words, it requires understanding the political, social, legal, economic, technological, ecological, cultural, or public health dimensions of the issue. Because these categories encapsulate, in a generic way, classes of social concern, they also describe the social institutions that have evolved to meet the concerns. Within a corporation, the recall of a defective product may raise issues that are owned by several different business units: design, manufacturing, legal, and others. Governments institutionalize their areas of concern in the form of departments or ministries. Examples of departmental focus include: the Environmental Protection Agency (ecological concerns), the Department of Health Services (public health concerns), or the Department of the Interior (cultural concerns). The corporation issue analyst can get a "feel" for the current active issues by monitoring government organizations.

Deciding on the dimensions of an issue makes it possible for the analyst to identify institutions, special publics, or interest groups that have a stake in the issue. A Washington corporate office head described how the issues of concern to his organization tend to cluster into groups that relate to specific House and Senate committees:

> Members of my staff follow their issues into the House, the Senate, executive branch agencies—wherever they lead. And their bundles of issues change very little because they relate to congressional committees. Tax and trade issues, for example, center in the House Ways and Means Committee and the Senate Finance Committee, falling into one natural bundle. The same with the Public Works Committee and the Environmental Committees. The Committee structure on the Hill dictates the issues assignments.[21]

If an organization does accept responsibility for answering for an issue, it must decide to what extent the responsibility is shared by other organizations or units within its administration. Within government, for example, several departments may have a stake in the same issue. Departments as diverse as marine life, natural resources, and transportation may be stakeholders in an issue generated by a major oil spill. Routine investigation into the possible failure of a tanker captain to observe required procedures and laws requires, at minimum, the involvement of the Coast Guard and/or special maritime regulatory bodies. For the company, the oil spill will probably have an impact on finance, legal, public relations, and planning units and any unit set up to deal with environmental cleanup issues.

One example of an issue with links to more than one organizational stakeholder concerns a 1988 outbreak of food poisoning caused by contaminated mussels. Three Canadians died as a result of eating contaminated mussels, making the public safety/public health dimension a major component of media coverage throughout the development of the issue. The contaminated mussels case was, first and foremost, a public health issue, owned by the Department of Health and Welfare. However, there was also a secondary stakeholder in the issue—the Department of Fisheries and Oceans. This department had a stake in the economic dimensions of the issue. Acting together, these two federal departments halted the distribution and sales of all shellfish originating in the presumed area of contamination, while government researchers at the National Research Council carried out tests to identify the toxin and uncover the source and extent of the contamination.

The ban on shellfish threatened the national and international credibility of the product. Because a sizeable amount of the shellfish from the Eastern seaboard is sold in foreign markets, the implications for international marketing were significant. The toxin responsible for the food poisonings was later identified as a rare organic substance with a limited zone of contamination. These findings prompted swift and virulent criticism of the government's handling of the issue in the area of the country responsible for producing the mussels crop. What had been predominantly a public health issue in its early stages became an economic and political issue in its latter stages. Accordingly, in the months that followed the crisis, the Department of Health and Welfare relinquished its stake in the issue to the regional office of the Department of Fisheries and Oceans. This office could better respond to the economic concerns of East Coast fisheries. The Prime Minister's office became involved in responding to the political aspects of the issue.

Another incident, which occurred early in 1989, had clear public health dimensions. An environmentalist disclosed the fact that PCBs and other highly toxic waste materials were being moved across the U.S./Canadian border through the spiking of bulk fuel oil and gasoline shipments. Although the public health threat was implicit in government statements and media coverage of the issue, the Department of Health and Welfare became a relatively minor player in the incident. As the issue developed, the largest part of media discussion centered on the criminal aspect of the scam, with a tax evasion component of the issue receiving major attention. At the same time, public health concerns came to be housed under the umbrella of environmental concerns. In some regards, environment became a euphemism for public health. Health threats were depersonalized as threats to the environment, and ownership of the issue changed hands. The political component was also stressed, with claims that both the U.S. and Canadian governments had known about the problem for some time but chose to take no action until the media disclosure. Subsequent spot checks of tankers were carried out. No toxins were found, and the issue wound down, with the public health threat claiming no more than 3 percent of media comment on the issue. This situation could have been very different, had any toxins been found. Because there were no bodies and no trace of a smoking gun, so to speak, the issue was played as a criminal and political one.

Most issue management specialists agree that few issues go away because the organization ignores them. Nonetheless, responding to issues that fall outside an organization's mandate or a department's jurisdiction can be dangerous. Only if an organization owns an issue will it have the authority to both deal with the issue and make a difference. If the organization answers for an issue, the public may assume it can do something about the area of concern. If, in reality, the organization has little or no authority to effect any real changes, it assumes responsibility for an issue that is basically out of its control. Because of the increasing tendency toward "boundaryless" organizations (a trend discussed in Chapter 1), questions of ownership become complicated. Many issues have shared ownership.

If the organization does not own the issue, a "Type 1" response would involve ignoring the issue or educating concerned publics on the matter of ownership. If the organization does own the issue, either alone or jointly, it will need to consider the subsequent questions on the decision tree.

USING ISSUE VARIABLES TO IDENTIFY "TYPE 2" ISSUES

The second question asked in the issue-screening decision tree is: Does the issue have characteristics that would make it a potentially high-impact issue? Characteristics of an issue that influence impact on the organization are *salience, value potency, maturity*, and *field of influence*.

Salience

Salience has to do with the visibility of an issue,[22] and *agenda setting* refers to the ability of the mass media to direct attention to specific issues, thus establishing their salience.[23] It is assumed that if the news media devote sufficient time to a specific issue (e.g., "executive salaries, perks and power"),[24] this topic will become elevated in the public's list of priorities. For that reason, organizations are often anxious to know how headlines will affect their business.[25] If a story dominates the news for several days, then a large percentage of the letters received will relate to this story, whether the story concerns taxes, corporate misconduct, or foreign policy.[26] Media also influences the *standards* by which we judge governments and corporations. It does so by priming us to judge CEOs and public servants by their performance on issues to which it accords importance. If employment issues are front page news, we will judge our leaders by how well they manage these concerns.[27] If, on the other hand, free trade issues capture headlines, these become the standard by which we measure the performance of bureaucrats and politicians. The audience is "primed" to alter the centrality of issues to which they accord importance.[28] The following example illustrates this point:

> Prior to one of his election campaigns, Governor Nelson Rockefeller was confronted with bad news when he met with his advertising and polling consultants. The research showed that on almost every issue which the New York electorate viewed as important, Mr. Rockefeller's opponents had considerably more favorable ratings. The only issue that he held a significant advantage on concerned the construction of roads and highways—an issue that was viewed as important by less than 5 percent of the electorate. Being an astute politician, Rockefeller turned to his advertising agency and told them, "Make that an issue." Over the next few months, voters in New York State were deluged by advertising which glorified that state's highway system, with the result that by the end of the campaign, roads and highways became the most important issue and Mr. Rockefeller was reelected.[29]

Executives in both private and public sector organizations are interested in the question: What keeps an issue on the media agenda? Sustained media coverage can result from the following influences:

1. The seeming inability of competing parties to reach a workable compromise may keep an issue alive indefinitely.
2. The sensational content of an issue (i.e., its potential to be dramatized) may sustain the issue for long periods of time.
3. The attractiveness of an issue to opposition stakeholders may keep the issue indefinitely before the public.
4. Interest groups may find it useful to keep a specific issue alive because other issues in which they have a larger stake may depend on the issue for enhanced visibility.

The issues that someone recognizes as being most important to the community or nation (issues on the public agenda) may not be the same issues the person regards as being most important on a personal level (issues on one's private agenda).[30] Issue fatigue occurs when the public wearies of hearing and reading about an issue. This phenomenon is most likely to occur when the importance accorded an issue by the media and by politicians—in other words, its ranking on the public agenda—fails to correspond to its ranking on people's private agendas. In the recent presidential campaign, Bush tried to prime the U.S. electorate to accept Clinton's military record as a critical campaign issue. The public refused to do so; defense-associated issues ranked very much lower on people's private agendas than did economic and employment issues. In the end, the press responded to public cues of disinterest and weariness with such rhetoric. In a real sense, the public had suffered issue fatigue on defense-related issues, and in the cases where people did hold strong views, they favored downsizing rather than emphasizing the role of the military. Attempts by George Bush to evoke the kind of emotions that had characterized middle America's response to draft dodgers in the 1960s only served to date Bush as a politician. It could also be speculated that issue fatigue is related to a feeling of impotency, a sense that no answer will satisfy all interested parties or meet the standards that have been set for a solution. The public is not apathetic or uncaring, but people lose faith in their own ability, as well as the competency of others, to generate answers to some problems; for example, free trade issues.

Value Potency of Issue

Deciding the priority level of an issue implies making a judgment on whether the issue could have a critical influence on the organization's survival or success. Understanding the social values that an issue resonates aids the organization in making this judgment. The most enduring issues have a *high value potency,* or connections into the central value system. Pension and employment issues, employee safety, and quality-of-life work programs connect with values such as material comfort, hard work, consideration of others, and worth of the individual. When companies are accused of taking more than their due in profits, they are accused of violating the values of generosity and social responsibility. Issues management implies making judgments on the rank ordering of values housed in an issue.

Some issues will be more strongly tied to first-order values than will others. Many corporate and political campaigns, for example, use family values as an "organizing concept."[31] The abortion issue is so value laden that public figures regard it as an issue to avoid: Not since Viet Nam has any issue generated such high levels of involvement on the part of the American public.[32] Pro-life groups identify the abortion issue with the first-order value of right-to-life, whereas pro-choice groups tie the issue to individual determinism. Because right-to-life has a higher ordering than individual determinism on an absolute scale of priorities, the task of the pro-choice groups is more difficult. Even in cultures that place a strong emphasis on individual determinism, pro-choice groups find their attempts to persuade easier when they are able to relate the rights of the woman to life-and-death concerns. In this way, they connect lower-order values with higher-order ones. Many believe that understanding and appreciating societal values will bring success and leadership to corporate executives and politicians.

When interest groups argue against corporate positions on environmental concerns such as toxic waste and protection of the ozone layer, they connect their arguments with right-to-life concerns, quality-of-life concerns, and social responsibility. This focus on first- and second-order values is a change from the focus of the 1970s when environmental campaigns used the slogan "Keep America Clean." Lady Byrd Johnson appealed to the value of cleanliness, a much lower-order value than is being addressed by environmentalists in the 1990s.

An issue may relate directly to a first-order value, or it may relate indirectly to the first-order value through a series of associated connections with lower-order values. For example, issues related to women in conflict with the law may be linked to the broader cloak of women's rights, which is in turn linked to equality of opportunity, a primary value in Western cultures. Issues that can be related directly, or indirectly, to first-order values such as the sanctity of life or protection of the public assume the status of first-order issues. Abortion and capital punishment are among the more notable of such issues. These qualify as first-order issues, even though they may remain relatively dormant for long periods of time. This is true not only because they are connected to the most strongly held of our social values, but also because they are of concern to virtually all of the general public.

Values are slow to change.[33] The most potent values in Western society are, and probably will continue to be for some time, core values such as individual freedom of choice, social responsibility, sanctity of life, and equal opportunity. Over time, however, the rank-ordering of certain values tends to shift: For example, the emphasis on achievement and equality has changed over time. Two recent national surveys of American youth have shown a "modest turning away from the public interest," a "sharp decline in emphasis on personal self-fulfillment," and a "sharp shift toward private materialism" from the 1970s through 1987.[34] There has been a "marked increase in support for capitalist institutions, such as profit making and advertising, and increased belief that corporations are doing a good job."[35] At the same time, there has been a "retreat from support for government action in areas such as cleaning up the environment."[36] More youths today call themselves "conservative," and fewer are politically active.[37] A number of surveys have demonstrated that religion has become a significant factor in how Americans view social and political issues. Other trends include shifts toward religious pluralism, a move away from organized religions, and a move toward more conservative, fundamentalist churches.[38] It is these kinds of value shifts that trend-monitoring firms seek to discern and to pass on to client organizations. When value priorities in a population begin to shift, new issues find their way onto the public policy agenda and ultimately receive the attention of government and corporations.[39] Older issues may assume new value profiles.

Psychographic research, which attempts to construct a psychological profile of stakeholders, can include a value component. Other studies combine analysis of lifestyles and analysis of values. For example, SRI International of Menlo Park, California, developed a Values and Lifestyle (VALS) system in 1980.[40] The researchers who generated this system identified nine lifestyle/value clusters into which Americans could be grouped. In addition to identifying value orientations, the researchers generated profiles of consumer behavior and media usage for people in the different lifestyle/value clusters. The original VALS classification system was modified in 1989 to account for shifts in consumer orientation. Eight clusters were identified in the new system. The excerpt from Dozier and Repper[41] discusses specifics related to the early version of these value groupings.

In recent years, many social marketing firms such as Yankelovich, Skelly, and White in the United States and Environics in Canada (working in association with Yankelovich) have conducted studies to identify the most important values in contemporary American and Canadian society and to track changes, over time, in value orientations.[42] They sell the results of their studies to business and government organizations, who, in turn, use the information for marketing and strategic planning. The Yankelovich *Monitor,* for example, is a "cost-shared annual census" that "charts the growth and spread of new social values, the types of customers who support the new values and the types who support traditional values, and the ways in which people's values affect purchasing behavior."[43]

FIGURE 3.3
Excerpt from "Research Firms and Public Relations Practices" by
David M. Dozier and Fred C. Repper

The VALS Typology. The nine clusters include two types of Americans defined as need driven. They are the *Survivors* and the *Sustainers.* Survivors (some 6 million Americans) are poor, often elderly, and poorly educated. They are unhappy, sometimes bedridden, and see no hope of escaping their lot in life. Sustainers (some 11 million Americans) are generally younger than survivors, but are almost as poor. Described as streetwise and angry at the system, many young minority Americans make up this cluster.

Three clusters are outer directed: *Belongers, Emulators,* and, *Achievers.* The values and lifestyles of these clusters are responses to perceptions of how others—how society—expects them to live and the values that others expect them to hold. The Belongers (some 57 million Americans) are "middle Americans." Conservative, ethnocentric, conforming, resistant to change, these Americans want to belong, to be part of the mainstream. Integrated into communities and voluntary associations, they adhere to a strict puritanical code. Emulators (some 16 million Americans) are striving to make it big, to be rich. They are competitive, upwardly mobile, status conscious. With many minority group members in this cluster, Emulators are distrustful of the system. Achievers (some 37 million Americans) are high-income materialists who lead American businesses and professions. Disproportionately male, white, and Republican, Achievers are hard working, successful, and comfortable.

The inner-directed clusters are people whose lifestyles and values come from within, rather than in response to their perception of the expectations of others. The three inner-directed clusters are: *I-Am-Mes, Experientials,* and *Societally Conscious.* The I-Am-Me cluster (some 8 million Americans) is viewed as traditional, a step from the outer-directed clusters to the Experiential or Societally Conscious clusters. Young, individualistic, self-absorbed, exhibitionistic, the I-Am-me cluster is typified by insecurity, impulsiveness, and inventiveness. They tend to be young, female, and single, sustained by parental support. They tend to be liberal but do not vote. The Experientials (some 11 million Americans) are theorized as a maturation of the I-am-me orientation. Less egocentric, these Americans are concerned about others. Adventuresome, direct, and involved, the Experientials are attracted to natural foods, fitness, and the exotic. Politically liberal, political involvement creeps into their lives, usually through the women's movement and environmentalism. The Societally Conscious (some 14 million Americans) are affluent, but unlike the Achievers, they see the need for social change. They typically are leaders of activist publics and single-issue campaigns. Not as materialistic as Achievers, these Americans value the quality of life in less material ways. Educated and reformist, the Societally Conscious hold intellectual jobs in the professions. Like Achievers, they see America as playing an active global role. Unlike Achievers, they favor cooperation rather than domination. They are supportive of peace movements and environmentalism.

The *Integrateds* blend elements of outer-directed and inner-directed orientations in their values and lifestyles. A small minority (only 3 million Americans make up this cluster), the Integrateds tend to be self-assured, self-actualized, and self-expressive. According to the implicit developmental psychological model of human personality, the Integrateds are fully mature. They "have it all" and are "above it all." They are the special leaders.

Source: Excerpted from edited volume by James E. Grunig, *Excellence in Public Relations and Communication Management* (Hillsdale, N.J.: Lawrence Erlbaum Associates, Publishers, 1992), pp. 205–6. Used with permission.

Maturity of the Issue

The *maturity of an issue* will also influence the issue's ability to have an impact on the organization. For the most part, decision makers have little interest in fledgling issues. Until an issue is adopted by an advocacy group and becomes important to a sufficiently large number of people, the organization will accord low priority to the issue. It is generally assumed that the more advanced the issue is in the public policy cycle, the greater will be the number of its adherents and its potential to have an impact on the operations of the organization. Likewise, the more advanced the issue is on the policy continuum, the higher the likelihood that the issue will have garnered media attention and the lower the likelihood that the organization can influence its development.[44] The most common stages through which an issue progresses are as follows:[45]

Emergence Phase

1. A gap between organizational performance and public expectations generates public discontent.
2. People begin to discuss the issue and form opinions on the topic.
3. Business firms and government departments start showing interest in issues that relate to their jurisdiction.

Organizational Phase

4. Activist groups, composed of people who share common attitudes and opinions on the issue, are formed.
5. Many interest groups become part of broader social movements that seek to effect systemic changes.

Legislative Phase

6. Negotiations begin.
7. One or more politicians adopt the group's issue and introduce it into the formal policy process.
8. The issue is placed on the public policy agenda.
9. The legislative phase begins.

Implementation Phase

10. Finally, the new rules and policies are implemented,
11. Negotiations may take place between government and business over enforcement standards and timetables, sometimes making this final stage adversarial in character.

Issues progress at different rates through the public policy cycle. It is generally accepted that early identification of issues can give the organization a wider range of alternative actions. When Reagan was elected to the presidency in 1980, issue analysts at Atlantic Richfield foresaw the possibility of federal budget cuts that could result in higher state taxes. Atlantic Richfield had operations in 28 different states at that time. When the issue of budget cuts later surfaced, the oil company was prepared to argue its case. In the late 1970s, the Bank of America identified a "holds on deposits" issue that didn't mature until 1982. In 1982, the issue received national publicity on *Meet the Press* and in the *San Francisco Examiner*. These discussions stimulated 5,000 people to write letters. As a consequence of this public outcry, House and Senate committees were convened to hold hearings on the subject. Because the Bank of America had foreseen the possibility of an inquiry into its "holds on deposits" practice, it was prepared. Members of the Bank of America presented the results of their research to the committees, and they received subsequent praise for their policy. If bank officials had waited to respond to the issue until it was a crisis, they would have been less able to influence the issue's development.[46] Crisis events, however, sometimes generate full-blown issues that do not follow the normal issue-development cycle. The bombing of Pan Am's aircraft over Lockerbie, Scotland, and the tragic deaths of American astronauts aboard the *Challenger* spacecraft exemplify this point.

Identifying the stage that an issue has entered is an important prerequisite to deciding upon the potential impact of the issue. It has been said that policy makers are most likely to have a knowledge gap on issues that are narrow in focus, complex, political in nature, and at an emerging stage of development.[47]

Field of Influence of the Issue

Is the issue of local, state, regional, national, or international interest? With what other issues does the issue interact? These questions identify the field of influence of the issue. The term *field of influence* refers to both the range of an issue's influence and linkages between issues; in other words, it refers to the extent to which certain issues activate or interact with other issues. Determining the nature of these interactions is important. For example, if construction is begun on a new city hall at the moment that the city council levies new taxes or cuts services, the two issues may interact significantly. Similarly, if a utility company imposes a rate increase at the moment that government announces inflation is down, people will interpret one event against the other. Environmental issues, in turn, are played against economic issues, native rights issues, and many other areas of public concern. When environmentalists press for protection of Malaysia's rain forests and argue for changes in the patterns of meat consumption, they are infringing upon strong commercial interests. In the national arena, campaigns for CFC-free products now have a high level of public acceptance, but moved into the international arena, management of this environmental issue requires different communication strategies. In Third World societies, the production and consumption of freon is seen as a development indicator; many people believe concern over environmental issues is a luxury they cannot afford when they are faced with day-to-day survival. For many poor Columbians, the drug issue has more than just a moral dimension; it also has economic and political dimensions, because the drug lords use some of their profits to provide education and to build roads.

Extradition requests will generate debate over the specific case in question; they will also activate discussion of broader concerns such as levels of criminal activity. Murders committed by repeat offenders will raise questions related to parole; they will also provoke renewed discussion of gun control. Media coverage of drug-related events in the United States will stimulate discussion of the drug problem; this coverage will also raise questions related to organized crime and international relations with certain countries. Homosexual rights issues interact with AIDS questions and pension questions, and AIDS questions interact with the debate over euthanasia. Activating certain issues can trigger activity in related areas, prompting renewed coverage of a more enduring issue.[48] Some issues ride piggyback on other issues. Legislation slated for introduction in Congress will assure coverage of a slate of issues that can be known in advance and plotted on an issues agenda. Heightened concern over immigration levels, for example, will almost always accompany periods of increased economic difficulty and bloated levels of unemployment. The burning of Windsor Castle raised more than the issue of who should foot the bill; it also activated renewed discussion of the place of monarchy in modern society. The separation of Sarah Ferguson and Prince Andrew and rumors of a divorce involving Diana and Prince Charles provoked similar speculation and debate. In the same way, many corporate issues will interact with economic, political, and health-related concerns.

The impact of an issue on the organization will be governed, in part, by the field of influence of the issue (the range of the issue and the number of related issues with which it interacts). Some studies indicate that organizations assign more resources to issues that are perceived as being interdependent with other issues.[49]

CONCLUSION

Using the issue-screening decision tree, an appropriate "Type 2" organizational response (to an issue with limited salience, value potency, maturity, and field of influence) would be continued scanning to detect future changes in the character of the issue. If the issue is sufficiently salient, value potent, mature, and has a significant field of influence, the organization will proceed to the next issue-screening step.

"TYPE 3" RESPONSES

The third question addressed in the issue-screening decision tree is: Does the issue attract opposition stakeholders with sufficient power capability and credibility to propel its development? The term *stakeholder* refers to "any individual or group who can affect or is affected by the actions, decisions, policies, practices, or goals of the organization"[50] or "groups of individuals whose interests coincide in one or more ways with the organization."[51] The stakeholders in an issue may be defined by a region (i.e., community, city, state, national or international grouping), by an ethnic or racial grouping, by political orientation, or by other demographic factors. Detailed study of interest-group formation and activity is an important part of environmental analysis.

For business and industry, stakeholders can potentially be shareholders, consumer advocates, customers, suppliers or distributors, competitors, the media, employees, managers, lobby groups, environmentalists, governments, or local community groups. The list will be much the same for government, with the addition of business and industry. Stakeholders that are relevant to a particular issue may oppose or support the organization's position on a specific issue. Opposition stakeholders are groups and individuals that advocate a stance different from the one taken by the organization. Stakeholders who support the organization's stance are also important because they can help the organization to negotiate critical issues. Some researchers suggest assigning weights or ranks to stakeholders, based on their potential impact on the organization.[52]

Power Capability

The strategic decisions that an organization makes in response to an issue will be governed, at least in part, by the power capability of the advocacy groups that have a stake in the issue. The term *power capability* refers to the property of an individual or group that enables the party to be politically influential.[53] In order to be taken seriously, an individual or group must be able to demonstrate this power capability. Not everyone's opinion exerts the same influence on the policy process. Some opinions matter more than others. Within a North American context, access to the media is one of the strongest capabilities an advocacy or other opposition group can boast. Media access is a critical variable; it has the power to overcome size, funding levels, and staffing shortages.[54] This access may result from any one of many different conditions, including newsworthiness of the issue, newsworthiness of the stakeholders, popular support for the advocacy position, economic resources of stakeholders, and technical skills.

Some issues have an inherent media appeal. Groups associated with these issues have a natural ability to access the media. The Earth Island advocacy group, for example, succeeded in getting H. J. Heinz, Van Camps, and Bumble Bee to announce they would stop purchasing tuna that had been caught using techniques that kill dolphins. The group did so by making a videotape of the dolphin slaughter, which "catapulted the issue to the top of the media agenda."[55] Issues with emotional impact are easily dramatized.

The newsworthiness of stakeholders also increases the chances that an issue will receive media attention. For example, the Natural Resources Defense Council (NRDC) sponsored one successful advocacy campaign that forced manufacturers of the pesticide Alar to withdraw their product and "sent waves through the business community."[56] Celebrity spokesperson Meryl Streep's involvement with the Alar issue secured the media's attention and "helped keep food safety on the front pages for weeks."[57]

Assessing the popular support of an activist group means going a step further to determine whether the group has a large grass-roots membership or only a few "important-sounding names on letterhead."

Groups that support causes lacking in media appeal, celebrity support, or popular appeal are still able to access the media if they have enough money. Some groups are well-funded and have professional staffs that include attorneys, public relations and issue specialists, and lobbyists; others rely on volunteers. Thus, a power capability based on financial assets commands the attention of the establishment in the same way as newsworthiness and advocacy support, because money buys time and visibility:

> Resource-rich sources enjoy certain advantages that place them in a much stronger position to bargain with reporters and to manage the news than resource-poor groups. These advantages stem from conventional criteria of newsworthiness applied in newspapers, from the structure of the beat and specialist systems, and from the capabilities of rich sources to ease the reporter's job in collecting the news.[58]

Technical skills can also enhance the power capability of a group.[59]

Credibility

The *credibility of stakeholders* can influence the level of impact that an issue has on an organization. The higher the level of credibility of the opposition stakeholders, the more substantial the threat:

> Ralph Nader and other public interest lawyers have become respected celebrities, often interviewed for response statements, photographed in suits and ties and sitting squarely behind desks or in front of bookshelves, embodying solid expertise and mainstream reliability. They have learned how to make the journalistic code book work for them.[60]

Credibility considerations can be applied to individual or group stakeholders in issues. It is equally possible to judge the credibility of a firm's chief executive officer, a candidate for public office, or a competitor's CEO. Also, an analyst may assess the credibility of an interest group or an opposing organization, entities that have a certain image with the public. In making these applications, the analyst will need to consider the credibility of the stakeholder in terms of the following six factors.

The first factor, *dynamism*, has to do with the extent to which a stakeholder is depicted or perceived as forceful, bold, active, involved, energetic, busy, assertive, progressive, or advocating change. An organization that wants to further this dimension of its credibility would promote the idea of its adaptability to changing world conditions, its interest in the future, and its adoption of progressive policies.

The *qualification* factor relates to the degree to which a stakeholder either is perceived to be or is depicted as being expert, knowledgeable, intelligent, from a relevant background, and experienced as an administrator, a bureaucrat, a politician, or a professional. In the recent presidential debates, Ross Perot had a high credibility rating with the business community when he talked about economic issues, but he had a low rating on experience in government. Bill Clinton tried to increase his qualification dimension by citing numerous statistics and examples of economic growth in his home state.

The *status* factor is an extension of the qualification dimension. People who are depicted as having a prestigious occupation or an association with influential people are believed to possess status. A person's dress also affects perceptions of the individual's status. Those who wish to acquire higher status in the eyes of others may arrange to be televised in settings with well-established status symbols such as a flag, a presidential jet, or a coat-of-arms. Appearing in world fora with other international spokespersons can lend an aura of respectability to a national leader or a business executive. Through association with status events such as the Olympics, businesses can enhance their credibility in the same way. In good economic times, being filmed in a penthouse office enhances the credibility of an executive on the status dimension; the person is viewed as affluent and successful. However, in difficult economic times, the same setting can reinforce a negative public perception that corporations are getting more than their share of the "good life." This consideration has led some organizations to become wary of "glossy" publications that may appear irresponsible to people who have lost their jobs or who are enduring wage freezes.

The *sociability* factor relates to the extent to which a stakeholder is depicted as likeable, friendly, associated with people in all walks of life and sharing the values and aspirations of the target audience. To be viewed as more sociable, politicians visit shopping malls and attend ground-breaking ceremonies. They don baseball caps and engage in games of pitch with the children of constituents. They even kiss babies! In the same way, corporation presidents put in an appearance at annual Christmas parties or do "walkabouts" in the plant. The Japanese regard this interpersonal dimension of credibility as particularly important for their CEOs, who often have highly accessible offices and are facilitators in the organization.

The *composure* factor is concerned with the extent to which a stakeholder is depicted as confident, articulate, in control, not stumbling or stammering (verbally or nonverbally) and maintaining direct eye contact. Former President Gerald Ford learned the importance of the composure dimension when he found the media noting every mistake he made after he stumbled, before television cameras, disembarking from an aircraft. On a second occasion, Ford was shown walking into a helicopter's doors. Meanwhile, *Saturday Night Live* aired a comedy routine parodying Ford's seeming clumsiness. Chevy Chase, acting out the part of Ford, stumbled over pieces of furniture and became entangled in a telephone cord. The situation deteriorated to the point that, in the presidential debates, a media advisor braced Ford's water glass to the podium to prevent any possibility that the glass could be overturned before a national television audience.[61] This media depiction of Ford as lacking in composure was an interesting example of the ability of the media to distort reality. Ford was, in fact, an ex-football player, noted for his dexterity and physical prowess. Organizations can also be depicted as out of control, confused, unable to respond to criticisms, or not able to articulate their views.

Minor and temporary lapses in composure can sometimes be a positive factor for an individual, causing others to perceive the person as spontaneous and sincere, even if less composed. Being too "smooth" can detract from the safety dimension, which has a greater weighting with most audiences than the composure dimension. Interpersonal communication theory tells us that we like people who are competent but "human."[62] Corporations are also discovering that it is sometimes better to admit a mistake or confess a shortcoming than to adhere doggedly to an untenable position.[63]

The *safety* factor concerns the extent to which a stakeholder is depicted as sincere, trustworthy, family oriented (in a North American context), honest, hard working, supportive of laudable causes, socially responsible, willing to take a stand (although it may be personally damaging) or sharing a common fate with the target audience. The safety factor is generally accepted as the most important credibility factor. No matter how composed, expert, or forceful, an executive, a public figure, or an organization that is perceived to be dishonest or socially irresponsible will lose the confidence of others. Richard Nixon, Gary Hart, Donald Trump, and many other top politicians and corporate executives have learned this lesson at high cost.

The protocol in Figure 3.4 illustrates one means of evaluating stakeholder credibility. The protocol may be applied to the evaluation of any stakeholder (e.g., institution, politician, or CEO).

The focus in surveys and reports is often on what competitors *can* do. But what competitors *can* do is often quite different from what they *will* do. For that reason, corporations are looking more carefully at the profiles of managers and decision makers (e.g., CEO, chairman, functional/operating vice president or manager, or R&D executives) as well as at organizational culture and behavior patterns. They now realize that organizational decisions are very much influenced by both the personality of the CEO and the culture of the organization.[64] Furthermore, the ability of the CEO to garner the necessary support for policies will be, in no small measure, the product of his or her credibility.

Some stakeholders have high credibility but lack the means to propagate their points of view. Whistleblowers often fit into this category.[65] A scientist who has learned that a chemical used in body implants is highly toxic may lose his job before he is able to convince the media and the public of the validity of his research. Whistleblowers go to the media in a last desperate effort to garner public support for their causes. Their success is often, but not always, limited. The level of credibility that is possessed by such individual stakeholders and advocacy groups can influence the degree to which an issue affects the organization.

"Type 3" responses, which are appropriate for issues that are not opposed by stakeholders with a significant power capability or high credibility, include the initiation of monitoring procedures. Through monitoring an issue on an ongoing basis, it is possible to track changes in the level of stakeholder capability and credibility. If opposition stakeholders acquire an enhanced capability and credibility over time (becoming more threatening to the organization), the organization will proceed to the next issue-screening step.

"TYPE 4" RESPONSES

Question four on the issue-screening decision tree asks: Does the organization have the power capability and credibility to defuse the threat? Any organization will need to assess its own power capability and level of credibility, in the same way that it assesses the power capability and credibility of opposition stakeholders. If the answer to this question is "no," the organization will continue monitoring efforts. It will also initiate low-cost, low-profile public relations strategies (e.g., consulting with elite opinion leaders or conducting focus groups) to lower the threat potential. It will respond with more resources, as required, to handle specific threats (e.g., a crisis situation).

"TYPE 5" RESPONSES

If the answer to question four is "yes" (a "Type 5" response), the organization will probably invest in high-cost, high-profile strategies (e.g., advertising and lobbying campaigns, extensive consultations, or surveys).

CONCLUSIONS

High-priority issues command the attention of the organization. They affect the company's bottom line, and they influence the government's potential to function with optimum effectiveness. The issues that are judged to be most critical will call for a different level of investment from those judged to be noncritical.

FIGURE 3.4
Stakeholder Credibility Protocol

Depicted in media as dynamic (forceful, bold, active, involved, energetic, busy, assertive, progressive, advocating change)

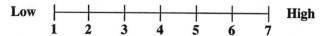

Low 　1　2　3　4　5　6　7　 High

Depicted in media as safe (sincere, trustworthy, family oriented, honest, hard working, supportive of laudable causes, socially responsible, believing what he/she says, willing to take a stand even when it may be personally damaging, depicted as sharing common fate with audience)

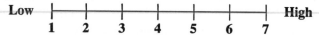

Low 　1　2　3　4　5　6　7　 High

Depicted in media as qualified (expert; knowledgeable; intelligent; having relevant background to hold position; able to cite statistics and evidence to back up stance on issues; experienced as administrator, bureaucrat, politician, or professional)

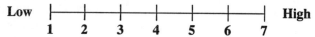

Low 　1　2　3　4　5　6　7　 High

Depicted in media as composed (confident; articulate; in control; not stumbling or stammering, nonverbally or verbally; maintaining direct eye contact)

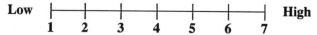

Low 　1　2　3　4　5　6　7　 High

Depicted in media as having status (associated with a prestige occupation or people; well-dressed; depicted with influential and respected authority symbols such as a flag, presidential jet, crest-of-arms; or with respected authority figures such as leaders of other countries, celebrities, etc.)

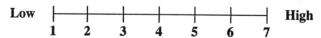

Low 　1　2　3　4　5　6　7　 High

Depicted in media as sociable (likeable; friendly; associated with people in all walks of life, including the young, the old, factory workers, professionals; sharing the values and aspirations of the audience)

Low 　1　2　3　4　5　6　7　 High

Overall Source Credibility Rating (average of above ratings): _____
Strengths or Opportunities: _____
Weaknesses or Threats: _____

Understanding what makes an issue critical or noncritical to the organization will assist decision makers in deciding issue priority. Issues with different impact potential will call for different levels of investment on the part of the organization.

NOTES

1. Interview with Alan Morgan, Director, Communication Strategy Directorate, External Affairs, Government of Canada, Spring 1989.
2. Survey conducted by Sherry Ferguson, to which 15 Fortune 500 companies responded, Spring 1992.
3. Jan P. Herring, "Senior Management Must Champion Business Intelligence Programs," *Journal of Business Strategy*, September/October 1991, p. 50.
4. Ibid.
5. Robert L. Heath and Richard Alan Nelson, *Issues Management: Corporate Public Policymaking in an Information Society* (Newbury Park, Calif.: Sage Publications, 1986), p. 149.
6. André G. Gib and Robert A. Margulies, "Making Competitive Intelligence Relevant to the User," *Planning Review*, May/June 1991, p. 18.
7. Anthony J. F. O'Reilly, "Leading a Global Strategic Charge," *Journal of Business Strategy*, July/August 1991, p. 13.
8. Seymour Lusterman, *Managing Federal Government Relations* (New York: Conference Board, 1988), p. 12.
9. Ferguson, Spring 1992.
10. Constance S. Bates, "Mapping the Environment: An Operational and Environmental Analysis Model," *Long Range Planning*, October 1985, pp. 98–102.
11. Gabriel Amond, *The American People and Foreign Policy* (New York: Praeger Publishers, 1960).
12. Heather Haveman, "Between a Rock and a Hard Place: Organizational Change and Performance Under Conditions of Fundamental Environmental Transformation," *Administrative Science Quarterly*, March 1992, p. 73.
13. For additional insights, see discussion by George Cheney and Steven L. Vibbert, "Corporate Discourse: Public Relations and Issue Management," in *Handbook of Organizational Communication: An Interdisciplinary Perspective*, eds. Fredric M. Jablin, Linda Putnam, Karlene H. Roberts, and Lyman W. Porter (Newbury Park, Calif.: Sage Publications, 1987), pp. 165–94.
14. Max Meng, "Early Identification Aids Issues Management," *Public Relations Journal*, March 1992, p. 22.
15. James K. Brown, *This Business of Issues: Coping with the Company's Environments* (New York: The Conference Board, 1970), p. 33.
16. Ibid.

17. Meng, p. 22.

18. Brown, pp. 30–32.

19. John M. Bryson, "A Strategic Planning Process for Public and Non-profit Organizations," *Long Range Planning,* February 1988, p. 76.

20. Ibid.

21. Lusterman, p. 3.

22. Howard Schuman, Jacob Ludwig, and Jon A. Krosnick, "The Perceived Threat of Nuclear War, Salience, and Open Questions," *Public Opinion Quarterly,* Winter 1986, pp. 519–36.

23. The development of agenda-setting research is traced in the article by Robert G. Meadow, "Politics and Communication," in *Annual Review of Political Science,* Vol. 2, ed. Samuel Long (Norwood, N.J.: Ablex Publishing Corporation, 1987), pp. 219–21. See also David Weaver, "Media Agenda-Setting and Elections: Assumptions and Implications," in *Political Communication Research,* ed. David L. Paletz (Norwood, N.J.: Ablex Publishing Corporation, 1987), pp. 176–93. Classical references include the following: Walter Lippmann, *Public Opinion* (New York: Free Press, 1922); V. O. Key, Jr., *Public Opinion and American Democracy* (New York: Alfred A. Knopf, 1961); Gladys Lang and Kurt Lang, *Politics and Television* (Chicago: Quadrangle Books, 1968); Maxwell E. McCombs and Donald L. Shaw, "The Agenda-Setting Function of the Media," *Public Opinion Quarterly,* Summer 1972, pp. 176–87; and Maxwell E. McCombs, *The Emergence of American Political Issues: The Agenda-Setting Function of the Press* (St. Paul, Minn.: West Publishing, 1977).

24. John Pound, "Beyond Takeovers: Politics Comes to Corporate Control," *Harvard Business Review,* March/April 1992, p. 93.

25. Adam Shell, "Speakers Jolt Business with Dose of Reality," *Public Relations Journal,* April 1992, p. 13.

26. W. Phillips Davison, James Boylan, and Frederick T. C. Yu, *Mass Media: Systems and Effects,* 2nd ed. (New York, N.Y.: Holt, Rinehart and Winston, 1982).

27. Shanto Iyengar and Donald Kinder, *News that Matters* (Chicago: University of Chicago Press, 1987). John G. Geer, "Do Open-Ended Questions Measure 'Salient' Issues?" *Public Opinion Quarterly,* Fall 1991, p. 367, found newspapers prime attitudes as much as does television. The impact of priming may be greater on issues perceived to be more important.

28. Richard A. Brody, respondent in "The Future Study of Public Opinion," edited by Leo Bogart, *Public Opinion Quarterly,* Winter 1987, p. S176.

29. Angus Reid, "Public Affairs Research: Quantitative and Qualitative," in *The Canadian Public Affairs Handbook: Maximizing Markets, Protecting Bottom Lines,* eds. W. John Wright and Christopher J. DuVernet (Toronto: Carswell, 1988), pp. 136–37.

30. Maxwell E. McCombs, "Public Response to the Daily News," in *Women and the News,* ed. Laurily K. Epstein (New York: Hastings House, 1978).

31. Reid, p. 138.

32. Claire Badaracco, "Religious Lobbyists in the Public Square," *Public Relations Quarterly*, Spring 1992, p. 31.

33. Some of the most often-cited studies that reached these conclusions include the following: Seymour Martin Lipset, *The First New Nation* (New York: Anchor Books, 1967); Robin M. Williams, Jr., *American Society: A Sociological Interpretation*, 3rd ed. (New York: Alfred A. Knopf, 1970), p. 455; Milton Rokeach, "Change and Stability in American Value Systems, 1968–1971," in *Understanding Human Values: Individual and Societal*, ed. Milton Rokeach (New York: The Free Press, 1979), pp. 17, 129, 143; Gordon Allport, *Personality* (New York: Holt, 1954), p. 231; Harold Lasswell, *Power and Personality* (New York: Viking Press, 1967), p. 17; Daryl J. Bem, *Beliefs, Attitudes and Human Affairs* (Belmont, Calif.: Brooks Cole, 1970), p. 17; and Robin M. Williams, Jr., "Change and Stability in Values and Value Systems: A Sociological Perspective," in *Understanding Human Values: Individual and Societal*, ed. Milton Rokeach (New York: The Free Press, 1979), p. 18.

34. Richard Easterlin and Eileen M. Crimmins, "Private Materialism, Personal Self-Fulfillment, Family Life, and Public Interest: The Nature, Effects, and Causes of Recent Changes in the Values of American Youth," *Public Opinion Quarterly*, Winter 1991, pp. 500–501, 529.

35. Ibid., p. 529.

36. Ibid.

37. See also Frank S. Levy, *Dollars and Dreams: The Changing American Income Distribution* (New York: Russell Sage Foundation, 1987) and John L. Hammond, "Yuppies," *Public Opinion Quarterly*, 50 (1986), pp. 487–501.

38. Badaracco, p. 32.

39. Rogene A. Buchholz, "Adjusting Corporations to the Realities of Public Interests and Policy," in *Strategic Issues Management*, ed. Robert L. Heath and Associates (San Francisco: Jossey-Bass Publishers, 1988), pp. 55–56.

40. SRI International, *VALS Typology* (Menlo Park, Calif.: Author, 1984). Also SRI International, *VALS–Values and Lifestyles of Americans* (Menlo Park, Calif.: Author, 1985). James E. Grunig and Fred C. Repper, "Strategic Management, Publics, and Issues," in *Excellence in Public Relations and Communication Management*, ed. James E. Grunig (Hillsdale, N.J.: Lawrence Erlbaum Associates, Publishers, 1992), p. 142, point out that although SRI charges corporate and other users a fee (ranging from $20,000 to $150,000 per year), other researchers have developed instruments that are in the public domain. According to Grunig, the following sources describe alternative systems: H. Assael, *Consumer Behavior and Marketing Action*, 3rd ed. (Boston: Kent, 1987); R. D. Blackwell and W. W. Talarzyk, "Life-Style Retailing: Competitive Strategies for the 1980s," *Journal of Retailing*, Winter 1983, pp. 7–27; and M. Hanan, *Life-Styled Marketing* (New York: AMACOM, 1980).

41. Excerpt from David M. Dozier and Fred C. Repper, "Research Firms and Public Relations Practices," in *Excellence in Public Relations and Communication Management,* ed. James E. Grunig (Hillsdale, N.J.: Lawrence Erlbaum Associates, Publishers, 1992), pp. 205–6. For further discussion, see B. Rice, "The Selling of Lifestyles," *Psychology Today,* March, 1988, pp. 46–50.

42. For example, they prepared one report titled "The American Social Climate in 1987," Yankelovich Environmental Scanning Program, 1988.

43. William G. Zikmund, *Business Research Methods* (Chicago: Dryden Press, 1988), p. 106.

44. Kathleen Getz, "Selecting Corporate Political Tactics," in *Academy of Management Best Papers,* eds. Jerry Wall and Lawrence R. Jauch, 51st Annual Meeting, Miami Beach, Florida, August 11–14, 1991, p. 328.

45. Rogene A. Buccholz, William D. Evans, and Robert A. Wagley, *Management Response to Public Issues: Concepts and Cases in Strategy Formulation* (Englewood Cliffs, N.J.: Prentice-Hall, Inc., 1985), pp. 7–8, outlined 7 of the 11 individual steps.

46. Meng, p. 22.

47. Getz, p. 328.

48. Meng, p. 22.

49. Jane E. Dutton, Stephen A. Stumpf, and David Wagner, "Diagnosing Strategic Issues and Managerial Investment of Resources," in *Advances in Strategic Management,* vol. 6, eds. Paul Shrivastava and Robert Lam (Greenwich, Conn.: JAI Press, 1990), p. 163.

50. R. E. Freeman, *Strategic Management: A Stakeholder Approach* (Boston: Pitman, 1984), p. 25.

51. E. W. Brody, *Public Relations Programming and Production* (New York: Praeger Publishers, 1988), p. 81.

52. Grunig, p. 126.

53. Richard Adams, "Political Power and Social Structures," in *The Politics of Conformity in Latin America,* ed. Claudio Veliz (Oxford: Oxford University Press, 1967), p. 26. See similar discussion by Charles W. Anderson, *Politics and Economic Change in Latin America: The Governing of Restless Nations* (New York: Van Nostrand and Reinhold, 1967), p. 90.

54. Ibid.

55. Merrill Rose, "Activism in the 90's: Changing Roles for Public Relations," *Public Relations Quarterly,* Fall 1991, pp. 29–30.

56. Ibid., pp. 28–29.

57. Ibid.

58. Edie N. Goldenberg, *Making the Papers* (Lexington, Mass.: D. C. Heath, 1975), p. 145.

59. Meng, p. 24.

60. Todd Gitlin, *The Whole World is Watching* (Berkeley, Calif.: University of California Press, 1980), p. 284.

61. Ibid., p. 248.
62. Ronald B. Adler and Neil Towne, *Looking Out, Looking In* (New York: Holt, Rinehart and Winston, Inc., 1990), p. 286. Also Stephen Worchel, Joel Cooper, and George R. Goethals, *Understanding Social Psychology,* 5th ed. (Pacific Grove, Calif.: Brooks/Cole Publishing Company, 1991), p. 250, discusses the results of studies that suggest that blunders, mistakes, and errors of judgment can be endearing in a person of high competence.
63. Prema Nakra, "The Changing Role of Public Relations in Marketing Communications," *Public Relations Quarterly,* Spring 1991, pp. 43–44.
64. Walter D. Barndt, Jr., "Profiling Rival Decision Makers," *Journal of Business Strategy,* January/February 1991, pp. 8–11.
65. Lea P. Stewart, " 'Whistle Blowing': Implications for Organizational Communication," in Sherry Devereaux Ferguson and Stewart Ferguson, *Organizational Communication* (New Brunswick, N.J.: Transaction Books, 1988), pp. 303–16.

CHAPTER 4

TRACKING PRIORITY ISSUES IN THE MEDIA: ASKING RELEVANT QUESTIONS

Organizations may monitor many categories of information: political and socio-logical trends, competitors, technological innovations, and patent applications, among others. In an information society, one of the most relevant categories of information to be tracked is public and other stakeholder opinion as it relates to the organization's issue environment (e.g., the opinion of brokers, employees, shareholders, attorneys, bankers, and the general public).[1] This opinion often surfaces in the media. Organizations monitor the media in order to:

- Respond proactively to critics of policies and programs.
- To learn more about what their competition is doing and saying.
- To learn more about what dissident investors are saying and doing.[2]
- To stay informed on public response to legislative proposals and "trial balloons" floated by governments.
- To understand perceived client needs.
- To learn the response of stakeholder publics to new products and ser-vices.
- To understand the public response to a crisis situation (e.g., a product recall, accusations of deceptive advertising, fraud charges, or other scandal.[3]
- To ascertain the extent to which the organization's preferred messages are reaching the public via media channels (which will, in turn, facilitate evaluation of media strategies).
- To identify threats, opportunities, and challenges in the organization's issue environment (including the extent to which the organization is being given appropriate credit for its strengths or being assigned blame for its weaknesses).
- To identify threats and opportunities in the issue environments of com-

petitors, vendors, subcontractors, financiers, venture and alliance partners, and others.

- To identify likely partners for future ventures (those with similar issue stances, compatible goals, high credibility, etc.).
- To learn stakeholders' responses to proposals for a strategic alliance (Do they perceive that the venture will be successful? How do they believe it will affect the company's reputation? How will the stock market respond? Are key members of top management on board, or do they see the alliance as a threat to their careers or power? How will customers, suppliers, existing alliance partners, financiers, and competitors react?[4]
- To learn how the organization's issues rank on the media agenda, thus facilitating appropriate organizational responses to threats and opportunities.
- To learn more about how the media is depicting organizational performance and leadership on specific issues.[5]
- To identify the extent to which the media is portraying the organization as being in control of its issue environment.
- To identify opinion leaders on specific issues, in order to respond to their concerns.
- To identify stakeholders' and organizational recommendations regarding future research, policies, and programs.

Vital intelligence regarding the plans of competitors can be found in the media. For example, in March 1989, a television interviewer asked Sir John Egan, head of Jaguar, about his interest in pursuing a merger. Egan said he was not interested, but his nonverbal language failed to reinforce his words. He spoke in a "slightly hesitant" tone of voice, and his manner and choice of words suggested that his decision was not firm. Less than a year later, in December 1989, Ford acquired Jaguar.[6] An increasing number of conflicts between industry and advocacy groups are being aired in the public arena, as advocacy groups use the media to push their causes. Many consumer and environmental activists, ousted from the inner policy circles of the government in the 1980s, learned to advance their social and public policy initiatives through strategic use of the media. Advocacy institutes have established training centers for "grass roots activists," where they are taught to frame their issues for media consumption. For example, a campaign against smoking might use a colorful analogy to bring life to statistics: "1,000 people quit smoking every day—by dying. That is equivalent to two fully loaded jumbo jets crashing every day with no survivors."[7] An advocacy group arguing against advertising policies laces the facts with emotional appeals: "Children can name more cans of beer than presidents."[8]

When researchers analyze issues in the media or other content sources, their first important step is to decide what to obtain from the analysis. In most large organizations, the issue analyst typically consults with others before beginning the monitoring. This collaboration allows for the framing of relevant research questions. Organization researchers ask themselves: Considering the goals of the organization and current demands on the organization, what are the most important questions to be addressed in any research effort?

A MENU OF QUESTIONS

One approach to issue analysis could be called the "menu approach." An analyst operates from a list of questions, or a menu, that can apply to almost any issue. It is possible to construct this menu from the questions raised in this chapter. In any given situation, the analyst examines such a list and tries to determine the questions to be answered in the analysis. The researcher eliminates some questions and adds others. This is a flexible approach because the analyst should not feel bound to answer all, or even most, of the questions. Rather, the purposes to which the analysis will be put, the character of the material being analyzed, and the intended readership for the issue analysis report will determine which questions will be answered.

The issue analyst commonly looks for the (1) *ranking of the issue on the media agenda;* (2) *stakeholders in the issue;* (3) *control of the media agenda;* (4) specific *arguments and reasoning* applied to the issue; (5) *opinion leaders;* (6) *focus of media coverage;* (7) *recommendations, cautions,* and *assignment of blame;* (8) *tone* of discussions, (9) *preferred messages* picked up by the media (10) general levels of *awareness and understanding* of issues evidenced in public discussions, (11) the extent to which the organization is depicted as having the *situation under control;* (12) levels of expressed *optimism that the issue will be favorably resolved;* (13) the *emergence of related issues;* and (14) *trends in media coverage.*

Ranking of Issue on Media Agenda

Where a story appears in the newspaper implies its importance, relative to competing items. A scandal involving a company official may receive headline coverage or be relegated to page eight, depending upon what else happens on that particular day. The announcement of a congressman's trip to Lebanon to barter for the release of hostages may be placed on page one or page six. An airplane crash or a summit meeting can give the news story a lower priority than it would normally occupy. Assessing the news value of other items that appear on the same broadcast or in the same newspaper can give additional information on the news value of the issue being tracked. Tracking the placement of a news item, over time, can suggest the long-term priority of the item.

Similarly, in the case of television, it is necessary to ask: Does the story appear in the first third of the television news lineup? Middle third? Final third?

Lead stories have more influence than stories at the middle or end of broadcasts.[9] How long has the story been in that position? What resources has the station invested in the story (e.g., location shots, on-the-spot interviews, or interstation hookups)? An analyst can determine when a story that first appeared in newspapers achieved broadcast status. The analyst can also ascertain the issue's survival time (how long it has been on the media agenda in first, second, third, or other ranking).

The following are other questions that researchers consider. Relative to other news media, how is a particular medium (e.g., television) treating the news item? What is the relative space or time devoted to the issue by different media? Analysts can answer these questions by studying context (i.e., the location and interaction of news items with other items).

Stakeholders in the Issue

Decision makers are interested in knowing which stakeholders (e.g., interest and lobby groups, opinion leaders, competitors, public figures, or other "categories of people or groups who are affected by an organization")[10] are speaking out on an issue. They want to know who opposes the organization's position on specific issues (or offers an alternative explanation) and who supports the organization's stance (or offers a similar interpretation). Issue monitoring enables the organization to acquire this information.

Groups with sufficient resources to prepare background materials, factual reports, and analyses have the best chance of having their views represented in the media. For the "resource-poor" groups to be given coverage, they must be defined as "newsworthy." This usually translates into group members doing something unusual or associating with someone who is prominent.[11] Speaking at a celebrity dinner, Elizabeth Taylor may argue the cause of AIDS activists; Michael Jackson may push pro-environment concerns. On *Saturday Night Live,* Sinead O'Connor tore up a picture of Pope John Paul in protest of the Church's stance on women's rights in Ireland. In issues management, the political orientations and levels of activism of stakeholder publics play an important role in defining their importance.[12]

Stakeholders may include customers, employees, managers, owners, stockholders, vendors, the general public, and public officials. Businesses are placing an increasing emphasis on the activities and plans of government bureaucrats. It has been said that the "absolute importance score" of government bureaucrats has increased by almost 25 percent over the last decade.[13]

Control of the Media Agenda

On many occasions, when seemingly highly critical coverage of an organization's handling of an issue has appeared in U.S. newspapers, the coverage has resulted from capture of the media agenda by specific interest groups, which are not necessarily representative of general public opinion. Because of the highly charged emotional content of issues associated with disposal of hazardous wastes, rising health care costs, abortion, gun control, and capital punishment, activists associated with these causes can secure sometimes a disproportionate amount of media coverage.

From time to time, foreign groups or governments manage to dictate the national media agenda. For example, on one occasion when the Canadian Minister of External Affairs was touring southern Africa, speaking in favor of increased sanctions against Pretoria, the South African government engineered a number of diversions to capture international media attention. Among these tactics was an invitation extended to two Canadian native leaders to visit South Africa. Upon their arrival, Pretoria encouraged the native leaders to compare the conditions of South African blacks to the living conditions of Canadian aboriginal people. Both the Canadian press and the international press responded to this public relations ploy by publicizing the antics of South Africa's President Botha. In so doing, the press unintentionally aided Botha in his attempt to discredit Canada and at the same time diverted attention from the foreign minister's tour. In a second case, the Canadian press gave extensive coverage to a U.S. lobby against a Canadian film-distribution bill. Such examples illustrate the occasional ability of individuals or interest groups outside the country to gain control of the media agenda and subvert the domestic government's efforts to get across its preferred messages.

In the above instances, the issue analyst is attempting to discover *who is in control of the media agenda.* When issues involve multiple stakeholders, the media may take the point of view of one or another stakeholder. The analyst asks: Whose attitudes appear to dominate the coverage? From whose *point of view* are arguments presented? A lobby or interest group? A foreign influence? Industry? Government? What time or space has been allocated by the media to views expressed by different stakeholders? With what frequency have the views of different groups been reported in the print and broadcast media?

The protocol that follows (Figure 4.1) illustrates an effort to collect information on point of view and focus of coverage. Logging the amount of air time or newspaper space that is devoted to different points of view or different facets of an issue can help the analyst to determine (1) the salience of the issue, (2) the dominant points of view, and (3) the grounds on which the issue is being argued. Knowledge is the foundation of all good communication strategies.

Arguments and Reasoning

An organization can best answer its critics if it knows the basic grounds on which issues are being argued. Decision makers are interested in knowing what lobby groups and opinion leaders are saying about the organization and its policies. They want to know what arguments are being used to support the

FIGURE 4.1
Stakeholder Perspective and Topic Focus

Time devoted to different stakeholder perspectives:

	Stakeholder	Time devoted
1		
2		
3		
4		
5		
6		
7		
8		

Dominant perspective(s) of newscast from list above:

Time devoted to different content topics:

	Topic	Time devoted
1		
2		
3		
4		
5		
6		
7		
8		

Dominant topic(s) of newscast from list above:

FIGURE 4.2
Protocol for Analysis of Arguments and Reasoning

I. Key concerns as defined by the press

  A. Concerns relating to . . .
    1.
    2.
    3.

  B. Concerns relating to . . .
    1.
    2.
    3.

  C. Concerns relating to . . .
    1.
    2.

  D. Concerns relating to . . .

II. Major criticisms of policy

  A. Criticisms relating to . . .
    1.
    2.

  B. Criticisms relating to . . .
    1.
    2.
    3.

  C. Criticisms relating to . . .
    1.
    2.

III. Major arguments articulated in favor of policy

  A. Arguments relating to . . .
    1.
    2.

  B. Arguments relating to . . .
    1.
    2.

  C. Arguments relating to . . .
    1.
    2.

  D. Arguments relating to . . .
    1.
    2.
    3.

IV. The anticipated effects of policy or event on stakeholders

  A. On stakeholder #1
    1. In area of . . .
    2. In area of . . .
    3. In area of . . .

  B. On stakeholder #2
    1. In the area of . . .
    2. In the area of . . .

  C. On stakeholder #3
    1. In area of . . .
    2. In area of . . .
    3. In area of . . .

  D. On stakeholder #4

  E. On stakeholder #5
    1. In area of . . .
    2. In area of . . .

V. Cautions urged

A. Cautions in area of . . .
   1.
   2.
   3.

B. Cautions in area of . . .
   1.
   2.
   3.

C. Cautions in area of . . .
   1.
   2.

VII. Trends evidenced in argumentation

A. In areas of . . .
   1.
   2.

B. In areas of . . .
   1.
   2.
   3.

C. In areas of . . .
   1.
   2.

D. In areas of . . .
   1.
   2.
   3.

E. In areas of . . .
   1.
   2.
   3.

VI. Recommendations for action explicit or implicit in press accounts

A. Recommendations relating to . . .
   1.
   2.

B. Recommendations relating to . . .
   1.
   2.
   3.
   4.

C. Recommendations relating to . . .
   1.
   2.

D. Recommendations relating to . . .
   1.
   2.

Please note: It is important to find some means of differentiating between arguments that appeared in editorial or other comment and arguments presented by stakeholders who are quoted in the coverage.

organization's position. They also want to know the key concerns that surface in the press. For example, a corporation that wants to retool and shift product emphasis may assess employee and community support for this change. One aspect of this assessment may be to identify the arguments in support of and against the manufacturing shift. Industries may track coverage of environmental issues (e.g., to learn what solutions are being proposed and supported by different members of the community). They may also want to know what groups are offering the strongest opposition and what elite opinion leaders are saying. A government that plans to revise its Freedom of Information legislation may want to examine experts' responses to loopholes in the present legislation and to identify problems that need to be corrected. An industrial organization may be interested in learning more about criticisms regarding its safety practices.

An analyst must evaluate the validity of arguments made by interest groups and other stakeholders. For example, are the arguments substantiated by reliable evidence? To what extent does the stakeholder rely on emotion rather than logic? The organization must weigh the evidence brought against its position and decide whether a change of position or clarification is required. At the very least, the organization will need to answer its critics. Understanding the logic of the opposition's position will facilitate this end. A sample format for analyzing arguments and reasoning in media, correspondence, or other content sources is presented in Figure 4.2. This format may be applied to any organizational issue. To use the format, identify the issue and then catalog:

- Key concerns related to the issue.
- Major criticisms of the organization in terms of this issue.
- Major arguments in support of the organization's position.
- The anticipated effects of the policy, the program, or other organizational decision on various groups of stakeholders.

IDENTIFICATION OF OPINION LEADERS

It may be relevant to ask where new arguments originate.[14] Pack journalism has become a much-discussed phenomenon in recent years.[15] Do some journalists or commentators act as opinion leaders on specific topics? Are some newspapers or television stations setting the direction for comment on an issue? What points of view do different newspapers take regarding an issue? For example, the researcher may note: "Journalists who have expressed an interest in the proposed organizational restructuring are. . . . Those who support restructuring are. . . . Those who have taken a relatively neutral stance on the issue of restructuring include. . . . Those journalists who have argued against restructuring the organization are. . . ." By identifying specific journalists, the organization can initiate a dialogue and plan its communication strategies.

Other opinion leaders may be important members of the community. Some consultancy groups specialize in generating profiles of elite opinion leaders. If you know who the elite opinion leaders are, you can consult with them, gain useful information and insights, and present your organization's point of view. Consultations at early stages of an issue's development can sometimes prevent deterioration of relations and facilitate negotiation of differences in viewpoint.

FOCUS OF MEDIA COVERAGE

Identifying the *focus of media coverage* can be important. For example, does media discussion of a company's dismissal of its personnel director center on legal or moral arguments? Does discussion of elder abuse concentrate on physical or psychological violence? In publicizing women's issues, does television focus on employment concerns, family violence, or other aspects? Does coverage of a proposed airline merger concentrate on social or economic dimensions of the merger? Legislation concerned with equal rights may have many components (rights for women, homosexuals, people over 65, or racial groups). The media may tend to concentrate on only one element of the legislation. Over time, the focus of coverage may shift, from rights of homosexuals in the armed forces, for example, to rights of people over 65 who want to remain in the work force. Strategic issues management necessitates isolating the sections of the legislation that appear to be the focus of media comment and planning to accommodate this reality.

Recognizing *shifts in focus* can be important to understanding the development of an issue. Shifts in focus will call for adjustments in strategies for addressing issues. An example that illustrates this point relates to the nuclear industry. The incident involved a rupture of pressure tubes at a Pickering, Ontario, plant that allowed radioactive material to move from one area of the reactor to another. Shutting down the plant and replacing major components in the nuclear reactor cost close to a billion dollars. Had the utilities industry been tracking media coverage of the incident, it would have made an interesting discovery regarding shifts in the focus of coverage:

> A review of clippings on the nuclear industry over the past six months indicated there was frequent mention of things such as the cost of nuclear power when compared to coal-generated power, the cost of replacement power for the Pickering shutdowns, the cost of repairs for the Pickering plants, etc. These references to costs were labeled as a "concern about the economics of nuclear power." When this coverage was compared to coverage in the six weeks before the Pickering incidents, it was found that in the earlier period, there was a greater concern with topics such as arms, war, bombs, disarmament. These concerns were labeled "armament/ disarmament." These findings provided a basis for the conclusion that one of the impacts of the Pickering incidents was to change the focus of media coverage on the nuclear industry from one on armament/disarmament to one on the economics of nuclear power.[16]

Shifts in the focus of coverage or in arguments and reasoning may necessitate the revamping of strategic approaches. If the press, for example, is arguing for rehabilitation of criminals on economic grounds and the government is answering with arguments based on moral or humanitarian grounds, then adjustments in communication strategies will be required. If a company is placing its public relations emphasis on pay-related issues and the media is stressing workplace safety, the firm will need to reframe its strategy.

RECOMMENDATIONS, CAUTIONS, AND ASSIGNMENT OF BLAME

The central concerns of interest groups and other organization stakeholders often appear in the press before there is a meeting or a public briefing. Issue-monitoring teams try to keep on top of breaking developments by tracking issues daily. They report this information to the staff members who brief organization executives and act as liaisons with the public. An organization can learn from its critics. The organization may want to know: of those who criticized a particular policy, how many offered specific direction for change? How much agreement was there on the approach that should be taken by the organization? Sometimes experts in specific areas will speak out, making concrete and valuable *recommendations*. Consumer groups, for example, may urge companies to undertake more research in specific areas or to correct problems. At other times, experts may accept the broad course of action pre-selected by the organization but urge *cautions* in proceeding. In the weeks following the reunification of Germany, many experts speaking on American foreign policy accepted the reunification of Germany as a political fact but urged that the U.S. government obtain clarification on certain points related to NATO commitments.

Organizations are also interested in learning when *blame* is assigned and on what grounds. If the media does set the public agenda, then the priorities of the press today will determine the questions asked by the public tomorrow. The politician who anticipates being met by a contingent of reporters when he or she steps off the plane, or the chief executive officer who must listen to representatives from a vocal interest group, wants to know, in advance, what questions will be on the agenda. Proactive issues management requires current information.

TONE OF COVERAGE

Researchers are often asked to assess the tone of news coverage to decide whether the coverage is positive (favorable to the organization's stance), negative (unfavorable to the organization's position), mixed (presenting a balanced view), or neutral (lacking a point of view). Assessing the tone of articles is the result of an organization's felt need to determine if public and media response is favorable to its policies. The practice of assigning tone to articles is a common one, often used by government. In a democracy, the rule of the government in power is subject to acceptance by the public. Therefore, it is important for governments to determine, on an ongoing basis, the level of public acceptance of their policies. This end is accomplished most often through public opinion polling, media monitoring that assesses the tone of news coverage, and consultations with stakeholders.

In the same way, business and industry want to know how their operations are perceived and how their policies are viewed by the public. Such insights will be particularly sought during periods of controversy; for example, when a company receives negative publicity about a product or service. Analysis of tone can also indicate the intensity of public opinion regarding the company, its chief executive officer, its operations, and its policies. To classify direction, researchers sometimes rate material on a seven-point semantic differential scale.[17]

```
Positive ____ ____ ____ ____ ____ ____ ____ Negative
Strong ____ ____ ____ ____ ____ ____ ____ Weak
Active ____ ____ ____ ____ ____ ____ ____ Passive
```

Such scales enable the analyst to classify the news story according to the intensity of direction. Sometimes researchers substitute a three-point nominal scale, as follows:[18]

```
1. Favorable          2. Neutral          3. Unfavorable
```

In assessing tone of coverage, it is important to differentiate between comment related to the *merit of a concept* and comment related to *implementation of the concept*. Public opinion may favor free trade as a concept but oppose specifics of an agreement. Research may indicate that the public supports the concept of parole (as a means of providing supervised reentry of offenders into society) but believes that inadequate administration procedures and inefficient communication in the system afford some parolees an unjustified opportunity to commit unprovoked and brutal crimes. The analyst who is making a judgment on the directionality or tone of an article must decide whether he or she is assessing tone of coverage toward the *concept* or toward the *implementation of the concept*. Failure to make this differentiation results in a less than credible, and generally useless, analysis of tone or directionality of coverage. When two analysts disagree on the tone of a particular news item, it is sometimes because one analyst is assessing the merit of the concept and the other is assessing the way in which the concept is being operationalized.

Alternatively, the disagreement may surface because the analysts are using different criteria for deciding tone. Researchers assess tone or directionality on the basis of bias that is evidenced in the news coverage. Many types of bias may appear in a news story. Some of the most common manifestations of bias include:[19]

- Attribution bias.
- Language bias.
- Explicit opinion bias.
- Graphic bias.
- Contextual bias.

If an analyst places more weight on one type of bias, ignoring or deemphasizing the other categories of bias, he or she may assess the tone of the coverage as significantly more or less favorable than another analyst looking at the same content.

Attribution bias refers to the sources that are cited in any news story. For example, were competing views presented? Whose views dominated? Did the overall coverage favor one point of view? For example, if a corporation is announcing a new emissions policy, the newspaper may quote both the chief executive officer and members of lobby groups that have been pressing the industry to put more effective controls in place. The amount of space devoted to comment by different stakeholders could potentially bias the coverage. Whether a point of view is presented at the beginning, middle, or end of a news story may influence its acceptance.[20] The number of sources that are quoted in support of, or opposition to, a specific point of view may contribute to bias in the news coverage.

Television demonstrates attribution bias when it chooses to televise an interview with one individual in preference to another. This bias may originate at the time individuals are selected to be interviewed or at the time of editing. Person-in-the-street interviews will be edited, for example, before broadcast. Some comments will be incorporated into the news coverage, and others will be dropped. A talk show will invite some people to appear on the program and will not invite others.

Language bias refers to choice of words and the use of "loaded" language. Sentences employing the terms *dislike* and *detest*, for example, will have different intensity ratings. Similarly, news stories that are characterized by strong language will have a different intensity rating from stories that employ weak language. Whether you choose the word *says* or *vows* makes a difference to the meaning of a sentence. To say that someone *staggered* into a room carries a different impact from saying the person *entered unsteadily*.

Headlines may also be biased (e.g., "Major Airline Ditches Excess Corporate Baggage"). The term *ditches* has connotative meaning that goes beyond its dictionary definition. The following headline appeared recently in the Toronto *Globe and Mail:* "Canada Shackling Some Deportees." The subtitle read: "Banning of Forcible Sedation Results in Gagging of Unwilling Passengers."[21] Such headlines are usually written by an individual other than the journalist who writes the news story. The particular part of the news story that the headline writer selects to feature in the headline lends bias. For example, the headline "Company Hedges on Environmental Policies" could have been written "Company Pauses to Consider Alternatives." The headline "Lobby Group Warns President that Problems Are Ahead" could have been "President Meets with Lobby Groups." The headline writer has a special mission: capturing the interest of the reader. The bias that the headline writer injects into a news caption often has little to do with his or her personal prejudices. As a professional, the person is following the formula for getting reader notice: Grab the reader's interest. Nonetheless, whether intentional or unintentional, the result is bias in news coverage.

Explicit opinion bias refers to editorial or other commentary that explicitly states a point of view. In many regards, this type of comment is the least dangerous to an organization. Unlike cases where bias enters a news story more subtly through loaded language or attribution, opinion bias is obvious to a reader. The reader chooses to agree or not to agree with the columnist or editorial writer. Moreover, there may not be as much personal identification with a point of view that originates outside the reader. If there is less directive comment, or if opposing considerations are presented, the reader must engage in higher-level critical thinking to arrive at a point of view. Having made a decision, the reader may feel more committed to the point of view than would otherwise be the case.

Graphic bias refers to bias that may be present in photographs or other visuals carried in newspapers or on television. At the time of Argentina's invasion of the Falklands, for example, a poignant picture of an Argentine widow bowed in grief over her husband's casket achieved international news coverage. The picture appeared in the British and American press, as well as in other newspapers around the world. Some Britons believed it was inappropriate for the press to convey images that generated sympathy for the Argentinians. Negative political campaign ads often contain graphic bias. One U.S. public relations firm edited a speech by their client's opposition in a way that depicted the opposing candidate repeatedly nodding his head as he spoke. The head nodding transmitted the nonverbal message that the candidate was a "yes" man, an individual without strength of opinion or views. On another occasion in

Canada, a photograph of the incumbent prime minister, carried by newspapers across the country, gave the distinct impression that he had horns. The visual association of this person with the devil no doubt gave the opposition more than a little satisfaction.

On television, the graphics that appear in the upper corner of the television screen or that serve as a backdrop for commentators may carry nonverbal information that biases the viewer's perception of the verbal message. Like the headline writer, the graphic artist who composes the picture will be disconnected from the source of news comment. The artist takes the news item and designs a picture to attract viewer attention. In designing a visual for news coverage of contaminated oysters, for example, the artist has many choices. The artist can draw a skull and crossed-bones emerging from a oyster shell. Alternatively, the designer can draw a picture of normal healthy-looking oysters, clean and shiny. A designer who wants to convey the message that the problem has been solved may print the word *safe* across the visual. These three possibilities for visuals transmit different information to the viewer. In all instances, bias is being conveyed by the graphic. In some instances, there may be a lack of congruence between audio and video content in television messages. Communication theory tells us that when such inconsistencies exist, people will generally favor the nonverbal or graphic message.[22]

Contextual bias refers to the relationships between items carried in the news. For example, a news story on famine in Somalia that appears opposite an advertisement on food will be interpreted against the advertisement. An article on war and poverty in the Third World will be read against the glamorous men and women who populate the perfume and liquor advertisements of the magazine in which both appear.[23] The announcement of strike action taken by a union will be read against the visual images of unruly union members shoving police officers.[24] A television address by a CEO, broadcast to the local community, will be interpreted against the backdrop of the dog food commercial that precedes the address and the soap commercial that follows it.[25] The significance of one item is tempered by the import of an adjacent item. The congruence or lack of congruence of the two will carry meaning to the reader. A university newspaper recently carried a banner on its Christmas edition that read "Season's Greetings." Beneath the banner, the headline read: "Government Cuts Funds to Universities." Beside the article was the smiling portrait of the responsible government official. The inconsistencies in these three adjacent items created a grim and not-so-pleasant irony. The concepts of graphic and contextual bias relate to a complex but interesting area of study, semiotics. According to semioticians, nothing can be viewed in isolation from all that surrounds it.[26]

The protocol (Figure 4.3) that follows can be used to assess bias in print news coverage. You fill out a separate protocol sheet for each news item, logging the following basic data: *issue* being tracked, *newspaper source, wire service* (if applicable), *journalist* who wrote article (if name is given), *date of publication,* and *type of article* (column, editorial, news, feature, or letters to the editor). See

FIGURE 4.3
Protocol for Analysis of Bias in Print Media Coverage

Issue:	Type of Article:	— Column
Newspaper		— Editorial
Wire service:		— News
Journalist:		— Feature
Date of Article:		— Letters to the Editor

Place on Media Agenda

In terms of space devoted to topic:	In terms of layout salience:
____ Column inches of coverage (including headlines and photographs)	Position in journal — Significant * or newspaper — Insignificant ** Visual impact — — Prominent — Average
* Significant—(e.g., page 1 or 2 of major or specialty section, back page) ** Insignificant—other	

Analysis of Bias of Coverage

Bias from perspective of which stakeholder? _____

Is bias being assessed in terms of degree of favorability toward the organization's position on the issue or toward the concept (e.g., toward the organization's position on free trade or toward free trade as a concept)? _____

Source Bias	Newspaper	Journalist
Perceived as positive		
Perceived as neutral		
Perceived as negative		

Attribution Bias (Other sources quoted or cited)	In space devoted to sources	In numbers of sources cited	In placement of citation
Predominantly positive			
Balanced			
Predominantly negative			

FIGURE 4.3 (*concluded*)

Language Bias	Choice of words	Explicit opinion expressed
Slanted positive		
Neutral		
Slanted negative		

Graphic Bias (Photographic, cartoon, etc.)	
Slanted positive	
Neutral	
Slanted negative	

Setting or Contextual Bias (Congruency of adjacent materials with content of article)	
— Congruent	— with positive slant
— Incongruent	— with neutral tone
	— with negative slant

Level of Organizational Control of Issue Implied in Article

— Situation under control
— Situation in flux
— Situation requires monitoring
— Situation out-of-control

Chapter 5 for definitions of these article types. You can also log *column inches of coverage, location of the article* (in terms of its salience), and assessment of *visual impact*. If an article is located on the front or back page of a newspaper or at the beginning of a specialty section, the placement is considered *significant*. Any other location would be considered *insignificant*.

In assessing bias of coverage, the protocol suggests the need to identify the perspective of the person doing the analysis. For example, in broad terms, does the analysis take an industry perspective or a government perspective? The name of the unit commissioning the study will generally be represented in the stakeholder perspective section of the protocol (i.e., unless the analysis is being carried out on behalf of another group or another business unit).

The protocol also suggests the need to indicate whether the analyst is identifying media reaction to a *general concept* or to some form of *operationalization of the concept*. Operationalization means how the decision is being implemented, what procedures are being applied, or what specifics of an agreement are being negotiated. If you are monitoring employee and community response to the announcement of a proposed merger, you may be interested in differentiating between support for the *idea of a merger* and support for *this specific merger*. Employees may recognize the economic exigencies that are driving a company to consider a merger and may accept this reality, but they may oppose the present offer. In contrast, they may oppose both the idea of a merger *and* this specific merger. In this section of the protocol, you specify whether your approach is *conceptual* or *operational*.

In the last section of the protocol, you place check marks in the appropriate categories, indicating the nature of bias in the coverage. The possible categories of bias include *source* (the newspaper and/or the journalist sometimes have a known disposition toward the issue), *attribution* (the newspaper quotes some individuals but not others), *language* (some journalists use slanted terminology), *graphic* (bias is expressed through visuals), and *setting or contextual* (incongruent items are placed adjacent to each other). *Level of organizational control* refers to the extent to which the article depicts the organization as being in control of this issue.

The second protocol (Figure 4.4) was designed to analyze television news content. You fill out a separate sheet for each broadcast item. In the first section of the protocol, you log the following basic data: *issue* identification, *origin of the broadcast, time of broadcast, length of the story* (in seconds or minutes), and *placement of the story* (first, second, or third part of the news lineup). Listing the names of other issues or events in the news enables a more sophisticated assessment of the item's priority. For example, a breaking news story on a major scandal will cause most other issues to assume a lower priority than they would normally have. The section labeled *implied level of organizational control of the issue* refers to the extent to which the organization has retained or reacquired control of its issue.

In the section labeled *analysis by source,* place check marks in the following appropriate categories: *studio newsreader/anchor, reporter,* and *spokesperson.* For any given news show, there will generally be one newsreader/anchor for the story and one reporter on site (if applicable). The reporter may interview more than one spokesperson. The protocol allows for up to four spokespersons. You then assess each category (newsreader/anchor, reporter, and spokespersons) in terms of specifics such as *nature of the source's contribution* (was it factual comment, interpretative comment, or advocacy of a specific point of view), *relationship of the source to the event* (was the source called upon as an expert to offer an opinion, as someone who had participated in the relevant event, as a witness to the event, or as a member of the general public who was asked to comment on the event or issue), *source credibility* (what was the level of credibility of the newsreader/anchor, reporter, or spokesperson—high, medium, or low), *source bias* (does the source have a preexisting reputation for being biased on this topic—positively, negatively, or other), *location of commentary* (did the commentary or interview take place in the studio, on the street or at another field location, through an interstudio hookup, or at a press conference), *setting or contextual bias* (did the general setting of the commentary or

FIGURE 4.4

Protocol for Analysis of Bias in TV News Content

Issue:	Origin (Station): ____ Local ____ Network					
Time of Broadcast:	Length of Story:					
Priority of Coverage: ____ First Third ____ Middle Third ____ Final Third						
Other stories on newscast:	Implied level of organizational control of issue: ____ Situation under control ____ Situation in flux ____ Situation requires monitoring ____ Situation out-of-control					

	Analysis by Source					
	Studio news-reader/anchor	Reporter	Spokesperson #			
			1	2	3	4
Source Contribution						
Factual comment						
Interpretative comment						
Advocacy argument						
Relationship of Source to Event						
Expert opinion						
Participant						
Witness						
Member of general public						
Source Credibility						
High						
Medium						
Low						
Source Bias						
Predominantly positive						
Neutral						
Mixed						
Predominantly negative						
Location of Commentary						
In studio						
Field—live interaction						
Interstudio hookup						
Press conference						
Setting or Contextual Bias						
Positive						
Neutral						
Mixed						
Negative						
Language Bias						
Positive						
Neutral						
Mixed						
Negative						

interview impart any sort of bias, for example, shoving and pushing on the part of striking union members), or *language bias* (did the commentator or spokesperson use loaded verbal or nonverbal language). Place check marks in the appropriate categories, cross-referencing the headings from top to bottom and left to right.

The third protocol (Figure 4.5) allows you to log the time devoted to supportive or critical comment on a specific organizational issue. If an issue receives a large amount of media coverage, interest groups may mobilize around it. Related issues may also acquire a higher profile. It is often important for the organization to track the amount of attention that is given to an issue, an organization, or the organization's leaders.

The fourth protocol (Figure 4.6) was generated to log correspondence according to bias (letters for, against, or presenting a balanced perspective on an issue). The protocol covers basic demographic information such as the date the letter was written or received, the sex of writer (for issues that may divide people along gender lines), and the writer's state of residence (for analysis of regional differences, if applicable). Analysis of demographic information can sometimes suggest the need for customized communication strategies for different groups.

PREFERRED MESSAGES

Most organizations utilize "free" advertising techniques (public service announcements, press conferences, interviews, speeches, press releases, backgrounders, and pseudo-events) designed to draw media attention. Because even these free techniques are costly to orchestrate, organizations look for ways to evaluate the effectiveness of such efforts. One way to measure the success of their public relations efforts is to track the extent to which "preferred messages" have been picked up by the media and transmitted to the public. In other words, organizations do usage counts to find out which magazines, association newsletters, or newspapers have carried specific points made in press releases, press conferences, public speeches, or interviews with journalists. They track the extent to which the organization was mentioned in the print or broadcast media. They may pay for media-monitoring services to report which radio and television stations have broadcast their public service announcements and the frequency of the broadcasts. Traditional evaluation methods include "counting press slips, comparing column inches and broadcast time to the equivalent advertising costs, and counting the number of generated consumer impressions."[27] A typical client media-clipping book might report:

> Media coverage included 3,500 column inches of news and photographs in 350 publications with a combined circulation of 79.4 million; 2,500 minutes of air time on 290 radio stations and an estimated audience of 65 million and 660 minutes of air time

FIGURE 4.5
Protocol for Analysis of Bias in TV/Radio News Content

Time devoted to supportive comment:

	Comment	Time devoted
1		
2		
3		
4		
5		
6		
7		
8		

Dominant supportive argument(s) from list above:

Time devoted to critical comment:

	Comment	Time devoted
1		
2		
3		
4		
5		
6		
7		
8		

Dominant critical argument(s) from list above:

FIGURE 4.6
Protocol for Analysis of Bias in Correspondence

	For/Against/Balanced				Sex of Writer		
	F	A	B	Date of Letter	M	F	Writer's State of Residence
1							
2							
3							
4							
5							
6							
7							
8							
9							
10							
11							
12							
13							
14							
15							
16							
17							
18							
19							
20							
21							

FIGURE 4.6 (*concluded*)

22							
23							
24							
25							
26							
27							
28							
29							
30							

on 160 television stations, with an estimated audience of 91 million. If this time and space had been purchased at advertising rates, it would have amounted to $1,047,000.[28]

Ketchum Communications developed a Publicity Tracking Model that produces a computerized audience analysis of groups reached by messages. The messages must have appeared in media in the top 120 U.S. markets to be picked up by the Ketchum tracking system.[29] The Newlin Company uses a similar publicity tracking system that equates product publicity with advertising value.[30]

The media-monitoring services that carry out usage counts are costly because of the time-consuming nature of the work, but many governments and commercial institutions, as well as a growing number of nonprofit organizations, consider it a necessary investment. Although they cannot ascertain, by such means, the direct relationship between public voting or buying habits and their social marketing strategies, they can at least learn the extent to which the public has or has not been exposed to the organization's messages.

In the process of strategic planning, the organization decides upon the messages that it wants to reach stakeholders and the general public. Through tracking these preferred messages, the organization finds out whether it has been successful in getting the messages to its target audiences.

AWARENESS AND KNOWLEDGE OF ISSUES

An issue analyst may be asked to comment on the level of public awareness of an issue and/or the sophistication of media treatment of the issue. In a recent situation involving a group of native Canadians and Americans who were arguing a land claim in Oka, Quebec, few journalists understood the issues underlying the land claim dispute when hostilities erupted.[31] Few knew the history of the relationship between the natives of American and Canadian origin who were involved in the dispute. The large number of journalists assigned to cover the crisis at Oka did not understand the long-standing acrimony, within the native camp, of groups with conflicting claims to leadership. Early coverage did not explain that another native tribe deeply resented the Mohawk land claim. Initial coverage failed to differentiate between the Warriors, the most pugnacious of the dissenting group, and natives who took a less warlike stance (and, in fact, many of whom were opposed to the Warrior position). Later analyses of the armed Warrior standoff at Oka, which deteriorated to the point where one police officer died in cross-fire, suggested that there had been a major problem with news coverage.[32]

In short, the journalists showed little appreciation of the complexities of the situation, and media coverage tended to be simplistic and geared toward the sensational elements in the case. With the exception of the army, most stakeholders in the dispute—the natives, the Quebec police, and federal government ministers—received uniformly bad press. The most flamboyant of the Warriors, as certain elements in the native camp were termed, were the focus of media attention. Television cameras zoomed in on tatoos of "Mother" written on Warrior arms; Warriors enhanced their media status by assuming code names such as "Lasagna"; an evening news broadcast showed a native woman shoving a military youth into a barbed wire fence. Other shots showed Warriors cleaning their guns. The media, at the same time, depicted federal political figures as shirking responsibility for the conflict and Quebec police as "bad guys," who kept food and medical supplies from everyone who was, willingly or unwillingly, behind the barricade. The fact that the journalists were largely unschooled in the history of the native land claim dispute led to distorted and superficial coverage and contributed to the volatility of an already bad situation. At the other extreme, journalists who stayed behind the barricades with the Warriors tended to give highly sympathetic coverage; they were later accused of falling victim to the "Stockholm syndrome."[33] A perceptive analysis of media coverage of Oka would have pinpointed media ignorance of the issue as a primary characteristic of the situation.

Some issue analyses contain a *myth versus fact* sheet that identifies common misconceptions evident in public perception or media coverage of the organization's issues. This information is necessary for planning appropriate issue-management strategies. It is equally important to know if essential facts are being omitted. These omissions may be as important as the distortions.

Examples of myth versus fact sheets follow. The first example (Figure 4.7)

FIGURE 4.7
Myth versus Fact

Myth	Fact
Natives were united in their support of the barricade at Oka, Quebec.	There was dissension in the native camp, with a number of people opposing the barricade.
The Warriors were the accepted leaders of the natives.	There were two groups, traditionally opposed to each other, competing for leadership.
The Warriors were a group of American natives with no right to be involved at Oka.	The situation was much less clearcut, with both Canadian and American natives involved. Neither recognized the Canadian/U.S. border as a legal designation affecting native territory.
The land claim dispute concerned only Mohawks.	A second native tribe had a conflicting claim to the disputed land and opposed a government settlement with the Mohawks.

relates to the Oka situation. The second example (Figure 4.8) was generated to illustrate concerns that might be relevant to an airline firm that has experienced recent difficulties.

While "there is no direct relationship between *exposure* to information and *learning* of information" (people can be exposed repeatedly to an idea but may not remember it), the mass media can raise the information level about a topic significantly—especially if people can find a use for the information or if it is in line with their existing attitudes."[34] If people do not appear to be learning from public discussions, and media coverage remains distorted or superficial over a period of time, the organization may respond by developing background materials to distribute to journalists. In large organizations, the preparation of backgrounders is routine. In some cases, if it is evident that certain interest groups are poorly informed, the organization can mount a public relations campaign to educate them. If there is deliberate distortion of an issue in news material, the organization can respond more aggressively with an advertising campaign, or it can present its case to higher echelons of the media.

SITUATION CONTROL

In an environment where everyone, at the top and the bottom of the societal pyramid, can obtain information at the same time, it is difficult for people at the top to appear always to be in control. The decision maker is often running to

FIGURE 4.8
Myth versus Fact

Myth	Fact
There is an inherent weakness in the design of the engine mountings on the BR 126 medium-range turbo jet.	Two cases of failure to fix bolts on BR 126 flight frames involved gross disregard of flight time replacement specifications.
There are more accidents involving BR 126 aircraft than any other medium-range aircraft.	BR 126s account for more than the total of all other types of aircraft flown by medium-range operators. The percentage of accidents among BR 126s is one of the lowest in the industry.
Deregulation of airlines will result in corner-cutting in maintenance.	Failure to comply with manufacturer-specified inspection maintenance and replacement schedules can result in an operator's license being withdrawn.
A spate of structural failures and crashes can be expected in the near future, as a consequence of an aging fleet of aircraft.	Schedules of aircraft inspection and maintenance are drawn up by manufacturers and are enforced by international airline authorities.

keep abreast of current developments. Sometimes, the chief executive officer for a public corporation obtains vital information after his or her shareholders secure the same information. The president of the United States may be watching the same television newscast, brought live from across the world, as his or her constituents. These situations are frightening to people at the top, whose power has traditionally depended on control of information.

A question frequently asked by the issue analyst is, "To what extent does the media present the organization as being in control of its issue environment?" Every corporation and government wants to be perceived as being in control. That is a primary aim of the public relations efforts of almost every organization. One of the most frequent criticisms of corporations and governments is that they failed to act when action was required. Corporations may be accused of dealing, in an apathetic or disinterested way with important issues (e.g., matters pertaining to the environment or airline safety). Government may be accused of letting situations, like Oka, get out of control because they did not act decisively or they failed to establish appropriate policies. Thus, a relevant question that the issue analyst may ask is: Does the media depict the organization as having an agenda and a direction, or does it paint the organization as reacting, in a knee-jerk fashion, to developments outside its control?

LEVELS OF EXPRESSED OPTIMISM REGARDING FAVORABLE RESOLUTION OF THE ISSUE

Associated with the concept of situation control is assessment of the optimism or pessimism of media coverage of an issue. The analyst asks: Does the coverage suggest that a bad situation is likely to improve? Does local news coverage imply that Company X will stave off bankruptcy or file for bankruptcy in the near future? Does electronic media coverage of Sarajevo suggest that its problems will be solved in the not-so-distant future? Does comment on Yeltsin's personal situation suggest that he is likely to remain in power or that he will be impeached. Do journalists writing on South Africa paint a continuing bleak picture, or do they suggest that the situation is improving? In other words, is the tone of the coverage optimistic or pessimistic? In many cases, deciding upon the extent to which media coverage of an issue is optimistic or pessimistic in tone will be more productive than examining the directionality of the coverage (positive, negative, mixed, neutral). In a business context, optimistic coverage can bolster shareholder support, whereas pessimistic coverage can precipitate actions that follow lost confidence.

EMERGENCE OF RELATED ISSUES

Identifying spin-off issues is also important. Related issues will often piggyback an issue that achieves media prominence. Noting the emergence of these related issues may be relevant to developing strategies for dealing with the primary issue. A current extradition case can provoke renewed discussion of the merits of capital punishment. The Mohawk standoff at Oka, Quebec, can yield media opportunities for the Haida Indians of British Columbia to protest clear-cut logging practices or for other native groups to protest the building of a dam on disputed territory in the West. The announcement of additional plant layoffs can give union spokespersons the occasion to speak out on job-security issues that affect many different workers.

News coverage was recently given to a group of businesspeople who had been retroactively billed for shipping charges incurred some years before. The failure of some shipping companies to file the discount rates that they were charging clients meant that shippers could later demand the legally filed rates for their services. As a result, businesses were billed thousands of dollars for services they assumed they had paid in full. The publicity that *Sixty Minutes* gave to these irate clients opened up an opportunity for unions to state their case. In this particular example, the unions backed collection of the additional shipping charges on the grounds that the money was owed to Teamster members. These recent events have given union leaders the opportunity to air their grievances, not only on this matter but also on related concerns. The analyst must be sensitive to related issues that can influence the development of a primary issue.

TRENDS

The quest for insights into the future is probably as old as humanity. The study of history is justified on the basis of offering metaphors or models that improve our understanding of the present and, hopefully, enable us to anticipate and influence the future. The preoccupation of political and business theorists with analysis of trends in the development of current issues reflects these same concerns. Modern soothsayers, however, have a much more impressive array of tools to assist them than did their ancient counterparts. There is a massive amount of data available to the analyst (in print, in sound and video recording, and in computer memory). This databank of information has negative as well as positive implications. When large amounts of information are available, overload can occur. Thus, it becomes difficult for the analyst to distinguish between the significant and the trivial. Traditional wisdom tells us that in overload situations, success depends on the researcher's ability to detect significant patterns. Although modern computer technology greatly enhances pattern recognition, the technology does not suggest the *significance of the patterns*. Deciding on the significance of patterns remains a matter of judgment. Thus, the judgment of the analyst is the critical factor in determining the quality of an analysis:

> Good research must embody a level of excellence in such factors as sampling and statistical analysis in the case of quantitative studies and in respondent recruitment and the choice of a moderator in the case of qualitative studies. Beyond this, however, good research must involve an analytical edge—an appreciation not only of technique but also of how social and psychological forces lead to behavioral and attitudinal changes and the implications of these for the practice of public affairs.[35]

At the same time, the organization must guard against allowing the analyst-judgment criterion to become a justification for impressionistic or superficial analyses.

An analyst can make different kinds of comparisons.[36] He or she can compare messages from a *single source over time,* with the intention of drawing inferences about trends: for example, media depiction of a company before and after a major environmental disaster or Bill Clinton's image as depicted in U.S. media in the period before and after the Presidential debates.

An analyst can compare messages from a *single source in differing situations:* for example, a company's image before and after an announced layoff policy (using the same media in both instances) or Clinton's television image in the pre-campaign period versus his television image during the election campaign.

An analyst can compare messages produced by a *single source across different audiences:* for example, media coverage of a company in different regions of the United States or media coverage of Clinton as he traveled in different states.

An analyst can compare messages produced by *two or more different sources.* Perhaps the *New York Times* will have the most favorable coverage of a particular issue and the *Washington Post* will have the least favorable coverage. Perhaps the broadcast media will treat a particular issue with a greater degree of neutrality than will the print media. On another occasion, the researcher may choose to compare the way radio covered a company announcement of layoffs with the way television covered the layoffs, or the way the print media depicted Clinton with the way the electronic media depicted him. Organizations often want to know how the press is lining up on specific issues that concern their mandates and jurisdiction.

An analyst can relate content data to some *performance standard.*[37] Meaningful interpretation of content data involves comparisons with other data or with some standard. For example, to note that 75 references to U.S. human rights policies appeared between July and December 1991 is meaningless unless one compares this information with past trends. Is the media increasing its coverage of human rights issues? Does this increased coverage reflect growing public concern with human rights issues? How does the coverage compare with last year's coverage in the same time frame? The researcher can compare typical broadcast media coverage of the seal industry with coverage after a major protest by Greenpeace members. To set a performance standard for analysis of coverage of a firm, the researcher may need to look at typical coverage of companies in the same sector. Alternatively, in a government context, an analyst could compare the way the media treats Clinton during his first term in office with how the media typically treats presidents. Some theories suggest, for example, that presidents first undergo a period of alliance with the media; next there is a competitive phase, characterized by media criticism; finally there is a period of detachment, in which relations become more formal and routine.[38] To comprehend the meaning of the media's coverage of Clinton's first year in office, one needs to be aware of the standard treatment given presidents.

Sometimes the analyst must construct standards for comparison. For example, if a researcher wants to know the relative emphasis given by California papers to federal issues, he or she will need to construct an index for the purposes of comparison.[39] The analyst will need to code sample coverage of federal issues in other states (e.g., Texas, Montana, and New York) to use as a reference point for gauging typical measures of coverage. Carrying out this task will allow the researcher to establish a standard against which to compare California's performance. The analyst can compare the average amount of space devoted to federal issues in California with the average amount of space devoted to federal issues in other states. He or she can also compare frequency of articles published on a topic in California over a given period of time with frequency of articles published on the same topic in other states, over the same period of time. The same can be done with coverage of a company's issues.

Finally, the analyst can compare content data with *products other than content indexes, such as expert opinion or aggregate data.*[40] For example, the researcher can compare Clinton's performance against some standard established by reference to expert opinion. A group of political scientists may point out that democrats typically receive more support in the South than do republicans. This information can help the researcher to interpret the data on Clinton's campaign. Communication specialists maintain that headlines tend to stress the sensational, and they tend to be more often negative than positive. This may be true regardless of newspaper bias toward the subject matter. This knowledge can help in interpreting the findings of a specific study. On other occasions, as in research concerned with seniors, youth, or minority groups, aggregate data (such as census data) can help the researcher to interpret his or her findings. To determine how much public confidence is being expressed in a company, the firm may want to take additional measures into consideration such as stock market performance or other standard performance indexes.

EXAMPLES OF QUESTIONS ASKED IN ANALYSES OF PUBLIC OPINION ENVIRONMENT

The following questions could apply in an analysis of media coverage of layoffs at an automotive plant:

- What priority was given to the issue in local news coverage?
- What stakeholders received media attention? Whose point of view dominated the coverage (the union's, the company's, or other stakeholder's)? Who appeared to be in control of the media agenda? Local unions? The company? The national union?
- What arguments and reasoning appeared in support of the company's position? What criticisms were levied against the company? What concerns were expressed?
- Did any opinion leaders speak out on the topic? If so, who? What was their point of view? How did journalists line up on the issue? What were the views of newspapers? What were the views of other media?
- Where did the press concentrate its discussion? On economic dimensions of the problem? On social dimensions? On political dimensions? On technological dimensions? In other areas?
- Were alternative solutions to the economic problems of the company proposed? What recommendations were made? Were any cautions urged? On whom was blame placed: The company for lack of commitment to its workers? The unions for making unreasonable demands? The

workers for failure to meet production schedules? The banking system or the government for refusal to bail out the company?

- What was the tone of coverage? Was it favorable toward the company's position? Unfavorable? Neutral?
- To what extent did the press transmit the preferred messages of the company in its coverage of the issue of layoffs?
- Did journalists demonstrate a good understanding of the nuances and complexities of the issue? Was there a fair and accurate representation of the situation? What inaccuracies, if any, appeared in the coverage?
- Did the coverage suggest that the company is still viable? Is it capable of retaining the support of the community and overcoming its present economic difficulties?
- Did any related issues emerge from the coverage of the layoffs? For example, pension issues? Retraining? Top-heavy management?
- Did any trends emerge? Did electronic media coverage vary from print media coverage of the layoffs? Did the coverage vary over time? Did any shifts take place in the period preceding and after the CEO appeared on local television to explain the layoffs?

An analysis of press and public reaction to the native barricade at Oka, Quebec, might have asked the following questions:

- What were the perceptions of government leadership in the crisis?
- To what extent was the government seen to have the situation under control?
- How were army actions viewed?
- To whom was blame assigned in the crisis? Natives? Quebec police? Provincial or federal government? Others?
- How was native leadership perceived? To what extent did the press depict native leadership as coherent?
- Whose point of view was represented most often in the coverage?
- What related issues received press coverage in the period under consideration?
- To what extent were there overtones of racism in the public discussions generated by Oka?
- What were the recommendations for resolving the issues generated by Oka?

Policy makers often analyze public and media reaction to positions that they have taken or intend to take. A U.S. policy maker concerned with public reaction to proposed participation in the Arias Peace Plan might have asked the following questions:

- What was the level of interest that the press displayed in Central American issues between August 1, 1987, and November 11, 1987?
- What was the tone of media comment on the possible participation of the United States in the Arias Peace Plan?
- What arguments were presented in favor of U.S. participation in the peace plan?
- What arguments were given against participation? Where did negative comment originate?
- How sophisticated was the media's treatment of Central American issues? Did there appear to be an appreciation of the complexities of the situation?
- Was there any consensus on which countries had the best chance of experiencing success with the Arias Peace Plan?
- What references to the government's human rights policies appeared in the coverage?
- What references to U.S. foreign aid policies appeared in the coverage?
- What references to U.S. immigration policies appeared in the coverage?
- What interest groups were represented in the coverage?
- Which newspapers actively reported on Central American issues in the period under consideration?
- What trends in coverage can be anticipated?

The sample analysis of U.S. press coverage of Central American peace issues illustrates an attempt to answer the above questions (see Figure 4.9).

Assuming that company X has announced its intention to subcontract the manufacture of parts that it previously made on site, an analyst asked to report journalistic comment on the proposed action might respond to the following questions:

- How many news commentaries addressed the topic?
- What arguments were presented in favor of subcontracting the work?
- What arguments were presented against subcontracting the work?
- What additional actions and cautions were urged?
- What interest groups were represented in the coverage?
- What points of view were espoused by the interest groups?
- What trends appeared in the press commentaries?

FIGURE 4.9
**Press Coverage of Central American Issues August 1, 1987–
November 11, 1987**

In the period under consideration, the press showed a sustained interest in
Central America, publishing numerous editorials and commentaries, even
when no news events were being reported. Press response to the idea of U.S.
support for the Arias Plan was unabashedly positive, with fewer than 10
percent of the editorialists and columnists opposing U.S. involvement.

Arguments in favor of U.S. participation in the peace plan were as follows:
(1) The United States could make a valid and important contribution to peace.
(2) The United States could answer critics who accuse the government of
continuing to pursue the role of aggressor in world politics. (3) The United
States could gain further friendships in the international community. (4) The
United States could reaffirm its position of leadership in the foreign policy
area.

The domestic press appears to recognize that the role of the U.S. military is
changing, and the large majority of journalists express approval for the shift
from a more aggressive posture to the role of peacekeeper.

Journalists did not appear to underestimate the complexity of the Central
American issues or the influence of economics on the politics of these
countries. For example, they saw Nicaragua as the key country that could
influence a sequence of events in other countries; and they saw upcoming
decisions in the U.S. Congress as critical to future developments in Central
America. The press did not reach consensus on which countries had the best
chance of experiencing success with the Arias Plan; however, El Salvador
probably received fewer votes of confidence than did the other countries.

Recent accusations that the U.S. government has behaved inconsistently in its
treatment of human rights violators did not influence the coverage of Central
American issues. While human rights abuses were mentioned, as was
suspension of personal freedoms in other countries, no journalist suggested
that these practices should influence the U.S. decision to give support to the
Arias Peace Plan.

A dissenting point of view on the question of financial aid to Central America
came from a Guatemalan organization whose representative was visitng the
United States. The group expressed the view that the United States should
encourage dialogue rather than offer financial aid to the Guatemalan
government. Few interest groups were represented in the news coverage in
the August to November period.

Relatively few references to the government's Central American refugee and
immigration policy appeared in the August to November press; journalists
writing on the topic championed a more open policy and argued against
closing U.S. borders to Central Americans.

Newspapers in the Southwestern United States were by far the most active on
Central American issues. To date, the journalists who have been most critical
of the U.S. position on other current foreign affairs issues, such as the U.S.
stance on sanctions against South Africa, have been silent on Central America.
If, however, these writers choose to become active on Central America, it is
anticipated that their arguments could be drawn from a stock selection
including references to (1) the political motives of the government,

FIGURE 4.9 (*concluded*)

---

(2) Communist/Marxist affiliations of countries we are aiding, (3) human rights records of countires to whom we are giving assistance, (4) the risk of military involvement, (5) shirking responsibilities at home in favor of engagement abroad, and (6) the economic burden of helping Third World countries.

* This is a fictitious example.

FIGURE 4.10
Media Response to Bill X, Refugee Determination Legislation

This analysis is based on a sample of 187 articles published in the print media between January 1, 1993, and January 15, 1993. Newspapers and magazines included in the sample are *The Wall Street Journal*, the *Baltimore Sun*, the *Los Angeles Times*, the *Washington Post*, the *New York Times*, the *Richmond Times-Dispatch*, *Newsweek*, *U.S. News and World Report*.

Commentaries

Fifty opinion articles were published between January 1 and January 15, 1993; half originated in the Northeast, especially Washington, D.C.; New York City; and Boston. A large number were published in the first three days after Bill X came into effect; however, journalists continued to comment on the legislation throughout the first two weeks in January.

Arguments in Favor of Legislation
1. The processing of applications will be speedier.
2. The new procedures are less complicated, with fewer steps.
3. The new legislation ensures admission of genuine refugees while steming the flow of bogus refugees.
4. The legislation has Constitutional validity.
5. The new legislation meets both physical and emotional needs of claimants.

Arguments Against Legislation
1. The new legislation imposes unduly strict regulations.
2. The new legislation is costly to implement.
3. The legislation will eventually generate its own backlog, just as the earlier legislation did.
4. The legislation ignores the emotional and human dimension of refugee claims.
5. The legislation violates Constitutional rights (right to appeal, right to full and impartial hearing, right to legal counsel, guarantee against arbitrary search and seizure, and right to fundamental justice).
6. The legislation puts the physical safety of refugee claimants at risk.
7. The legislation prevents external agencies from legally helping claimants.

Additional Actions and Cautions Urged
1. Regulate immigration consultants.
2. Refute portrayal of United States as an easy haven for bogus refugee claimants.
3. Reconsider issue of safe Third World countires.

FIGURE 4.10 (*concluded*)

---

4. Apply the same regulations to all refugee claimants—no matter what the claimant's position in the public realm be.

Interest Groups

Those opposing Bill X included church organizations such as the Inter-Denominational Committee for Refugees, immigration lawyers, immigration consultants, Citizens Against Violence, and the World Amnesty Organization.

Those supporting Bill X included some refugee claimants and various refugee aid organizations.

Trends

Over the two-week period, comments by the press became increasingly positive towards the new legislation. Although journalists tended to give sympathetic coverage to those refugees being sent home, they also praised the government for taking a firm stance. Some interest groups that had initially voiced the strongest opposition to the bill began to comment on positive aspects of the bill as well.

* This is a fictitious example. Ilona Koszegi assisted in developing this example.

The sample analysis represented in Figure 4.10 addresses similar questions that the federal government could ask on the occasion of passing new refugee determinism legislation.

A government policy analyst, at the time of the tabling of new state abortion legislation, could ask the following questions about the public opinion environment surrounding the abortion issue:

- How does the public (as reflected through the media) view the abortion issue?

- What are the dominant arguments developed by the right-to-life and the pro-choice groups?

- How have the arguments of these groups shifted over time?

- Does the press appear to be giving greater coverage to one group, as opposed to the other?

- Does the press appear to be championing one point of view over the other?

- Does the coverage signal the emergence of a third major point of view on the issue?

- How is the government position on the abortion issue portrayed by the media?

- Have specific messages that were sent out by the government, via the media, reached the public?

Some common questions asked by the issue analyst can be inferred from the outlines in Figures 4.11 through 4.16. Reports generated on the basis of these outlines would be organized by region, stakeholder, dimensions of issue, time,

FIGURE 4.11
Common Patterns of Organization, by Region

Reaction to Telephone Rate Increases
1. Reaction in Louisiana to rate increases.
   a. Pro-corporation perspective.
   b. Anti-corporation perspective.
2. Reaction in Arkansas to rate increases.
   a. Pro-corporation perspective.
   b. Anti-corporation perspective.
3. Reaction in Alabama to rate increases.
   a. Pro-corporation perspective.
   b. Anti-corporation perspective.
4. Reaction in Mississippi to rate increases.
   a. Pro-corporation perspective.
   b. Anti-corporation perspective.
5. Reaction in Texas to rate increases.
   a. Pro-corporation perspective.
   b. Anti-corporation perspective.

FIGURE 4.12
Common Patterns of Organization, by Stakeholder

Subsidized Child Care
1. Perspective of parents providing in-home care for children.
   a. Proposed policy places unfair additional tax responsibility on Americans.
   b. Government should give better tax breaks to homemakers.
   c. Government should give the same tax allowances to parents of children receiving in-home care as to parents of children receiving out-of-home care.
   d. Government should not be using public funds for private purposes.
   e. Day-care subsidies contribute to the economic, political, and/or moral decline of the country.
2. Perspective of parents requiring out-of-home care for children.
   a. Government should give more financial support to parents requiring out-of-home care for children.
   b. Government must ensure the availability of more spaces for children in nonprofit centers.
   c. Government should ensure access to better quality out-of-home care.
   d. Government must ensure continuing subsidies for low-income families.
3. Perspective of profit day-care centers.
   a. Government must not abandon profit centers.
4. Perspective of state government.
   a. Government has a responsibility to subsidize out-of-home care for children.
   b. Government does not have a responsibility to subsidize out-of-home care for children.

FIGURE 4.13
Common Patterns of Organization, by Dimension of Issues

Drug Testing in the Workplace
1. Legal.
    a. Arguments in favor of testing.
    b. Arguments against testing.
    c. Interest groups speaking out on issue.
2. Social.
    a. Arguments in favor of testing.
    b. Arguments against testing.
    c. Interest groups speaking out on issue.
3. Moral.
    a. Arguments in favor of testing.
    b. Arguments against testing.
    c. Interest groups speaking out on issue.
4. Economic.
    a. Arguments in favor of testing.
    b. Arguments against testing.
    c. Interest groups speaking out on issue.

FIGURE 4.14
Common Patterns of Organization, by Chronological Order

Changing Attitudes of Consumers Toward Energy Efficient Products
1. Attitudes of consumers in 1973.
    a. Priority given to fuel consumption as a criterion for purchasing an automobile.
    b. Priority given to home energy efficiency by buyers.
    c. Priority given to energy guide rating by buyers of home appliances.
2. Attitudes of consumers in 1983.
    a. Priority given to fuel consumption as a criterion for purchasing an automobile.
    b. Priority given to home energy efficiency by buyers.
    c. Priority given to energy guide rating by buyers of home appliances.
3. Attitudes of consumers in 1993.
    a. Priority given to fuel consumption as a criterion for purchasing an automobile.
    b. Priority given to home energy efficiency by buyers.
    c. Priority given to energy guide rating by buyers of home appliances.

FIGURE 4.15
Common Patterns of Organization, by Cause/Effect/Solution

Air Safety
1. Speculation regarding causes of present air safety problems.
   a. Aging planes.
   b. Inadequate maintenance.
   c. Inadequate regulation.
   d. Inadequate enforcement of regulations.

2. Effects.
   a. Pan-Am crash.
   b. United Airline disaster.
   c. Gander crash.

3. Recommendations or solutions suggested.
   a. New planes required.
   b. Better maintenance.
   c. Better regulation.
   d. Better enforcement of regulations.

FIGURE 4.16
Common Patterns of Organization, by Issue/Theme

Senior Issues
1. Housing.
   a. High rent costs.
   b. Lack of availability of services.
   c. High taxes.
   d. High property maintenance costs.

2. Transportation.
   a. Air costs and services.
   b. Rail costs and services.
   c. Bus costs and services.

3. Income.
   a. Pension reform.
   b. Retirement planning.
   c. Grants for seniors.
   d. Impact of free trade.

4. Health.
   a. Diseases.
   b. Fitness.
   c. Abuse.
   d. Euthanasia.

5. Leisure.

cause/effect/solution, or theme. The questions that the analyst asks will influence the organizational scheme for the issue-monitoring report, and different organizational patterns will emerge from answering different questions.

A WORD OF CAUTION

A word of caution is necessary. Although the questions to which an analyst seeks answers may be reasonable and appropriate, the researcher may find that the material does not yield answers to all or even most of the questions. Sometimes the questions that the researcher chooses in advance will be far less appropriate than questions that become apparent as the person carries out the analysis.

Assume that Congress is considering legislation that would tighten controls over Japanese investment in U.S. industries. Industry researchers could initially decide to analyze media response in terms of directionality; that is, to look for indications of positive, neutral, or negative reception of the proposed legislation. After reading a sample of the articles written on this topic, the researcher may realize there is virtually no disagreement between American journalists and industry spokespersons that some controls should be placed on Japanese investment in the United States; however, most news articles may appear to focus on the Japanese lobby's negative response to the bill. The analyst may decide that tabulating the number of news articles that focus on directionality of coverage would serve more to misrepresent than to illuminate understanding of American response to the proposed legislation. A sorting of news articles on the basis of directionality could suggest, erroneously, that the American press opposed a bill that sought to place tighter controls on Japanese investment in the United States; however, all the opinion articles may have almost uniformly supported the bill. A more interesting and appropriate approach to take in this report would be to analyze the percentage of time that the Japanese business lobby was in control of the American media agenda. Recognition of this fact could lead to an attempt to deal with a significant feature of the situation.

In summary, a reseacher of the public opinion environment may discover, sometime after a media or other analysis is begun, that the original questions posed may be far less important than other questions implied by the material. Although it may be useful to define an introductory format for consideration of an issue, the analyst should be flexible enough to accept the possibility that the format will not, on all occasions, be compatible with the material. Discovering the hidden structure of arguments and reasoning can be much more rewarding than trying to plug round holes with square pegs. Answering questions that the data does not address and sorting extremely complex developments of arguments into simple categories can sometimes be fruitless exercises. Sometimes what is most important in a body of data is what has been left out. The messages that an organization attempts to convey may be completely lost and never emerge from a set of data, while other messages may surface. If the analyst either feels bound by a preconceived structure or a finite set of questions or, alternatively, is unable or incompetent to locate and define the significance of the material, the result may be a useless, or worse, a misleading product.

JUDGING THE ISSUE ANALYSIS REPORT: A SUMMARY OF KEY POINTS

In judging the quality of an issue analysis report, the following criteria are relevant to consider:

- Does the analysis have a "value-added" component? Does it go beyond summarizing content to weighing favorable and unfavorable reactions, identifying strengths and weaknesses, and making a statement on the significance of the content?
- Does the analysis identify the extent to which preferred messages have been picked up in the coverage? Does the analysis point to distortions of the organization's messages?
- Does the analysis reveal linkages to other issues and programs? Has the analysis defined the parameters of the issue?
- Does the analysis point to regional differences in coverage, if applicable?
- Does the analysis point to possible impact on different constituencies or stakeholders?
- Does the analysis point to cautions for future action, or criticisms of past actions?
- Does the analysis suggest, wherever possible, recommendations for action (as represented in both the media coverage and in conclusions reached by the analyst)? Does the analysis suggest opportunities that could or should be seized?
- Is the analysis sensitive to shifting focus in arguments and reasoning?
- Is the analysis based on evidence rather than on loose impressions?
- Does the analysis provide organized commentary rather than "stringing together" a series of quotations? Is the analysis focused?
- Does the analysis identify trends in coverage (departures from previous coverage and new themes, directions and emerging issues)?
- Does the analysis consider the relevance of missing data?

All of these points are significant when judging the quality of a media-monitoring report.

NOTES

1. Joseph J. Penbera and Charles Bonner, "The Director's Role in a Takeover Bid," *Journal of Business Strategy,* May/June 1990, p. 39.
2. John Pound, "Beyond Takeovers: Politics Comes to Corporate Control," *Harvard Business Review,* March-April 1992, p. 91.
3. Paul K. Chaney, Timothy M. Devinney, and Russell S. Winer, "The Impact of New Product Introduction on the Market Value of Firms," *Journal of Business,* October 1991, p. 581.
4. Peter Lorange and John Roos, "Why Some Strategic Alliances Succeed and Others Fail," *Journal of Business Strategy,* January/February 1991, p. 27.
5. George Cheney and Steven L. Vibbert, "Corporate Discourse: Public Relations and Issue Management," in *Handbook of Organizational Communication: An Interdisciplinary Perspective, eds.* Fredric M. Jablin, Linda L. Putnam, Karlene H. Roberts, and Lyman W. Porter (Newbury Park, Calif.: Sage Publications, 1987), p. 191, conclude that organizations have become "vitally concerned with controlling the terms of their presentation to various publics, both 'inside' and 'out there' "—including value, issue, image, and identity.
6. This example was given by Andrew Polland in *The Competitive Intelligence Review,* Summer 1990. Howard Sutton, *Competitive Intelligence,* The Conference Book Report No. 913, 1988, discussed the experiences of 315 companies who were surveyed on the topic of competitive intelligence. Sutton also discussed case studies that included the experiences of AT&T, Kraft, Motorola, Adolph, Coors, Pfizer Combustion Engineering, and other major companies in setting up competitive intelligence systems.
7. Merrill Rose, "Activism in the 90's: Changing Roles for Public Relations," *Public Relations Quarterly,* Fall 1991, p. 29.
8. Ibid.
9. See, for example, Shanto Iyengar and Donald Kinder, *News that Matters* (Chicago: University of Chicago Press, 1987).
10. James E. Grunig and Fred C. Repper, "Strategic Management, Publics, and Issues," in *Excellence in Public Relations and Communication Management,* ed. James E. Grunig (Hillside, N.J.: Lawrence Erlbaum Associates, Publishers, 1992), p. 127.
11. Edie N. Goldenberg, *Making the Papers* (Lexington, Mass.: D.C. Heath, 1975), p. 66.
12. David M. Dozier and Fred C. Repper, "Research Firms and Public Relations Practices," in *Excellence in Public Relations and Communication Management,* ed. James E. Grunig (Hillsdale, N.J.: Lawrence Erlbaum Associates, Publishers, 1992), p. 203.
13. Barry Z. Posner and Warren H. Schmidt, *California Management Review,* Spring 1992), p. 84. Posner and Schmidt reported the results of a survey of 1500 managers, to which two-thirds responded.

14. A Strength of Personality Scale was developed by Allensbach Survey Center in Germany to identify opinion leaders. This scale is discussed in Gabriel Wiemann, "The Influentials: Back to the Concept of Opinion Leaders," *Journal of Communication,* Summer 1991, pp. 267–79. Some commerical firms also compile profiles of opinion leaders and other elites.
15. See, for example, discussions in "History on the Run: Media and the '79 Election," directed by Peter Raymont and produced by Sidney Riley and Peter Raymont, National Film Board, Canada, 1979; also David Taras, *The Newsmakers* (Scarborough, Ont.: Nelson Canada, 1990), pp. 89–91; and Dan Nimmo and James E. Combs, *Mediated Political Realities,* 2nd ed. (New York: Longman, 1990), pp. 168–74.
16. Peggy Binns, communication analyst, Privy Council Office, Government of Canada, 1989.
17. This scaling was suggested by Charles E. Osgood, George J. Suci, and Percy H. Tannenbaum, *The Measurement of Meaning* (Urbana, Ill.: University of Illinois Press, 1957).
18. In workshop situations, I have often asked groups to classify print and television news items into favorableness categories, using ranking and rating scales. I have found that, with a limited number of items (three or four), they can almost always agree on *relative degrees* of favorability (in other words, there is a high level of intercoder agreement when three or four items are ranked as *relatively* more or less positive than other items), but agreement is much less rare when respondents classify articles into *positive, neutral,* and *negative* categories.
19. J. C. Merrill, "How *Time* Stereotyped Three U.S. Presidents," *Journalism Quarterly,* Autumn 1965, pp. 563–70.
20. The terms used to refer to the influence of items appearing early or late in a series are *primacy effects* and *recency effects.*
21. The *Globe and Mail,* August 7, 1991, p. 1.
22. See Paul Ekman, *Telling Lies: Clues to Deceit in the Marketplace, Politics, and Marriage* (New York: Norton, 1985).
23. See John Berger, *Ways of Seeing, Part IV: "The Language of Advertising,"* BBC Enterprises, 1972.
24. See discussion by John Hartley, *Understanding News* (New York: Methuen, Inc., 1982). See also John Fiske, *Introduction to Communication Studies* (New York: Methuen, Inc., 1982).
25. Sherry Ferguson, "The Apologia: 1971 Genre," *Southern Speech Journal,* Spring 1972, pp. 280–91.
26. See classic works by Umberto Eco, *A Theory of Semiotics* (Bloomington, Ind.: Indiana University Press, 1979); Roland Barthes, *The Semiotic Challenge* (New York: Hill and Wang, 1988); and Ferdinand de Saussure, *Course in General Linguistics,* trans. Wade Baskin (New York: Philosophical Library, 1959).
27. Extracted from Arthur M. McRims, "Marketing Step Child: Product Pub-

licity," *Harvard Business Review,* November/December 1979, pp. 111–12, reported in Prema Nakra, "The Changing Role of Public Relations in Marketing Communications," *Public Relations Quarterly,* Spring 1991, p. 44.

28. Ibid.

29. Dozier and Repper, p. 196. The Ketchum Model is also discussed in Scott M. Cutlip, Allan H. Center, and G. M. Broom, *Effective Public Relations,* 6th ed. (Englewood Cliffs, N.J.: Prentice-Hall, 1985).

30. William P. Ehling and David M. Dozier, "Public Relations Management and Operations Research," in *Excellence in Public Relations and Communication Management,* ed. James E. Grunig (Hillsdale, N.J.: Lawrence Erlbaum Associates, Publishers), 1992, p. 264. Patricia Newlin describes her system in *PR Week,* 1988, p. 10.

31. In the fall of 1990, the Department of National Defence, Canada, invited journalists, participants in the Oka crisis, and specialists in media and in Indian and northern affairs to a conference to discuss media coverage of the Oka confrontation. The consensus appeared to be that journalists had been largely unschooled in the issues prior to the time of the land claim dispute.

32. Ibid.

33. Ibid., a presentation by Joe Scanlon, journalism professor at Carleton University, Ottawa, Canada, Fall 1990.

34. Ibid.

35. Edgar M. Arundell, "The Publics of Public Affairs," in *The Canadian Public Affairs Handbook: Maximizing Markets, Protecting Bottom Lines,* eds. W. John Wright and Christopher J. DuVernet, (Toronto: Carswell, 1988), pp. 135–36.

36. Ole R. Holsti, *Content Analysis for the Social Sciences and Humanities* (Reading, Mass.: Addison-Wesley Publishing Company, 1969), pp. 28–31.

37. Ibid., p. 31.

38. Michael Grossman and Martha Kumar, *Portraying the President* (Baltimore: Johns Hopkins University Press, 1981).

39. Roger A. Wimmer and Joseph R. Dominick, *Mass Media Research: An Introduction,* 3rd ed. (Belmont, Calif.: Wadsworth Publishing Company, 1992), p. 171, discuss the importance of establishing benchmarks or bases for comparison.

40. Ibid.

CHAPTER 5

ANALYZING MEDIA AND OTHER CONTENT

An organization that wants to know more about its media visibility or its public image will engage consultants or in-house researchers to track and analyze media coverage of the organization, its executives, or issues confronting the organization. A number of media-monitoring firms have come into being during the past 10 years to serve these organizations, and many consultancy firms now specialize in media analysis and trend monitoring.[1] Naisbitt's *Megatrends* and his monthly newsletter *The Trend Report,* which offers the results of studies based on content analysis, generated much interest in this area in the 1980s. In more recent works such as *Trend Watching,* management specialists have suggested techniques by which organizations can use systematic means to track their most prominent issues.[2] Others have generated mathematical models for predicting public opinion based on the appearance of items in the mass media.[3] These techniques are the result of efforts to move away from "reactive accommodation" and to move toward "proactive formation."[4] The questions to which an organization and its top executives will want answers have been posed in the previous chapter. Content analysis is one of three research tools most often used to answer these questions (the other two are surveys and focus groups, which are discussed in following chapters).[5] The most common sources analyzed are newspapers, magazines, radio, and television. Other sources include correspondence received by the organization (from the general public, from experts in certain fields, and from interest and lobby groups), House and Senate debates, and association newsletters.

Although content analysis has been applied for many years to the study of political communication, its popularity as a research tool within organizations is more recent. American Telephone and Telegraph Company was one of the first firms to recognize the value of this research technique.[6] For over 10 years, AT&T has used content analysis methods to track issues carried in the mass media. As increasing numbers of organizations engage in formal strategic planning, others are adopting this practice. Organizations use the information they acquire from monitoring and analyzing media, as well as information they gain from other sources, to project trends. Knowledge of trends can help the organization to cope with an unstable environment.

Content analysis first became popular in the 1930s.[7] During World War II, the U.S. government sponsored a number of reviews and analyses of the Nazi press.[8] The researchers aimed to gain a better understanding of propaganda techniques and, ultimately, to learn how best to counter them. Interest in content analysis as a research tool faltered in the late 1950s and early 1960s. The National Conference on Content Analysis, held in November 1967, was the first major conference since 1955 that was devoted to this topic.[9] Today social scientists use content analysis to study a wide range of media trends, including the depiction of women and minorities, levels of violence in the media, and political campaigns and rhetoric.

The classical question asked in most communication research is, "Who says what, to whom, how, and with what effect?"[10] Content analysis involves asking the additional question, "Why?" Sometimes we study messages in order to make inferences about characteristics of a message or a text, to suggest what conditions may have generated the message, and to speculate on the possible effects of the message. Those engaging in content analysis assume that messages *have* an effect. In the case of media analysis, they assume that an issue's place on the media agenda may influence how the public perceives it. They further assume that how the media treats the organization and its chief executives (i.e., whether it gives them favorable or unfavorable coverage) will influence public perceptions of the organization and, ultimately, the organization's capacity to manage the issue.

Content analysis involves examining the *message* component of the communication process. When engaging in content analysis, you classify the message, using as precise and objective standards as possible. Then you summarize and interpret the results of your efforts. In content analysis, you attempt to follow rules and procedures and to apply these rules and procedures consistently. In that sense, content analysis is both *objective* and *systematic*.[11] In the analysis process, the researcher seeks to arrive at generalizations based on consensus among all those who analyze and classify information.

The following discussion is organized to correspond with the steps most often followed in content analysis of media. The discussion has been adapted, however, to the specific demands of current issue analysis.

LIMITING YOUR STUDY: DECIDING WHAT TO INCLUDE AND WHAT TO EXCLUDE

Defining what you want to study means limiting your study or deciding in advance what to *include* and *exclude*. Assume that your organization has a stake in the North American free trade initiatives. Certain manufacturing sectors, for instance, may want to learn more about press coverage of the trade negotiations. They may be curious to know: Who is supporting or opposing the organization's position on certain issues? How much visibility is being given to the views of these stakeholders? Are U.S. government spokespeople indicating any flexibility in positions they are taking on topics of concern to manufacturers?

Some of the questions to be answered in deciding the limits of a study relate to *scope;* others relate to *sources.* Examples of questions related to scope follow:

- *What aspect of the topic do you want to consider?* North American free trade initiatives in general? Negotiations between the United States and Mexico? Position of General Agreement on Tariffs and Trade (GATT) on the U.S.-Mexico negotiations? Mexico's response to the U.S. proposals? Free trade as a general concept?

- *Will you restrict the content to certain kinds of materials?* News coverage? Opinion coverage? Will your study be confined to front-page news items? The business section? If you are analyzing television coverage, will you look only at the evening news? Documentaries? Phone-in shows?

- *What is the geographical focus of your study?* International? National? Regional? Local? In analyzing broadcast news, you may decide to limit your analysis to three local networks. On the other hand, you may decide to eliminate all regional *and* local network coverage.

- *What time period will the study cover?* Three weeks? Six months? Two years? The overall time period for an analysis will probably be determined by the purpose of the research.

Thus, if you want to analyze media reaction to a proposed policy or merger, you might choose a sample of materials drawn from the period immediately following announcement of the proposal. In contrast, if you are studying reaction to a product recall, you might want to examine the coverage immediately preceding, during, and following the recall. In such a case, it is important to establish a benchmark.[12] A researcher who tracks coverage of generic issues such as women's rights may study even longer time frames. These issues, rather than being event driven, are long-term, self-sustaining issues.

Analyzing Americans' response to a new tax policy may require studying no more than two weeks' coverage following the announcement because the event is short lived. On the other hand, if you believe it is important to include background material, you may need to include a much longer time frame, perhaps a period of weeks or months before the announcement was made. Sometimes you may shorten the time period covered in the analysis in order to get more specific information. Perhaps the first week's coverage is more important than the fifth week's coverage of the issue, especially with short-term crisis issues such as oil spills. On the other hand, it may be important to find out if coverage is continuing beyond the crisis period. How long does a scandal involving a company official remain front-page news? Moreover, there is often a five to seven-day lag between news coverage following a major event and editorial coverage of the event. Tracking the numbers of articles appearing in the different time frames may be critical to gaining a full understanding of the issue.

Sample questions related to *sources* include the following:

- *What media do you want to consult?* Print news media? Broadcast media?

- *Where will you go to find sources?* The index to the *New York Times?* A media clippings service? Your in-house clippings or videotaping service?

- *What kind of criteria will you use to select sources?* Will you use the most well-known or well-established newspapers? Will you eliminate all newspapers with circulations under a certain number? Will you look at daily newspapers? Weekly newspapers?

- *Do you need to access specialized databases or acquire extraordinary materials?* Would it be advisable or useful to examine expert opinions found in academic publications? Would examination of futurist journals add quality and interest to your analysis?

You may want to learn more about the circulation of various newspapers or magazines before deciding which sources to sample. Some figures can be obtained from the Audit Bureau of Circulation. Sources of information on television stations are Arbitron Company and A. C. Nielson Company. The advertising departments of newspapers and radio and television stations can provide detailed information regarding circulation and audience analysis.[13]

The decision to limit a study will probably be, at least partially, determined by factors such as time and resources. How much time is available to carry out the analysis? The more in-depth the analysis, the more time required to read and assimilate the information into meaningful patterns. How much will the analysis cost in resources? Consulting firms that offer such services are expensive, and staff analysts usually deal with multiple issues. The time spent on crisis management often makes it difficult for firms and governments to devote extensive resources to media monitoring. Does the analyst's background on the topic mean that the person will require only a minimal amount of time to study the topic area? Using the same individuals to track issues on an ongoing basis should mean that the cost in time and money declines. Much of the work in content analysis derives from the demanding task of deciding upon frameworks for understanding the content. All of these points will be taken into consideration when decisions are made to limit a study. In the end, you may make a statement such as, "This study considers the news content on the front pages of the *Washington Post* and the *New York Times,* excluding Sundays, from January 1 to December 31 of the past year."[14]

PICKING A SAMPLE

Once you have decided the scope of your study and identified the sources you want to examine, you select a representative sample of material from the choices that are available. Except in the case of a short-lived crisis or an emerging issue, it is usually not possible to examine every item from the available material. In these latter cases, you may have a limited number of items to analyze. In studies involving larger quantities of data, sampling procedures become necessary.

The term *random sample* refers to a sample in which every source has an equal (or if not equal, at least *known*) chance of being selected. To select a random sample, you can use a table of random numbers (see pp. 207–9, Chapter 6). Alternatively, you can assign numbers to individual articles in your sampling frame (all available choices) and then pick randomly from the list. Other methods of sampling are discussed in a following chapter on survey techniques.

If you are examining U.S. media response to a new policy or product, you should include all geographic regions in your sample. To obtain a *stratified* sample, group newspapers by region and then randomly draw a certain number of papers from each region. Chapter 6 discusses this technique in more depth. In some cases, you may need to oversample certain populations. For example, drawing a simple random sample of all newspapers listed in certain indexes would mean that newspapers with varying circulations have an equal chance of being selected. Yet it may be important to ensure that the sample selected for analysis includes more than a representative number of daily newspapers with large circulation. In other instances, stratified sampling techniques may yield a limited number of items to study; therefore, you need to oversample in order to get stratified samples that are large enough to give meaningful information.

In selecting your media source sample, you may choose to draw the sample from all potential calendar dates, for example, every fifth issue of a newspaper or every third broadcast day. To ensure distribution across a month, you can limit your selection to four items from each week of the month, picked randomly. Alternatively, you can randomly select six items per day over a two-week period. You may want to draw your sample from different days of the week, for example, one Monday, one Tuesday, one Wednesday, one Thursday, one Friday, and one Saturday. To choose the specific Monday, pick randomly from all choices of Monday, following the same procedure for other days of the week.

It is important to get an undistorted population. For example, weekend news may be different from weekday news. If you choose to analyze every seventh day's coverage, you may be examining all Sunday newspapers, a different variety from other days of the week. Some types of content vary by season. Election years, for example, will generate a different type of media coverage from other years. Likewise, anniversary dates such as Human Rights Day and the Fourth of July will produce coverage different from other periods of time. To avoid bias entering into your results, you will need to consider these kinds of factors. The choices made in selecting the sample will limit or expand the available information. Therefore, decisions regarding sources and dates are critical ones.

In most content analyses, it is assumed that the larger the sample, the better. Too small a sample may not be representative. Limiting the analysis to 30 clippings out of a possible 500 may give few insights into the nature of the coverage. However, there are points beyond which increasing sample size makes little difference. One study analyzed samples of 6, 12, 18, 24, and 48 issues of a newspaper. The researcher found each of the sample sizes to be adequate; he also found that increasing the sample size beyond 12 did not improve the accuracy of the results.[15] A study of television programming, conducted for the purposes of producing a violence index, found that one week of fall programming produced results similar to that of a larger sample drawn throughout the year.[16] Another study compared the results obtained from four different types of samples: odd-day samples, every-fifth-day samples, weekly samples, and every-tenth-day samples. The researchers found no noticeable difference between the results obtained from data representing all days of the month and those obtained from odd-day and every-fifth day samples. They did, however, find that weekly samples and every-tenth-day samples were inferior.[17] In carrying out a series of content analyses on a single topic, you may want to determine these optimum sample size cut-off points.

In conclusion, you should consider the preceding factors when you decide which and how many materials to analyze. At the same time, however, you should recognize that these procedures are sometimes more realizable in an academic study than in the day-to-day functioning of an organization that is attempting to track many issues simultaneously. In an organizational context, you will often be working with a sample chosen by individuals over whom you have little control. The most that you can do, in such a situation, is to give the staff of the media-monitoring or in-house clippings service a list of criteria that they will use to make their selections.

Rigid conformity to sampling procedures may be less than useful in other organizational contexts. Purposive sampling (e.g., drawing on a small sample of carefully selected media sources) sometimes makes more sense than using probability sampling procedures.[18] You could, for example, learn more about investment opportunities in Asia by examining major financial newspapers,

newspapers that subscribe to international wire services, and newspapers that have correspondents in relevant Asian countries than you could by drawing a random sample from a newspaper index. At the other extreme, in some situations, it may not be possible to ignore *any* piece of information, because if you do, you may be discarding an important news item. Any staff member who has been called to task for not informing the CEO or a political representative of some relatively obscure news item or editorial will appreciate this particular point. The culture of some organizations demands that all items of information be given at least cursory examination. A much more detailed and systematic description of the steps to be followed in sampling appears in the chapter on survey techniques.

WHAT DO YOU COUNT?

Content analysis involves counting: counting the number of stories that refer to lobby activities, counting the number of times a CEO achieves visibility for a new company patent, counting the number of times editorials argue for or against a government policy to subsidize first-time home buyers. To know what to count, you must decide on your unit of analysis. What is the smallest unit you will count? For example, will you count every time the CEO is mentioned in an article, or will you limit your count to one reference per article, no matter how many times the president is mentioned in that article?

The unit of analysis that you count in written content (a newspaper or magazine article) might be a "single word or symbol, a theme . . . or an entire article or story. In television and film analyses units of analysis can be characters, acts, or entire programs."[19] Some units of analysis are easier to count than others:

> It is easier to determine the number of stories on the "CBS Evening News" that deal with international news than the number of acts of violence in a week of network television because a "story" is a more readily distinguishable unit of analysis than an "act." The beginning and end of a news story are fairly easy to see but suppose that a researcher trying to catalog content was faced with a long fistfight between three characters? Is the whole sequence one act of violence, or is every blow considered an act? What if a fourth character joins in? Does it then become a different act?[20]

Similarly, in analyzing press coverage of a technological innovation, it is easier to count the number of *stories* or *items* that mention the innovation than to count the number of *references within stories* to the topic. To count the number of internal references, you must answer questions such as the following: Does each person speaking constitute a different unit of analysis? Does every reference to the topic, no matter how many times the same speaker is involved, count as separate units of analysis? If Barbara Walters speaks at three different points on a topic, does that count as one reference to the topic or as three? Is the unit of analysis the speaker or the paragraph or the time period (e.g., every 30 seconds of the newscast or every minute)?

The unit of analysis for locating arguments, criticisms, cautions, and so forth, could be the *article* or the *paragraph* or the *sentence*. If the unit of analysis is the sentence, it is necessary to count every time a particular idea appears. Assume that, as a government researcher, you are trying to determine the number of *positive, negative* and *neutral* references to the introduction of new gun-control legislation. Every time a sentence such as "The new gun-control legislation means that ordinary citizens no longer have the means to protect themselves" appears, you count the sentence as *negative*. When a sentence such as "The new gun-control legislation is likely to result in major drops in homicides" appears, you designate the sentence as *positive*. A statement such as "The new gun-control legislation will be in place by the first of the year" falls into the *neutral* range. In each case, the unit of analysis is the sentence.

If references to a product defect appear in 15 sentences of an article on a company, and the unit of analysis is the sentence, the frequency count will be 15. However, if the unit of analysis is the paragraph and references to a product defect appear in five paragraphs of the article, the frequency count will be five. This will be true even if there are multiple references to the product defect within any one paragraph. If the unit of analysis is the entire article, you will only count one for any item.

On other occasions, you may decide to use more than one unit of analysis. For example, you may consider headlines as a separate unit of analysis from the articles that they introduce. Headlines, which many believe can have a significant influence on how people read articles, can sometimes be skewed, even when the articles are neutral or balanced.

Another possible unit of analysis is the *theme*.[21] It may be more meaningful to categorize data by themes than by sentences because a sentence may contain more than one theme. Consider the sentence, "Rumors suggest that the CEO of Company X may be resigning, and some say the company may be in financial trouble." There are two themes in this sentence: the CEO's possible resignation and the company's financial difficulties. If the unit of analysis is the sentence rather than the theme, then you will have a problem categorizing the sentence.

Consider some other examples. Different themes may be present in a State of the Union address, including social justice, economic renewal, and constructive internationalism. In an analysis that seeks to study press coverage of issues pertaining to the mentally retarded, themes such as human rights, safety, housing, and employment may be present. A theme may appear in only one sentence or may span several paragraphs. One theme ends when another theme begins. It is more difficult to define the boundaries of themes than to define the boundaries of sentences, paragraphs, and articles. Coding themes is also very time-consuming. Nonetheless, on many topics, the *theme,* or a "single assertion about one subject,"[22] is the most useful unit of content analysis.

In some studies, analysts will consider individual *words* or *phrases* as units of analysis.[23] A study of Ross Perot's campaign rhetoric could, for instance, involve an analysis of adjectives used by journalists to describe Perot. In this case, words or phrases would be the unit of analysis. For example, to learn more about how journalists responded to Perot's campaign rhetoric, you could look for the appearance of "appreciative" or "depreciative" adjectives. Examples of appreciative adjectives are *down-to-earth, concerned, colorful,* and *interesting;* examples of depreciative adjectives are *irrational, patronizing,* and *inexperienced.* Research into a company's image could similarly reveal trends in references to the company, with applied adjectives ranging from *innovative* and *committed* to *outdated* and *financially overextended.* Computer content-analysis programs have reduced both the financial costs and the time it takes to carry out this kind of analysis. Readability studies also use this type of program.

As a general rule, you will find it is much too tedious to count every reference to an issue or argument that appears in a broadcast or in a newspaper article. In an organizational context, the usual tendency will be to code for *the presence or absence of an attribute* within a document, or to engage in what has been termed *contingency analysis.*[24] For example, if you are tracking the ebb and flow of arguments pertaining to grain subsidies, you would count the number of articles in which relevant arguments appeared. The next stage of the analysis would involve charting the appearance of the arguments in graph form, depicting the shifts in emphasis over time. Sometimes, it is important to locate how often two arguments appear in conjunction with each other. A contingency analysis can identify which ideas appear concurrently in issue coverage. The term *innovative,* for example, may appear most frequently in discussions of the country's foreign aid policies or the company's personnel policies. Some ideas will appear almost always in conjunction with other ideas.

It is important to note that you can obtain different results when using different units of analysis. Assume, for example, that you are judging the tone of the financial press's response to your company's announced intention to restructure its operations and seek new markets. Assume that the unit of analysis, in the first instance, is the individual paragraph or the theme. Then for comparative purposes, consider the entire article as one unit. Theoretically, your results could be as follows (see Figure 5.1):

In the first instance, when the theme is the unit of analysis, the content is 41 percent favorable, 19 percent neutral, and 40 percent unfavorable, as represented in the four editorials. In the second instance, when the entire article becomes the unit of measurement, there is 25 percent favorable and 75 percent unfavorable content represented in the four commentaries. In the latter case, each commentary represents 25 percent of the coverage.[25] It is clear that the

FIGURE 5.1
Financial Press Reaction to Restructuring

Editorial #	Theme as Unit of Analysis	Entire Article as Unit of Analysis
1	12 favorable 9 neutral 15 unfavorable	1 unfavorable
2	7 favorable 6 neutral 10 unfavorable	1 unfavorable
3	0 favorable 0 neutral 8 unfavorable	1 unfavorable
4	15 favorable 1 neutral 0 unfavorable	1 favorable

response of the financial press would appear to be far more negative in the second than in the first instance, although the same material is being analyzed. Which interpretation is correct depends on your point of view. In the first instance, you are assuming that the best way to assess the impact of an editorial is to count the number of favorable and unfavorable assertions in the comment. Using this technique, a relatively lukewarm editorial will be scored differently from a more favorable one. In the second instance, you are assuming that the impact of the message derives from the overall positive, negative, or neutral impression that it creates: "The first view is that the effect of the whole is equal to the sum of its parts, the second position is that the impact of the whole is different from the sum of its parts."[26]

Studies have also demonstrated that the longer the coding unit (articles are longer than paragraphs; paragraphs are longer than sentences), the more likely it is that the unit will be rated as biased, either favorable or unfavorable in tone. Shorter units produce more neutral ratings than do longer units of content.[27]

It is important to remember that the smaller the unit of analysis, the more time you will require to complete the analysis. You must determine the degree of fineness of detail that you require: "Generally, the greater the need for precision, the higher will be the costs of the analysis. Often the nature of the categories and data are such that the search for maximum precision will not only entail considerably higher costs, but also may sacrifice reliability."[28] The reason for the decline in reliability is that it is less likely that three or four people will agree on a number of references within an article than that they will agree on a single evaluation of the article. *Reliability* derives from the ability to get the same results from "repeated measurements of the same material."[29] *Intercoder reliability* refers to "levels of agreement among independent coders who code the same content using the same coding instrument."[30]

The examples that follow illustrate how you may select different units of analysis, depending upon the purposes of your research[31] (see Figures 5.2 and 5.3).

CREATING "PIGEONHOLES" FOR YOUR DATA

After you have (1) *decided what you want to study*, (2) *picked your sample*, and (3) *decided on your unit of analysis*, you can begin the process of (4) *coding your content*. Coding involves putting content in subject-matter categories. In other words, you are attaching labels to your units of analysis. Subject categories are the "pigeonholes" into which you put your content units.[32]

The process of analyzing issues usually entails identifying the frequency with which certain arguments appear in media or other related materials. For example, if you want to assess objections to new regulations imposed by a federal aviation board, you might use the following subject categories: *increased likelihood of flight delays, threats to economic viability*, and *undermining of uniform standards agreed to by members of the International Civil Aviation Organization*. If you are analyzing press reaction to an impending plant shutdown, you might find that appropriate subject categories are *impact on employees, impact on management, impact on community, impact on alliance partners, impact on investors*, and *impact on financial institutions*.

Relevant categories in the analysis of women's issues might be *housing, child care, employment*, and *pensions*. Each of these subcategories could be broken into additional subcategories. For example, *employment* could be further broken down into *equity concerns, financial concerns*, and *safety concerns*. Each of these major categories could, in turn, be broken down into subcategories, requiring the analyst to make increasingly finer levels of distinction regarding content characteristics. The appropriateness of broad or narrow categories depends on how you plan to use the analysis. For example, if you are examining a week's news broadcasts, you may want to know the relative amount of attention given to different topics such as the *economy*, *social welfare* issues, *health, justice*, or other broad content categories. In that case, defining subcategories may not be important. On the other hand, if it is important to know the amount of attention given to different aspects of one of these areas, you may choose to break down your material into multiple subtopics.

There are costs related to both broad and narrow categories. If the categories are extremely broad, you may not be able to answer your questions. Assume, for example, that you are a government researcher who wants to answer the question, "What are American attitudes toward the United

FIGURE 5.2

Introduction to Vocabulary (Examples of Content Analysis of Print Media)

Topic	Purpose of Analysis	Universe	Sample	Unit of Analysis
Natural gas pipeline	To learn the response of southern residents to government's subsidizing the piping of gas to the northern United States.	All southern daily newspapers, September to October 1976.	Systematically selected sample of southern daily newspapers, September to October, 1976.	Any newspaper story over five lines in length on the piping of natural gas from the southern United States to the northern United States.
FDA test results regarding drug X	To learn the response of U.S. consumer groups to announcement of FDA test results regarding drug X.	All AP stories appearing in top-10 daily circulation newspapers, August 1992.	70 randomly selected stories discussing FDA announcement, August 1992.	Headlines.
Plywood tariffs	To examine the response of the U.S. and Canadian lumber industries to the announcement of new plywood tariffs.	Lumber-related U.S. and Canadian trade journals, April 1988.	All articles discussing plywood tariffs, April 1988.	Introductory abstract to all articles discussing plywood tariffs.

134

Oil spill	To acquire information on the reaction of Western environmental groups to the spill.	All western daily newspapers, April 1–8, 1993.	All front-page articles, April 1–8, 1993.	Any newspaper story and photographs relating to oil spill.
Cruise missile testing	To examine the reaction of the international press to cruise missile testing.	All major international newspapers, June to August, 1987.	50 randomly selected articles from the *N.Y. Times, Le Monde, London Times,* and *Globe and Mail,* June to August 1987.	Any newspaper article on topic of cruise missile testing.
Elder abuse	To learn the frequency with which references to elder abuse are appearing in newspapers published by senior organizations.	All 1992 stories on elder abuse appearing in newspapers published by senior organizations.	Random sample of 100 articles from 30 newspapers published by seniors groups.	Any references within newspaper articles to elder abuse.

FIGURE 5.3
Introduction to Vocabulary (Examples of Content Analysis of Broadcast Media)

Topic	Purpose of Analysis	Universe	Sample	Unit of Analysis
Equality rights legislation	To determine which equality rights themes received the most frequent mentions in TV news coverage.	All TV news coverage.	Two weeks local TV news coverage in March 1990 in 10 U.S. cities, randomly selected.	Any reference to one of four major equality rights themes.
Prison furlough policies	To gain information on public opinion regarding furlough policies.	All TV talk shows.	Talk shows on three national networks, May 1990, randomly selected.	Individual speakers on talk shows.
Utilities rate increases	To acquire insight into public perception of rate increases.	All local TV news coverage.	Evening newscasts on three local TV stations March 20–30, 1993, randomly selected.	Individual interviews on topic, with members of the public.
Derailing of train carrying toxic waste	To learn extent to which derailment activated renewed debate over toxic waste transportation issue	All TV news coverage.	Four weeks of midday news broadcasts on eight regional channels, randomly selected.	Any segment mentioning public response to the incident.

Defence cuts	To check reaction of interest groups to announced closing of military bases.	All local TV coverage.	One week's coverage, April 26–May 3, 1992, on local TV outlets in affected areas, randomly selected.	Statements by any spokespersons of organized interest groups in affected areas.
Impaired-driving campaign	To ascertain the level of visibility given to the state government's impaired-driving campaign on state television.	All public service announcements aired in state.	Three weeks TV coverage during campaign period between 8:00 and 12:00 each evening.	Any public service announcements.
Employee layoffs at company X	To learn nature of coverage given to issue during and after layoff announcements.	All TV news coverage on networks.	One week's network news during September 1992—early evening broadcasts on three national networks.	All references to layoffs.
Hostage taking	To check to see if local live TV coverage compromised the police's handling of a hostage incident.	All local TV coverage of hostage incident.	All footage showing activity at hostage site.	Any individual video shot, depicting incident.

States' involvement in Somalia?" You could establish subcategories such as *attitudes toward economic assistance to Somalia, attitudes toward military assistance to Somalia,* and *attitudes toward technical assistance to Somalia.* Under the category *attitudes toward military assistance to Somalia,* you could have additional lower-level subcategories such as *attitudes toward short-term involvement* and *attitudes toward long-term involvement.* The subcategory *short-term involvement* could be further subdivided into *involvement that minimizes the use of force* and *involvement that maximizes the use of force.*

Increasing the levels and numbers of subcategories involves costs. For example, it is possible to generate hundreds of categories and subcategories on a specific topic. But the results may be many categories that include single items. The purpose of any analysis is to acquire more sophisticated insight into an issue or problem; if the end result of an analysis is the cataloging of long lists of arguments or points, the meaning of the material may well be lost. The most important function of content analysis should be to help you to organize data into meaningful patterns, in order to examine and predict trends. Generating too many categories confuses interpretation, reducing the reliability of your analysis. Reliability can also suffer when different coders, working with the same content, must make fine distinctions between categories. Everyone may agree that a reference to a plant fire falls under *plant safety,* but not everyone will agree that it belongs under the subcategory *violations of plant safety.* Still fewer people would agree on the subset *deliberate violations of plant safety.* Some might believe the reference fits under *accidental violations of plant safety.* At each category level, you must make finer distinctions in content type; at each progressive level, judgment becomes more arbitrary and agreement among multiple coders becomes more difficult.

How do you solve your problem? How do you know how many categories to establish? One answer that has been given to this question is the following:

> Common sense, pretesting and practice with the coding system are valuable guides to aid the researcher in steering between the two extremes: developing a system with too few categories (so that essential differences are obscured) and defining too many categories (so that only a small percentage falls into each, thus limiting generalizations).[33]

There are several rules governing choice of categories.[34]

The first rule says that categories should reflect the purposes of your research. Categories will be specific to the topic being studied. You read or view a representative sample of the materials, using an initial set of categories. Judging the worth of the categories means that you must ask, "Do the categories help me to ask the kinds of questions that I need to answer with this analysis?" For example, in attempting to identify media/public reaction to a hostile buyout, you might find that the following arguments have surfaced in the news coverage: (1) *Buyout is seen as threat to the future well-being of the company*. (2) *Buyout is seen as a probable drag on the company's profits.* (3) *Buyout is seen as a precursor to many job losses.* These three arguments could appear on your data sheet as major content categories. Categories that might be less useful in identifying public attitudes toward the buyout are *historical details leading up to the buyout, financial profile of the company, equipment liabilities, employment practices,* and *environmental problems.* Even though facts and statistics related to these latter categories may appear frequently in articles that discuss the buyout, counting or noting the number of times they appear may be irrelevant to answering the main question of the analysis.[35] It is important to construct content categories so that they answer the questions that appear to be most salient to your study.

As an analyst, you could use several different approaches to answer the question, "Does press coverage suggest that Zimbabwe is manifesting a strong spirit of national reconciliation?" For example, assume that you have decided to carry out a content analysis of all the press coverage specific to Zimbabwe over a six-week period. An examination of newspapers for this six-week period suggests many different content categories. There is much discussion of alleged corruption on the part of government officials. There are historical references to Zimbabwe's earlier colonial status. Journalists talk about Zimbabwe's attempt to revitalize its economy. One journalist discusses the problems generated by an overeducated population and limited employment opportunities. Other articles point to ways in which the blacks have preserved the privileges of white Zimbabweans, while at the same time creating a situation where the two groups have learned to live together in harmony.

Obviously, in this example, you could generate many different content categories. You must, however, always keep in mind the purposes of your research. If you are seeking to confirm or reject the idea that a strong spirit of national reconciliation exists in Zimbabwe, you will disregard potential content categories such as *unemployment problems, historical details* (except as they relate to present relations between blacks and whites), and *corruption charges against government officials.* You will concentrate instead on categories such as *references to recognition of minority political rights, references to accord between Nkomo and Mugabe,* and *references to improved relations between warring tribal factions.*

A second rule for defining content categories states that categories must be exhaustive. There must be a slot into which every *relevant* unit of analysis can be placed. To decide if the categories are appropriate, you must apply them to a sample of material. If some units do not fit, you must modify the categories to accommodate the idea. You may use a category titled *other* or *miscellaneous,* into which you place ideas that don't fit elsewhere. You should, however, reexamine any analysis in which 10 percent or more of the content is placed in the miscellaneous category. Such a situation would mean that new categories should be generated to include some of the miscellaneous content.

A third rule for constructing content categories says that categories should be mutually exclusive. For women's issues, you may initially define categories such as *housing, child care, financial,* and *pensions.* Once your analysis is under way, you may discover that the financial category overlaps with *housing, child care,* and *pensions* categories. To deal with the problem, you can eliminate the *financial* category. Thus, it is necessary to modify and refine categories whenever they overlap.

Another example would be categorizing media reaction to an event, for example, the Tylenol-related deaths. Categories such as *effects on pharmaceutical manufacturers, effects on consumers,* and *effects on retailers* would be mutually exclusive. However, the category *effects on international distributors* should be excluded because references to international distributors could overlap with the retailer category.

A fourth rule for constructing categories says that categories must be derived from a single classification principle. For example, in analyzing the possible repercussions of the reunification of East and West Germany, you could create major categories labeled *economic repercussions, cultural repercussions,* and *legal ramifications.* You would not combine these categories with the categories *anticipated reactions of Western bloc countries* and *anticipated reactions of Eastern bloc countries.* There may be, in fact, a place in the analysis for both concepts, but the categories must be organized so that there is a clear distinction between categories that are derived from different classification principles. You could solve your problem by placing one set of categories under the other set (i.e., using different levels of categories). For example, *anticipated reactions of Western bloc countries* and *anticipated reactions of Eastern bloc countries* could become major category headings. Then *economic, cultural,* and *legal ramifications* could become subheadings under each of the other two major categories. Making this adjustment maintains the integrity of your classification principle.

Consider a second example that illustrates this point. In an analysis of free trade issues, combining the following categories under one heading would be inappropriate: *support free trade, reject free trade, regional responses to free trade,* and *industry responses to free trade. Regional responses* and *industry responses* make sense as one category level. *Support free trade* and *reject free trade* also make sense as a category level, but these involve a different classification principle. Both supporting and rejecting arguments can fit under *regional responses to free trade* and *industry responses to free trade.* Therefore, they should be subcategories under the other headings.

A final example that illustrates this point particularly well involves trying to fit target audiences into gender-based and class-based groupings, for example, into slots such as *male, female, upper class, middle class,* and *working class.* The first classification principle that you will be using relates to gender, the second to socioeconomic class. To solve the problem, you could create two major headings, *male* and *female,* under which you create class groupings.

Alternatively, you could create major headings related to *class*, with male and female subgroupings under each. Which one of these two alternatives is most appropriate will be determined by the questions you are asking in your research.

Some attempts have been made to construct *standard* categories for analyzing newspaper content, especially in areas such as values and attitudes. A media analysis of copyright infringement could involve identifying values such as *right to own property, social responsibility, individual freedom,* or *protection of the individual.* An analysis of response to Japanese investment in the United States could entail a search for the values such as *cultural sovereignty, autonomy, expansion, innovation,* and *competitiveness.* Many researchers caution against relying on standard categories, (i.e., ones that don't emerge from the specific material being analyzed). Even within relatively short periods of time, discussion may shift on topics, where only the major headings within subject areas remain the same. Specific arguments get dropped and are modified. Most analysts agree that the "most interesting content analyses will probably always depend on categories developed especially for the data at hand."[36] The quality of any analysis is dependent upon the quality of the categories constructed from the data: "Content analysis stands or falls by its categories. Particular studies have been productive to the extent that the categories were clearly formulated and well adapted to the problem and to the content."[37]

The term *coding* refers to the process of classifying data, or units of analysis, into content categories. This part of the task is the most "time-consuming and least glamorous."[38] Examples of protocols with subject matter categories can be seen in Figures 5.4 and 5.5. In the first example, these protocols were developed as a result of reading materials pertinent to a CEO's resignation. In the second example, the materials related to Freedom of Information legislation. To use the protocols, read an article on the same topic; then place a check mark or an entry indicator by all categories that were addressed in the article. Use a new protocol sheet for each article that you analyze. After analyzing the necessary sample of articles, tabulate frequencies for the categories. These points are considered in more depth in the discussion that follows.

LOGGING YOUR INFORMATION

As was indicated in the previous section, you will need to transfer your subject matter categories and subcategories to a data sheet that you can use for logging individual items. Your data sheet may be hard copy or a spread sheet on the computer. There should be a place on each data sheet for logging in the basic information on the item, including the following:

- Source (name of newspaper or television station).
- Date of appearance of news item in the print or broadcast media.

FIGURE 5.4
Individual Data Sheet: CEO Resignation

Place check marks in all categories that apply to a given news item, either press or television.

1. *Long-Term Positive Effects of Resignation*

On general visibility of parent company	
On product sales	
On strategic direction of company	
On shareholder value	
On employee well-being	
Total	

2. *Short-Term Positive Effects of Resignation*

On general visibility of parent company	
On product sales	
On strategic direction of company	
On shareholder value	
On employee well-being	
Total	

3. *Long-Term Negative Effects of Resignation*

On general visibility of parent company	
On product sales	
On strategic direction of company	
On shareholder value	
On employee well-being	
Total	

4. *Short-Term Negative Effects of Resignation*

On general visibility of parent company	
On product sales	
On strategic direction of company	
On shareholder value	
On employee well-being	
Total	

FIGURE 5.5
Sample Subject Category Sheet

Freedom of Information and Privacy Legislation*

1. Key concerns as defined by the press.
   a. Concerns relating to specific exemptions that restrict the public's ability to access government documents.
      __ Broad use of provision totally exempting Cabinet information.
      __ Broad use of provision allowing government officials to conceal records containing policy advice.
      __ Broad application of exemption to any meeting attended by government officials.
      __ Discretionary exemptions allowing information blackout on records affecting international and federal/state affairs & police investigations.
      __ Inability of courts to intervene when a document is described as Cabinet confidence or falls into an exempt category under the Act (becomes subject to the discretion of head of government institution).
      __ Practice of identifying person requesting government documents.
      __ Issue of whether quasi-government organizations should be exempt from legislation.
      __ Inadequate records kept by government departments.
      __ Too many records destroyed too soon.
      __ Issue of lobbyist relationship with client.
   b. Concerns related to personal data that is protected (relating to inadequate safeguards or inadequate ability of individual to access his or her own records).
      __ Increasing size of government data banks; general threat to personal privacy.
      __ Cross-indexing of government records.
      __ Lack of deadlines for destruction of government records.
      __ Failure of exempt banks to meet the criteria of containing predominantly personal information or cases of persons questioning the validity of exempt banks.
      __ Provisions in earlier acts that permit a federal court judge to order evidence withheld from trial court process on national security grounds.
      __ Inability of public to determine, in the case of exempt banks, whether a file exists.
      __ Inability of courts to order release of government files on individuals when exempt banks are involved.
      __ Inability to access criminal record files.
      __ Lack of internal safety checks in dealing with outside contractors and with files containing personal information on Americans.
      __ Threat posed by growth of microcomputers.
   c. General concerns.
      __ High costs for users.
      __ Limited knowledge of legislative provisions, lack of use by public, skepticism.
      __ Long delays and excessive red tape.
      __ Lack of aggressiveness on the part of the government officials in publicizing provisions of legislation.
      __ Lack of cooperation on part of civil servants.
      __ High costs and time involved for government to process requests.

FIGURE 5.5 (*concluded*)

---

2. Recommendations explicit or implicit in press accounts.

   a. Recommendations relating to specific exemptions that restrict the public's ability to access government documents.

     __ Need to narrow range of exemptions, making them specific, necessary, and limited.

     __ Need to empower courts to weigh injury against likely benefits of release of information and to make decision.

     __ Need better record management/preservation of records.

     __ Need to bring Cabinet documents under legislation, subject to court review.

   b. Recommendations relating to personal data that is protected (related to inadequate safeguards or inadequate ability of individual to access his or her own records).

     __ Need new guidelines for all government projects that collect, use, and destroy personal information.

     __ Need safeguards to ensure respondents to surveys are told why they have been selected.

     __ Need specific clauses in all contracts with outside firms to govern protection of personal information on Americans.

     __ Need new process to ensure approval for release of personal information by government departments.

     __ Need better safeguards to protect against improper release of personal information by government departments.

     __ Need to empower courts to weigh injury against likely benefit of release of information and to make decision.

     __ Need to "stay" trial proceedings until a judge can hold a hearing to identify evidence that can be released to the defence without damaging national security.

   c. Recommendations relating to general concerns.

     __ Need to educate public regarding rights and procedures in using legislation.

     __ Need to eliminate complex wording.

     __ Need to eliminate excessive fees.

     __ Need to eliminate delays and excessive red tape.

     __ Need to eliminate cumbersome appeal procedures.

  * The analyst uses one set of these sheets for each news item analyzed. He or she places a check mark beside all categories that appear in the article. There may be a number of items checked.

  ** This example is fictitious.

- Type of article (news, feature, editorial, letter to the editor, column, interview, or other).
- Journalist or commentator.

In some instances, you may omit some of the demographic data. In other cases, the specific needs of your organization may require that you note other kinds of basic information. See Figure 5.6 for a sample coding sheet for demographic data. The names of journalists and newspapers will vary, depending on the issue you are tracking.

The following definitions may be used as a basis for categorizing stories as *news, editorial, column, feature,* or *letter to the editor* (see Figure 5.7).

In logging correspondence, you will probably want to record some types of demographic data. The information that you acquire when you research and analyze issues will later become the foundation for the design of your organization's strategic messages. You will be targeting audiences on the basis of factors such as age, sex, income, and region. These are key determinants of attitudes and behavior patterns.[39] Claritas, Inc., of Alexandria, Virginia, for example, developed a system called PRIZM that divides the United States into 300 markets; 3,000 counties; 30,000 zip code zones; 80,000 neighborhoods; and 300,000 block groups. Within these geographic, demographic, psychographic, and consumer groupings, the members share certain common characteristics. The researchers at Claritas found 12 social groupings and 40 lifestyle clusters to be associated with the 80,000 neighborhoods identified in their studies.[40] For that reason, it is important to discover the geodemographic characteristics of your correspondents. With this information, you can better understand how to communicate effectively with these stakeholders. Typical demographic data that you may choose to log (as exemplified in Figure 5.8) includes:

- Name of writer.
- Sex of writer.
- Place of residence.
- Region of country from which letter originates.
- Date on which correspondence was written or received.
- Whether letter represents an organized lobby effort.

In a content analysis of correspondence, you should keep the following points in mind:

- People who write to organizations, expressing their point of view on issues, constitute a special public, who may or may not represent the general public. Most issues have their crusaders. For example, Gary Rosenfeldt of British Columbia, father of one of the victims of mass murderer Clifford Olson, writes on a regular basis to Canadian newspapers. He argues for stronger victims' rights and for the death penalty.

FIGURE 5.6
Definitions of Types of Newspaper Articles

Genre	Description	Examples
News Story	An article that chronicles the who, what, where, why, and how of timely occurrences. "Hard" news or "straight" news. Designed to inform. Often based on information drawn from wire services (e.g., AP or Knight-Ridder). May or may not include name of journalist. Ostensibly impersonal, presenting unopinionated facts. Bias may enter through selection of quotations, details, or headlines.	Reports of a speech by a ranking official. The announcement of a new economic policy. The initial revelation of an airplane crash. Reports of an oil spill.
Editorial	An article that analyzes an event, public question, or current issue. Appears on editorial page. Contains no specific reference to writer in most cases. Assumed to have originated with editor of newspaper or, at least, to reflect management's views.	Comment on recent layoffs by local plant. Statement of newspaper position on political candidacy. Comment on government's monetary policies. Reaction to embezzlement charges against industry official.
Column	An opinion article, usually written continuously by one person. Appears in one or more newspapers. Set apart from editorial by the fact that it is the opinion of one individual, as opposed to the opinion of the newspaper management. Name, and often a photograph, of the columnist will appear.	Comments on inappropriate behavior by union workers. Comments on implementation of equity policies in local university. Comment on spending policies of municipal government.

| Feature | An umbrella term that refers to a number of different types of stories.
Analyzes the news; entertains an audience; or describes people, places, or things in or out of the news.
Not governed by same rules of formal objectivity that govern news story.
Often adds personal comment to basic news content.
Uses more graphic language than is case with straight news stories. | Human interest stories.
Personality profiles.
Stories that add interpretative comment to news events. |
| Letter to the Editor | Expression of individual point of view, often a stakeholder in an issue.
May reveal institutional or other affilliation of writer.
Number of letters received may, or may not, reflect general public opinion on topic (e.g., newspaper may publish equal number of articles from opposing camps, but they may have received more letters from people who oppose policies than from people who support them). | Letter on education funding issue, written by university professor.
Letter on violence in the media, written by father of a victim.
Letter on plant hiring policies, written by president of a minority rights group. |

FIGURE 5.7

Sample Logging Sheet for Recording Basic Data on Newspaper Articles (Coding Information on Articles)

Type of Article:
☐ News
☐ Feature

Newspaper:
☐ Wall Street Journal
☐ USA Today
☐ Daily News (New York)
☐ Los Angeles Times
☐ New York Times
☐ Chicago Tribune
☐ Newsday (Long Island)

☐ Editorial
☐ Column

☐ San Francisco Chronicle
☐ Philadelphia Inquirer
☐ Boston Globe
☐ Newark Star-Ledger
☐ Cleveland Plain Dealer
☐ Baltimore Sun
☐ Houston Chronicle

Placement:
☐ Prominent
☐ Not Prominent

☐ Washington Post
☐ New York Post
☐ Detroit News
☐ Detroit Free Press
☐ Chicago Sun-Times
☐ Miami Herald

Wire Service:
☐ AP
☐ New York Times

☐ Los Angeles Times
☐ Chicago Tribune

☐ Knight-Ridder

Month in which Article Appeared:
☐ January
☐ February
☐ March
☐ April

☐ May
☐ June
☐ July
☐ August

☐ September
☐ October
☐ November
☐ December

Journalists:
☐ R. W. Apple, Jr.
☐ Maureen Dowd
☐ Aaron Epstein
☐ David Hess

☐ Susan Moffatt
☐ Clarence Page
☐ Anna Quindlen
☐ James Rowley

☐ William Safire
☐ Jenny Scott
☐ Roberto Suro
☐ Calvin Woodward

FIGURE 5.8
Protocol for Logging of Correspondence

	For/Against/Balanced			Date of Letter	Sex of Writer		Writer's State of Residence
	F	A	B		M	F	
1							
2							
3							
4							
5							
6							
7							
8							
9							
10							
11							
12							
13							
14							
15							
16							
17							
18							
19							
20							
21							
22							
23							

FIGURE 5.8 (*concluded*)

24						
25						
26						
27						
28						
29						
30						

- People who are negatively disposed toward a proposed policy or course of action may be more likely to be moved to write than those who either agree with or have no strong feelings on the subject. For example, people who are against a proposed merger are more likely to write than those who support the merger.
- Many of the letters received on any issue may be the product of write-in campaigns generated by advocacy groups. Rightly or wrongly, organizations tend to attach less weight to form letters than to original correspondence.
- Some organizations differentiate between correspondence from "experts" on a topic and correspondence from the general public, attaching more weight to expert opinion.
- There may be a time lag between the occurrence of events or announcements and any correspondence they stimulate.

In coding information on House and Senate debates, you may choose to include basic data such as the following:

- Name of speaker.
- Region or state represented by speaker.
- Party represented.
- Date on which question was asked.
- Interest groups represented in the questions.

CALCULATING FREQUENCIES AND SPACE/TIME

After completing the logging of information on individual news items, correspondence, or other research materials, you total what is contained on the individual data sheets. In other words, you calculate the frequency with which specific topics appeared in the information that you analyzed. In some cases, you translate frequency into percentages. The purpose of these frequency counts is to enable you to make the following kinds of judgments.[41]

Frequency counts to determine the *journalists and newspapers* that covered a particular issue enable you to make statements such as "The news-

FIGURE 5.9
CEO Resignation

This cumulative spread sheet reflects the total number of times that the following content categories appeared in the sample of articles selected for analysis. Subtotals appear to the right of each subcategory. Each number represents an article. The number 20, for example, indicates that this topic category appeared in 20 articles.

1. *Long-Term Positive Effects of Resignation*
   On general visibility of parent company   0
   On product sales   0
   On strategic direction of company   0
   On shareholder value   20
   On employee well-being   9
                                    Total   29

2. *Short-Term Positive Effects of Resignation*
   On general visibility of parent company   3
   On product sales   0
   On strategic direction of company   0
   On shareholder value   4
   On employee well-being   1
                                    Total   8

3. *Long-Term Negative Effects of Resignation*
   On general visibility of parent company   69
   On product sales   1
   On strategic direction of company   11
   On shareholder value   2
   On employee well-being   5
                                    Total   88

4. *Short-Term Negative Effects of Resignation*
   On general visibility of parent company   11
   On product sales   2
   On strategic direction of company   6
   On shareholder value   1
   On employee well-being   15
                                    Total   35

FIGURE 5.10
Proposed Merger Media Response, Analyzed for Directionality
December 19, 1992–December 26, 1992*

Source	Number of Articles				
	Positive	Negative	Neutral	Mixed	Totals
Wall Street Journal			7		7
USA Today		14			14
Daily News (New York)		21			21
Los Angeles Times		28			28
New York Times		7	7		14
Chicago Tribune		42	7		49
Washington Post		49	21		70
New York Post		7			7
Detroit News		28	14	7	49
Detroit Free Press		14	49		63
Newsday (Long Island)		5			5
Chicago Sun-Times		12	4		16
San Francisco Chronicle				6	6
Philadelphia Inquirer			6	2	8
Boston Globe		32			32
Newark Star-Ledger		40			40
Cleveland Plain Dealer	4				4
Baltimore Sun		17		5	22
Houston Chronicle		8	2		10
Miami Herald			4	3	7
Totals	4	324	117	20	465
Percentage	1%	70%	25%	4%	100%

* This is a fictitious example. The total number of articles with references to the proposed merger is shown in the last column of numbers above. The additional breakdown of numbers reflects tone of comment.

paper showing the highest level of interest in the issue of the impending repatriation of Hong Kong is the *Chicago Sun*. The journalists who most often speak out on the issue are. . . . Leading critics of Britain's position are. . . ."

Frequency counts of the *number of articles appearing on a given topic over a period of time* enable you to make statements such as "Coverage of the plywood lumber dispute declined in volume between September and November but increased in volume again in the new year."

Frequency counts of *types of articles* enable you to make a statement such as "Although news accounts of plant shutdowns increased in the month of March, editorial comment on these issues declined during the same period of time."

Frequency counts of major *themes* enable you to make statements such as "Recent coverage of the controversy related to Company X's takeover of Company Z reveals several major themes such as. . . ."

Frequency counts of major *issues* appearing in New York newspapers in a given time period allow you to make statements such as "The number one ranked issue appearing in the month of March related to employment; the number two issue related to pensions; the number three issue was taxes."

Frequency counts of *major arguments or criticisms* enable you to make statements such as "The three major arguments raised in support of a merger were. . . ." or "The most frequent criticisms of National Revenue appearing in the press over the past six months have been. . . ."

FIGURE 5.11
Calls for Stiffer Regulations Governing Occupational Safety
January 1993–March 1993*

Location of Nonopinion Items in Newspapers			
Location of Articles	*Page 1*	*Page 2/3*	*Other*	*Total*
Number of Articles	9	18	21	48

Number and Type of Articles, by Newspaper				
Source	*News*	*Column*	*Feature*	*Editorial*	*Total*
Wall Street Journal	3	1	2	0	6
USA Today	4	1	2	2	9
Daily News (New York)	4	2	2	0	8
Los Angeles Times	5	3	3	2	13
New York Times	1	4	0	0	5
Chicago Tribune	2	2	1	1	6
Washington Post	2	1	1	2	6
New York Post	6	4	3	1	14
Detroit News	1	0	0	1	2
Detroit Free Press	2	0	1	0	3
Newsday (Long Island)	3	0	2	1	6
Chicago Sun-Times	8	2	4	2	16
San Francisco Chronicle	2	0	1	0	3
Philadelphia Inquirer	3	1	2	0	6
Boston Globe	0	1	0	0	1
Newark Star-Ledger	4	2	0	1	7
Cleveland Plain Dealer	1	1	1	1	4
Baltimore Sun	0	2	4	0	6
Houston Chronicle	2	5	1	2	10
Miami Herald	7	1	3	1	12
Totals	60	33	33	17	143

* This is a fictitious example.

FIGURE 5.12
Demands for Recall of Product X April, 1993–May, 1993*

		Number and Type of Articles, by Region			
Region	*News*	*Column*	*Editorial*	*Feature*	*Totals*
Northeast	4	2	2	0	8
Southeast	8	8	4	4	24
Midwest	24	7	4	8	43
Southwest	10	2	3	5	20
Northwest	2	0	0	1	3
Totals	48	19	13	18	98

Column Inches of Coverage, by Region	
Region	*Column Inches*
Northeast	84
Southeast	225
Midwest	413
Southwest	164
Northwest	26
Totals	912

* This is a fictitious example.

Frequency counts of *statements defending an organization's actions or position* enable you to say the following, "Statements most frequently appearing in defense of the company's position on layoffs are. . . ." or "Positive perceptions related to the U.S. postal service's performance are. . . ."

Frequency counts to determine *who controlled the media agenda in a particular period* enable you to make a statement such as "During the recent abortion debate, the pro-life group appeared to be in control of the media agenda more than 75 percent of the time."

Frequency counts of *references to major stakeholders* enable you to make statements such as "The key players in the long-range missile testing controversy appear to be. . . ." "The key players in the controversy surrounding the company's refusal to withdraw product X from the market are. . . ."

The cumulative data sheets on pages 151 to 157 (Figures 5.9–5.16) illustrate such tabulations of frequency, sometimes in the form of charts and other times in the form of graphs. The information contained on these data sheets will later be incorporated into narrative. You use the information on the data sheets to generate the basic structure of your report, adding other points, quotations, and

FIGURE 5.13
Television Coverage of Acquisition X by Six Local Stations

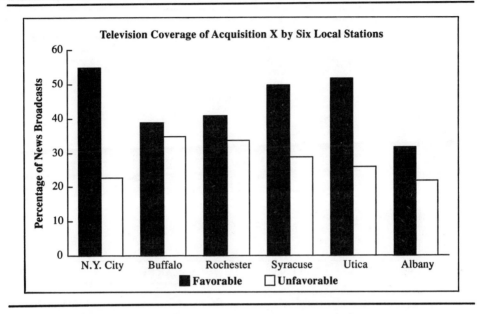

FIGURE 5.14
Expressed Support for Industry Position on Four Current Issues, by Region
August 1986–October 1986*

Eastern U.S.	Supported	Opposed	No Stand
Free trade	9%	81%	10%
Tax reform	67%	13%	20%
Acid rain	22%	31%	47%
Agricultural subsidies	51%	22%	29%
Western U.S.	Supported	Opposed	No Stand
Free trade	46%	21%	33%
Tax reform	56%	33%	11%
Acid rain	22%	33%	45%
Agricultural subsidies	27%	41%	32%

* This is a fictitious example. The percentages refer to numbers of newspapers in the Eastern and Western United States that supported, opposed, or took no stand on the industry position on these issues.

FIGURE 5.15
Dominant Content Themes Appearing in Media Coverage of Waste Disposal Industry

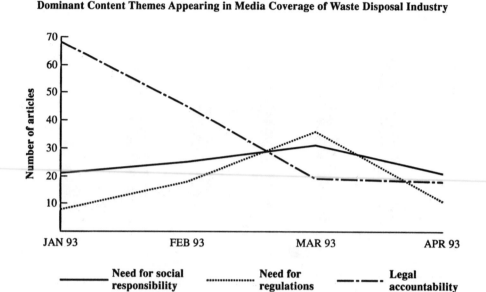

Dominant Content Themes Appearing in Media Coverage of Waste Disposal Industry

examples as required. The data sheets typically appear in the appendix to the issue analysis report.

Most debates over content analysis occur because some researchers claim that frequent appearance of an idea does not necessarily denote concern, value, intensity, or focus of attention. Others say that not all units of content should be given equal weight. In other words, they say that some themes, characters, articles, and words are more important than others. For this reason, some attempt is made to differentiate items appearing on the front page from those printed elsewhere in a newspaper, either by coding the articles separately or by giving front-page items a greater weight. Others use similar techniques to differentiate the position of items on a page or to give greater weight to larger-print headlines. Some have advocated the usefulness of distinguishing between different typefaces and identifying column placement.[42] Some studies adjust ratings to reflect the circulation of the newspaper in which they appear. These same kinds of adjustments can be made when analyzing the broadcast media. Items appearing early in a broadcast or announced early may be judged to have greater prominence or potential for impact than those appearing later.

Some researchers measure column inches as an alternative to computing frequency. Many early content analyses employed measures of *space* to describe the relative emphasis given to different topics appearing in newspapers.

Since the news hole remains constant, organizations can get a sense of the importance being attached to a specific issue.[43] Measurement of column inches enables you to make statements such as, "The percentage of the news hole allocated to discussion of the hostile buyout of company Z increased between January 1989 and May 1989" or "The total amount of space devoted to the topic of industry violations of the National Safety Code has increased dramatically since 1984." Measurement of column inches also enables you to make statements such as "The journalists who have given the most in-depth treatment to the issue of agricultural subsidies are. . . ." or "Compared to issue X, issue Y drew much more attention in. . . ."

FIGURE 5.16
Dominant Focus of Network News Coverage of Communist Coup in Soviet Union*

Dominant Stakeholder Perspective Conveyed in News Segment Analyzed:

	Number of News Segments			
	CBS	NBC	ABC	Total
Gorbachev	20	22	17	59
Yeltsin	45	48	50	143
Coup leaders	6	3	1	10
Leaders of Baltic states	11	9	10	30

Orientation Implied in Tone and/or Content of Newscast:

	Number of News Segments			
	CBS	NBC	ABC	Total
Pro-recognition	15	6	13	34
Anti-recognition	67	76	65	208

Policy Recommendations (Explicit or Implicit):

	Number of News Segments			
	CBS	NBC	ABC	Total
Pro-intervention	6	11	8	25
Anti-intervention	5	20	10	35
Wait-and-see	71	51	60	182

* This is a fictitious example.

FIGURE 5.17
Space Devoted to Issue of Deceptive Advertising January 1993–March 1993*
(Column Inches of Coverage, by Newspaper

Newspaper	Column Inches
Wall Street Journal	480
USA Today	210
Daily News (New York)	506
Los Angeles Times	400
New York Times	304
Chicago Tribune	215
Washington Post	220
New York Post	508
Detroit News	400
Detroit Free Press	315
Newsday (Long Island)	210
Chicago Sun-Times	180
San Francisco Chronicle	509
Philadelphia Inquirer	800
Boston Globe	430
Newark Star-Ledger	308
Cleveland Plain Dealer	252
Baltimore Sun	653
Houston Chronicle	310
Miami Herald	600
Total	7010

* This is a fictitious example.

One study compared the total space in column inches devoted to issues, the frequency of appearance of different issues, and the size of headlines employed in articles. The study found that all three measures (column inches, frequency, and size of headlines) yielded similar results, but the fastest and easiest method involved measuring space.[44] Other researchers have cautioned, however, that the measurement of space does not allow you to answer sophisticated questions. Using this technique on its own, they say, enables you to assess space devoted to a topic but not manner of treatment.

The equivalent unit of measurement for film, radio, and television is *time*. It has been said that the continuing popularity of space/time measures grows out of the ease in applying them.[45] Some say that space/time measures are most suited to analysis of mass media, but even so, they are too crude to be adequate indexes of attitudes, values, or style. The cumulative data sheets (Figures 5.17–5.19) illustrate the application of space and time measures to content analysis of current issues.

FIGURE 5.18
Time Devoted to Union Position on Issue X, by Network

Date	ABC (sec)	NBC (sec)	CBS (sec)	Totals (sec)
13-Mar-93	50.3	46.7	58.6	155.6
14-Mar-93	70	68.3	55.3	193.6
15-Mar-93	94.9	89.8	73.4	258.1
16-Mar-93	89.5	88.6	75.4	253.5
17-Mar-93	91	67.5	76.7	235.2
18-Mar-93	95.8	35.2	61.4	192.4
19-Mar-93	77.9	84.2	86.6	248.7
20-Mar-93	66	51.5	49	166.5
21-Mar-93	48.7	32.2	42.6	123.5
22-Mar-93	46.9	53.6	70.7	171.2
23-Mar-93	64.6	43	55.9	163.5
24-Mar-93	67.6	37.6	63.7	168.9
25-Mar-93	90	62.1	65.4	217.5
Totals	953.2	760.3	834.7	2548.2

Time Devoted to Industry Position on Issue X, by Network

Date	ABC (sec)	NBC (sec)	CBS (sec)	Totals (sec)
13-Mar-93	20.2	11.7	15.6	47.5
14-Mar-93	44.8	52.9	34	131.7
15-Mar-93	21.3	23.7	11.2	56.2
16-Mar-93	30.5	26.4	25.7	82.6
17-Mar-93	29.8	26	34.1	89.9
18-Mar-93	26.2	23.5	36.9	86.6
19-Mar-93	41	35.2	42.3	118.5
20-Mar-93	38.5	29.3	32.7	100.5
21-Mar-93	24.9	23.8	18.6	67.3
22-Mar-93	13.8	16.4	11.2	41.4
23-Mar-93	13.2	16.5	14	43.7
24-Mar-93	9.8	10.2	16.3	36.3
25-Mar-93	8.6	5.4	7.8	21.8
Totals	322.6	301	300.4	924

FIGURE 5.19
Financial Difficulties of Company X*

Newspaper	Column Inches Devoted to Topic
Indianapolis Star	38
Christian Science Monitor	84
New York Times	84
Chicago Sun	50
San Francisco Examiner	20
New Orleans Times-Picayune	28
Washington Post	65
Total	369

* This is fictitious example.

TRAINING AND UTILIZING THE ANALYST

Media analyses carried out within the organization will usually be the product of one analyst. Outside firms, however, often use multiple analysts to study a single large issue that is being tracked on an ongoing basis. Also, in the case of correspondence, the task of reading, analyzing, coding, and answering correspondence may fall to more than one person. In all instances where multiple analysts are employed in the study of a single issue, careful training of the analysts is essential. Training will enhance the possibility that different analysts agree on categorizing and interpreting data. The more precise and clear the categories used by the analysts, the greater will be the reliability of the results that are obtained. Ill-defined and overlapping categories, on the other hand, will yield unreliable results.

Pretesting a category system is one way to increase the validity and reliability of the results. Results obtained from working with a test sample are evaluated and discussed with analysts. Analysts are given the opportunity to compare their interpretation of categories with the interpretations of others who are involved in the study. The analysts can then reach a common understanding of what is meant by different categories. They contribute to the renaming of categories and the revision of category sheets. They become comfortable with the definitions and the procedures. Furthermore, the training sessions allow analysts the opportunity to talk over any problems or to question the organization of the data.

Because learning the language of any new area takes time, it is advantageous for an organization to designate expert analysts for specific content areas. It is true that an issue rarely remains static and usually takes on new forms over time; however, an analyst who is acquainted with the history and development of an issue can more easily detect variations in form. If one individual who has tracked a topic over a long period of time conducts training sessions with new analysts, the organization can short-circuit the inconsistencies that would otherwise surface in a situation involving multiple analysts. Media analysis is one of the most subjective of processes. Because issues do take on new dimensions over time, one training session will not suffice to ensure quality analyses. Ongoing sessions, conducted at regular intervals, will be a better guarantee of consistency in interpretation of data. The end result of these training sessions is a set of detailed instructions to all those who will be participating in the study.[46] These instructions, which typically include examples, serve to shorten the learning time for new analysts who join the team.

Using computers to classify material yields perfect intercoder reliability but can also generate a situation where important information is missed. The computer is used most often to seek out words or phrases as units of analysis. Computers can assist but not replace the analyst. Although some programs help the analyst to identify the recurrence of words, phrases, and themes, no computer program understands narrative.[47] Consequently, fine distinctions are lost when single words have multiple meanings. People working in their native language make these distinctions; computer programs do not. Also, people make inferences about matters that are implied but not directly stated; no computer program, at present, is capable of drawing these inferences. Researchers at the Yale Artificial Intelligence Laboratory have attempted to create a computer program that understands narrative and answers questions about text. They have tried to program into the computer the capacity to make inferences about matters that are only implied. Their efforts have necessitated that they experiment with 10 knowledge areas: knowledge about syntax and language, objectives, plans for achieving objectives, affect or emotions, events and scripts concerning events, interpersonal relations, social roles, reasoning and beliefs, settings, and abstract themes.[48] Despite the ambitious efforts of researchers in artificial intelligence, most scientists still regard this field of study as being in its infancy. The Yale system, for example, can understand only a limited number of topics, and experts say it is dangerous to expect too much too soon, especially considering the cost of developing appropriate techniques and programs.

In conclusion then, it is not realistic to assume, given the present situation, that computers can take over the work of the analyst. At best, computers offer limited assistance, storing data or the results of analyses already completed, so that trends in content, themes, and other areas can be tracked over time. Many organizational specialists caution against overreliance on computer technologies.[49]

SUMMARY OF KEY POINTS

When engaging in content analysis of media, remember to:

- Consider the purposes of your research.
- Limit your study, deciding what to include and exclude.
- Pick a sample, taking different factors (including organizational culture) into account.
- Decide what will be your smallest unit of analysis.
- Generate categories, or "pigeonholes," for your data.
- Log your information.
- Tabulate frequencies and space/time measures.
- Train your company's analysts in order to achieve reliability of results.

If you pay an outside contractor, or if you ask someone in the company to carry out an analysis, you should keep in mind the following points:

1. The smaller the unit of analysis that you want studied, the more time will be required to carry out the analysis. Therefore, you should expect to pay more for an analysis that makes these discriminations.

2. The more questions you want answered, the greater will be the time expended to find the answers.

3. Determining the frequency of appearance of different arguments and deciding directionality and focus of content require significantly more time than measuring column inches of coverage and listing topic areas. The former activities also require a higher level of expertise and should cost more.

4. Trend analysis based on frequency should cost more than trend analysis based on column inches of space or logging of broadcast material by time. Finer discriminations and more judgment calls are required.

5. The more "impressionistic" an analysis, the less time required to carry out the task.

6. Unless a transcript is furnished, analysis of audio materials will cost more than analysis of print media materials because few people can skim or speed read an audio tape. Analyzing the material will require stopping and starting the tape, rewinding, and making notes before you can even begin the analysis.

7. The same rationale applies to video material, but the process of analysis becomes even more complex and, thus, more time-consuming and costly. More variables than the spoken word become important in the analysis of video materials. The part that judgment plays is even greater.

8. If you opt for analysis of video transcripts, the cost will be less, but you will lose a large part of the content. The most reliable information you acquire from video transcripts will be the frequency with which specific questions and arguments appear. It is almost impossible to make complex judgments on content, based on transcripts alone.

9. The greater the time involved in completing an analysis, the higher the likelihood that multiple persons will be involved at some stage in the analysis. For example, analysis of video content will almost never be carried out by one person and will almost never be done in-house. Therefore, the conclusions reached in the analysis may be based on information gleaned from the work of many people over whom you have little or no control. Unless you conduct adequate training sessions with personnel and refine categories of analysis over time, you will probably obtain meaningless results. For these reasons, if you commission this kind of work, you will be best served by setting up a long-term contract with one consulting firm rather than asking many different firms to carry out the analyses. You will also do well to take some steps to ensure quality control (i.e., asking to meet and talk with the individuals who are engaged in the analysis). Ask to see examples of categories of analysis applied at different stages to determine whether any steps are being taken to refine concepts. Ask whether formal and ongoing training sessions with personnel are planned. Attend a training session. Analysis of video materials is so costly that it is hardly justifiable under any other conditions.

10. Correspondence analysis and large-scale print media analyses involving topics such as free trade will similarly involve multiple coders under most conditions. The same cautions are urged.

11. Whether dealing with print or broadcast media, you should expect to pay more (based on time requirements) to an analyst who is learning a content area than to one who has carried out work for you on the same topic over a longer period of time. Learning a content area requires time. A large part of analysis is recognizing what is new, what is no longer present, and what subtle shifts have taken place in arguments over time. Acquiring this contextual framework is time-consuming, but an analysis carried out without the necessary background risks being superficial. A firm that requests more time for a first analysis on a topic is not being unreasonable.

12. Generating a media analysis is a labor-intensive activity. Because the work involves research and constant exercising of judgment, it is also a fatiguing activity. Employees who are expected to do this type of work five days a week, seven and a half hours a day, will soon experience burnout and/or will look for another job. Press clippings services experience high turnover for similar reasons. Because training and experience are important factors in carrying out good media analyses, supervisors should recognize when a project is done well and attempt to induce some variety into the work of the media analyst. At the same time, the organization should recognize that analytical work requires immersion in the task for relatively long periods of time. The analyst should be given these large time segments, as it is anti-productive to come and go from a task that requires "entry time," the time necessary to reconnect with the subject matter.

NOTES

1. See James E. Grunig (ed.), *Excellence in Public Relations and Communication Management* (Hillsdale, N.J.: Lawrence Erlbaum Associates, Publishers, 1992) for discussion of firms that do this type of work.
2. John E. Merriam and Joel Makower, *Trend Watching: How the Media Create Trends and How To Be the First to Uncover Them* (New York: Tilden Press, AMACOM, 1988).
3. David P. Fan, *Predictions of Public Opinion from the Mass Media: Computer Content Analysis and Mathematical Modeling* (New York: Greenwood Press, 1988).
4. George Cheney and Steven L. Vibbert, "Corporate Discourse: Public Relations and Issue Management," in *Handbook of Organizational Communication: An Interdisciplinary Perspective,* eds. Fredric M. Jablin, Linda L. Putnam, Karlene H. Roberts, and Lyman W. Porter (Newbury Park, Calif.: Sage Publications, 1987), p. 191.
5. David M. Dozier and Fred C. Repper, "Research Firms and Public Relations Practices," in *Excellence in Public Relations and Communication Management,* ed. James E. Grunig (Hillsdale, N.J.: Lawrence Erlbaum Associates, Publishers, 1992), pp. 196–99.
6. Ibid, p. 198.
7. The Payne Fund film studies, carried out between 1929 and 1932, contained some of the early examples of content analysis. Edgar Dale, for example, reviewed, classified, and analyzed the content of 1,500 films. These studies were published by the Arno Press and *The New York Times*. Other examples of such early content studies included Howard P. Becker, "Distribution of Space in the *American Journal of Sociology, 1895–1927*," *American Journal of Sociology* November 1930, pp. 461–66; and Howard P. Becker, "Space Apportioned Forty-Eight Topics in the *American Journal of Sociology, 1895–1930*," American School of Sociology July 1932, pp. 71–78.
8. Walter K. Lindenmann, "Content Analysis," *Public Relations Journal,* July 1983, p. 24. See, for an example of this type of study, Jerome Bruner, "The Dimensions of Propaganda: German Shortwave Broadcasts to America," *Journal of Abnormal Social Psychology,* July 1941, pp. 311–37.
   The most influential publication of the 1940s in terms of contribution to content analysis is said to have been Harold D. Lasswell, Nathan Leites, and associates, *The Language of Politics: Studies in Quantitative Semantics* (Cambridge, Mass.: MIT Press, 1949). For an earlier article addressing some of the same ideas, see Harold D. Lasswell, "Communications Research and Politics," *Print Radio and Film in a Democracy* (Chicago: University of Chicago Press, 1942), pp. 101–17.
9. George Gerbner, Ole R. Holsti, Klaus Krippendorff, William J. Paisley, and P. J. Stone, eds., *The Analysis of Communication Content: Developments*

in Scientific Theories and Computer Techniques (New York: John Wiley & Sons, 1969).

10. Harold D. Lasswell, "The Structure and Function of Communication in Society," in *The Communication of Ideas,* ed. Lyman Bryson (New York: Harper & Brothers, 1948), pp. 37–51.

11. Bernard Berelson, *Content Analysis in Communications Research* (Glencoe, Ill.: Free Press, 1952), p. 18. Berelson's book is a classic. Also frequently referenced is Klaus Krippendorff, *Content Analysis: An Introduction to Its Methodology* (Beverly Hills, Calif.: Sage Publications, 1980).

12. Roger A. Wimmer and Joseph R. Dominick, *Mass Media Research: An Introduction,* 3rd ed. (Belmont, Calif.: Wadsworth, 1992), p. 171.

13. Dozier and Repper, p. 196.

14. Wimmer and Dominick, p. 162.

15. Guido H. Stempel, III, "Research in Brief: Sample Size for Classifying Subject Matter in Dailies," *Journalism Quarterly* 29 (1952), pp. 333–34.

16. George Gerbner, Larry Gross, Marilyn Jackson-Beeck, Suzanne Jeffries-Fox, and Nancy Signorielli, "One More Time: An Analysis of the CBS 'Final Comments on the Violence Profile,' " *Journal of Broadcasting,* 21 (1977), pp. 297–303.

17. Alexander Mintz, "The Feasibility of the Use of Samples in Content Analysis," in Lasswell, pp. 127–52.

18. Guido H. Stempel, III, "Content Analysis," in *Research Methods in Mass Communication,* eds. G. H. Stempel, III, and Bruce H. Westley, 2nd ed. (Englewood Cliffs, N.J.: Prentice-Hall, 1989), pp. 119–31.

19. Wimmer and Dominick, pp. 164–65.

20. Ibid.

21. See Lindenmann, pp. 24–26.

22. Wimmer and Dominick, p. 165.

23. Robert Philip Weber, *Basic Content Analysis,* 2nd ed. (Newburg Park, Calif.: Sage Publications, 1990), pp. 49–53.

24. Charles E. Osgood and Evelyn G. Walker, "Motivation and Language Behavior: Content Analysis of Suicide Notes," *Journal of Abnormal and Social Psychology* 59 (1959), p. 63. See also Richard W. Budd, Robert K. Thorp, and Lewis Donohew, *Content Analysis of Communications* (New York: The MacMillan Company, 1967), pp. 78–79.

25. Ole R. Holsti, *Content Analysis for the Social Sciences and Humanities* (Reading, Mass.: Addison-Wesley Publishing Company, 1969), p. 120. Holsti used a similar example to illustrate the point that different units of analysis can produce widely varying results.

26. Ibid.

27. A. Geller, D. Kaplan, and Harold D. Lasswell, "An Experimental Comparison of Four Ways of Coding Editorial Content," *Journalism Quarterly* 19 (1942), pp. 362–70.

28. Holsti, p. 119.

29. Wimmer and Dominick, p. 171.

30. Ibid.

31. These models are based on a similar format suggested by Wimmer and Dominick.

32. Ibid., p. 95.

33. Wimmer and Dominick, p. 167.

34. See Holsti, pp. 95–101.

35. This example is based on a discussion by Joseph J. Penbera and Charles Bonner, "The Director's Role in a Takeover Bid," *Journal of Business Strategy,* May/June 1990, pp. 39–42.

36. Ibid., p. 102.

37. Berelson, p. 147.

38. Wimmer and Dominick, p. 168.

39. Angus Reid, "Public Affairs Research: Quantitative and Qualitative," in *The Canadian Public Affairs Handbook: Maximizing Markets, Protecting Bottom Lines,* eds. W. John Wright and Christopher J. DuVernet (Toronto: Carswell, 1988), p. 139.

40. Dozier and Repper, pp. 207–08.

41. The format for the presentation of material in this section was suggested by Peggy Binns, communication analyst, Privy Council Office, Government of Canada, 1989.

42. M. W. Klein and Nathan Maccoby, "Newspaper Objectivity in the 1952 Campaign," *Journalism Quarterly* 31 (1954), pp. 285–96.

43. See discussion in Merriam and Makower, pp. 63–64.

44. James W. Markham and Guido H. Stempel, III, "Analysis of Techniques in Measuring Press Performance," *Journalism Quarterly,* Spring 1957, pp. 187–90.

45. Holsti, p. 121.

46. Wimmer and Dominick, p. 171.

47. Weber, p. 72–73.

48. M. G. Dyer, *In-Depth Understanding: A Computer Model of Integrated Processing of Narrative Comprehension* (Cambridge, Mass.: MIT Press, 1983).

49. See, for example, discussions by Leonard Fuld, "A Recipe for Business Intelligence Success," *Journal of Business Strategy,* January/February 1991, p. 14; and Jan P. Herring, "Senior Management Must Champion Business Intelligence Programs," *Journal of Business Strategy,* September/October 1991, p. 52.

CHAPTER 6

WHY AND HOW TO
CONDUCT SURVEYS

As spending is cut, organizations must determine what it is that people want and need the most. Surveys have become one of the most popular means of acquiring the information needed to establish these priorities.[1] In the issues management domain, governments and corporations use surveys to track public opinion on priority issues. Survey results also help organizations to evaluate the usefulness of their services and programs.[2]

Governments of all political persuasions appear to be accepting the view most colorfully expressed by consultant Lionel Sosa: "If you fly by your guts, you're nuts."[3] The popularity that public opinion surveys enjoy with U.S. governments has spread to other countries. First, the Liberal government and later the Conservative government in Canada have followed the U.S. lead: government under Pierre Trudeau was accused of "leadership by Goldfarb" (a Canadian polling firm) and government under Brian Mulroney similarly has been accused of leadership by polls. Under Conservative government, Decima Research developed from a fledgling organization into a "polling powerhouse with an international reputation."[4] Critics accused the Conservative government of commissioning almost 800 surveys in its first term in office.[5] Governments in power have the advantage over opposition groups because they are able to use public money to subsidize survey research of an ostensibly nonpartisan nature.

On the flip side of the coin, private and voluntary sector organizations use surveys to learn more about what pressures are being exerted on top-level government officials. When American CEOs were asked what they considered to be the major challenge of the next century, they responded: "the threat from government regulation."[6] Corporate America has become increasingly cognizant of the need to keep a close check on the pulse of government because government has the power (a) to decide who wins and who loses in disputes between firms and their publics, (b) to close down one firm and protect another, (c) to exercise discretion regarding environmental and regulatory policies, and (d) to provide support in the form of public goods and services.[7] Aware of the significance that government at both the national level and state level attaches to survey results, corporate decision makers are avid followers of the latest results of Harris, Gallup, Roper, and other polls.

Businesses sometimes undertake similar polling projects in order to understand shifting public priorities and attitudes. For example, a chemical producer might routinely track (either independently or through its association) public attitudes on environmental issues: "This ongoing monitoring, coupled with intelligence on possible future government initiatives, will provide the company and association with 'early warning' when perceived environmental threats are likely to translate into new regulatory action."[8] Establishing formal mechanisms for soliciting the views of stakeholders can short-circuit the need for company representatives to spend the year on the road "talking to and placating" major institutions.[9]

Ten out of 15 Fortune 500 companies that responded to a 1992 survey said that they use surveys as a scanning tool; eight said surveys assist them in prioritizing the company's issues; and nine reported that they use surveys as a monitoring tool. Some assert that the use of surveys is the "most powerful tool in the practitioner's arsenal of scanning and evaluation tools."[10] The development of modern survey research is tied closely to marketing practices. Corporations have, for a long time, invested large sums of money in surveys that solicit consumer response to products, organization image, publicity campaigns, and marketing approaches.[11]

Because the cost of conducting large surveys is generally greater than other means of tracking public opinion (media analysis, focus groups, and some forms of consultation), the survey option is not available to all organizations. Because surveying is more common at the national level rather than the state level, a group at Rutgers University spearheaded the establishment of the Network of State Polls.[12] The local government, however, shows the most dramatic increase in public opinion survey practices: "More and more local units of government are turning to citizen surveys, community polls, or citizen planning to elicit residents' opinions concerning such things as the quality of the city's services, satisfaction with the city as a place to live, or priorities for future projects."[13]

The *omnibus* survey is a cooperative response to the high cost of surveying. With omnibus surveys, clients buy the right to add a designated number of questions to a multipurpose survey. The omnibus survey may contain a mix of questions pertaining to products, issues, policies, and personalities. In such instances, the organization purchasing the service will probably provide their own questions or, at least, the substantive content.

Even if organizations do not conduct their own surveys on public issues, the majority appear to recognize the benefits of becoming sophisticated consumers of surveys conducted by other groups. Although governments do not always volunteer the results of their opinion research (especially if public policies do not correspond to public sympathies) businesses, universities, and nonprofit organizations can nonetheless acquire access to the results of most surveys. Freedom of information legislation will usually ensure access to information generated with public funds. Pressure groups use the results of surveys to support their demands for public funds, and money traders and members of elite groups read and act upon survey results.[14]

Despite the widespread popularity of surveying with almost every kind of group (from nonprofit groups to corporations to governments) surveying is considered by many to be a "black art" and anti-democratic or the impetus for centralizing control, shaping policies, and "leading to principles being fudged."[15] Pollster Angus Reid says that "like prostitution, polling has become one of the most controversial professions,"[16] subject to much hypocrisy, with leading citizens and journalists publicly rebuking surveying practices but privately commissioning the services of pollsters. This jaundiced view of surveying is so widespread that governments are careful to differentiate between the term *surveying* and the term *polling*. It is not difficult to understand the reasoning behind these distinctions. Because surveying is an expensive process and governments are not supposed to use public funds for furthering party agendas, they must carefully define the purposes and the uses for their surveys. Democratic countries do not typically sanction the use of public funds to gain insight into voter intentions and party image. These governments may, however, request people's policy preferences and their issue priorities. Although some would contend that this is a circuitous route to the same door, it is nonetheless legitimate to ask people such questions.

Therefore, *surveying* has come to be regarded as a more respectable term, a term with potentially broad connotations and applications. A survey may imply anything (i.e., from a census to academic research into supervisor-employee relations in the workforce). It may also include the practice of soliciting the views of citizens toward the policies and practices of their governments. *Polling,* on the other hand, has political connotations. Its use is typically restricted to the acquisition of information of an unabashedly political nature, for example: What party platform do you prefer? For whom do you intend to vote? What is your party affiliation? *Polling,* therefore, is a subset of *surveying;* a *poll* is a survey that solicits information of a partisan nature.

Those who argue against the reliance of politicians on public opinion polls say our political process is being compromised; they say that polls now decide who stays and who leaves in a political race. Because television must "winnow down" the number of people that can be covered, it must decide upon frontrunners.[17] Polls are one of the easiest ways of making this determination; at the same time, they are highly attractive to the media. An increasing number of media organizations are commissioning their own polls. At least five polling organizations in the United States work for major newspaper chains, and the situation in Canada has been described in the following way:

> Media's stake in polling reached unprecedented proportions in 1988, with virtually all of the major news organizations becoming players in the game. Goldfarb Consultants polled for the Liberals as well as for Baton Broadcasting, owner of several CTV stations. Southam commissioned four polls by Angus Reid; soon after the election, the polling firm was taken over by Southam. Gallup Canada did surveys

for the *Toronto Star* and their polls were carried in other newspapers as well. The *Globe and Mail* featured four polls conducted by Environics. Canadian Facts and Insight Canada Research did surveys for the CBC and CTV, respectively. The mating dance between polling firms and news organizations is facilitated by the fact that polling firms often agree to do polls for media outlets at bargain basement prices in the hope of gaining a windfall of publicity.[18]

Some researchers criticize the growing involvement of the media in public opinion polling, saying that media organizations use polls as a "vehicle for self-promotion," celebrating their own polls and downplaying or ignoring polls carried out by other news organizations.[19] Furthermore, it is claimed, many journalists lack the expertise to interpret either poll or survey results.[20] One observer noted, "I could count on one hand the number of journalists that are competent to analyse polls."[21] Some theorists criticize the potential for a bandwagon effect to be created by media reporting of polls; others say that following the polls creates "finger-to-the wind" politicians and organizations that are focused on the short term.[22] Some critics say such practices create an apathetic public. Others claim that few attempts are made to cross-check the results of surveys.

The proliferation of surveys in all areas of our lives and the often-conflicting results are leaving many people, including the general public, confused. Some people argue the necessity for the average citizen in a democracy to acquire a better understanding of how to interpret survey results.[23] Journalist Neil Reynolds speaks about the level of cynicism with which many people approach polls. Reynolds cites instances where the results of polls conducted during the 1988 U.S. presidential campaign varied by dramatic degrees, even within the same time frames. The *Los Angeles Times* published one poll, for example, that gave George Bush a nine-point lead over Michael Dukakis. On the same day, it published a second poll that tied the two contenders. In essence, the newspaper let the readers decide for themselves which poll to believe. The same day that the *Washington Post* gave Bush his "breakthrough" lead, the *New York Times* published a poll that showed the two men were neck-in-neck. In September 1988, seven survey organizations published polls regarding the presidential election within a three-day interim; the results varied from an eight-point lead for Bush to a six-point lead for Dukakis. To explain these widely varying results, it is necessary to examine some points about surveying. Why do we engage in surveying? What are the best ways to survey? What are the potential pitfalls?

WHY SURVEY?

Surveys provide information, that is, useful *input* to the organization. They provide another source (along with media tracking, focus groups, and consultations) of environmental data to assist the organization in strategic and operational planning. Acquiring information on the external environment and stakeholders is essential to the survival of most organizations (large and small, corporate and political). If you don't understand what people are saying and thinking, you will be out of touch with the people whose needs you are trying to meet. Understanding one's audience is critical to the communicator; understanding one's clients is critical to the organization. Furthermore, in the public policy realm, it is widely accepted that public opinion surveys contribute to the policy-making process. This view is held most strongly by those who consider the policy-making process as an interactive one, whereby the public influences the policy maker and the policy maker influences the public. Surveys give useful feedback to decision makers, allowing them to evaluate and sometimes to modify and explain their policies.[24]

In terms of issues management, surveys aim:

1. To describe the opinions, beliefs, and attitudes held by stakeholders toward particular issues and toward the organizations associated with these issues (i.e., to generate opinion profiles of stakeholders).
2. To identify the ordering of issues in terms of audience priorities.
3. To explain motivations and relationships (For example, what is the basis for stakeholders' beliefs? What are the perceived linkages between different issues? What cause-effect relationships are perceived?)

Discussing the rationale behind his organization's use of surveying, Canadian broadcast executive Elly Aboim said: "The only way I can evaluate what is really germaine . . . is by polling. I have to see what the issue subset is. I have to know what the rank order is. I have to understand the relationship between leadership and issues."[25] As a marketing strategy, newspapers often conduct surveys of their readership to identify issue priorities. (This type of information is often accessible to interested parties.) Organizations that commission surveys to gain a better understanding of their clients tend to use criteria that conform to the best survey practices. They take care to see that their sample is representative. They order their questions to eliminate bias. They avoid "leading" questions and "loaded" wording. In short, they attempt to obtain objective and reliable information.

A second important use for survey information is *output* from the organization to the public. The information collected in surveys gives the organization data to back up its claims. Governments and corporations can use the results of surveys as evidence to support proposed policies, acquisitions, research and development activities, and programs. Individuals in the Marketing Science Institute's group of companies say that more than 60 percent of the studies they undertake are confirmatory, that is, "designed to reinforce or sell a decision that has already been made."[26] This second function of surveys can cause problems.

Organizations that conduct surveys to obtain feedback that will assist them in selling their policies and programs to the public use a different set of criteria in framing the survey. They regard the survey as a means of proselytizing. If this point of view prevails, the individuals who decide upon sampling techniques or who design the questionnaires may have less concern with valid and reliable information than with *usable* information. This may explain the sometimes wild variations among survey results. It may also legitimize the claims of those who say that public opinion surveys can "manufacture" public opinion.[27]

Although some problems with survey research may stem from incompetent researchers, most survey firms, polling firms, and in-house researchers know their business. It is more probable that a sizeable number of poorly designed surveys derive from a client's desire to order and frame the questions · in order to get desired results. In the case of custom-designed surveys for a specific client, the survey organization usually advises the client on appropriate ways to word questions. The clients purchase not only the administration services of the survey group, but also their expertise. In such instances, clients have the option of listening to the experts or ignoring them.

The exact wording of questions is often omitted in discussions of survey results, and the order of questions is rarely reported in news accounts of government-sponsored surveys. The kinds of bias that can creep into results (e.g., callbacks are not made to respondents and samples are not representative) will not be obvious to the average reader. In a society where we are accustomed to receiving information in small, manageable quantities, we are not likely to question brevity of reporting; the average American still pays homage to numbers, attaching almost automatic credibility to statistics. Corporate and government leaders are not likely to be more exacting in their demands on those who report the results of surveys. The restraints on an executive's time mean that he or she rarely receives the complete version of any report; therefore, summaries are the rule of thumb (hence the term *executive summaries*). Under such circumstances, decisions made at operational levels of the organization (middle management) may never be queried by those concerned with strategic decision making (senior management).

HOW DO YOU DO IT? SEVEN EASY BUT SLIPPERY STEPS

The steps in conducting a survey include:

1. Designing the survey.
2. Selecting a sample.
3. Constructing the questionnaire.
4. Deciding on question order.
5. Preparing introductory materials.
6. Administering the questionnaire.
7. Analyzing and presenting the results.

1. Designing Your Survey

After specifying your survey objectives and identifying your target population, you may choose from several research designs. The most common are

cross-sectional surveys,

longitudinal surveys, and

multiple-sample surveys.

Cross-Sectional Surveys

In a *cross-sectional* survey, you collect data from a sample at a *single point in time*. An example would be a survey to determine employee support for a collective agreement prior to a union vote or, alternately, exit interviews after the vote.

Longitudinal Surveys

Longitudinal surveys collect data at different points in time, sometimes from different people and sometimes from the same people. The longitudinal survey seeks to identify *shifts in opinion over time*. This survey may take several different forms:

trend studies,

cohort studies, and

panel studies.

Trend studies consider a *general population* at *different points in time*, with *different people* participating each time the survey is conducted. For example, researchers may want to find out how first-year employees view their jobs. They may be interested to know whether there is any shift over time in how first-year employees view the company and their jobs. Their study design may call for sampling first-year employees in 1992, 1996, and 2000. The specific employees who are queried will be different each time the survey is conducted. Some employees will have moved; some will have left the company; none will qualify as first-year employees after their initial year with the company. This is the nature of a trend study: same general population, different points in time, different individuals in the sample. In this case, the results of the study will tell the company whether first-year employees in 1996 and 2000 have different workplace attitudes and values than do employees in 1992.

Cohort studies are similar to trend studies, except that cohort studies focus on a specific subgroup of the larger population (i.e., cohort studies consider a *bounded population* at *different points in time*, with *different individuals* participating each time the survey is conducted). Assume, for example, that you want to know how employee attitudes toward a company change as employees acquire seniority. An example of a cohort design is sampling from all workers first employed by the company in 1992. Then you sample again from this same 1992 population in 1996 and 2000. You might have different employees participating in each survey because a random sample will not give you the same employees each time you survey. Also, some employees may have left the company, moved, died, or otherwise become inaccessible. Still, you are drawing your sample from the population of people employed in 1992. You are not looking at employees who joined the company in any other year.

Panel studies involve surveying the *same individuals* within a population at *different points in time*. Assume you are studying how employee attitudes toward their work change as they gain additional years with the company. If Joe Smith is in your first survey on employee attitudes, he must also be in your next survey if you use a panel design. Panel studies are sometimes used to learn about people's attitudes toward parties and candidates for office. In this case, the pollster meets, at several different times over the course of an election campaign, with the same panel of people. He or she questions the panel members about their voting intentions and probes if switches have occurred. There are obvious problems with panel studies. For example, it is difficult to keep track of individuals over time. It can be costly to locate panel participants and survey them. Some people refuse to participate in subsequent sessions. Still, this study is useful in answering some kinds of questions. For example, if you want to know how people who were prescribed different medications fared over time, you might want to go back to the same individuals you included in your first study. Panel studies are most feasible in short time spans.

Multiple-Sample Surveys

The *multiple-sample* study is an alternative to cross-sectional and longitudinal surveys. With this design, you study *more than one sample at the same time*. In this way, you can identify, describe, and explain relationships between or among two or more populations. For example, you could survey a sample of lower-level employees, a sample of middle managers, and a sample of senior managers to compare how their views on employment equity differ or converge.

2. Choosing your Sample

It's unrealistic to think you can reach all members of a population; if you want to know the views of a particular group, you must select a *representative sample* from that population. A *sample* is a smaller group that, ideally, has the most important characteristics of the larger group that you wish to study. The smaller group must be sufficiently like the larger group (in terms of the characteristics you wish to study) to allow you to generalize your survey findings to the larger group. Two broad kinds of sampling procedures, *probability* and *nonprobability,* can be used in the selection of a sample group.

Probability Sampling

The most popular sampling techniques used by pollsters and academics are probability-based techniques. It is said that public opinion survey research resulted from the development of statistical sampling theory. Probability theory tells us that a sample will be representative of the population from which it is selected if "all members of the population have an equal chance of being selected in the sample."[28] Furthermore, probability theory enables us to calculate, mathematically, the chances that we are in error and by how much.

Probability sampling techniques include:

- Simple random sampling.
- Systematic sampling.
- Stratified sampling.
- Multistage cluster sampling.

The most common probability sampling technique is *simple random sampling.* Random sampling techniques ensure that all members of the target population have an equal chance of being selected. A random sample is drawn from what is called a *sampling frame.* A sampling frame is a "population roster"[29] or a list of all members of the target population (e.g., a telephone directory of all organization employees, a voter registration list, or a list of shareholders for a given corporation). First, you number all the members of your population. Then to get your random sample, you can use a table of random numbers,* use a computerized random selection, or even pull names from a hat. If your desired sample size is 150, you draw 150 names. Assuming that all potential members of the population are included and that people are not missing from your list, you should get a representative sample using these means.

A second probability technique is *systematic sampling.* Systematic sampling can also generate a representative sample. First, you randomly pick a starting point for drawing your sample. For example, close your eyes and place your finger at some point on a table of random numbers. Then system-

---

* Several pages of random numbers are included at the end of the chapter (see pages 207–209). To use these tables (a) Select one of the tables, close your eyes, and randomly point your finger to the page. (b) Open your eyes and read the closest number from the table. (c) Multiply this number by your population size and round up (e.g., if you have a list, or sampling frame, of 200 people and the number to which you pointed is 0.4271, multiply $0.4271 \times 200 = 85.42$; therefore, you would select the 86th person on your list). (d) Continue until you have reached your sample quota.

atically draw the rest of your sample (e.g., draw every 10th member of the population represented in your sampling frame until you fill your sample quota).

A problem that can arise from systematic sampling is sampling frame *periodicity,* a situation wherein a cyclical sequencing pattern occurs. For example, in a World War II study of soldiers, researchers drew their sample from a list of all men in a military unit. Each roster had 10 names. Using systematic sampling techniques, the researchers selected the first name on each list. Had the names appeared randomly on the list, there would have been no problems; however, in this case, the men were listed by rank, with sergeants' names appearing first on the rosters, followed by corporals and privates. Thus, the final sample contained only sergeants, scarcely representative of the military squads they headed.[30] If, after examining your sampling frame, you believe there is a problem with periodicity, randomize your lists. The ease of using systematic sampling makes it very popular, even with this one potential problem.

A third type of probability sampling is *stratified sampling*. Rather than being an alternative to simple random sampling or systematic sampling, it is a variation on the two forms. Before drawing your sample, break your population into relatively homogeneous subgroupings. The criteria for forming the subsets depends on your research purposes. For example, do you want to know the differences in attitudes expressed by male and female employees? If so, separate your population into males and females before sampling. Do you want to know how people in different parts of the company view a given issue? If so, break your population into different business units (e.g., finance, marketing, manufacturing, R&D). To consider both sex and sector variables, organize your population by males and females, then subdivide the population at a second stage into different sectors of the company. In other words, you classify your population into different strata before drawing your sample.

Once stratified, you can use simple random sampling or systematic sampling techniques to choose your sample. Stratified sampling ensures that all relevant subgroups are represented in your final sample. With stratified sampling, you should have the same representation of members in your final sample that you have in the larger population. For example, if the population is 55 percent male and 45 percent female, your stratified sample should be 55 percent male and 45 percent female.

If you want to sample from a very large population (e.g., all members of a multinational corporation) you may need to use still another variation, *multistage cluster sampling*. Multistage cluster sampling breaks the process of drawing the sample into two or more stages. The number of stages varies, depending on the size of the population. For example, if you want to draw a sample of hospital administrators from across the United States, you can do so in three or more stages. In the first stage, you select *states* to be included in your study by drawing a sample from a list of 50 states. In the second stage, you select *towns* large enough to include hospitals from your sample of states. In the third stage, you pick hospitals to be studied from a list of all possible hospitals in these towns. The administrators of these hospitals will constitute your final sample. If you had been studying nurses, you would have needed a fourth stage of sampling.

It doesn't matter how careful you are in selecting a sample frame and in picking a sample; your results will probably stray, at least a little, from the values of the larger population. Factors that affect the degree to which your sample might be representative are the *size of your sample* and the *homogeneity of the population* from which you have drawn your sample.

Size of Sample. The larger the sample, the smaller the margin of error, which means the less the chance that you have made a mistake. If your sample size is large enough, you can compensate for personal idiosyncrasies in your sample population.

Homogeneity of the Population. The more homogeneous the population, the smaller the margin of error. In homogeneous groups, almost all people are alike, so it is easier to generalize from a smaller number of the group.

Probability theory gives a way of calculating both the odds that the results are in error and the probable degree of divergence. Two terms used to express such error are *confidence level* and *confidence interval. Confidence level* refers to how confident we can be that our statistics represent the population we are trying to understand, for example, 95 times out of 100 we will be right. *Confidence interval* tells us how far out we are likely to be in our estimates. For example, a confidence interval of +/−3 percent tells us that support for a corporate takeover might be as low as 45 percent or as high as 51 percent in a survey that reports 48 percent of the employees favoring the takeover. You can obtain both a desired, or acceptable, confidence level and confidence interval by selecting a sufficiently large sample size.

You can use figure 6.1 as a guide to determine the appropriate sample size. First, decide on a confidence level and a confidence interval that you feel would be acceptable. For example, perhaps it is sufficient that your survey be accurate to within, say, +/−5 percent of your population's true division on an issue, and you would be willing to carry out the survey if it were 95 percent probable that the survey would yield results within this confidence interval. Next, cross-reference the desired confidence level with the desired confidence interval to arrive at a minimum sample size. For example, for the above given confidence interval of +/−5 percent and confidence level of 95 percent, the minimum recommended sample size would be 384 persons.

Commercial polling firms, such as Gallup and Harris, often aim for a confidence interval of about +/−3 percent, with a confidence level of about 95 percent. Samples of 1,200 to 1,500 people are typically used in their national surveys.

FIGURE 6.1
Sample Sizes Required for Different Confidence Levels and Intervals

Confidence Level	Confidence Interval									
	1%	2%	3%	4%	5%	6%	7%	8%	9%	10%
99%	16,577	4,144	1,842	1,036	663	460	338	259	205	166
98%	13,533	3,383	1,504	846	541	376	276	211	167	135
97%	11,772	2,943	1,308	736	471	327	240	184	145	118
96%	10,547	2,637	1,172	659	422	293	215	165	130	105
95%	9,604	2,401	1,067	600	384	267	196	150	119	96
94%	8,836	2,209	982	552	353	245	180	138	109	88
93%	8,190	2,048	910	512	328	228	167	128	101	82
92%	7,656	1,914	851	479	306	213	156	120	95	77
91%	7,183	1,796	798	449	287	200	147	112	89	72
90%	6,765	1,691	752	423	271	188	138	106	84	68
89%	6,400	1,600	711	400	256	178	131	100	79	64
88%	6,045	1,511	672	378	242	168	123	94	75	60
87%	5,730	1,433	637	358	229	159	117	90	71	57
86%	5,439	1,360	604	340	218	151	111	85	67	54
85%	5,184	1,296	576	324	207	144	106	81	64	52

The numbers given in Figure 6.1 are based on the Standard Normal Distribution and apply to relatively heterogeneous populations. With more homogeneous populations, as is the case with many stratified samples, a smaller sample size may yield representative results. The decision to reduce sample size, however, is highly subjective.

Nonprobability Sampling

Unlike probability sampling techniques, *nonprobability sampling* techniques do not usually claim to generate a representative sample. Nonrandom selection methods are used in nonprobability sampling. Some of the most well known of these techniques are convenience sampling, quota sampling, and purposive or judgmental sampling.

Convenience sampling is availability sampling, that is, selecting your sample from people who are readily accessible to you (people walking on the streets, people in supermarket parking lots, or people in malls). The sampling process is nonrandom, so there is *no guarantee that the sample will be representative* of the larger population you want to study. For example, morning shoppers in suburban malls will have a certain demographic profile (probably more females than males, usually more old than young shoppers, and probably more unemployed than employed individuals). People intercepted on city streets or in parking lots may have other profiles. Shoppers coming out of Neiman Marcus will scarcely represent the general public. The benefits of convenience sampling derive from its *ease* and *low cost*.

Quota sampling aims to generate a *representative sample,* but it is not a probability technique. Quota sampling involves the following steps:

- Construct a matrix based on stratification of the population, using all relevant subsets (e.g., "gender, educational level, income, age, ethnic origin, geographic region, political orientation, and other demographic variables"[31]).
- Decide what percentage of the population falls into each cell of the matrix.
- Collect data from individuals who have the characteristics of a given cell.
- Use proportionate weighting in terms of the larger population to determine the sample size for each cell.
- Use nonrandom techniques to select your sample.

Essentially, quota sampling gives interviewers quotas to fill (e.g., two black male urban respondents, three white female urban professionals). The procedure is time-consuming and offers little guarantee that you will have generated a sample with the characteristics of the larger target population. Nonetheless, it can be useful in situations where you know the type of respondents that you require.

With *purposive or judgmental sampling,* the researcher or pollster decides who is to be included in the sample. He or she makes a personal judgment about who is representative, or typical. For example, a pollster might decide that, based on historical precedent, certain voting districts will be key to an election victory for the democrats. The researcher then samples only from the districts that are perceived to be critical. In some cases, there are bellwether precincts, which indicate trends. A pollster might sample the potential voters in bellwether precincts in order to obtain an idea of how other precincts will vote. In some cases, a researcher is interested in certain subgroups within a population (e.g., employees with a specific profile, travelers who have certain characteristics, or companies with a unique management style). The researcher decides which employees, travelers, or companies fit the profile. After making this judgment, the person may use probability sampling techniques to acquire the final sample. The quality of the final sample depends on the quality of the researcher's judgment in the initial selection phase.

The processes involved do not differ greatly from judgments that are made by Customs officials who stop some travelers and let others go by. The randomness of the checks is mediated by the control that is exercised by Customs officers.

Note. Some populations are rarely reached by surveys (e.g., the homeless and drug addicts). Although these populations are not important to some surveys, they are critical to others. Failure to include street people in a survey about drugs will give a distorted view of the subject.

3. Constructing Your Questionnaire

Designing a survey questionnaire involves:

- Deciding what type of questions to ask.
- Writing the questions.
- Organizing the questions in such a way as to encourage a high response rate.
- Developing appropriate instructions.
- Designing an attractive format for the questionnaire.

Regarding surveys, studies have found that, as a general rule, it is best to use short, simple, and clear sentences.[32] The federal Office of Management and Budget recommends that no survey should exceed 30 minutes in length.[33] These ideas are important if you want to maximize your chances of getting people to participate in your survey.

Questionnaire construction and wording will depend on the nature of your research problem, the population you are surveying, and your resources. Limited organizational resources may require that you prioritize questions so that you can later drop some questions, if necessary.[34] You should avoid extraneous and repetitious questions unless you need to mask the purposes of your study. Questions can elicit *facts* (demographic details or behavioral patterns) or *opinions* (beliefs, motives, intentions, likes, and dislikes) from people. Most surveys contain a mix of the two.

Sometimes, a fine line exists between fact and opinion. What may be *fact* to one person may be *opinion* to someone else. For example, if you ask someone for basic demographic information (employment status, marital status, etc.) you may get varied responses to the terms.

> **Example 1.** Someone who is actively looking for work may consider himself or herself unemployed. Someone who gave up looking for work three years ago also may consider himself or herself unemployed.
>
> **Example 2.** The legal system may not accord a gay couple the benefits of marriage, but the individuals may nonetheless define themselves as married.

The same kind of ambiguity can come into play when you elicit other kinds of information. For example, the researchers who carried out a national crime survey in the United States discovered that not all people consider the same acts as "crimes."[35] They discovered (as have many groups who work with victims of elder abuse, child abuse, and spouse abuse) that it is necessary to educate people to recognize certain forms of family violence as "crimes." Given this ambiguity of interpretation, it is easy to see that if you asked survey respondents to identify past experiences in which they have been a victim of crime, some might limit their list to acts of theft or robbery. In the past, many people, even victims, did not consider family violence as crime. Pretesting a questionnaire can sometimes help you to anticipate these kinds of discrepancies of interpretation.[36]

Questions usually elicit one of ten categories of information. You may be seeking to learn more about respondents' *knowledge* (how much they know about the topic), their *degree of concern* (level of interest in the topic), their *attitudes* (predisposition to act), their *motivations* (why respondents act as they do), the *intensity* with which they hold their beliefs and attitudes, *saliency* (the perceived importance of the topic), respondents' *readiness to act,* their *perceptions* (how respondents view the issue or topic), their *background characteristics* (demographic variables such as age, sex, place of residence, etc.), and their *behavior* (in terms of participation, voting, and consumer habits, as well as other categories of information).[37]

Questions can be *closed* or *open ended.* Open-ended questions call for unstructured responses.

> **Example 1.** *What are the most important issues on the public agenda?*
>
> **Example 2.** *How do you feel about the new abortion legislation?*

Example 3. *If a democrat were to walk into the room today, what might the person look like?*

Vignettes, or stories, are sometimes used in open-ended questionnaires to encourage the expression of opinions and attitudes. If you know the consequences of a particular piece of legislation, for example, you could depict the situation in vignette form.

Example 1. A state government, considering legislation that would result in more mentally disturbed people being dismissed from hospitals, could write a vignette that gives several different alternatives to the status quo, one of which is the legislation to tighten the criteria for admitting and keeping mentally disturbed individuals in hospitals. The respondent is asked to discuss his or her views on the topic.

Example 2. A teacher's association, interested in surveying the public on their attitudes toward rising classroom enrollments, could translate enrollment statistics into vignette format and elicit public reaction.

Example 3. A committee, formed to deal with the problem of prostitution in the city's market area, could write a vignette that describes the situation. The public is asked to suggest solutions to the problem.

The attractiveness of vignettes, or scenarios, is their concreteness. People can relate to specific situations. To avoid respondents becoming fatigued or bored, however, you should limit the number of vignettes in a survey to 15 or fewer cases. Examples of surveys that have included vignettes are a Detroit area study, in which the general public was sampled, and a national cross-sectional survey by the National Opinion Research Center.[38]

You can learn much from open-ended questionnaires, especially in the exploratory stages of research:

- Open-ended questions do not anticipate a response.
- Open-ended questions give people the freedom to generate their own answers.
- The basic premises of open-ended questions can be contested.
- Open-ended questions encourage in-depth answers.
- Open-ended questions can help an interviewer to find out why the person answered in a certain way.

But there are also problems with using open-ended questionnaires:

- This technique is time-consuming.
- Quantifying open-ended responses is more difficult than quantifying closed responses.
- Analyzing open-ended results is more subjective than analyzing closed results.

- Responses to open-ended questions are sometimes ambiguous. For example, when asked what is most important in a job, employees may say "pay." When you later attempt to interpret this answer, you won't know whether the person meant good pay or steady pay.[39]
- Open-ended questions sometimes tap only the superficial concerns of people and fail to reveal their fundamental attitudes.[40]
- The person conducting the survey has less control than is the case with closed questionnaires.

In order to anticipate these kinds of problems, researchers may ask open-ended questions in *pretests* and closed questions in the *larger confirmational phase of research.*

With *closed* questions, the researcher provides survey respondents with a list of options:

Example 1. Some questions call for yes-no or agree-disagree answers.

Example 2. Some questions are multiple choice.

Example 3. Some questions are inventory types that ask respondents to check all applicable items on a list.

In the case of closed questions, the respondent can pick only from the alternatives that are provided. In that sense, a survey that employs closed questions forces choices on respondents. The type of learning that takes place with closed questions has been termed *single-loop* learning, that is, you can only learn within pre-set parameters. On the other hand, with *double-loop learning* (exemplified by open-ended questions), you can question what is given.[41] Double-loop learning is interactive; learning takes place on the part of both the interviewer and the interviewee.

Compared to open-ended questions, closed questions require little time or effort to answer. The results are easy to analyze and quantify.[42] If, however, the choices do not reflect the true range of possibilities, the data generated by closed questions will be less than useful. Situations may change between the time a questionnaire is written and the time it is administered. Especially with regard to issues management, this can be a problem. A crisis issue can completely wipe other issues off the public agenda, yet the questionnaire may not reflect this new, and significant, variable. If you ask people to select the most important issue facing the country, but you omit a critical emerging issue from the list, you will obtain misrepresentative data.[43]

Categories such as *other* and *no opinion* are sometimes added to forced-choice answers to compensate for these kinds of problems. Some researchers, however, don't like to include a *no opinion* or *don't know* category because too many people will mark that category. Studies have demonstrated that between one eighth and one third of people surveyed will choose such a response when given the option.[44]

Regarding closed questions, it is important that there be no overlapping categories from which people must choose. In other words, the response categories should be mutually exclusive. One of the most common mistakes made in composing surveys is the problem of overlapping numbers and dates. The following examples illustrate this point.

Example 1. A person is asked to indicate an age category. The choices are less than 20, 20–30, 30–40, 40–50, etc. A person who is 30 won't know which category to mark; the same is true for people who are 40.

Example 2. The same mistake occurs with periods of time (e.g., less than six months, six months to one year, one to two years, two to five years, etc.).

A special type of closed question is the *filter question,* which allows certain questions in surveys to be targeted to subgroups of the sample population. An example of a filter question follows.

Example 1. *Do you subscribe to any monthly news magazines? If yes, please continue. If no, skip to Part II of the questionnaire.*

If a survey is attempting to find out what people consider to be the advantages of career planning, it could include the following filter question:

Example 2. *Do you agree or disagree with the statement: Implementation of career planning is key to the future development of the company? If you agree, continue with the next question. If you disagree, skip to question number five.*

Rating Scales: Measuring Attitudes

Some closed questions employ rating scales such as the *Likert scale.*[45] A Likert scale involves an opinion statement or question, followed by a list of five or seven options. The following are examples of questions employing Likert scales, which are designed to solicit attitudes.

Company X's products are environmentally friendly.

☐ Strongly agree.
☐ Moderately agree.
☐ Neither agree nor disagree.
☐ Moderately disagree.
☐ Strongly disagree.

Clinton administration policies demonstrate a concern for middle-class Americans.

☐ **Always.**
☐ **Often.**
☐ **Sometimes.**
☐ **Seldom.**
☐ **Never.**

How do you feel about mandatory drug testing in the workplace?

☐ **Strongly approve.**
☐ **Somewhat approve.**
☐ **Neither approve nor disapprove.**
☐ **Somewhat disapprove.**
☐ **Strongly disapprove.**

Another popular rating scale is the *semantic differential*.[46] Semantic differential scales use bipolar adjectives, placed at opposite sides of a seven-point continuum. Respondents are asked to place a check mark along the continuum, corresponding to how they would rate the organization, its products, or its handling of an issue. Three dimensions are represented in semantic differential scales:

- The first is the *evaluative* dimension, indicating the degree of favorableness someone feels toward a word. Examples are *good-bad, cold-warm, efficient-inefficient,* and *fair-unfair*.
- The second dimension is the *potency* dimension, exemplified by adjectives such as *strong-weak, heavy-light,* and *hard-soft*.
- The third dimension is the *activity* dimension, represented by bipolar adjectives such as *fast-slow, dynamic-static,* and *active-passive*.

Issues, personalities, companies, governments, and policies can be rated on a semantic differential scale such as the one that follows.

Efficient	___ ___ ___ ___ ___ ___ ___	Inefficient
Fast	___ ___ ___ ___ ___ ___ ___	Slow
Static	___ ___ ___ ___ ___ ___ ___	Dynamic
Active	___ ___ ___ ___ ___ ___ ___	Passive
Progressive	___ ___ ___ ___ ___ ___ ___	Regressive
Dull	___ ___ ___ ___ ___ ___ ___	Sharp
Cold	___ ___ ___ ___ ___ ___ ___	Warm
Soft	___ ___ ___ ___ ___ ___ ___	Hard
Dirty	___ ___ ___ ___ ___ ___ ___	Clean
Expensive	___ ___ ___ ___ ___ ___ ___	Inexpensive
Moral	___ ___ ___ ___ ___ ___ ___	Immoral
Unfair	___ ___ ___ ___ ___ ___ ___	Fair
Strong	___ ___ ___ ___ ___ ___ ___	Weak
Light	___ ___ ___ ___ ___ ___ ___	Heavy
Old-fashioned	___ ___ ___ ___ ___ ___ ___	Modern
Good	___ ___ ___ ___ ___ ___ ___	Bad

A *Stapel* scale also measures the intensity and direction of a person's attitude.[47] The Stapel scale substitutes a single adjective or a phrase for the bipolar adjectives used in a semantic differential scale. This word (or words) will appear above a seven-point scale that ranges from +3 to −3. With this scaling device, you are attempting to measure the proximity of a concept to the descriptive term. Stapel scales are easy to construct and use. An example follows:

Company X

+3	+3	+3
+2	+2	+2
+1	+1	+1

Salary Policies   **Environmental Policies**   **Hiring Policies**

−1	−1	−1
−2	−2	−2
−3	−3	−3

A special type of rating scale sometimes used in surveys is a *magnitude estimation scale*.[48] This technique is used to measure various aspects of public opinion (e.g., the perceived usefulness of a piece of legislation, the perceived effectiveness of a policy, or the seriousness of a crime). The researcher might ask: "If robbery is given a rating of 6, what would sexual assault be?" Alternatively, a survey could ask, "If the earlier policy had an effectiveness rating of 4, how would you rate the current policy?" It is interesting to note that this same technique is employed with patients who believe that they may be experiencing a heart attack. The doctor in attendance will typically ask, "How would you rate this pain on a scale of 1 to 10?" Or he or she might ask, "Think about the worst pain you have ever experienced. What was it, and what would its intensity be on a scale of 1 to 10? Compared to this pain, how would you rate your present level of discomfort?"

Some rating scales employ *graphic techniques*.[49] With the *line-production method*, a person is asked to draw a line to represent the importance of an issue to the organization. The individual may then be asked to draw a second line to indicate how important the issue *should be* to the organization. Rather than representing absolute values, this technique assesses the intensity with which a person holds certain opinions. In another instance, a graphic scale might request that the respondent place an X at the place along the continuum that best represents the person's attitude. An example relevant to a corporation follows:

Please indicate your assessment of each of the following options by placing an "X" at the appropriate location on the line.

Takeover by competitor Z

Beneficial _____ Not Beneficial

Strategic alliance with supplier Y

Beneficial _____ Not Beneficial

A government department might include questions of the following type on a survey questionnaire:

Please rate each of the following issues in terms of their perceived importance to you. Indicate your position by placing an "X" at the appropriate location on the line.

Gun control   Not important _____ Important

Employment   Not important _____ Important

A third example relevant to business is:

Please rate the following options in terms of their (1) practicality and (2) acceptability to you. Indicate your position by placing an "X" at the appropriate location on the line.

Lowering costs by lowering salaries
Practical _____ **Impractical**
Acceptable _____ **Unacceptable**

Lowering costs by reducing number of hours worked
Practical _____ **Impractical**
Acceptable _____ **Unacceptable**

Lowering costs by lowering overhead
Practical _____ **Impractical**
Acceptable _____ **Unacceptable**

Lowering costs by reducing product material costs
Practical _____ **Impractical**
Acceptable _____ **Unacceptable**

To analyze the results, the individual or group conducting the survey will need to divide the line into intervals and assign a quantitative value to each response. Not all graphic scales involve straight lines. If you are trying to assess public attitudes toward Party X's proposed health care policies, economic policies, etc., you could use *ladder scales:*[50]

On health care, I believe that Party X will give us:

Best Possible Health Care Policies

10
9
8
7
6
5

4
3
2
1

Worst Possible Health Care Policies

In the economic realm, I believe that Party X will give us:

Best Possible Economic Policies, etc.

A similar rating instrument is the *feeling thermometer,* which was developed by the National Election Study (NES):[51]

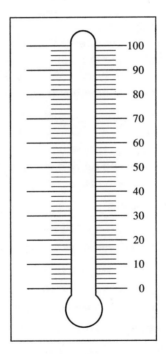

This thermometer was originally designed to measure a person's feelings toward political candidates, but it has been adapted to measure issues, policies, and organizations. If you feel warmly toward a policy, for example, you place the policy close to the 100-degree mark on the thermometer. If you feel fairly neutral toward the policy, you place it near the 50-degree mark. If you have cold feelings toward the policy, you locate it at or near the zero point.

You do the same in representing your feelings and attitudes toward personalities and organizations.

Rating Scales: Measuring Behavioral Intentions and Expectations

Whereas the previous examples of rating scales involve the measurement of attitudes, other scales measure *behavioral intentions*. For example, you could ask a respondent:

How likely is it that you will switch to product X?

☐   **I definitely will switch to product X.**
☐   **I probably will switch to product X.**
☐   **I might switch to product X.**
☐   **I probably will not switch to product X.**
☐   **I definitely will not switch to product X.**

Some scales measure *expectations*. The U.S. Bureau of the Census, for example, uses a probability scale that ranges from 100 percent for absolutely certain to 0 percent for absolutely no chance.[52] This scale can be applied to the study of attitudes toward actions taken or policies pursued by a company or government, as in this case:

Please indicate how likely you think it is that policy X will result in full economic recovery for the company.

_____ **100% (Absolutely certain) recovery will follow.**

_____ **90% (Almost sure) recovery will follow.**

_____ **80% (Very big chance) recovery will follow.**

_____ **70% (Big chance) recovery will follow.**

_____ **60% (Better than even chance) recovery will follow.**

_____ **50% (About even chance) recovery will follow.**

_____ **40% (Smaller chance) recovery will follow.**

_____ **30% (Small chance) recovery will follow.**

_____ **20% (Very small chance) recovery will follow.**

_____ **10% (Almost certainly no chance) recovery will follow.**

_____ **0% (Certainly no chance) recovery will follow.**

Ranking Scales

Ranking scales typically ask the respondent to rank-order a series of items, from most preferred to least preferred. In earlier years it was common to ask respondents to rank-order 12 or 13 items. Today surveys typically employ no more than four or five ranking items. Sometimes, a person is asked to select the top three or four choices from a longer list. In value surveys, it is better to ask people to *rank-order* values rather than to *rate* them on scales.[53]

The difficulty with forcing choices, however, is that sometimes two or more values will be equally important to an individual (e.g., loyalty and morality may have equal weighting). Forced to choose, the person makes arbitrary selections. The process is much akin to the dilemma of Meryl Streep in *Sophie's Choice,* where she must decide which child is to live and which is to die.

Some ranking scales involve *paired comparisons.*[54] An example of a paired comparison is the following question asked of Sutherland Oil Company shareholders.

Sutherland Oil Company is considering the following two policy options. Policy A would mean that the company enforces an embargo against Iraq, which would result in higher oil prices. Policy B would mean that the company abandons its embargo against Iraq, which would result in lower oil prices. Which policy do you think is better?

☐ **A is better**   ☐ **B is better**   ☐ **Unsure**

A second example follows:

We would like to know your opinion of the following two approaches to foreign aid. Approach A says that we should emphasize technical assistance. Approach B says that we should emphasize monetary assistance.

☐ **A is better**   ☐ **B is better**   ☐ **They are the same**

Sorting techniques ask respondents to indicate their attitudes by arranging cards or other items. Each card represents some concept, product, or other item. A respondent, for example, may be asked to sort issues into groups on the basis of perceived importance, visibility, or impact on the organization.

The cafeteria reward system asks respondents to assign priorities to ideas or issues. The person is given a set sum of money or points, which he or she can divide among different categories.[55] An example follows:

Suppose you had $100, and you could allocate varying amounts to different organizational areas. How would you divide the money?

____ **Marketing and advertising.**

____ **New product development.**

____ **Public relations activities.**

____ **Manufacturing.**

____ **New equipment and technology.**

____ **Training.**

---

4. Deciding on Question Order

There are few rules to guide the researcher in deciding question order. The most common view is that general questions should precede specific ones and related topics should appear together. Researchers say that survey respondents are most comfortable moving from the general to the specific, making it more likely that they will continue the interview if questions are presented in this order.[56] On the other hand, not everyone agrees on this point. Some people argue that the "inverted funnel" order (specific to general) is best. They say the ease in answering more specific questions motivates people to continue the survey or interview.[57] Some potential problems associated with question order appear in Chapter 7.

5. Preparing Introductory Materials

All questionnaires need to be introduced by some preface materials, for example:

- A short informal cover letter that includes a general explanatory statement.
- The name of the organization or individual conducting the survey.
- The nature and purposes of the survey.
- Assurances that confidentiality will be maintained.
- A promise to send results of the survey to participants.

- References to incentives (if incentives are offered).
- Assurances that answering the questionnaire will not consume too much of the person's time, if the questionnaire is relatively brief.
- An explanation of why the questions are necessary, if your survey includes personal questions.

General directions for responding to the survey will often appear in a paragraph that precedes the first survey question. More specific directions will accompany individual sections of the survey. Key terms should be identified.[58] Survey questionnaires should be typed neatly, appear uncluttered, and use sufficient white space.

6. Administering the Survey

In administering an oral survey, don't go too fast. If there are no written instructions, you may need to explain why you are conducting the survey. With a written questionnaire, these instructions will appear in preface materials, as discussed above. Additional rules apply to the administration of different types of surveys.

Personal Interviews

Personal interviews are generally conducted in the workplace or at the respondent's home. They may be *structured* or *unstructured*. In a *structured* interview, there is little room for the interviewer to exercise discretion regarding the content or format of the interview. In an *unstructured* interview, the interviewer can generate new questions, can probe freely, and can shift the order of questions. In-depth information can be acquired in this type of survey situation.

The unstructured interview has been called "a conversation with a purpose."[59] In this case, questions are open ended, and the respondent plays an important role, sometimes guiding a discussion in directions not foreseen by the interviewer. Although unstructured interviews are more costly (in time) and require a higher level of interviewing expertise, they can yield unexpected insights. If good rapport is established, the interviewer can sometimes obtain responses to sensitive questions. Unstructured interviews are particularly valuable in pilot studies or in the exploratory stages of a study. Using the results of such unstructured surveys, organizational researchers can frame closed questions to be asked to larger numbers of people at a later time.

It is common for personal interviews to last 45 minutes or an hour. The interviewer can, and often does, make use of "show cards," photographs, and other visual materials. His or her observations can supplement other kinds of data obtained from the interview. Large amounts of information can be acquired in a relatively short time from the personal interview. In personal interviews, questions should be grouped by topic, and demographic data should be obtained at the beginning of the interview.[60]

Interviewer training and instruction manuals are important to obtaining the results desired from any survey. The manuals tell *whom to interview, when to interview, how to dress,* and *how to behave* during the interview. They also tell the interviewer *how to record information* and *what to do when people are not available.* They outline *procedures for callbacks,* which are necessary when people are busy or unavailable. They also outline *procedures for verification of results.*

Some disadvantages of the personal interview include:

- Its relatively high cost.
- The possibility for interviewer bias (with the age, sex, race, dress, verbal or nonverbal behavior of the interviewer influencing the results).
- The possibility that the respondent may try to please the interviewer.
- The overload of data that may be obtained from an unstructured interview.
- The possibility that the interviewer will not be competent or honest.
- The tendency to suspect people who come to the door requesting an interview.

Interviews conducted during the day have been found to elicit the views of a different group of people than interviews conducted at night.

The *elite* interview is a special type. *Elites* are "the influential, the prominent, and the well-informed people in an organization or a community."[61] Information acquired from these individuals can be of more than ordinary value to the organization. They are selected for interviews on the basis of the expertise they hold in the social, political, financial, or administrative spheres. They often have a sophisticated understanding of the legal and financial structures of their organizations, and they occupy positions that allow them to influence policies, plan future courses of action, and place past events in context.

It is necessary, however, to realize that some interview techniques work better than others with elites. Elites respond best to broad, open questions that allow them to expand the focus of the inquiry into areas that they deem relevant. They tend to enjoy an active exchange with the interviewer and dislike closed questions.

> Elites respond well to inquiries related to broad areas of content and to a high proportion of intelligent, provocative, open-ended questions that allow them the freedom to use their knowledge and imagination.[62]

It is not uncommon for elite respondents to assume the questioner's role, from time to time, in an interview session. This type of interview places considerable demands on the interviewer, who must establish competency by displaying a thorough knowledge of the topic areas discussed or must demonstrate an "accurate conceptualization of the problem through shrewd questioning."[63]

Obtaining appointments with elites may not be easy; the interviewer may have to rely on referrals, recommendations, and introductions to gain an audience with these influential individuals. It is necessary to recognize that, although it is possible to gain many valuable insights from elites, their views may not be generalizable to the larger population.

Telephone Interviews

Special materials will need to be prepared for telephone surveys: an interviewer instruction manual and training materials. The instruction manual will include information such as *whom to call, when to call,* and *how to record information.* Training sessions will include simulations of the survey situation and a chance for the interviewers to discuss problems. A central location will be designated for receipt of survey information and for monitoring.[64] It is necessary to make callbacks when respondents are not available the first time they are called; usually interviewers make no more than two callbacks to "busy lines" or "no answers." It has been found that 95 percent of all targeted individuals can be successfully reached with three callbacks.[65] Interviewers often try to reach respondents in the evening who were not available during the day. A recent study found that answering machines do not appear to be generating serious problems for telephone interviewers, because most answering machine owners are reachable and willing to communicate."[66] The answering machine is used more often on weekends than on weekday evenings.

To verify results obtained from telephone interviews, select a small subsample of respondents to call back; ask these individuals to respond to two or three of the original questions. The most likely questions to be omitted from telephone interviews are the sensitive questions that interviewers don't like to ask; you may wish to include these questions in your callbacks. Tabulation of the final data will involve a computation of the response rate, including the number of disconnects, no answers, and refusals.

In administering telephone surveys, interviewers should observe the following:

- Speak clearly and slowly.
- Read the questions as written and in the order in which they appear in the questionnaire.
- Repeat questions that are not understood.
- Probe unclear responses with neutral questions.
- Appear interested and appreciative.
- Record responses verbatim for open-ended questions.

- Thank respondents for their participation.

Behaviors for telephone interviewers to avoid include:

- Prompting answers.
- Showing approval or disapproval for responses.
- Explanations that are not part of the planned interview.

Advantages of telephone interviews include:

- The higher level of control that is possible.
- Higher response rates than with mail surveys.
- The lack of transportation costs.
- Access to WATS lines that facilitate the collection of national survey data.
- Reasonable costs.
- Fast responses.
- Ability to reach almost everyone.
- Less likelihood of interviewer bias.

Disadvantages of this interviewing medium include:

- Limited kinds of questions can be asked.
- Cost (telephone interviews are more expensive than mail surveys).
- Possibility for the interviewer to influence the results.
- Inability of the interviewer to use visual aids.
- Tendency of some respondents to view the telephone interview with suspicion.
- Lack of commitment that comes with anonymity.
- Lack of nonverbal feedback.
- Incompleteness of some telephone listings and the inaccuracy of others.

Some telephone surveys are computer assisted. These surveys are more error free because the interviewer does not skip questions or ask the wrong questions. However, they do take somewhat more time to complete. In such a case, questions should be grouped by topic.[67]

Mail Surveys

Mail surveys entail a minimum expenditure of time and money; they are the least expensive of the survey techniques. They also do not require a large survey team. Yet the mail survey can generate large quantities of information drawn from many different constituencies. Specialized mailing lists and selective sampling make it easy for the organizational researcher to reach target audiences. Respondent anonymity is possible with mail surveys. People can complete the questionnaires anywhere, in the privacy of their own homes and at their own pace. In this case, interviewer bias is eliminated.

An analysis of 115 studies that appeared in over 25 journals from business, education, marketing, political science, psychology, sociology, and statistics, among others, indicated five ways to increase response rate from mail surveys:[68]

- Use a cover letter that includes appeals.
- Limit your survey to less than four pages.
- Include a stamped or metered return envelope.
- Include a small incentive.
- Give preliminary notification that the survey will be arriving at a later date.

It is best to begin self-administered questionnaires with the most interesting questions. Group the questions by topic, and save the demographic questions for the end. Questions that elicit sensitive information should appear after the middle or near the end of the questionnaire.[69]

If you use business reply envelopes for mailing questionnaires, you will pay mailing charges only for those questionnaires that are returned. For best results, the first follow-up mailing should take place after two weeks; the second follow-up mailing should take place after four weeks. Some studies indicate that telephone calls may be as effective as letters in "prodding nonrespondents to return mail questionnaires."[70] Studies also confirm the advantages of *sponsorship, personalization, anonymity, prior commitment,* and techniques affecting *questionnaire appearance.*[71] Questionnaire *format* and *layout* are important in all forms of interviews—written as well as oral.[72] Other specific suggestions that relate to the content of the mail survey questionnaire include the following:

- Closed-ended questions are preferable to open-ended questions.
- The length of the questionnaire is important; long questionnaires elicit low response rates. Response rates increase with a survey of less than four pages.
- Explanations should be clear and concise.

A number of professional associations and marketing research organizations sell mailing lists to researchers and advertisers, but obtaining the results of mail surveys is often a slow process. Furthermore, we don't always know for certain who has answered the survey. The *major* disadvantage of the mail survey, however, is its low return rate; many people discard surveys. A typical survey achieves a return rate of 20 percent to 40 percent, even with follow-ups.[73] Only the most interested people may participate, and high-status groups are more likely than low-status groups to return mail surveys.

Group-Administered Surveys

In some cases, surveys are administered to groups. For low-literacy groups, the interviewer may read the questions aloud. Response rates in group interviews are generally high, and because the interviewer is available to both

FIGURE 6.2
Survey on Environmental Policy

Survey on Environmental Policy

Of the total sample, 48% reported being in favor of the company's environmental policies; 37% reported being opposed to these policies; and 15% reported holding no opinion, one way or the other.

Survey on Environmental Policy	Number of Employees	Percentage of Employees
In favor of	46	48
Opposed to	35	37
No opinion	14	15
Total	95	100

(A)

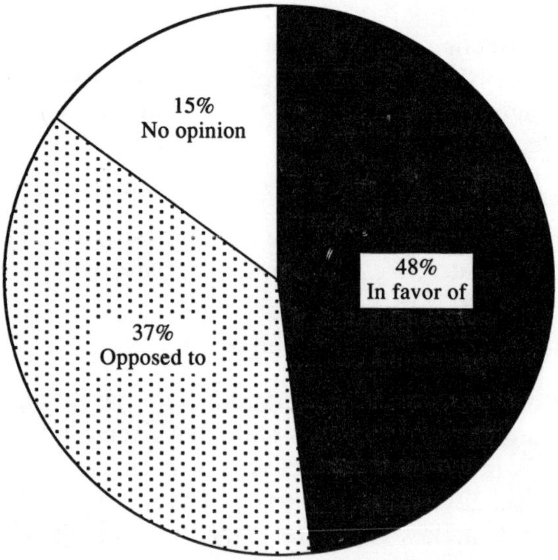

(B)

answer questions and address problems, respondents leave few blanks or unanswered questions. Group interviews are less costly than face-to-face interviews or telephone interviews. Respondents may assume, however, that group-administered surveys have received the sanction of upper management; this conclusion may influence responses to individual questions. Respondents may also fear that their responses will be made known to management. Mixing different classes of respondents (e.g., respondents from different levels of the organization) is not recommended.

7. Analyzing and Presenting Your Results

You may or may not decide to use computers in analyzing your data. Whatever your choice, however, you must plan in advance how you will analyze your results. Some of the points to be taken into consideration include the following.

Your first task is counting the number of survey participants who fall into each category. Perhaps you want to know, for example, how many people support or oppose a company policy. You can then translate these numbers into percentages. Simple frequency distribution tables are often used to present these numbers and percentages. See Figure 6.2(A). Simple frequency distributions may also be presented graphically with the use of pie graphs. See Figure 6.2(B).

Sometimes you will choose to *compare* percentages (e.g., between the responses of different groups of respondents or different regions). *Contingency tables* depict the relationship between a respondent characteristic and answers given to survey questions. The contingency table in Figure 6.3(A) compared responses obtained from employees who hold shares in a company and those who do not. While pie charts are useful in displaying simple frequency distributions, bar graphs are more useful when presenting the kind of information found in contingency tables. See Figure 6.3(B).

Complex breakdown tables show the relationship between respondent answers and more than one variable. A complex breakdown table, for example, breaks respondent data down by variables such as *gender, age, region,* and *income bracket.* A contingency table includes only one of these variables. Complex breakdown tables also include total numbers of respondents in each subgrouping. See Figure 6.4 for an example.

To identify the kinds of relationships that are depicted in these tables, your survey must have collected the necessary kinds of data from participants (e.g., age, gender, race, place of residence, memberships, etc.). The nature of the survey will dictate the specific questions asked.

Inadequate numbers of respondents in a given category may mean that you cannot break down the percentages by subgroups. This point is discussed in a previous part of the chapter. Unless you have oversampled to compensate

FIGURE 6.3
Survey on Corporate Merger

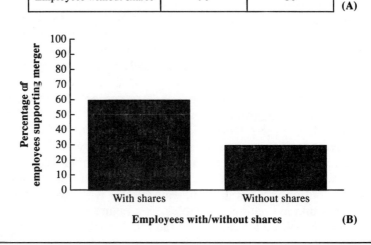

Survey on Corporate Merger

On the question of a merger, the responses of those employees who hold shares in the company varied significantly from the responses of those who do not hold shares. Sixty percent of the employees with shares favored the merger, as opposed to thirty percent of those without shares.

Survey on Corporate Merger	Number Surveyed	Percentage for Merger
Employees with shares	65	60
Employees without shares	90	30

(A)

(B)

for limited numbers of respondents, you may have to forego looking at certain relationships.

Sometimes, you are looking for changes over time, or the emergence of trends. See Figure 6.5(A). Both bar graphs and line graphs are useful formats for presenting changes over time. Bar graphs tend to be more appropriate when the number of time periods is relatively few and/or you wish to view the data as being given at discrete points in time. Line graphs, on the other hand, are useful when there are a fair number of time intervals and/or the data can be viewed as being continuous over a period of time. See Figure 6.5(B) for an example of information best presented in bar graph form.

FIGURE 6.4
Views on Abortion

VIEWS ON ABORTION	Number Surveyed	Percentage Pro-Life	Percentage Pro-Choice	Percentage No Opinion
Gender:				
Male	285	26	55	19
Female	333	35	59	6
Age:				
16–18 years	115	37	42	22
19–25 years	237	21	64	16
26–39 years	164	35	61	4
40 and older	102	41	53	6
Income Bracket:				
Under $20,000	257	37	60	3
$20,000–$39,999	175	20	56	24
$40,000–$64,999	141	30	53	16
$65,000 and over	45	40	56	4
Total	618	31	57	12

See Figure 6.6 for an example of tabular data that best translates into line graph format.

Multiple line and multiple bar graphs may be used to compare trends between or among two or more sets of data.

In the following example, the percentage of companies with 500 or more employees that have initiated sexual harrassment policies over a five-year period *are compared with* the percentage of companies with fewer than 500 employees that have initiated sexual harrassment policies over the same period. See Figure 6.7.

If you choose to refer to averages in your discussion of survey results, your analysis might read as follows:

On a 5-point Likert scale, with 5 representing "strongly agree," 4 representing "agree," 3 representing "neither agree nor disagree," 2 representing "disagree," and 1 representing "strongly disagree," the average response to the statement, "I support patrolling air space around Iraq" was 4.

Sometimes you have to include, in your discussion of survey results, reference to landmark events that have taken place since the time that your survey was conducted, for example, the election of a new government or the replacement of a company CEO.

FIGURE 6.5
Employee Confidence

Employee Confidence in Company Surviving Without Layoffs

The confidence of Detroit automobile plant workers that the
company will survive the current recession without layoffs has
dropped steadily over the past six months.

Month	Number Surveyed	Percentage Confident	
March, 1992	203	77	
April, 1992	187	72	
May, 1992	190	68	
June, 1992	215	58	
July, 1992	167	52	
August, 1992	185	45	**(A)**

(B)

For more in-depth consideration of analyzing survey results, you should
use one of the many textbooks that explain how to calculate average and
median responses to questions; it will also show you how to apply advanced
multivariate techniques to the analysis of your data. The concepts of validity
and reliability will also be discussed in these more specialized books. Some
useful references are mentioned in end notes to this chapter and some of the
other methodology chapters. Chapter 7 will discuss some of the problems that
can occur in the writing and administering of surveys.

FIGURE 6.6
Acceptance of Genetic Engineering

Acceptance of Concept of Genetic Engineering

Attitudes toward genetic engineering have changed significantly since the first surveys were conducted in 1972. Significantly more people accept the concept of genetic engineering than was the case 20 years ago.

Year	Number Surveyed	Percentage Accepting Genetic Engineering
1972	10,000	23
1973	11,456	21
1974	12,765	24
1975	14,765	27
1976	13,356	25
1977	12,645	28
1978	11,653	32
1979	11,973	33
1980	10,954	37
1981	12,048	42
1982	9,854	45
1983	13,083	47
1984	15,083	51
1985	16,033	58
1986	14,083	64
1987	13,038	67
1988	12,093	65
1989	14,022	69
1990	16,004	70
1991	17,922	78
1992	17,234	82

(A)

FIGURE 6.6 (*concluded*)

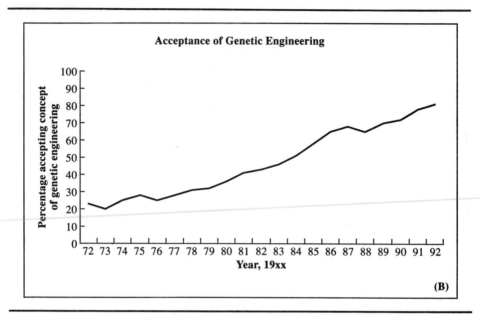

(B)

KEY POINTS TO REMEMBER

Surveys can function as *input* (an instrument for learning) or as *output* (a means of legitimizing what the organization has already decided to do). When the function of a survey is confirmatory (to be used as output), the procedures for planning and carrying out the survey may depart from practices that are usually followed when the organization has a genuine desire to learn from the survey. The steps in conducting a legitimate survey should include:

- Using standard techniques to select the sample.
- Constructing the questionnaire.
- Deciding on question order.
- Preparing introductory materials.
- Pretesting.
- Administering the questionnaire.
- Analyzing and presenting the results.

Few corporations, governments, or voluntary associations have the necessary expertise and resources to carry out all of their own research projects. Sometimes, the company will contract out the entire research project; at other

FIGURE 6.7
Companies Initiating Sexual Harassment Policies

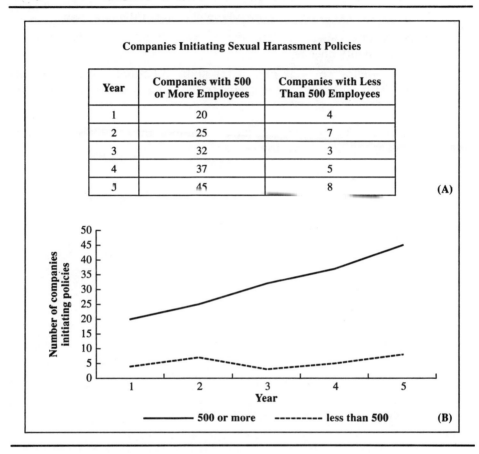

Companies Initiating Sexual Harassment Policies

Year	Companies with 500 or More Employees	Companies with Less Than 500 Employees	
1	20	4	
2	25	7	
3	32	3	
4	37	5	
5	45	8	(A)

times, it will subcontract components of the project. The following points should be kept in mind if you are purchasing research services from outside suppliers:[74]

- For projects requiring high levels of senior management input, request the involvement of a senior-level researcher; for more field-intensive projects, you can lower the cost of the project by using junior researchers.
- Expect the research firm to introduce you to a range of alternatives and to explain the strengths and weaknesses of each.
- Request detailed information on how the sample will be selected. Consider not only sample size but also other factors such as the potential quality of the sample.

- Ask how much of the work will be carried out by the firm from whom you are buying services and how much will be subcontracted.
- Evaluate the expertise of those who will conduct the interviews.
- Visit the interviewing centers from time to time during the project to conduct quality checks.
- Attend briefing sessions or ask for audio recordings of pretest interviews. This will help you to evaluate the validity of the survey instrument.

The more complex your issue, the more important it is for you to assess the research capabilities of the firm you are hiring.[75]

Table of Random Numbers

0.7113	0.1538	0.6222	0.8312	0.3387	0.8088	0.5426	0.3543	0.5063	0.7160	0.0013	0.2245	0.7621
0.9462	0.9103	0.8950	0.9264	0.4716	0.4932	0.2767	0.0450	0.3014	0.4918	0.1791	0.0675	0.8563
0.8424	0.4192	0.8407	0.4426	0.4095	0.2052	0.1097	0.2637	0.6032	0.5552	0.0969	0.4796	0.5978
0.9948	0.0894	0.6738	0.0601	0.9168	0.7269	0.4976	0.8654	0.3236	0.2244	0.7793	0.0081	0.2186
0.2505	0.3084	0.0176	0.0665	0.7866	0.1768	0.6388	0.9974	0.7407	0.3581	0.1199	0.6805	0.2301
0.6465	0.5078	0.0623	0.6470	0.7349	0.3481	0.3530	0.6722	0.6621	0.1422	0.6191	0.1816	0.1726
0.4502	0.2930	0.0302	0.7578	0.9151	0.0224	0.8806	0.1503	0.0404	0.9677	0.9497	0.7582	0.5099
0.3105	0.6730	0.1673	0.2937	0.9670	0.0785	0.6958	0.0755	0.5297	0.7230	0.9759	0.9224	0.1520
0.4266	0.2999	0.5726	0.7585	0.0115	0.3014	0.3598	0.9609	0.0400	0.3689	0.5164	0.6563	0.2843
0.9063	0.3298	0.0545	0.3296	0.0678	0.7242	0.5562	0.8142	0.6759	0.9319	0.6748	0.2904	0.3594
0.8092	0.3180	0.3864	0.8791	0.3762	0.5314	0.6336	0.2050	0.0587	0.5413	0.3262	0.3080	0.9426
0.0351	0.2784	0.1914	0.8203	0.4614	0.9392	0.3200	0.0538	0.4246	0.9425	0.2939	0.3268	0.8624
0.3581	0.6653	0.0089	0.2588	0.4016	0.9264	0.9565	0.7977	0.1631	0.7113	0.1571	0.4414	0.4429
0.1919	0.3057	0.4128	0.0142	0.3466	0.8021	0.3336	0.7188	0.3177	0.0406	0.5258	0.3077	0.7026
0.8625	0.0718	0.2476	0.5750	0.5103	0.1655	0.6673	0.8784	0.4142	0.1008	0.5553	0.6856	0.5007
0.5065	0.7610	0.4209	0.4872	0.9663	0.3972	0.5032	0.9137	0.6802	0.0622	0.2681	0.8673	0.5283
0.8095	0.2714	0.1411	0.9229	0.1705	0.6026	0.0164	0.0446	0.2169	0.7957	0.7441	0.9509	0.7542
0.5704	0.2735	0.1623	0.0693	0.8544	0.3719	0.7513	0.1284	0.6787	0.5150	0.9776	0.3545	0.5610
0.3791	0.3549	0.1964	0.0769	0.3103	0.4066	0.1487	0.0769	0.9257	0.4070	0.6932	0.9507	0.0154
0.5225	0.5652	0.5906	0.3451	0.3579	0.2215	0.5656	0.7529	0.0730	0.4056	0.5786	0.2201	0.6771
0.1943	0.9025	0.6296	0.6625	0.9329	0.0184	0.6839	0.5548	0.0034	0.1927	0.7807	0.0912	0.6235
0.5897	0.8078	0.4646	0.8368	0.1613	0.8011	0.3022	0.0307	0.5403	0.4930	0.4898	0.0162	0.7288
0.8831	0.1817	0.8945	0.0499	0.0278	0.3793	0.7622	0.9360	0.2094	0.9091	0.5704	0.3401	0.2073
0.8879	0.8121	0.0821	0.9393	0.6669	0.5825	0.1867	0.1850	0.2236	0.3732	0.3320	0.8829	0.5581
0.6744	0.7728	0.3623	0.2689	0.6678	0.8993	0.2975	0.0848	0.4991	0.8384	0.5601	0.2660	0.2088
0.3457	0.1117	0.1553	0.3324	0.8359	0.0173	0.8659	0.6572	0.8232	0.0606	0.5440	0.8065	0.7075
0.5039	0.4899	0.7745	0.2486	0.8744	0.1714	0.4328	0.5503	0.7997	0.1852	0.6185	0.4910	0.3928
0.2282	0.4433	0.8223	0.5353	0.7723	0.4297	0.6019	0.4561	0.7720	0.0994	0.8591	0.4051	0.5635
0.6975	0.9412	0.5625	0.2983	0.6380	0.2445	0.2558	0.6481	0.5371	0.1814	0.6193	0.1319	0.1319
0.3618	0.5827	0.7348	0.4670	0.4512	0.5389	0.4425	0.6735	0.9514	0.4806	0.5429	0.9837	0.4209
0.0768	0.9895	0.3734	0.7059	0.9864	0.1241	0.3888	0.0011	0.6537	0.1621	0.7230	0.3729	0.4947
0.7013	0.6096	0.8915	0.3841	0.6066	0.8931	0.4116	0.3400	0.0809	0.4294	0.8228	0.6327	0.8632
0.9658	0.5907	0.4921	0.3410	0.1626	0.7408	0.0534	0.0494	0.0374	0.0916	0.3626	0.1997	0.7949
0.7599	0.0578	0.5805	0.7109	0.6655	0.5752	0.4952	0.9843	0.4638	0.4196	0.7266	0.2817	0.4309
0.3686	0.6539	0.8318	0.4049	0.0440	0.0714	0.7134	0.5620	0.7160	0.5366	0.3577	0.0003	0.6057
0.9924	0.2535	0.0778	0.3347	0.7717	0.0812	0.2903	0.4187	0.3221	0.9937	0.3828	0.2208	0.5926
0.9281	0.8922	0.6073	0.3443	0.3390	0.9083	0.3107	0.7879	0.7538	0.6597	0.3966	0.0433	0.4077
0.7628	0.1919	0.2018	0.6173	0.4165	0.3715	0.6333	0.8576	0.4076	0.4094	0.7208	0.9184	
0.6973	0.7007	0.3486	0.2800	0.4041	0.9938	0.1611	0.4655	0.3964	0.9479	0.2710	0.3131	0.7952
0.5681	0.6132	0.0773	0.6934	0.1936	0.3346	0.0459	0.5181	0.0758	0.4301	0.0620	0.8353	0.1809
0.9129	0.1138	0.3316	0.8528	0.6262	0.0357	0.5814	0.0053	0.5779	0.2241	0.4662	0.2195	0.2931
0.3334	0.6750	0.3282	0.1233	0.3428	0.4213	0.8590	0.1231	0.4645	0.8046	0.0167	0.8609	0.3931
0.5260	0.3906	0.4538	0.2000	0.6861	0.5643	0.2884	0.2373	0.3974	0.6870	0.4664	0.3651	0.5487
0.4808	0.0330	0.9063	0.2913	0.7062	0.2793	0.9183	0.2103	0.2727	0.8304	0.8777	0.3344	0.1144
0.7004	0.0386	0.2859	0.8863	0.4788	0.4782	0.4901	0.1587	0.6451	0.7123	0.1590	0.3310	0.0679
0.6843	0.9188	0.0301	0.7566	0.2267	0.9853	0.6321	0.9001	0.0620	0.9460	0.9600	0.8305	0.1862
0.1238	0.6741	0.0128	0.3023	0.9699	0.4969	0.1581	0.7658	0.9534	0.0101	0.7064	0.8861	0.0541
0.9420	0.7701	0.9982	0.4596	0.6950	0.1352	0.1219	0.1274	0.5342	0.5928	0.0120	0.4350	0.2373
0.0038	0.7419	0.1635	0.3437	0.6703	0.8068	0.7243	0.4952	0.1654	0.2076	0.6761	0.8432	0.5819
0.6691	0.0644	0.6584	0.4603	0.0577	0.8068	0.2256	0.5801	0.3999	0.2733	0.9478	0.3329	0.4480
0.3580	0.4137	0.8756	0.8078	0.8157	0.7761	0.4582	0.6347	0.2741	0.8008	0.3954	0.2430	0.3471
0.7253	0.6590	0.8833	0.5676	0.5141	0.4005	0.2577	0.4748	0.4395	0.7228	0.2743	0.8623	0.1876
0.2052	0.5851	0.1321	0.8939	0.6850	0.9996	0.7373	0.6543	0.1256	0.3451	0.4123	0.7746	0.0728
0.7754	0.7582	0.9785	0.3067	0.4073	0.1865	0.5911	0.0798	0.5645	0.3121	0.2453	0.0552	0.3229
0.3267	0.5098	0.3044	0.8890	0.4470	0.1029	0.3849	0.7855	0.6558	0.3055	0.5702	0.8022	0.6612

Table of Random Numbers

0.4587	0.4830	0.6465	0.8537	0.7872	0.7367	0.2261	0.1747	0.2386	0.3483	0.6800	0.5788	0.5862
0.0712	0.7805	0.0881	0.5810	0.4717	0.4560	0.5538	0.4686	0.1366	0.3534	0.9219	0.8473	0.8054
0.0179	0.2099	0.5583	0.4226	0.2774	0.5486	0.0099	0.1213	0.8661	0.3373	0.4376	0.5755	0.4188
0.6970	0.7858	0.9365	0.6484	0.5850	0.0964	0.2099	0.5604	0.9583	0.1231	0.9485	0.5622	0.2032
0.0252	0.3322	0.8130	0.6424	0.8716	0.5464	0.7615	0.7119	0.2025	0.0556	0.1845	0.0857	0.6669
0.4980	0.2531	0.0812	0.3061	0.7627	0.2844	0.5206	0.3769	0.0218	0.0159	0.9693	0.3824	0.8747
0.2313	0.3451	0.5082	0.8518	0.4224	0.4343	0.4765	0.3184	0.2423	0.0550	0.2045	0.5433	0.7896
0.6492	0.8877	0.2797	0.3418	0.8049	0.4933	0.5485	0.0045	0.4865	0.7553	0.0304	0.0541	0.5244
0.6542	0.3938	0.9285	0.7845	0.8006	0.8592	0.4280	0.9403	0.9349	0.9987	0.1073	0.4441	0.3007
0.4283	0.3784	0.1225	0.8867	0.7595	0.4726	0.9182	0.0405	0.4173	0.2766	0.5454	0.0327	0.9197
0.3721	0.0200	0.4968	0.8479	0.5304	0.6373	0.4965	0.6255	0.5400	0.8841	0.5082	0.7673	0.6466
0.2119	0.9128	0.8664	0.7465	0.5586	0.8471	0.1906	0.0916	0.5486	0.6371	0.7570	0.5249	0.1611
0.6633	0.9535	0.3298	0.1389	0.3261	0.5123	0.3793	0.9638	0.3351	0.5778	0.4323	0.9785	0.2558
0.3124	0.1410	0.0923	0.3108	0.2510	0.1391	0.9830	0.4883	0.5541	0.8610	0.8690	0.3046	0.7291
0.1800	0.5569	0.6151	0.7312	0.1741	0.8580	0.4313	0.7858	0.3995	0.6682	0.5522	0.0261	0.2826
0.8605	0.1214	0.1048	0.1243	0.4504	0.0710	0.2005	0.9764	0.2148	0.3206	0.1651	0.0748	0.5551
0.0898	0.4430	0.7875	0.0674	0.5922	0.2416	0.3312	0.3807	0.6962	0.0298	0.3634	0.2874	0.3084
0.2239	0.7732	0.9809	0.9895	0.2805	0.0715	0.6850	0.8587	0.7411	0.2767	0.7131	0.3502	0.1672
0.3859	0.2267	0.9168	0.7496	0.8742	0.1111	0.3650	0.2077	0.9165	0.0157	0.4504	0.0299	0.8703
0.2444	0.2208	0.6347	0.4094	0.4684	0.7250	0.2221	0.3578	0.5079	0.2159	0.3342	0.9473	0.7662
0.0496	0.3964	0.9620	0.8338	0.4852	0.2619	0.4849	0.2923	0.9376	0.4115	0.0026	0.4057	0.9127
0.9409	0.0999	0.7744	0.0024	0.7602	0.7069	0.8768	0.9935	0.2378	0.7971	0.3983	0.4895	0.4690
0.3647	0.0470	0.5266	0.7050	0.3528	0.0774	0.7152	0.9395	0.7088	0.8141	0.2457	0.3991	0.4234
0.9078	0.4181	0.5649	0.9141	0.1789	0.6193	0.0298	0.7147	0.3191	0.7966	0.4653	0.3701	0.1245
0.1751	0.8580	0.7298	0.0324	0.9562	0.2773	0.2109	0.9327	0.4827	0.3666	0.3375	0.2818	0.6351
0.4333	0.9768	0.1488	0.4420	0.2325	0.7521	0.8106	0.2376	0.3160	0.8749	0.5305	0.8904	0.8138
0.5914	0.3464	0.7329	0.2593	0.1147	0.0193	0.1572	0.8020	0.1793	0.0783	0.4170	0.2491	0.2111
0.6532	0.4967	0.9164	0.3010	0.4560	0.9994	0.8442	0.9624	0.0555	0.0898	0.1110	0.3465	0.8552
0.9452	0.2937	0.5311	0.6999	0.0788	0.7376	0.7140	0.6809	0.3904	0.0225	0.9473	0.2491	0.6573
0.4821	0.4633	0.0976	0.0077	0.1586	0.5924	0.4129	0.8856	0.2823	0.8237	0.8625	0.3895	0.8052
0.3593	0.7210	0.1333	0.2588	0.9931	0.8804	0.7233	0.9593	0.0058	0.2600	0.1508	0.6375	0.1718
0.1519	0.7231	0.4214	0.7880	0.0782	0.3226	0.8139	0.5167	0.6587	0.6007	0.3613	0.9444	0.8259
0.7336	0.8402	0.6937	0.7557	0.6871	0.3110	0.6575	0.0607	0.8763	0.0231	0.3960	0.4256	0.7807
0.4342	0.3909	0.6399	0.7904	0.0066	0.2753	0.6300	0.4288	0.7440	0.2793	0.9135	0.5975	0.6706
0.5711	0.0544	0.4155	0.2403	0.9196	0.7157	0.2501	0.9153	0.3555	0.7320	0.9678	0.3901	0.6034
0.3057	0.7428	0.3816	0.5658	0.0356	0.9463	0.0027	0.0807	0.6445	0.0004	0.7408	0.8188	0.6898
0.9377	0.2395	0.2840	0.6409	0.1738	0.6474	0.9871	0.5886	0.7219	0.3615	0.2462	0.0817	0.4667
0.3193	0.2212	0.3166	0.1877	0.1832	0.5501	0.9060	0.9418	0.7487	0.5788	0.5659	0.7818	0.8285
0.6270	0.1315	0.2903	0.5456	0.7530	0.7254	0.2924	0.0772	0.2666	0.6542	0.5429	0.7143	0.9675
0.4516	0.3527	0.2320	0.0944	0.7248	0.7886	0.8314	0.7969	0.7822	0.0023	0.8059	0.0868	0.1223
0.3858	0.9052	0.5628	0.6951	0.4749	0.7705	0.0312	0.5893	0.2843	0.7285	0.2817	0.0122	0.0502
0.0216	0.8854	0.7355	0.0254	0.9907	0.4851	0.7842	0.4955	0.8825	0.6103	0.0388	0.2103	0.6520
0.6763	0.2939	0.6728	0.6165	0.3352	0.7367	0.2177	0.6088	0.2032	0.6033	0.2340	0.2612	0.8035
0.0645	0.4225	0.9200	0.9391	0.2440	0.2658	0.4301	0.8136	0.8256	0.5960	0.8270	0.7655	0.0556
0.3244	0.0647	0.9126	0.5941	0.9882	0.9595	0.0068	0.6070	0.1306	0.0988	0.8093	0.5806	0.2637
0.8176	0.2605	0.5388	0.4451	0.1910	0.0263	0.5341	0.2229	0.6034	0.7346	0.0028	0.5251	0.9105
0.1268	0.2575	0.1133	0.8367	0.0779	0.4367	0.6111	0.6317	0.7242	0.8251	0.8384	0.5897	0.8864
0.0749	0.1913	0.0321	0.7328	0.7253	0.5972	0.2353	0.9583	0.3268	0.3532	0.2632	0.8702	0.1386
0.4384	0.7256	0.2712	0.9177	0.9433	0.0141	0.0875	0.5653	0.8408	0.7318	0.3429	0.2410	0.7716
0.1724	0.5843	0.3500	0.8955	0.2095	0.9893	0.5877	0.6546	0.5232	0.8403	0.0657	0.7448	0.1476
0.4238	0.2624	0.0609	0.6333	0.2196	0.7784	0.6273	0.2497	0.0845	0.1805	0.5512	0.7929	0.1289
0.1901	0.1138	0.1592	0.5619	0.9074	0.8170	0.0751	0.0515	0.8067	0.5901	0.1528	0.7636	0.9542
0.2740	0.2131	0.6685	0.2969	0.2417	0.1343	0.8772	0.3440	0.5424	0.3354	0.5562	0.4246	0.2025
0.3776	0.7337	0.1531	0.9732	0.0106	0.2026	0.7368	0.2590	0.7389	0.0151	0.7859	0.3775	0.1662
0.6000	0.3815	0.5613	0.9721	0.3312	0.3305	0.4619	0.5525	0.4372	0.7328	0.6787	0.6530	0.4017

Table of Random Numbers

0.9362	0.5746	0.9227	0.9709	0.0833	0.7691	0.6576	0.1550	0.6710	0.1038	0.0070	0.5820	0.9538
0.2167	0.2135	0.4260	0.4698	0.2519	0.4913	0.5828	0.7256	0.0360	0.7859	0.7125	0.7074	0.6037
0.7386	0.0149	0.7637	0.0407	0.9268	0.2909	0.1021	0.2277	0.9410	0.6586	0.7376	0.9993	0.2618
0.5985	0.6205	0.3331	0.9982	0.1987	0.2474	0.7364	0.2725	0.1900	0.0249	0.8095	0.8890	0.4737
0.7786	0.9819	0.9724	0.3932	0.4185	0.6126	0.0804	0.0288	0.5027	0.1189	0.2046	0.7886	0.3737
0.4099	0.0015	0.9419	0.1658	0.0549	0.8186	0.2036	0.8028	0.0931	0.7828	0.6133	0.0926	0.1665
0.5477	0.5276	0.9450	0.8237	0.4571	0.8661	0.9040	0.9198	0.4827	0.1228	0.9411	0.4820	0.1138
0.2312	0.9841	0.7165	0.0957	0.9330	0.3295	0.5834	0.2578	0.6373	0.9016	0.8709	0.6526	0.1138
0.4665	0.2206	0.7653	0.9411	0.8061	0.2186	0.7142	0.8603	0.9940	0.1325	0.5512	0.4501	0.2154
0.0157	0.7803	0.5223	0.2097	0.5000	0.3926	0.3990	0.2168	0.1120	0.7201	0.1645	0.3839	0.8724
0.9551	0.5606	0.7258	0.8822	0.9271	0.2429	0.6632	0.3610	0.4177	0.3899	0.6254	0.6736	0.5762
0.0350	0.5057	0.3128	0.0593	0.9335	0.1156	0.8705	0.3788	0.4744	0.9323	0.2559	0.5663	0.1577
0.2545	0.4527	0.2599	0.1249	0.2800	0.0084	0.4575	0.1164	0.4786	0.5336	0.3595	0.4706	0.9461
0.8778	0.4396	0.6349	0.8241	0.7694	0.6820	0.9856	0.2223	0.8034	0.8429	0.2797	0.0077	0.6393
0.5475	0.5387	0.1177	0.4615	0.1404	0.5246	0.1837	0.6951	0.0602	0.5341	0.0166	0.7991	0.4604
0.3960	0.5091	0.8545	0.9530	0.7291	0.9799	0.1589	0.9806	0.3602	0.3188	0.5687	0.3765	0.7448
0.5129	0.2643	0.1251	0.3070	0.0679	0.5318	0.1238	0.6785	0.7877	0.2562	0.0515	0.9016	0.3158
0.8470	0.3843	0.5907	0.8458	0.5026	0.3825	0.9163	0.8303	0.6870	0.6792	0.3729	0.4662	0.7041
0.2820	0.4950	0.4181	0.6525	0.1533	0.7900	0.0796	0.3331	0.4734	0.4670	0.6057	0.7790	0.2164
0.1888	0.0740	0.1208	0.8722	0.3940	0.5058	0.1111	0.9695	0.1532	0.1047	0.0119	0.3557	0.2227
0.9911	0.9503	0.4009	0.9722	0.2631	0.4887	0.7455	0.5971	0.4877	0.5800	0.7472	0.4311	0.4478
0.3244	0.4518	0.4860	0.3256	0.1890	0.4577	0.0689	0.6073	0.4631	0.5713	0.0082	0.5112	0.0592
0.0292	0.3198	0.2263	0.7669	0.1346	0.1841	0.4803	0.1361	0.1902	0.2225	0.8936	0.2932	0.4145
0.6840	0.6340	0.5874	0.4475	0.8860	0.8892	0.4534	0.2548	0.4663	0.4464	0.8505	0.8225	0.7632
0.3948	0.3328	0.2136	0.0341	0.0992	0.8506	0.8503	0.8182	0.3234	0.8489	0.4886	0.5404	0.6195
0.7123	0.3888	0.3147	0.2733	0.9508	0.0858	0.4935	0.5470	0.5418	0.5233	0.8654	0.6201	0.6249
0.6257	0.0537	0.6401	0.4804	0.8561	0.0251	0.5282	0.5269	0.3786	0.9322	0.7445	0.3389	0.1712
0.6093	0.3909	0.3067	0.7306	0.9599	0.8690	0.9593	0.1577	0.1414	0.6092	0.5343	0.7374	0.9481
0.2882	0.1733	0.1046	0.0690	0.4880	0.1791	0.2324	0.5005	0.1121	0.4663	0.4199	0.5295	0.6672
0.5064	0.7965	0.3323	0.6758	0.4447	0.2612	0.4226	0.9222	0.3689	0.6435	0.8469	0.0460	0.7157
0.0148	0.5084	0.0140	0.8849	0.7862	0.1879	0.1837	0.6343	0.8571	0.4751	0.0456	0.1765	0.4458
0.2433	0.5095	0.2034	0.0933	0.2236	0.8397	0.4638	0.7389	0.0605	0.2388	0.5219	0.1822	0.6157
0.7548	0.0754	0.8955	0.3529	0.4565	0.9366	0.5327	0.9873	0.9045	0.2512	0.8366	0.5738	0.0688
0.8864	0.1446	0.7833	0.8466	0.9209	0.8241	0.1070	0.8224	0.3968	0.5061	0.3444	0.4734	0.5452
0.0815	0.3017	0.3766	0.7212	0.1712	0.7410	0.1944	0.6701	0.4791	0.0172	0.5189	0.7737	0.6867
0.7433	0.0343	0.3390	0.2529	0.7682	0.6880	0.1499	0.1684	0.8343	0.7789	0.5611	0.5743	0.6641
0.4558	0.3604	0.4938	0.2840	0.5823	0.9511	0.3529	0.4421	0.0239	0.4877	0.5534	0.4798	0.8115
0.9741	0.6645	0.2168	0.2877	0.4562	0.8188	0.6137	0.1224	0.6764	0.6514	0.2830	0.6466	0.1338
0.9188	0.2046	0.8323	0.8228	0.2167	0.5622	0.4806	0.3596	0.4498	0.1145	0.8195	0.9282	0.4547
0.7436	0.8421	0.6396	0.1197	0.0290	0.4749	0.1965	0.6659	0.5907	0.7237	0.5543	0.1438	0.8676
0.5297	0.7625	0.0212	0.9036	0.0711	0.2163	0.7902	0.3746	0.9346	0.0264	0.1536	0.2068	0.0615
0.4885	0.1134	0.6786	0.8578	0.7328	0.6025	0.3241	0.7548	0.4155	0.9666	0.1203	0.4987	0.2408
0.4547	0.4623	0.2493	0.9852	0.3453	0.5716	0.9096	0.7430	0.7771	0.4312	0.5113	0.2428	0.0737
0.7780	0.4297	0.5087	0.4539	0.2187	0.3474	0.4715	0.4450	0.7664	0.6508	0.0015	0.3487	0.7998
0.8861	0.6228	0.6316	0.0633	0.6040	0.5824	0.4814	0.1265	0.2999	0.4730	0.1062	0.3960	0.8899
0.7547	0.1865	0.8340	0.6867	0.1345	0.6144	0.4123	0.0798	0.3567	0.0289	0.0129	0.6016	0.2084
0.8125	0.3393	0.4222	0.9100	0.3470	0.0653	0.9596	0.0109	0.2213	0.4893	0.6621	0.3534	0.1833
0.0874	0.1138	0.6498	0.1051	0.5825	0.1866	0.8459	0.0620	0.0491	0.8572	0.5434	0.2063	0.0879
0.7359	0.2097	0.8805	0.3840	0.3773	0.9903	0.9162	0.2987	0.1839	0.3719	0.9104	0.4423	0.5006
0.4163	0.2670	0.8753	0.2424	0.7131	0.7658	0.7131	0.4953	0.5579	0.7780	0.2608	0.4515	0.5575
0.3107	0.2951	0.3185	0.8648	0.3682	0.8990	0.3491	0.6859	0.5568	0.2454	0.3849	0.8995	0.3914
0.3823	0.7123	0.4273	0.4732	0.3470	0.8423	0.5660	0.8255	0.1188	0.4618	0.8484	0.8957	0.1516
0.7310	0.4576	0.8273	0.0513	0.2286	0.5825	0.4656	0.0750	0.5339	0.9334	0.2730	0.0492	0.4245
0.2399	0.9083	0.0833	0.6007	0.9858	0.9310	0.6136	0.1434	0.3058	0.6410	0.8767	0.1293	0.7503
0.3517	0.4859	0.0484	0.1689	0.8146	0.7173	0.7355	0.8354	0.3473	0.4337	0.4807	0.3881	0.7793

NOTES

1. Otis Baskin and Craig Aronoff, *Public Relations: The Profession and the Practice,* 3rd ed. (Dubuque, Iowa: Wm. C. Brown Publishers, 1992), p. 114, claim that surveys are the most common type of public relations research.
2. Arlene Fink and Jacqueline Kosecoff, *How to Conduct Surveys: A Step-by-Step Guide* (Newbury Park, Calif.: Sage Publications, 1985), p. 20.
3. Quoted in John Witherspoon, "Campaign Commercials and the Media Blitz," in *Campaigns and Elections,* ed. Larry Sabato (Glenview, Ill.: Scott, Foresman, 1989), p. 62.
4. David Taras, *The Newsmakers: The Media's Influence on Canadian Politics* (Scarborough, Ont.: Nelson Canada, 1990), pp. 181–82.
5. Ibid.
6. Jan P. Herring, "Senior Management Must Champion Business Intelligence Programs," *Journal of Business Strategy,* September/October 1991, p. 48.
7. Edgar M. Arundell, "The Publics of Public Affairs," in *The Canadian Public Affairs Handbook: Maximizing Markets, Protecting Bottom Lines,* eds. W. John Wright and Christopher J. DuVernet (Toronto: Carswell, 1988), pp. 46–47.
8. Angus Reid, "Public Affairs Research: Quantitative and Qualitative," in *The Canadian Public Affairs Handbook: Maximizing Markets, Protecting Bottom Lines,* eds. W. John Wright and Christopher J. DuVernet (Toronto: Carswell, 1988), p. 131.
9. John Pound, "Beyond Takeovers: Politics Comes to Corporate Control," *Harvard Business Review,* March/April 1992, p. 92.
10. David M. Dozier and Fred C. Repper, "Research Firms and Public Relations Practices," in *Excellence in Public Relations and Communication Management,* ed. James E. Grunig (Hillsdale, N.J.: Lawrence Erlbaum Associates, Publishers, 1992), p. 200.
11. See discussion by Prema Nakra, "The Changing Role of Public Relations in Marketing Communications," *Public Relations Quarterly,* Spring 1991, p. 44.
12. Jerry L. Yeric and John R. Todd, *Public Opinion: The Visible Politics,* 2nd ed. (Itasca, Ill.: F. E. Peacock Publishers, 1989), p. 118.
13. Ibid., p. 119.
14. Gary A. Mauser, "The Short-Term Effect of Election Polls on Foreign Exchange Rates: The 1988 Canadian Federal Election," *Public Opinion Quarterly,* Summer 1991, p. 232.
15. Interview with Robin Sears, Ottawa, Ontario, June 4, 1987, reported in David Taras, *The Newsmakers: The Media's Influence on Canadian Politics* (Scarborough, Ont.: Nelson Canada), p. 183. See also Taras, p. 193.

16. "Pollsters Often Misunderstood, Reid Says," *Ottawa Citizen*, October 4, 1988, p. A4.
17. Dan Nimmo and James E. Combs, *Mediated Political Realities*, 2nd ed. (New York: Longman, 1990).
18. Taras, p. 187.
19. Ibid.
20. Alan Frizzell, "The Perils of Polling," in *The Canadian General Election of 1988*, eds. Alan Frizzell and Anthony Westell (Ottawa, Ont.: Carleton University Press, 1989).
21. Comment by Robin Sears, reported by Taras, p. 187.
22. Comment by Daniel Greenberg, reported in Herbert Asher, *Polling and the Public* (Washington, D.C.: Congressional Quarterly Press, 1988), p. 15.
23. Yeric and Todd, p. 239.
24. Ibid., pp. 100–102.
25. Elly Alboim, "Television and the Democratic Process," *Banff Television Festival*, June 6, 1989. Cited in Taras, p. 191.
26. George S. Day, "Continuous Learning About Markets," *Planning Review*, September/October 1992, p. 48.
27. Yeric and Todd, p. 241.
28. Earl Babbie, *Survey Research Methods*, 2nd ed. (Belmont, Calif.: Wadsworth Publishing Company, 1990), p. 71.
29. Mary John Smith, *Contemporary Communication Research Methods* (Belmont, Calif.: Wadsworth, 1988), p. 77.
30. Babbie, pp. 84–85.
31. Smith, p. 85.
32. Stanley Presser and Shanyang Zhao, "Attributes of Questions and Interviewers as Correlates of Interviewing Performance," *Public Opinion Quarterly*, Summer 1992, p. 239. Presser and Zhao found that brevity of questions facilitates the task of the interviewer.
33. Cited in Roger D. Wimmer and Joseph R. Dominick, *Mass Media Research*, 2nd ed. (Belmont, Calif.: Wadsworth, 1987), p. 118.
34. James H. Frey, *Survey Research by Telephone*, 2nd ed. (Newbury Park, Calif.: Sage Publications, 1989), p. 122–23.
35. Cited in Jean M. Converse and Stanley Presser, *Survey Questions: Handcrafting the Standardized Questionnaire* (Newbury Park, Calif.: Sage Publications, 1986), pp. 17–18.
36. Floyd Jackson Fowler, Jr., "How Unclear Terms Affect Survey Data," *Public Opinion Quarterly*, Summer 1992, p. 230.
37. Frey, p. 121.
38. Converse and Presser, pp. 26–27.
39. Ibid., p. 34.
40. Eric R. A. N. Smith, *The Unchanging American Voter* (Berkeley: University of California Press, 1989), p. 84.

41. Chris Argyris, "Leadership, Learning, and Changing the 'Status Quo,'" *Organizational Dynamics,* Winter 1976, pp. 54–64.
42. John G. Geer, "Do Open-Ended Questions Measure 'Salient' Issues?" *Public Opinion Quarterly,* Fall 1991, p. 360.
43. Converse and Presser, p. 34.
44. Ibid., p. 35.
45. Rensis Likert, "A Technique for the Measurement of Attitudes," *Archives of Psychology* 19 (1932), pp. 44–53.
46. Charles E. Osgood, P. H. Tannenbaum, and G. J. Suci, *The Measurement of Meaning* (Urbana: University of Illinois Press, 1957).
47. William G. Zikmund, *Business Research Methods,* 2nd. ed. (Chicago: Dryden Press, 1988), p. 279.
48. Converse and Presser, pp. 29–30.
49. Fink and Kosecoff, pp. 34–35.
50. Zikmund, pp. 281–82.
51. Yeric and Todd, p. 37. Also Wimmer and Dominick, pp. 113–14.
52. Cited in Zikmund, p. 283.
53. Converse and Presser, p. 29.
54. Zikmund, pp. 285–86.
55. G. David Hughes, "The Measurement of Beliefs and Attitudes," in *Handbook of Marketing Research,* ed. Robert Ferber (New York: McGraw-Hill, 1974), pp. 30–31, cited in Zikmund, p. 287.
56. Converse and Presser, p. 41.
57. Smith, p. 228.
58. Floyd Jackson Fowler, Jr. and Thomas W. Mangione, *Standardized Survey Interviewing: Minimizing Interviewer-Related Error* (Newbury Park, Calif.: Sage Publications, 1990), p. 86.
59. R. Kahn and C. F. Cannell, *Dynamics of Interviewing* (New York: John Wiley & Sons, 1957), p. 149, cited in Catherine Marshall and Gretchen B. Rossman, *Designing Qualitative Research* (Newbury Park, Calif.: Sage Publications, 1989), p. 82.
60. Babbie, p. 141.
61. Marshall and Rossman, p. 94.
62. Ibid.
63. Ibid.
64. Presser and Zhao, p. 239.
65. Wimmer and Dominick, pp. 124–25.
66. Peter S. Tuckel and Barry M. Feinberg, "The Answering Machine Poses Many Questions for Telephone Survey Researchers," *Public Opinion Quarterly,* Summer 1991, pp. 200–17.
67. Frey, p. 156.
68. Francis J. Yammarino, Steven J. Skinner, and Terry L. Childers, "Understanding Mail Survey Response Behavior: A Meta-Analysis," *Public Opinion Quarterly,* Winter 1991, pp. 619–27.

69. Babbie, p. 141.
70. Frey, p. 24.
71. Yammarino, pp. 613–14.
72. Maria Elena Sanchez, "Effects of Questionnaire Design on the Quality of Survey Data," *Public Opinion Quarterly,* Summer 1992, pp. 206–17.
73. Wimmer and Dominick, p. 122.
74. Reid, pp. 144–46.
75. Ibid.

CHAPTER 7

PITFALLS OF POLLING AND SINS OF SURVEYING

Properly designed and executed surveys can yield much useful information. Those who place their faith in surveys and polls must remember, however, that judgments made at all stages of the survey process will affect the quality of the results. Some classic examples illustrate surveys "gone wrong." Although some of these examples are drawn from politics, the principles are universal, and they can be applied to modern business and government. Because corporations do not tend to publicize the results of their public opinion surveys to the same extent as political parties (who are bound to higher levels of public accountability), it is easier to draw examples from the political sphere. Also, the very large sums of money that are expended by political parties in the area of polling make the failures all the more dramatic.

CONTAMINATED SAMPLES

The most well-known and often recounted incident of a poll gone astray occurred in 1936 when the *Literary Digest* predicted republican Alf Landon would soundly defeat incumbent democratic President Franklin Roosevelt by a margin of 57 percent to 43 percent. The results of the contest are history. Roosevelt was returned to office by a landslide, the biggest in history, garnering 61 percent of the popular vote and 523 electoral votes. Landon, on the other hand, received only eight electoral votes.[1] The inaccurate poll results were blamed on an unrepresentative sampling frame. Pollsters had drawn their sample from lists of telephone subscribers and automobile owners, people who were scarcely representative of a Depression-mired population. At that time, fewer than 40 percent of American households had telephones and only 55 percent of the population owned automobiles. Of the two million people sampled, the survey drew from a disproportionately large number of people who were wealthy, or at least, relatively so.[2] Yet it was the disillusioned poor who turned out in unprecedented numbers to vote in the 1936 elections. George Gallup, using a different sampling procedure, predicted that Roosevelt would win a second term. Through quota sampling, Gallup ensured that people at different levels of the social and economic strata were represented in his poll results.[3]

The time at which you draw your sample can influence the results. For example, in the United States, many polling firms refrain from polling on Friday evenings. More affluent members of the population are less likely to be home at that time. Polls conducted on a Saturday evening can also lead to underestimating the level of support for more liberal government policies. Younger voters are less likely to be at home on a Saturday night than are their older counterparts.[4] Conducting all your interviews during the day, when you are most likely to find seniors and women at home, can contaminate a sample. Failure to call back individuals that you don't reach the first time can generate additional problems.

LOADED AND LEADING QUESTIONS

Differences in survey results can be due to variations in wording.[5] Loaded questions are usually easy to spot, but the people who read the survey results may never see the wording of questions. Consider the following statements. The respondent is asked to agree or disagree:

I believe that the government should drop all surtaxes that could impair the ability of businesses to attract international investors. (A business coalition could ask this question on a survey intended for use by lobbyists.)

I believe that Americans should have the right to defend themselves against intruders. (This question could conceivably appear in a survey soliciting the opinions of Americans on gun control).

I would like my children to have the opportunity to receive quality day care. (This question could be part of a survey soliciting views on state funding of child care.)

I believe that we should help small businesses to stay competitive by allowing them to remain open on Sundays. (This question could be asked by a local small business association or an association of mall owners lobbying for the right to stay open on Sundays.)

I am proud that America helps people from other countries to flee despotic regimes. (This question could appear in a survey of attitudes toward U.S. immigration policies.)

I believe that every American should have the right to three good meals a day. (A coalition against poverty, lobbying for increased subsidies for meal programs in schools with low-income populations, could ask this question.)

Similar examples are *"Are you in favor of helping the needy?"* or *"Do you agree with the environmentalists who say that we must protect the seal population?"* *"Do you accept the popular belief that acid rain disturbs the chemical balance in our rivers and lakes?"* All of these examples cue the respondent as to the most acceptable answer. Lengthy preambles can also bias responses. Although favorable survey results may give some measure of reassurance to senior management, they will in the long run "distort their reading of the public mood and invite rather than deter external threats."[6]

QUESTIONS WITH A HIDDEN AGENDA: HAVE YOU GIVEN UP YOUR LIFE OF CRIME?

Questions sometimes contain underlying premises which may be erroneous. It is easy to recognize the most obvious of this genre of question. Most of us would see the inherent bias in the classic question, *"Have you stopped beating your wife?"* We don't, however, always recognize the more subtle ways in which questionnaires include hidden assumptions.

Example 1. Consider the question: *Do you support the idea of large multinational corporations controlling our economy?* This question contains loaded language and hidden assumptions. First, it is loaded by the use of terms such as *controlling*. Most Americans respond negatively to any suggestion of control, and they react to the term *multinational*. The question also contains the underlying assumption that multinational corporations do control the economy. Some studies have found that terms that suggest restraints on freedom or liberty will evoke negative responses (e.g., *constrain, ban, restrict, control,* or *forbid*). It is better to use more neutral terms such as *not allow*.[7]

Example 2. A second example also illustrates hidden assumptions. In this case, a coalition of physicians could ask respondents to agree or disagree with the following statement: *I believe that Americans should have the right to choose their own doctors.* By itself, this question is innocuous, and most Americans would agree with it. The problem arises when the question is asked in association with other questions. For example, if the question appears in a survey that asks about state-subsidized health care, this question (if asked early in the survey) implies that changes from the *status quo* could result in a loss of the right to choose one's own doctor.

If you want to gain insights into what people are thinking about these issues, you will learn little by asking such questions. If, however, you intend to use the survey results to support a lobbying campaign, you will probably get just what you want. In the latter case, the question of ethics arises, and many would contend that this approach to public relations is one that (in the end) ill serves the interests of the organization.

EMBARRASSING QUESTIONS: DO YOU CHEAT ON YOUR INCOME TAX?

Some questions elicit sensitive or embarrassing information. Because these kinds of questions can result in respondents breaking off an interview or refusing to go further with a questionnaire, sensitive questions should be placed last or, at least, in the middle of a questionnaire.[8] If you have already asked the most important questions, it will not matter so much if the interview is terminated.

An interesting example of people's lack of willingness to respond honestly to certain kinds of survey questions occurred with an anthropological study that took place a number of years ago. A group of anthropologists were studying patterns of food and drink consumption among people living in the southwestern United States. During the day, the researchers went door-to-door, asking people to describe what they ate and drank in a typical week. To confirm the quality of the data they were obtaining, the researchers went through their subjects' garbage cans in the evenings. What they learned is that people are not always honest when they are asked to describe such personal matters as diet. The subjects in the study had typically described themselves as following a healthy food regime and consuming few alcoholic beverages. What the anthropologists discovered, however, was that junk food composed a significant part of the diet of the people and consumption of alcohol was at a much higher level than reported.

In order to alleviate these kinds of response problems, it is necessary to frame sensitive questions in a neutral fashion that encourages honesty. Word your question so that you make it possible for people to give a socially acceptable response.[9] For example, these researchers could have said: "Some people include a certain number of foods in their diet that are quick and easy to prepare. Is this the case with your family? What do you eat in a typical week?" With a sensitive topic such as reporting income, you could say, "We want to learn more about how Americans view reporting of income. Some people report all of the income they earn in a year. Others report only part of their income. Into which category do you usually fall?"

Sometimes, people are more likely to tell the truth if you put the question in third-party terms. To learn more about how many people evade paying income taxes, you could say: "Let us assume that Ted and Mary Smith earn $30,000 a year. They report $15,000 of this income. How do you view their income tax reporting practices?" Bracketing age and income can also encourage people to respond to sensitive questions.[10] For example, instead of asking how much someone earns, ask the person to select the appropriate income bracket: *"less than $20,000" "20,000–$29,999," "30,000–39,999,"* etc. Include at least one bracket that is lower than you anticipate your respondents will require. Studies have found that people are more likely to be honest if they don't have to place themselves in the lowest income category. Be sure that your bracketing of numbers doesn't include overlapping figures. Instead of asking, *"What is your age?"* offer a choice of different age groupings (e.g., *21–30, 31–40, 41–50, 51–60, over 60*).

HARDLY EVER OR CONSTANTLY

The movie *Annie Hall* has been used to illustrate the difficulties inherent in using vague quantifiers in group comparisons:

> In the movie Annie Hall, there is a split screen. On one side, Alvie Singer talks to his psychiatrist; on the other side, Annie Hall talks to hers. Alvie's therapist asks him, "How often do you sleep together?" and Alvie replies, "Hardly ever, maybe 3 times a week." Annie's therapist asks her, "Do you have sex often?" Annie replies, "Constantly. I'd say three times a week."[11]

The question asked by the psychiatrist is evoking a relative response. Using semantic differential and other intensity scales can help to alleviate but not totally resolve these kinds of problems. The term *often* generates particular difficulties for survey respondents. In the case of an unusual event such as an earthquake, a hurricane, or a flood, "often" could be once every 10 years or more. For gunfire in action films, "often" could be 50 times in a movie. A person's feelings toward an event can also influence the response. For example, for someone who dislikes taking buses to work, "often" could be once a week. Providing choices such as "more than usual," "less than usual," and "about the same as usual" can elicit more accurate responses than relative terms such as "often."[12]

Some questions are ambiguous, leading to inconsistent responses and unreliable results.[13]

> **Example 1.** *"Do you believe that we should be conducting road checks for drunken drivers on a regular basis?"* (How often is *regular?* How would the new policy differ from the *status quo?*)
>
> **Example 2.** *"Should the United States be making more substantial contributions to the famine-plagued Somalians?"* (How much is *substantial?* What are we giving now? What must Americans give up to give more?)
>
> **Example 3.** *"Do you believe that government policies on the environment are effective?"* (Which level of government are you describing—national,

state, or local? What is meant by *effective?* Does the term imply short-term results or long-term results? Whose point of view is considered?)

Example 4. *"Do you agree or disagree with the following statement: The United States cannot afford to become involved in Yugoslavia."* (What do you mean by *afford?* Does the term have economic or social dimensions?) *Do you believe that U.S. policies regulating the flow of immigrants from Mexico to the United States are fair?* (*Fair* to whom? Mexicans or Americans?)

Example 5. *"Should we be taking stronger measures to protect the environment?"* (Are you referring to individuals or government? What do you mean by *stronger measures?* Do you mean stronger legislation? Stiffer penalties? Better enforcement of existing legislation? What will the trade-offs be regarding jobs and industry losses?)

Some questions just don't make much sense, no matter how you interpret them (e.g., asking people in different age groups whether they are satisfied with their level of physical activity). How is an 80-year-old individual to answer? What will a person with a physical limitation say? What does it mean if a 20-year-old indicates that he or she is *not* satisfied with the level of physical activity? Do they want more or less activity? The finding that 40-year-old individuals are *not* satisfied with their level of physical activity and that 70-year-old persons *are* satisfied is meaningless. You could interpret the data as saying that people in their 40s believe they could do more, and people in their 70s have accepted their limitations. On the other hand, you could interpret the data as saying that most 70-year-olds believe that they lead active lives, on the same terms as a 40-year-old person.

Before itemizing the choices available to a survey respondent, you should state the question. For example, don't say: *"Would you 'strongly agree', 'moderately agree', 'neither agree nor disagree', 'moderately disagree', or 'strongly disagree' that states should have more control than the federal government over equity issues?"* Instead, say: *"Some people say that states should have more control than the federal government over equity issues. Do you 'strongly agree', 'moderately agree', 'neither agree nor disagree', 'moderately disagree', or 'strongly disagree' "?*

"ACRONYMONIOUS" LANGUAGE

Survey questions should also be framed in simple, clear language. Use common terms to reach the lay public. Avoid compound and complex sentence structure. Restrict the use of jargon or specialized terms to interviews with professionals who understand the language. Bureaucrats, for example, often speak to each other in a language that means little to the average person. They talk about *target publics, politically correct decisions, strategies, people-at-risk, demonstration projects, bilateral programs, agricultural subsidies, immigration quotas,* and *initiatives.* They have very specific meanings for these terms, just as the lawyer who speaks of *moot court, affidavits,* and *habeas corpus.* The terms allow these groups and individuals to communicate with each other in a more precise way. Single words can carry a cargo of meanings to the insider, but to the lay public, the terms often sound like jabberwocky.[14]

Acronyms are also popular with bureaucrats and the military (e.g., SWAT teams, CEOs, the FDA, the FCC, POWs, MIAs, the GNP, ROTC). Such acronyms are useful; they allow people to communicate in shorthand. Sometimes, the abbreviated version of words becomes so common that people can't tell you what the acronyms stand for. Nonetheless, as a general rule, you should avoid the use of acronyms in surveys because the general public will not understand acronyms that evolve within a specific organizational culture.

DOUBLE-BARRELED QUESTIONS

Including two separate points in the same question forces the person being interviewed to make a choice between the two. The following examples illustrate this idea.

> **Example 1.** *"Do you support reducing taxes and restructuring the tax system to assist middle income families?"* It is quite conceivable that a person could support reducing taxes but not believe that restructuring of the tax system is necessary.
>
> **Example 2.** *"Do you find environmental measures to be effective and fair?"* A person may believe that current measures are effective but may also consider them unfair. Perhaps the individual thinks that the burden is being carried by the public instead of private industry.
>
> **Example 3.** *"Do you believe that immigration rules should give priority to seniors and children?"* Someone may believe that one group should have priority status but not the other.

Because each question in a survey should contain only one idea,[15] you should check carefully to see if you have used a conjunction such as *and* or *but* in a question. Also avoid questions that ask for both information and attitudes at the same time.

> **Example 1.** *"Do you engage in recycling, and how do you feel about your local community recycling programs?"*
>
> **Example 2.** *"Do you intend to vote in the next election, and would you support our candidate's position on make-work programs?"*

People can be confused by questions that use double negatives.[16] Suppose that you ask someone to agree or disagree with the following statements:

Example 1. *"The United States should not give further aid to Nicaragua."* If you disagree, you are saying that the United States should give additional aid.

Example 2. *"The company should not reduce salaries to protect jobs."* If you disagree, you are saying that the company should reduce salaries to protect jobs.

HYPOTHETICAL QUESTIONS

Be careful asking for reactions to hypothetical situations:[17]

Example 1. *"Would you volunteer for military service if the United States declared a second war against Iraq?"*

Example 2. *"Imagine our country is facing another world energy crisis. In such a situation, would you be willing to give up the use of your automobile for at least three days a week?"*

Example 3. *"If our airline merged with airline X, would you support the merger?"*

It is easy to respond "yes" so long as the situation is hypothetical, but a person might think twice before taking the actual step. Furthermore, it is rare that a hypothetical situation specifies all the ramifications or options. For example, employees might support a merger if they have guarantees their jobs will not be lost, that they will not be relocated, and that they will not have to take a pay cut. To improve the chances of obtaining valid information from a hypothetical question, you should be as specific as possible, for example: *"Would you support a merger if it meant that things basically remained the same for you in terms of job security, place of work, pay, etc.?"* The question is still hypothetical, but the specifics make it easier for the person to relate to the question on a realistic level. Some researchers suggest adding at least one question based on actual experience to balance any hypothetical questions; they also suggest probing at least one of the hypothetical questions.[18]

TRIGGERING RECALL

Survey respondents often have problems remembering fine details from the past. Most of us remember the most important life events (births, deaths, anniversaries, marriages). We may also recall major historical events (elections, wars, crises). Canadians will not soon forget, for example, the massacre of young female engineering students gunned down in the corridors of a Montreal polytechnical institute. Americans remember the assassination of John

Kennedy and the death of Marilyn Monroe. The British remember the Falklands, the Americans D-Day, and the Canadians Dieppe.

In general, it can be said that we remember the best and the worst. We are selective in what we recall, and we tend to allow lesser events to slip from our memories. In designing surveys, it is sometimes useful to place questions against some landmark event that people are likely to remember, in order to set the question in time. References to major holidays can also assist people in remembering.[19]

> **Example 1.** *Since the time of the Montreal Massacre, would you say that the women's movement in Canada has (a) grown stronger, (b) remained about the same, (c) grown weaker?*
>
> **Example 2.** *Since last Christmas, would you say that the company has made (a) steady progress toward its goal of achieving quality in customer service, (b) some progress toward its goal of achieving quality in customer service, or (c) no progress toward its goal of achieving quality in customer service.*

Using graphic, concrete terminology in a survey question can also trigger recall. Recall is aided by specificity.[20] For example, if you are eliciting people's views on television depiction of the fighting in Sarajevo, you could prompt recall in the following way:

> *Try to remember any scenes of people bleeding, bodies lying in the street, people in hospitals, graveyard mourners, etc. Would you say that this media coverage is probably (a) representative of the true situation in Sarajevo, (b) somewhat representative, or (c) not representative at all.*

Reducing the reference frame to six months or less sometimes helps:[21]

> **Example 1.** *Has your company established any new equity policies during the last six months?*
>
> **Example 2.** *Has correspondence from shareholders increased notably during the last four weeks?*

Even with a short reference frame, people will typically go beyond the period for which you are requesting information.[22] So if you ask what happened to someone in the last year, they might go back 18 months. If you asked what occurred in the past 6 months, they might take you back 9 or 10 months. Alternatively, they might *telescope,* or underreport, saying that an event occurred more recently than is actually the case. Respondents are telescoping when they say they attended a meeting last week but the meeting actually occurred three weeks ago.[23]

To cope with problems of overreporting and underreporting time periods, researchers have developed techniques such as *bounded recall.*[24] Bounded recall requires more than one interview with the same subject. In the first interview, you ask a subject to recall events of the preceding six months. In a subsequent interview, you ask the person what has happened in the six months since the first interview. By examining both sets of data, you can identify which events fell into the second time period. There are also other variations on the bounded recall technique. In one case, you ask about what happened in the time period previous to the one in which you have an interest; then you ask about the current time period.[25]

Other techniques for dealing with overreporting and underreporting of time periods include:

- Offer cues to stimulate recall (e.g., give a list of events or behaviors and ask about participation in these events or behaviors).
- Ask respondents to recall landmark events in their lives and to recount events that followed.
- Verify responses against more objective records (e.g., attendance records, calendars of events, ledgers, other official records, or accounts of other people).[26]

IT'S HARD TO SAY "I DON'T KNOW"

No one likes to appear uninformed or unintelligent. Most people assume that if a topic is important enough to appear in a survey that they should have a view on the issue or subject. Accordingly, some people will be reluctant to admit lack of familiarity with a topic. They may claim to have an attitude, even if they are uninformed. The number of people who are uninformed may be larger than we like to admit. As early as 1947, Gallup reported that public knowledge in some areas is extremely limited.[27] A number of other studies have reached similar conclusions. An attempt to test people's understanding of economics found that less than one third knew anything about the GNP.[28] Data derived from the University of Michigan Center for Political Studies confirmed the prevalence of voters who are "lamentably ill-informed" about issues and candidates:[29]

> Between 1956 and 1984 an average of 56 percent of the people queried were unable to identify the congressional candidates running for election from their district. The surveys were taken at the height of election campaigns, in an environment that has increasingly been saturated by a whole variety of media messages. In studies of more specific issues, citizen knowledge is also low.[30]

A California study that tested public knowledge of the nuclear power issue found the voters "highly skewed toward the low end of the knowledge scale," with 80 percent of those surveyed registering below the midpoint on the scale. This finding occurred, despite the fact that the researchers gave credit for partial answers.[31]

People will, nonetheless, often offer an opinion on topics about which they are ill-informed or uninformed. Studies demonstrate that between 10 percent and 15 percent of respondents "routinely lie to pollsters."[32] In one study, almost one third of those queried about an obscure agricultural trade act and a little-known monetary control bill voiced an opinion.[33] In another instance, one third of those surveyed expressed a point of view on a fictitious public affairs act.[34] Some studies have found significant support expressed for nonexistent politicians and bias against some fictitious groups.[35] University of Toronto political scientist Nelson Wiseman says that many people view surveys as tests they "don't want to flunk."[36]

Filter questions can be useful in eliminating or, at least, identifying uninformed respondents. Consider the following filter question. "Have you heard of company X's plan to invest in Russian industry? If *yes,* continue. If *no,* skip to Part II of the questionnaire." In this example, the survey identifies those who are basically uninformed on the details of the investment scheme. Having a second part to the survey (even if you do not intend to analyze the responses to this section) suggests to the uninformed that they are not alone in their lack of knowledge. In the second part of the survey, you could ask about other issues that respondents consider to be more important, or you could find out why they have not taken the time to become informed on the issue.

It can also be helpful to establish a frame of reference that will take the level of respondents' knowledge into account.

> **Example 1.** If you want to find out how employees would react to a revised policy that would allow some people to work at home, you could state in the preface to a questionnaire or in the introduction to an interview: *"Some people have expressed a preference for working at home. They believe they will be able to accomplish more if they spend fewer hours commuting. Under the present policy, all permanent employees are required to be physically present in the office. Do you agree that the company should allow interested employees the opportunity to work at home?"*
>
> **Example 2.** If a company is trying to find out whether people like its new logo better than the old logo, the person conducting the survey could ask: *"You may have noticed that company X recently changed its logo. By logo, I mean its trade symbol. If I show you a picture of the old logo and the new logo, could you tell me which one you like better."*

I HAVEN'T THOUGHT ABOUT IT LATELY, BUT IF I DID, I WOULDN'T CARE

Often people have limited knowledge of an issue or product, but if someone asks them to rank order the issue or evaluate the product, they will accommodate the interviewer and assign a value. They may, however, have never thought about the question or, more important, they may not care. Their responses will, nonetheless, receive the same weighting in the final analysis of results as the responses of people who know and care about the issue or product.

Example 1. *How important is it for the United States to build a dam in Ewaktotok?* Even if the public recognizes the issue, they may never have had reason to consider it.

Example 2. *Do you believe that U.S. corporations should adopt a more global focus?* The average American may have no idea what this orientation implies; moreover, those who do understand the question may never have had reason to form an opinion.

Example 3. *How important is it for company X to expand its product line into nontraditional areas?* Only individuals who have intimate knowledge of the functioning of the company may be equipped to answer the question. The average person and sometimes even the average employee may have no basis for forming an opinion.

There are many issues that are important to decision makers, but the public has relinquished responsibility for these issues to their leaders. Unless the issues bear directly on the well-being of the public, they may not follow the issues in the news or discuss them. Despite this fact, few surveys attempt to measure factors such as level of commitment.[37]

A classic study into the political belief systems of American voters concluded that ''large portions of an electorate do not have meaningful beliefs, even on issues that have formed the basis for intense political controversy among elites for substantial periods of time.''[38] Average people fail to develop more ''global points of view''; they are unable to respond to questions about policy in abstract or ideological terms, and they are unable to relate politics to policy.[39] During the 1960s and midway through the 1970s, this situation appeared to be changing as voters showed a higher level of ideological and issue orientation.[40] Viet Nam, civil rights, and law and order were but a few of many issues that claimed the attention of the public. More recent research, however, shows a tendency for today's youth to place considerably less importance on public interest issues than did their peers in earlier years.[41] Some studies are finding the U.S. public's factual knowledge of politics is lower than it was in the 1940s and 1950s; it is said that women, younger adults, and the less educated know less about political issues than men, older adults, and the more educated. This trend is said to have been influenced by this same factor of declining public interest.[42]

Researchers suggest that forcing an opinion toward a topic about which a person has little knowledge or interest is less than useful.[43] In order to avoid forcing opinions, some researchers use filter questions (discussed in the previous chapter). Filter questions allow a respondent to omit questions that they don't have an opinion on or that are not relevant to their circumstances. It is also possible to ask questions that elicit the frequency with which respondents have been discussing the issue with friends and family.[44] Alternatively, you can ask a series of questions that lead toward the major policy question.[45]

In the same way, people may not know *why* they believe as they do. If you ask "why," you may get misleading responses from people who search to find a socially acceptable reason for their beliefs or behavior. For that reason, some researchers caution against asking "why" questions.[46]

Some researchers have found that if you ask survey respondents to view an issue from different perspectives, their responses will vary, according to the perspective they take. For example, if asked to respond as consumers, they will answer one way. If asked to respond as citizens, they will respond differently.[47] As consumers, they may like the idea of legalized gambling. As citizens, they may oppose legalized gambling, believing it will bring crime into the community. How you frame your question will influence the response that you obtain.

IT SHOULD MATTER—SO I GUESS IT DOES

Sometimes, the public will recognize an issue as important on some idealistic scaling, but the issue will rate low on their private agendas. Ranked against domestic issues like employment, taxes, and health care, most foreign affairs issues will assume a low priority. Nonetheless, if queried, people will recognize some of these issues as embodying principles of importance to democratic society.

Example 1. If you ask the question, *"How important is it for this country to be a member of the United Nations?"* most people would say "very important." Forced to make a choice, they give the issue the rating that they regard to be appropriate to the values embodied in the issue.

To label some issues as unimportant is to violate the American dream.

Example 2. The issue of sanctions against South Africa is linked to human rights and minority rights—concerns that rank high, at least on a rhetorical level, in the American value system. The average American recognizes that he or she is supposed to care about these issues. From grade school on, Americans are told that everyone is created equal. They are told that race, sexual orientation, age, etc., should not matter. When asked in a person-on-the-street interview whether the issue of sanctions is *"very important," "important," "neither important nor unimportant," "not very important,"* or *"not important at all,"* many will respond in a predictable fashion. The largest number will probably agree that the issue is *"important"* or *"very important."* The value of equality is at the heart of the sanctions issue—a disenfranchised people discriminated against on the basis of the color of their skin. Yet when people are faced with a stagnant economy, runaway inflation, escalating health care costs, high gasoline prices, and the threat of military involvement in another part of the world, they do not place the issue of sanctions high on their everyday private agendas.

How useful are forced responses? They could be potentially valuable if you were compiling a psychographic profile of your audience. The information has less value if you want to predict the swell of public opinion on critical issues. You could be led, erroneously, to believe that some issues have a more important weighting to people than is the reality.

PLEASING THE INTERVIEWER

People who are being surveyed will often look to the interviewer to obtain cues about how they are expected to answer. People don't like to displease interviewers. The nonverbal behavior of the interviewer (e.g., a smile, a nod, a grimace, a frown, or a look of boredom) can influence the response to a question.

There is also a phenomenon called *acquiescence response set,* a tendency for some people to agree, no matter how a question is phrased.[48] For example, asking people to agree or disagree with the following statements encourages an acquiescence response: *"Government should see everyone gets adequate health care"* or *"Everyone should be responsible for his or her own health care."* Asking the question in a different way can help to control for this response tendency: *"Should government or the individual be responsible for health care?"*

I'M ALL IN FAVOR, BUT WHAT DID YOU SAY IT COSTS?

Sometimes, questions do not state what has to be given up in order to obtain an end result.

Example 1. If you ask the question, *"Do you think it is important to give increased job opportunities to disadvantaged minorities?"* most people would respond "yes." If, however, you asked the question, *"Would you support increased job opportunities for disadvantaged minorities if it meant fewer job opportunities for you?"* you might get a different response.

Example 2. If you asked the question, *"Do you support subsidized food banks for the poor?"* many people would respond positively. If you asked, *"Would you be in favor of subsidized food banks for the poor if it* *meant higher taxes?''* the answer might be different. Almost everything has its price, but questions often fail to mention what it is.

Some costs may be strategic rather than economic in nature. Polls during the first term of the Reagan administration showed support for a nuclear freeze, but only for a "verifiable and balanced freeze agreement." Of those who claimed to know or care about U.S. policy, many doubted whether the Soviet Union genuinely wanted a nuclear freeze. Still fewer individuals felt positive toward the political activists who were behind the debate.[49] Support for many issues is conditional; the most useful surveys will try to capture this kind of information.

PERCENTAGES CAN BE PROBLEMATIC

Many people have difficulty answering questions that involve estimating percentages. Yet surveys often ask people to report the percentage of time or money spent on different activities, for example:

- The percentage of time spent on activities external to the organization.
- The percentage of the budget devoted to media-monitoring activities.
- The relative emphasis placed on different issues.

People usually end up guessing about allocation of time and money, and the guesses may be reasonably accurate or very inaccurate. If you believe it is important to obtain percentages, ask a series of questions that will enable you to calculate the percentages.[50] Also, frame questions so that you ask for "typical" or "average" amounts of time spent on a task or activity, for example:

- *How many hours in a typical week do you spend watching television, listening to radio, and reading magazines and newapapers?*
- *How many hours in a typical week do you devote to reading magazines?*
- *How many hours in a typical week do you devote to reading news magazines?*

The answers to these three questions enable you to calculate percentages.

BIAS ASSOCIATED WITH PERSONALIZING OF ISSUES

Public opinion research over the last decade suggests a tendency for "the population to adopt right-wing attitudes on general issues but left-wing perspectives on specifics."[51]

Example 1. Canadian public opinion research shows high levels of support for "cutbacks in government expenditures" but strong opposition to "cuts in major expenditure areas such as education and health."[52]

Example 2. The public, in the same way, opposes the general concept of increasing immigration but supports allowing increased numbers of specific groups into the country.[53]

Personalizing more general concepts appears to make a difference to how people respond to a survey question.

PRESTIGE EFFECTS

Prestige effects can occur when you include a reference to a prestigious or well-known person in a question (e.g., the President of the United States or the company CEO).[54] The following question could evoke this type of bias: *"Do you support the CEO's environmental policies?"* This question has two weaknesses. The first weakness is its reference to the CEO. The position that this individual occupies is the highest position in the company, a position to which the average employee assigns credibility and prestige. Studies indicate that a certain number of people will agree with prestige figures, no matter what the question or issue. Second, this question includes a term that is very broad: *environmental policies.* Today, most companies have more than one component to their environmental policies.[55] Many companies have an entire unit devoted to dealing with environmental concerns. Framing such a broad question further encourages the person to rely on the prestige source.

It is possible that a source could also bias a question in the opposite direction, for example, including a reference to a union leader in a survey directed at corporate executives. *"Do you support union leader Robert White's position on the U.S.-Mexico-Canada free trade pact?"* If the executive has any doubts about the potential impact of the agreement on the industry, he or she might hesitate to agree with a union leader because the two have traditionally represented different interest groups.

ORDER EFFECTS

Several different kinds of order effects can occur. First, it has been found that people are more likely to agree to opinion items that appear early in a survey than to those that appear later in the same survey.[56] Second, people learn as they participate in a survey. They use cues from some questions to answer other questions. Early in a questionnaire, you may ask an employee to rate the quality of some employment equity practices that have been undertaken by an organization (e.g., "fast-tracking" women and visible minorities; affirmative action hiring policies; access to career counseling for employees who are members of minorities; increased access to training programs for these same individuals; and cross-cultural training for managers to sensitize them to minority group needs and cultures). If, later in the survey, you ask the respondent to evaluate the company's commitment to employment equity, you will have influenced the response that you obtain.

Third, some questions bias the responses given to other questions.

Example 1. Assume you are soliciting the views of people on the topic of free trade. Other questions you include in your questionnaire can influence the answers you get to your main question. For example, if you precede your question on free trade with the question, *"Do you believe in opening up more markets in which U.S. industry can sell its goods?"* you will prompt one answer. If, on the other hand, you precede the question on free trade with the query, *"Do you believe in allowing other countries freer entry to the U.S. market?"* you may get a different response.

Example 2. If you ask questions about job losses prior to asking a more general question about corporate performance, you will influence the response to the latter question.

Question order effects occur most frequently with less-educated respondents.[57] Some researchers recommend randomizing the order of questions to overcome these kinds of problems, but others say that randomizing question order results in a chaotically ordered and confusing questionnaire. Respondents may react negatively to the seeming lack of coherency to the questionnaire. Researchers may find it more difficult to identify contextual biases. The best approach may be to become sensitive to the potential for order effects. Alternatively, you can construct more than one version of your questionnaire and give different versions to different respondents. Some researchers recommend pretesting the questionnaire, using different formats, to determine order effects.[58] This latter approach would facilitate identification of problem areas.

"IT'S NOT OVER 'TILL THE FAT LADY SINGS"

Despite their 1936 experience, 12 years later in 1948, the pollsters, including Gallup this time, proved their fallibility when they predicted that Thomas Dewey would win over Harry Truman. It is now believed that the polling exercise finished too soon to predict the steady trend toward Truman. The largest number of those who were undecided apparently voted for Truman. Shortcomings in quota sampling techniques are believed to have contributed to this inaccurate prediction.[59] A more recent example of the same phenomenon occurred in 1980 when pollsters predicted that Ronald Reagan would win over Jimmy Carter by only the narrowest of margins. They reported the race as being "too close to call."[60] Like Truman's win, the extensiveness of Reagan's victory was explained by the failure of the pollsters to pick up last-minute voting trends. Those who continued to survey until election day were more successful in gauging the margin between victor and vanquished. Whereas Gallup and the *New York Times*/CBS polls ceased their operations four days prior to election day, the ABC News/Harris organizations polled up to election day. The earlier polls showed a 1 percent margin in favor of Reagan; the latter polls showed a 5 percent margin. More aware of what was happening, Patrick Caddell, Jimmy Carter's pollster, is said to have warned Carter of a "severe hemorrhage of support in the final days before the election."[61]

Canadian pollster Angus Reid says that it is important to keep track of undecided respondents. He describes an example of poll results being misinterpreted because people failed to keep track of the undecided vote:

> Soon after the first televised "leaders" debates in the 1984 election, a stunning verdict was delivered by the polls—Liberal support among decided voters had dropped a full seven points. For Canadians, this news implied that many thousands of Liberal supporters had switched their allegiance to the Conservatives. What actually happened was the number of undecided voters had dropped from 30 percent to 20 percent, and most of these went to the Conservatives.[62]

In any campaign, a certain percentage of the vote is "soft," (i.e., voters have only weak party allegiances). In the 1988 Canadian federal election, 23 percent of conservative, 37 percent of liberal and 23 percent of the new democratic supporters were soft in that they expressed uncertainty about whom they planned to support—they were " 'leaners' who can and will switch direction."[63]

This same tendency toward respondent indecision can be seen in other similar situations. Survey results taken a month before the Canadian referendum revealed that the "yes" camp for a new Constitutional accord had 42 percent public support, the "no" camp had 41 percent support, and the undecided vote was at 17 percent.[64] These figures fluctuated from day to day by a significant number of points, showing that public opinion was capable of being moved in either direction, depending on who was interviewed by the media on a particular day. The stock market reflected this uncertainty. When former Prime Minister Pierre Trudeau spoke against the accord, the Canadian dollar dropped to its lowest level in recent years.

In the above case, only 45 percent of those in the "yes" and "no" camps (as reported in one survey) said they were "certain" about their vote. It was not uncommon for politicians to boast that they had dramatically increased the odds for their point of view "since yesterday." When those voting "yes" were asked "why" they were voting "yes," they gave two major reasons. One of these two reasons was issue fatigue.[65] They wanted the Constitutional debate to end and business to go on as usual, scarcely a sound foundation for building confidence in a solid vote at the polls. Some analysts say that these kinds of results prove the fluidity of public opinion, which is attributable not to public apathy or ignorance of political process but to a growing cynicism and a general erosion of confidence in traditional institutions and authorities.[66]

For the above reasons, it is important for surveys to take commitment into account: "Measures of commitment are harbingers of what lies in store for the public opinion formation process. They can be used to detect areas of strength and vulnerability and should be included as a central element in any public affairs undertaking."[67]

It is important to remember that public opinion polls are only "snapshots in time,"[68] and we must remember their limitations. We must never accept the results of a single poll as an indicator of public opinion: "Polls cannot predict anything. Today's poll is tomorrow's history. The results of a good poll reflect the opinion of the target population when the questions were asked. People can—and will—change their minds for all sorts of reasons in an instant or over time."[69]

BIASED REPORTING OF SURVEY RESULTS

Not all the problems associated with surveys result from sampling or design error. Many originate with the people who interpret the surveys. Given a statistical analysis of survey results, news organizations translate survey statistics into language that is more palatable to the public. In doing so, they may inject bias, intentional or unintentional, into the survey results. Let us assume that a public opinion survey finds that 49 percent of Americans are in favor of military action against the Serbians in Yugoslavia and 51 percent are opposed. A newspaper that wants to push military involvement could legitimately publish the following headline: "Near Majority of Americans Favor Military Action Against Serbs." A newspaper that is against military action could use a very different headline: "Americans Oppose Military Action in Yugoslavia." Still another newspaper could publish the headline: "Americans Ambivalent about Military Move Against Serbs." In essence, the headline writer (usually an individual different from the one who writes the story) has the choice of reporting the glass as being "half empty" or "half full." If the headline writer is aware of a bias within the community or media hierarchy for one point of view over another, it is likely that the writer will opt for the more agreeable interpretation. It can be speculated that the more high profile the issue, the more likely it is that the majority opinion of the community and/or news organization will be represented in the headline.

Sometimes, reporting bias is unintentional. Canadian pollster Angus Reid said it is not unusual for polls to be "misunderstood and sometimes misinterpreted by the media."[70] In the example discussed previously, increases in support for one candidate may be read by the inexperienced as losses for the other candidate. In actual fact, it may be that the "undecideds" are making up their minds. There may be no loss of confidence on the part of those who earlier expressed support for a favored candidate. It is important in reporting survey results to include points such as *margin of error* so that the public can make their own judgments on what they read. This point is discussed in more detail in the preceding chapter.

Because of the problems associated with reporting of poll results, the U.S. National Council on Public Polls recently published a guide to interpreting poll results titled *Twenty Questions a Journalist Should Ask About Poll Results.*[71]

SUMMARY OF POTENTIAL POINTS OF BIAS IN SURVEYING

Some common problem areas in sampling procedures and questionnaire design include the following:

- Contaminated samples.
- Loaded and leading questions.
- Embarrassing questions.
- Questions with a hidden agenda.
- Relative wording.
- Unclear and ambiguous questions.
- Specialized jargon and bureaucratese.
- Double-barreled questions.
- Double negatives.
- Hypothetical questions.

Some common problems associated with the psychology of the respondent include the following:

- Attempts to please the interviewer.
- Memory problems on the part of the respondent.
- Knowledge gaps on the part of the respondent.
- Lack of respondent opinion on topic.
- Tendency to give answers that reflect socially acceptable values.
- Tendency of respondent to weigh cost-benefit factors.
- Difficulty with translating numbers into percentages.
- Tendency of respondent to be influenced by personalizing of issues.
- Tendency of respondent to be influenced by prestige effects.
- Tendency of respondent to be influenced by order effects.

Some common problems associated with administration of surveys and interpretation of surveys include the following:

- Tendency to extend the results of a survey beyond the date of surveying.
- Tendency to extrapolate too much from surveys.
- Biased reporting of survey results (intentional or unintentional).

Organizations will do well to take these kinds of factors into consideration when they design and administer their surveys.

NOTES

1. Peverill Squire, "Why the 1936 *Literary Digest* Poll Failed," *Public Opinion Quarterly,* Spring 1988, pp. 125–33.

2. James H. Frey, *Survey Research by Telephone,* 2nd ed. (Newbury Park, Calif.: Sage Publications, 1989), pp. 22–23.

3. Earl Babbie, *Survey Research Methods,* 2nd. ed. (Belmont, Calif.: Wadsworth, 1990), p. 67.

4. Angus Reid, "Pollsters Often Misunderstood, Reid Says," *Ottawa Citizen,* October 4, 1988, p. A4.

5. Jerry L. Yeric and John R. Todd, *Public Opinion: The Visible Politics,* 2nd ed. (Itasca, Ill.: F. E. Peacock Publishers, 1989), pp. 91–92.

6. Angus Reid, "Public Affairs Research: Quantitative and Qualitative," in *The Canadian Public Affairs Handbook: Maximizing Markets, Protecting Bottom Lines,* eds. W. Wright and Christopher J. DuVernet (Toronto: Carswell, 1988), p. 143.

7. Jean M. Converse and Stanley Presser, *Survey Questions: Handcrafting the Standardized Questionnaire* (Newbury Park, Calif.: Sage Publications, 1986), pp. 13–14.

8. Babbie, p. 141.

9. Charles F. Cannell and Robert L. Kahn, "The Collection of Data by Interviewing," in *Research Methods in the Behavioral Sciences,* eds. Leon Festinger and Daniel Katz (New York: Dryden Press, 1953), pp. 327–80. Cannell is probably the most often cited researcher in the area of survey interviewing. Some of his early studies, such as this one, became benchmarks in the literature on the best survey practices.

10. Arlene Fink and Jacqueline Kosecoff, *How to Conduct Surveys: A Step-by-Step Guide* (Newbury Park, Calif.: Sage Publications, 1985), p. 32.

11. Nora Cate Schaeffer, "Hardly Ever or Constantly: Group Comparisons Using Vague Quantifiers," *Public Opinion Quarterly,* Fall 1991, p. 395.

12. Ibid.

13. Floyd J. Fowler, Jr., and Thomas W. Mangione, *Standardized Survey Interviewing: Minimizing Interviewer-Related Error* (Newbury Park, Calif.: Sage Publications, 1990), pp. 86–87.

14. See Norma M. Williams, Gideon Sjoberg, and Andrée F. Sjoberg, "The Bureaucratic Peronality: An Alternate View," in *Organizational Communication,* eds. Sherry Ferguson and Stewart Ferguson (New Brunswick, N.J.: Transaction Publishers, 1988) for a discussion of how bureaucrats use ambiguity in language to communicate meaning to insiders.

15. Cannell and Kahn, pp. 327–80.

16. Converse and Presser, p. 13.

17. Ibid., p. 20.

18. Ibid., p. 23.

19. Converse and Presser, pp. 20–22.

20. Ibid., p. 31.

21. Ibid., p. 21.

22. Ibid., pp. 20–23.

23. Ibid.

24. Ibid.

25. This latter technique, *specific bounded recall,* is discussed by Converse and Presser, p. 21.

26. Frey, pp. 170–71.

27. Cited in Converse and Presser, pp. 24–25.

28. Lee Sigelman and Ernest Yanarella, "Public Information on Public Information: A Multivariate Analysis," *Social Science Quarterly,* June 1986, pp. 402–10.

29. Yeric and Todd, p. 105.

30. Ibid.

31. James H. Kuklinski, Daniel S. Metlay, and W. D. Kay, "Citizen Knowledge and Choices on the Complex Issue of Nuclear Energy," *American Journal of Political Science,* November 1982, pp. 615–42.

32. David Taras, *The Newsmakers: The Media's Influence on Canadian Politics* (Scarborough, Ont.: Nelson Canada, 1990), p. 189. Taras cites studies by I. Lewis and William Schneider, "Is the Public Lying to the Pollsters?" *Public Opinion,* April/May 1982, pp. 42–47, in support of this point.

33. Howard Schuman and Stanley Presser, *Questions and Answers in Attitude Surveys: Experiments on Question Form, Wording, and Context* (New York: Academic Press, 1981).

34. George Bishop, R. W. Oldendick, A. J. Tuchfarber, and S. E. Bennett, "Pseudo-Opinions on Public Affairs," *Public Opinion Quarterly* 44 (1980), pp. 198–209.

35. Lewis and Schneider, pp. 42–47, cited in Taras, pp. 189–90.

36. Claire Hoy, *Margin of Error* (Toronto: Key Porter Books, 1989), p. 90.

37. Reid, "Public Affairs Research," p. 137.

38. Phillip E. Converse, "The Nature of Belief Systems in the Mass Public," in *Ideology and Discontent,* ed. David Apter (New York: Free Press, 1964), p. 245. Converse's study is described by Yeric and Todd, p. 104, as "the model of the American citizen that has been accepted by the academic community and the popular press." It is considered a classic in the public opinion literature.
39. Converse, p. 247.
40. Norman H. Nie with Kristi Andersen, "Mass Belief Systems Revisited: Political Change and Attitude Structure," *Journal of Politics,* August 1974, pp. 540–91.
41. Richard Easterlin and Eileen M. Crimmins, "Private Materialism, Personal Self-Fulfillment, Family Life, and Public Interest: The Nature, Effects, and Causes of Recent Changes in the Values of American Youth," *Public Opinion Quarterly,* Winter 1991, pp. 500–501, 529.
42. Michael X. Delli Carpini and Scott Keeter, "Stability and Change in the U.S. Public's Knowledge of Politics," *Public Opinion Quarterly,* Winter 1991, pp. 583–612. The introduction to Chapter 8 suggests, however, that 1992 electoral and referendum results may contradict this trend.
43. Converse and Presser, p. 24.
44. Reid, "Public Affairs Research," pp. 141–42.
45. Converse and Presser, pp. 44–47.
46. Reid, "Public Affairs Research," pp. 142–43.
47. Ibid., p. 136.
48. Converse and Presser, pp. 38–39.
49. J. Michael Hogan and Ted J. Smith III, "Polling on the Issues: Public Opinion and the Nuclear Freeze," *Public Opinion Quarterly,* Winter 1991, pp. 534–69.
50. Ibid., p. 16.
51. Reid, "Public Affairs Research," p. 140.
52. Ibid.
53. Ibid.
54. Discussion of prestige effects is common in the literature on surveying. See, for example, Roger D. Wimmer and Joseph R. Dominick, *Mass Media Research: An Introduction,* 3rd. ed. (Belmont, Calif.: Wadsworth, 1992).
55. David T. Buzzeli, "Time to Restructure an Environmental Policy Strategy," *Journal of Business Strategy,* March/April 1991, pp. 17–20. Also Jacqueline S. Scerbinski, "Consumers and the Environment: A Focus on Five Products," *Journal of Business Strategy,* September/October 1991, pp. 44–47.
56. Mary John Smith, *Contemporary Communication Research Methods* (Belmont, Calif.: Wadsworth, 1988), p. 228.
57. J. Edwin Benton, "A Question Order Effect in A Local Government Survey," *Public Opinion Quarterly,* Winter 1991, p. 642.

58. Babbie, p. 141.

59. Ibid., p. 67.

60. See discussion in Yeric and Todd, pp. 231–33.

61. Ibid., quoted on p. 232.

62. Reid, "Pollsters Often Misunderstood," p. A4.

63. Ibid.

64. Julian Beltrame, "Yes Forces Trailing in Three Provinces," *Ottawa Citizen*, September 26, 1992, p. A1.

65. Ibid.

66. Everett C. Ladd and G. Donald Ferree, "Were the Pollsters Really Wrong?" *Public Opinion*, December/January 1981, pp. 13–14.

67. Reid, "Public Affairs Research," p. 136.

68. Yeric and Todd, p. 233.

69. Angela Mangiacasale, "The Problem with Polls," *Ottawa Citizen*, October 10, 1992, p. B3.

70. Reid, "Pollsters Often Misunderstood," p. A4.

71. Referenced by Mangiacasale, p. B3.

CHAPTER 8

RESEARCHING PUBLIC OPINION THROUGH FOCUS GROUPS

Focus groups have become increasingly popular in recent years. With the breakdown of traditional institutions, corporations, volunteer groups, and governments have come to rely on many techniques (including media tracking, surveys, and focus groups) to keep track of a volatile public opinion. The complexity of issues; the interplay of social, political, and economic forces in society; and the feeling that no one has the answers undermines the ability of leaders to persuade their publics and control their issues. Public confidence in politicians, government leaders, and corporate boardroom executives appears to be at an all-time low. Since the historical events of Watergate, the American public has developed a healthy cynicism for the positions taken by politicians. The popularity of a relative unknown, Texas billionaire Ross Perot, in the 1992 race for president demonstrated well the public disillusionment with establishment politics. Similar levels of skepticism and distrust characterize the response of many Americans to the perceived motives of big business and Wall Street traders.[1]

In general, there is a feeling among many that, as a country, America has lost the ability to generate leaders with either character or vision and foresight. The average citizen sees major corporations floundering, unsure how to save their failing industries and businesses. They read about record numbers of bankruptcies. They see politicians and government officials unable to take control of the deficit, the falling dollar, and other critical issues such as unemployment.

Recent events in other countries have suggested that this decline in public confidence in leaders is not unique to America. National referenda in France and Canada in 1992 confirmed this same public unwillingness to accept, without question, the decisions of those in positions of power. Joan Bryden, a Canadian journalist, wrote in October 1992, "After years of passively deferring to authority, Canadians seem poised to give a collective boot to all their political leaders. The October 26 plebiscite is supposed to be on the Charlottetown constitutional accord. Instead, for many Canadians, it's turned into a vote on the entire political system. So far at least, polls suggest a majority [of people] in at least two provinces . . . intend to use their vote to reject not only the accord but the first ministers who concocted it and the political, business, labor, academic and media elites who rushed to support it."[2] In fact, in the end, five provinces and the Yukon voted down the accord. Pollster Michael Adams of Environics said that many Canadians have come to the conclusion that "maybe these elites aren't all that smart after all," and the referendum offered an opportunity to repudiate them.[3] Former Prime Minister Joe Clark, who helped engineer the accord, stated that Canadians are, in essence, saying, "a plague on all your houses."[4] He said, "It seems the more you put out the so-called big boys . . . the more alienated people get. Someone said to me the other day, it's a good chance for people to say . . . No to politicians, No to big business, No to the unions and No to the media."[5]

In such an environment, marked by uncertainty and confusion, it is hard to fault corporate and government leaders for feeling that "tea leaves," "soothsaying journalists," "sorcerer consultants," and other "inside dopesters" may be about as reliable as any other sources for tracking public opinion.[6] So it is that leaders seek out the best prophets—the journalists who appear to be acting as opinion leaders for the pack, consultants who have a feeling for what the public wants and needs, legitimate pollsters, and the most reliable methodologies for assessing public opinion. Focus groups have come to be regarded as one of the more respectable means of acquiring these kinds of insights.

In the 1988 U.S. election, for example, the republicans boasted of the results that they obtained from New Jersey focus groups. Republican campaign advisers had conducted the focus groups to learn where Dukakis's weaknesses lay. Whereas surveys can tell where Americans stand on the most salient issues, focus groups can identify emerging or less-prominent issues that may not show up in surveys. In the case of the New Jersey focus groups, the results suggested that Americans strongly disagreed with Dukakis on two issues: his championing of weekend furloughs for criminal offenders and his rejection of a law that forced teachers to lead their students in the pledge of allegiance. It was on these two issues, rather than the critical pressing issues of the day such as the economy and unemployment, that Bush placed his campaign hopes.[7]

Although businesses most frequently use focus groups for marketing research, 53 percent of the Fortune 500 companies that responded to a 1992 survey said they use focus groups to prioritize issues and to scan and monitor their issues environment.[8] Thirty percent of the firms listed in *Canadian Business* (a directory of "top" performers in different sectors such as communications, mining, etc.), who responded to a similar 1991 survey, said they use focus groups as a means of prioritizing issues; 43 percent said they use focus groups for scanning purposes; and 33 percent said they employ focus groups for ongoing monitoring of opinion on priority issues.[9]

WHAT IS A FOCUS GROUP?

Focus groups are a special type of interview situation, a variant of quota sampling techniques (discussed in more detail in Chapter 6).[10] Focus groups involve a moderator and 7 to 12 participants, typically unacquainted with each other (researchers disagree on the optimum number of participants). Too few participants can mean that one or two individuals are able to dominate a discussion; too many participants result in inadequate opportunities for participation. Restricting the number of participants to four or five (as a few researchers have begun to advocate) does make it easier for the organization to fill the focus group and to establish a close friendly atmosphere, but the small number of participants have a more limited range of experiences to contribute to the group.

Organizational researchers often use focus groups as an exploratory technique to investigate new areas of interest, to look for unexpected insights, or to refine existing insights. They also use focus groups to gain a better understanding of why people hold certain attitudes and beliefs or why they behave as they do.[11] Some researchers argue that it is the only methodology that can be used successfully in the discussion of highly sensitive issues, for example, insurance fraud or human rights violations by corporations.[12] Focus groups permit an opportunity to acquire a more sophisticated understanding of people's reasoning processes. Senior management is said to be particularly drawn to this methodology.[13]

In a focus group, participants meet at a predetermined location at a given time to discuss a single topic. The topic may have more than one dimension, for example, legal, moral, economic, or other aspects of some issue. The discussions may be centered on:

- A candidate for office.
- An organization's image.
- A product.
- An idea.
- An issue.

Syracuse University used focus groups to help plan a major fund-raising drive. A county mental health department set up focus groups to plan a program.[14]

The focus group is relatively unstructured; it has a flexible format that can be adjusted by the moderator. The moderator introduces the subject and encourages the group members to discuss their perceptions, feelings, and opinions on the topic. From time to time, the moderator asks additional questions to stimulate interaction or to focus the discussion on areas that interest the researcher or the organization sponsoring the focus group.

COMPOSITION OF THE GROUP

Research has shown that homogeneous groups work best, in other words, groups of people who have similar characteristics in terms of education, expertise, income level, age, and social class.[15] People who perceive themselves to be inferior to other group members in educational accomplishments, socioeconomic status, or expertise tend to be poor participants; they are uncomfortable voicing their views and often defer to the opinions of other higher-status members. Bringing together individuals of widely varying ages can generate adult-child interactions, whereby some members behave paternalistically and others rebel against authority figures.

The introduction of too many different arguments and viewpoints into one focus group can also confuse the results. In an organizational setting, for example, it may be counterproductive to have too many different business units represented in one focus group. The members may tend to engage in territorial behavior, defending their special organizational interests.

Although some focus groups may be composed of experts, it is not wise to place one or two experts in a larger group of relatively uninformed individuals. The presence of the expert may act as a deterrant to group participation. In other instances, the expert will dominate the discussion.

Men and women communicate differently. Studies show:

- Men tend to dominate discussions in which women are present. They do this partly by "interrupting women or answering questions not addressed to them."[16]
- Men often initiate new topics of conversation rather than acknowledging or responding to comments by women.
- Delayed listening responses, overlapping comments, and interruptions serve to have a subduing impact on women.[17]
- Men tend to "perform" for women.[18]
- Women complain that they have a difficult time getting and holding attention in group situations with men.
- Women tend to take on "stroking" behaviors such as nodding and confirming the contributions of men with "yes," "mmh," etc.
- Women use tag questions; they make an assertion but ask for follow-up confirmation. An example of a tag question is *"Multinational organizations have too much power. Don't you think so?"*[19]

These kinds of differences in patterns of communication imply the need for separation of the sexes in some focus-group situations. It has been observed that, particularly in instances where husbands and wives are brought together in focus groups, wives tend to defer to the views of their husbands. Even when a wife disagrees with her husband, she may remain silent. Therefore, focus groups composed of four married couples yield the results that a focus group of four *individuals* might generate.[20]

If an organization wants to learn the perceptions and views of several different categories of people, the researcher should include these individuals in the testing procedure but conduct a *series* of focus groups, with different kinds of people in each group.[21] In such a case, a maximum of four focus groups, made up of individuals with similar characteristics, is generally required.[22] Some say that it is wise to evaluate the findings of the third focus group; if no new information is generated by the third group, the fourth focus group is probably not required. If additional insights are gained in the third group, plans for a fourth and, perhaps, additional focus groups may be warranted. More extensive focus-group testing may be necessary for statewide or nationwide studies, and as many as a dozen sessions may be required.[23] With heterogeneous groups, you will need more sessions than with homogeneous groups.[24]

SOLICITING PARTICIPATION

The purpose of any study should determine who is invited to join a focus group. Groups can be selected randomly or nonrandomly (see discussion on sampling techniques in Chapter 6). Names can be pulled from existing membership lists, directories, or organizational files. Alternatively, names can be solicited from relevant organizations, perhaps with a promise of a donation to the group. At the end of sessions, participants can be asked to suggest the name of a friend or family member to participate in some future group. Intercept techniques may also be used, whereby individuals are recruited "on location." For example, participants may be recruited at an exhibit or other activity, which is likely to be visited by individuals with the desired characteristics. Finally, telephone screening techniques can be used. With telephone screening techniques, names are randomly selected from a telephone directory; follow-up calls are made to determine if the individuals possess the required characteristics to become focus-group participants. Success with this last technique depends greatly upon the interpersonal skills of the person conducting the screening.

Snowball sampling techniques may be used (i.e., participants are invited to bring a friend to the focus group). Some researchers, however, caution against having friends in the same group, saying that the following problems can result:[25]

- Friends discourage anonymity.
- Friends can cause a breakdown in group process by "pairing off."
- Friends may engage in private conversation that disrupts and inhibits the expression of views by others.
- Friends tend to endorse each others' views.

Other techniques used by public institutions and nonprofit organizations to solicit participation in focus groups also have been found to yield poor results, for example, newsletter announcements, form-letter invitations, announcements at meetings.[26]

One focus group facilitator discussed the kinds of problems that can result when the wrong techniques are used to solicit focus group participation. He said he had found several major flaws in the traditional invitations that his firm used:[27]

- Our invitations were not personalized.
- We had no follow up to the original written invitation.
- We asked people to attend a discussion on a seemingly insignificant topic.
- We were unaware of the seasonal time demands on some audiences.
- We did not build on existing social and organizational relationships.
- We did not offer incentives.

People need to understand why they have been selected to participate in the focus group. Follow-up correspondence to the original invitation should include meeting times that don't conflict with work schedules, sporting events, or the beginning of fall network TV shows.[28] Follow-up letters should arrive approximately a week before the meeting time. Last-minute reminders, either via phone or mail on the day before the meeting are important for all participants. The anonymity of telephone screening methods suggests the need to overrecruit by 20 percent to ensure sufficient numbers in groups.[29]

A small incentive, in the form of money, a gift, or a meal, may be offered to focus-group participants. Cash incentives typically range from $10 to $100. Gifts (e.g., alarm clocks, calculators, and telephones) usually range in value from $5 to $20. The size of the incentive is often related to the difficulty researchers have securing the cooperation of people in that group of society. For example, an incentive of $15 to $25 is a typical amount paid to secure the participation of members of the general public (e.g., male or female heads of household). Middle managers or engineers would receive incentives in the $25 to $50 range.[30] Some researchers say it is not uncommon to pay in excess of $50 to professionals, and incentives paid to physicians and lawyers would probably exceed $100. "Substantial cash incentives may be required to secure the participation of top-level executives."[31] Holding a session at a prestigious location, serving refreshments, and explaining the value of the study further enhance the chances that people will agree to participate and will arrive at the designated place and time.[32]

Limited information on the purpose of the focus group is offered in introductory communications to prevent the likelihood that some individuals will plan their responses in advance by soliciting the views of friends and other family members. Specific information on the sponsorship and purpose of a study can be given at the end of the focus-group session.

ESTABLISHING A FRIENDLY ENVIRONMENT

Focus groups are conducted in many different kinds of settings, from "professional rooms equipped with two-way mirrors to motel rooms rented for the occasion."[33] Conference rooms are used when available. It is important that participants feel at ease in the focus-group situation. One of the ways of establishing this sense of well-being is by choosing a pleasant physical environment for the central meeting location. Buildings and their layouts influence the type of interactions that occur within. The nature and size of a room do make a difference; more positive exchanges have been found to occur in "beautiful" rooms. Level of noise, lighting, degree of privacy, colors, and location also can influence interpersonal interactions.[34] The room should be set up and the temperature should be adjusted before the participants arrive.

Some settings encourage interaction (e.g., chairs placed in circles bring people together); other settings discourage interaction (e.g., bolted down chairs in airports hold people apart).[35] The placement of chairs, desks, and sofas in a room influences both the quality and quantity of communication. Individuals seated at the end of long rectangular tables have an advantage over others in terms of perceived dominance. It has been found that persons occupying the corners of such tables contribute least to discussions. A squared-off or circular table, on the other hand, maximizes eye contact and minimizes distance between group participants, encouraging more participation and sharing of power.[36] Seating participants around such a table is a preferred arrangement.

It has been suggested that a "coffee klatch" or "bull session" atmosphere works best for focus groups.[37] A centrally placed table should be sufficiently large to accommodate the 7 to 12 people who attend the session. Some researchers recommend seating experts and loud participants next to the moderator and seating quiet participants directly across from the moderator. Eye contact encourages responses; lack of eye contact discourages interactions.[38]

Focus groups conducted at work locations can be problematic because superior-subordinate interactions can impede the process. Employees may be reluctant to speak openly and honestly in front of their superiors. Superiors may feel the need to mask their true feelings and motivations in front of subordinates. Status factors can be powerful inhibitors to group discussion.

The moderator must establish an atmosphere that is conducive to openness and sharing. People must be made to feel that their ideas and contributions are important to the success of the meeting. A facilitator who relates well to people will have the best chance of establishing this kind of tone. Name tags will help participants to become acquainted, and they will make it easier for facilitators to call on people by name. In some situations, however, especially if sensitive topics (e.g., sexual harassment, family violence, or supervisor-subordinate relationships) are discussed, participants may not want to be recognized by their last names. The moderator may want to invite individuals to share private thoughts or experiences on paper, which are then passed to the moderator. The moderator maintains the anonymity of the contributor but shares the idea or experience with the group.

Appointing an assistant can free a moderator to concentrate on the group discussion. The assistant attends to details such as videotaping or sound recording sessions, ensures that the physical needs of participants are met, and welcomes late arrivals.

STEPS IN CONDUCTING THE FOCUS GROUP

The following points should be included in the moderator's opening comments.

1. The moderator welcomes group members.
2. The moderator gives an overview of the topic.
3. The moderator previews the agenda for the focus-group session.
4. The moderator discusses the basis on which the participants were selected.
5. The moderator stresses the importance of hearing from all group members.
6. The moderator emphasizes that there are no right or wrong answers but only different points of view.
7. The moderator stresses that negative as well as positive observations are solicited.
8. The moderator should indicate if confidentiality is to be protected.
9. The moderator should mention if sessions are being recorded and explain the purpose for these recordings.
10. In the introduction to the session, the facilitator should refer to the length of the discussions, break times (if any), and availability of refreshments.
11. The moderator should explain policies on smoking.
12. The moderator should also establish ground rules (e.g., expectations regarding turn taking).
13. The group facilitator may begin the discussion by asking members to introduce themselves.
14. The moderator will ask group participants to withhold specific information in making their introductions if the information could bias later interactions (e.g., occupational status or position in the community).

In a focus group, the first question should be an "ice breaker" (e.g., focus-group members can be asked to share stories or anecdotes on the topic being discussed). Alternatively, a *stimulus* can be used to initiate discussion, for example, "an object, a drawing, a slide or transparency, a story board, or a complete communication product such as a public service announcement."[39] Sometimes, a group will be asked to react to a videotape or an audio recording.[40]

Most focus-group discussions move from the general to the specific. Moderators may open a discussion with open-ended questions and follow up with more closed ones. It is best to avoid becoming too specific too soon in a focus group. Given the proper context, participants will move in a natural way toward the topic of interest. Nonetheless, even though the discussion format will be flexible, the moderator should keep on hand prepared questions in case the issues are not raised or the discussion dies prematurely. The moderator should memorize key questions (usually no more than 10) in advance of the focus-group session. Rules governing the development of questions for focus groups will be similar to those discussed in the preceding chapter on survey questions.

Focus groups have purposes, and throughout the discussion the moderator should be consciously gauging the extent to which those purposes have been met. The moderator must never lose sight of where the group should be at the end of the discussion. At some point, it may be necessary to encourage a narrowing of focus in order to address the researchers' main areas of interest. Occasional summaries may help to refocus a group that has strayed too far off the topic. Gentle prompting can also lead a group back on track. The moderator must follow the mood of the group; when interest flags, he or she must be ready to move the group toward the next issue.

Focus group discussions can be divided into six stages:[41]

1. A rapport-building stage that establishes relations and clarifies the task.

2. An exploratory stage that allows participants to answer broad questions.

3. A probing stage that narrows the topic areas to those that are of special interest to the researcher.

4. A task stage that could entail, for example, writing a slogan or using projective techniques.

5. An evaluation stage that may include some stimulus to create interaction.

6. A closing stage that elicits any final input from the participants and allows the moderator to obtain any remaining information.

Not all stages will occur in every focus group. Some researchers use supplementary questionnaires to solicit additional information from the focus group. Other researchers argue that you should collect only demographic data on questionnaires; they say that responding to a questionnaire can bias later responses in the focus group or, alternatively, the focus-group interaction can determine how a person later fills out a questionnaire.[42]

Part of maintaining a friendly interpersonal environment is beginning and ending a focus group session on time. Group members may become openly hostile if held beyond the time for which they have been asked to meet. Therefore, the moderator must manage time well (i.e., keep the group sufficiently on track to cover all points that are raised, while not stifling or shutting off discussion too soon in important areas). The average focus-group session lasts for approximately two hours.[43]

INTERVIEWING STYLES AND MODERATOR CHARACTERISTICS

Facilitators for such groups can use directive or nondirective interviewing techniques. Nondirective techniques derive from the Hawthorne studies of the late 1930s and early 1940s when researchers discovered that they could gain more insight into employee motivations when they asked open-ended rather than closed questions. Nondirective interviewing allows control to shift from time to time during the interview (i.e., from the interviewer to the interviewee and back again.) The interviewer supplies the topic for discussion, but the focus group process is highly interactive.

A more directive interviewing style can result in a large number of topics being covered in a relatively short span of time; however, the facilitator may close off some avenues of discussion before they yield interesting results. In such a case, learning will be single-loop; that is, the moderator only elicits information within the confines of existing knowledge. Some of the most productive focus groups open up new avenues to moderators, areas of interest that they did not previously anticipate. A directive style of interviewing shuts off this option.

It has been said that the best approach to moderating focus groups may be somewhere between these two extremes. For a two-hour focus group, the moderator will generally ask 5 to 10 questions.[44] The facilitator maintains sufficient control to keep discussions on track and focused but allows temporary excursions into unforeseen territory. Moreover, before arriving at the discussion, the facilitator reviews the purposes of the session and chooses a style that is most appropriate to achieve these purposes. For example, if the intent of the focus group is to generate new and creative insights, a free-wheeling approach may be best. If the purpose of the gathering is to isolate problem areas, a more directive approach may be better. In a focus group, the moderator should limit the use of "why" questions.[45]

Although some people recommend calling directly on individuals to respond to questions or going around the table and asking for positions on an issue, such techniques can be counterproductive. Some researchers claim that a weakness of focus groups is a tendency for the moderator to "overdirect." An individual who doesn't have an opinion on a particular topic may feel pressured to take a stance. Uninformed individuals may be similarly forced into a position. Having stated a position on an issue, a person may feel obliged to defend that position. The moderator may embarrass a person by asking for an opinion on certain topics. Progressing systematically around a group can be boring for participants. The lack of spontaneity in the situation can generate disinterest in completing the session. Some group members will answer at length, while others will give short peremptory responses.

Moderators should be careful not to signal acceptance or nonacceptance of an idea through verbal or nonverbal behaviors (e.g., nodding the head or saying "that's an excellent point"). Moderators should treat participants as equals, being careful not to give responses that could be construed as championing some points of view and negating others. A focus-group moderator should avoid expressing or revealing personal opinions or biases. Moderators should be good listeners. Friendly, consistent behaviors exhibited throughout the session can make participants feel that their views are valuable.

A moderator who wants to encourage balanced group participation can catch and hold the eye of nonparticipants when asking a question. If the person closes off the communication channel by averting his or her gaze, the moderator should move on. *Avoiding* the gaze of an individual who tends to dominate the discussion can prove to be an equally useful technique. If a panel happens to include an individual with a much higher level of expertise than the rest of the group, the moderator may want to appoint this individual as a resource person to elaborate on designated points or to provide detailed factual information. The individual should be asked to refrain from expressing an opinion or point of view that could unduly influence the course of the discussion.

Some researchers claim that moderators should appear like the participants, in manner and dress. Some caution against having female moderators with all-male focus groups and male moderators with all-female groups.[46] Some moderators specialize by working exclusively with certain age or demographic groups (e.g., teenagers or immigrants).[47] A good background knowledge of the topic being discussed, an ability to recognize the critical dimensions of issues, and good group-facilitation skills are just a few of the characteristics that should be possessed by the successful focus-group moderator. Also helpful are a sense of humor, a basic respect for people, and an enjoyment of interacting with others. The ability to synthesize and see the relationship between ideas is essential. Training in areas such as marketing, psychology, communication, and psychotherapy can be useful preparation for a facilitator.[48]

COMMON PARTICIPANT BEHAVIORS

Participant behaviors are commonly grouped under the categories of *group task roles, group maintenance roles,* and *dysfunctional roles.*[49] Any group member may take on a number of these roles during the course of a group discussion. Awareness of the roles will help a group facilitator to understand the group dynamics and to maintain control.

Under *group task roles,* some group members act as *initiators,* proposing new ideas, goals, and solutions. Those classified as *information givers* contribute evidence and opinions to group discussion. *Information seekers* ask for information and seek clarification. *Opinion givers* state their own beliefs, opinions, and attitudes on a topic. *Opinion seekers* solicit the views of others and ask others to clarify their ideas. *Elaborators* clarify and build on ideas presented by other group members; they offer examples, illustrations, and explanations. *Integrators* try to pull together and make sense of the concepts and ideas contributed by the group. *Orienters* keep a group focused on its goal, offering periodic summaries of what has been discussed and clarifying positions of group members. *Energizers* call for higher levels of involvement from group members, soliciting participation.

Those in *group maintenance roles* work to increase group cohesiveness by building and maintaining the interpersonal relationships in a group. The *encourager* praises and compliments others for their contributions. The *harmonizer* works to mediate differences and conflicts, proposing compromise positions for the group. The *tension reliever* uses informality and humor to establish a relaxed interpersonal climate. Through body orientation and eye contact, the *gatekeeper* encourages balanced participation on the part of group members. The *follower* defers to the opinions of others.

Some roles are *dysfunctional.* Such roles do not contribute to the progression of a discussion or to the maintenance of interpersonal relationships. Rather, members who assume these roles can take a discussion off track or can cause friction and disruption. The *blocker* complains and offers only negative comments; she or he objects to more constructive suggestions by others. The *aggressor* insults and criticizes other group members, laughing at perceived faults or mistakes. The *anecdoter* takes the group off its course with irrelevant stories and personal experiences. *Recognition seekers* call attention to their own achievements and successes. *Dominators* monopolize group interaction either by flattering or interrupting others. The *confessor* uses the group as an audience for his or her personal problems, revealing inadequacies and fears. The *special-interest pleader* seeks favors or attention for an outside group. The *playboy/playgirl* relies on antics, jokes, and irrelevant comments to distract a group from more task-oriented goals and to direct it to more entertainment-oriented goals.

RECORDING AND OBSERVING THE SESSION

An assistant researcher often observes the focus group from behind a two-way mirror, taking notes on verbal and nonverbal behaviors of participants. Representatives of the group that has commissioned the study may also be present (e.g., company executives or senior managers).

Sometimes, researchers videotape or audiotape sessions for later study. In such a situation, it is best to use an omnidirectional microphone, which is compatible with the tape recorder. The microphone should be centrally located on the table in clear view of the participants. As the discussion proceeds, participants, and sometimes even the moderator and his or her assistant, will often tend to forget the equipment is present.

Even if the session is being taped, the moderator and assistant moderator should take notes. The moderator takes brief notes. The assistant moderator takes more detailed notes, being careful to record quotable statements. Observations and notes can be useful in postsession analyses. This extra measure is important because tape recorders don't always function, comments may be lost when tapes are switched, and background noise can interfere with the quality of the recording. However, the moderator's notetaking should not impede the flow or spontaneity of the discussion.

STRENGTHS AND WEAKNESSES OF FOCUS GROUPS

Some of the strengths of focus groups are:

- Focus groups are relatively easy to organize and execute.
- The focus group is a relatively inexpensive tool for learning about public opinion.
- Compared to the survey, the focus group has a flexible format, often evoking discussion on a large number of topics.
- The focus group is useful for gaining insights in new areas, for testing concepts, and for learning what motivates people to believe and behave as they do.
- The focus group has the potential to stimulate spontaneity and build on the ideas of others.
- The focus-group format allows the interviewer to probe and explore ill-defined areas of thought.
- Unexpected insights often emerge from the creativity of focus groups.
- Focus-group interviews allow people to speak when they want to speak, not on demand as in the individual interview situation.

- The focus group offers the possibility for more natural interactions than do other types of survey situations.
- It is easier for the organization to afford the services of one trained focus-group moderator than to afford the services of many skilled interviewers.
- In a focus group, data collection is fast, and data analysis is relatively easy.

Some of the problems with focus groups include:

- Seldom are focus-group results generalizable to the larger population.
- Few focus groups are representative samples, no matter how carefully the organization proceeds in recruiting participants.
- Without a competent facilitator, focus groups will be ineffectual.
- Focus groups tend to vary in characteristics and the quality of their contributions.
- In some cases, one or two individuals will dominate a focus group, sabotaging the group process.
- Tendencies of focus groups to move toward conformity can sometimes undermine the process.
- It can be difficult to coordinate the schedules of focus-group participants.
- Participants sometimes follow the lead of those in the group who are experts or who proclaim themselves to be the experts.
- Some moderators may "overdirect," reducing the number of opportunities for group members to interact spontaneously. To deal with this latter problem, some researchers suggest that companies should conduct "unfocus" groups with less rigid formats and more free flow of communication.[50]

Major cost factors in setting up and conducting focus groups include the cost of hiring a moderator, the investment in incentives for participants, rental fees for the research site, and the cost of making and transcribing tapes of the sessions.

Marketing researchers typically charge clients in excess of $2,000 to conduct focus groups whose membership is drawn from the general population. The cost can more than double if there is a requirement to obtain the involvement of individuals with specialized expertise or the involvement of more-difficult-to-reach parts of the population.[51]

Many researchers claim that focus groups results are most valuable when combined with results from other quantitative and qualitative techniques such as surveying and/or interviews with elite opinion leaders. For example, a company interested in learning more about public perceptions of its image might commission a focus group before investing in a larger study. The focus group would yield insight into what should be included in the survey questions.[52] Some researchers argue, however, that it is not always necessary to follow focus groups with quantitative studies; that is, the focus groups themselves can produce useful insights that stand on their own. It has been claimed that research firms with a considerable investment in their survey operations often use focus groups as a "stalking horse to lead clients into more expensive surveys."[53]

Focus Group Example 1: Representative Comments

Company X has recently received national publicity on one of its products. Some individuals have brought a legal suit against the pharmaceutical company, claiming that its product creates a health risk. The company has responded by placing a warning label on the product. It has also conducted a series of focus groups to determine the short-term impact of the negative publicity. The company is hoping to acquire insights from the focus groups that would enable it to address the concern of consumers.

	Responses by Region			
Question	**Southeast**	**Northeast**	**Midwest**	**West**
You're probably aware that pharmaceutical companies sometimes receive unexpected publicity on their products. Can you think of any examples in recent years to illustrate this point?	Silicon breast implants. Tylenol.	Tylenol.	Allergy medicines. Breast implants.	Tylenol. One of the allergy medications.
One of you mentioned product X. What have you heard about this product lately?	Side effects. Heart attacks.	Don't remember hearing anything. Heart problems.	Heard something on TV. Can't recall details.	Can induce heart conditions.
Where did you receive this information?	Television.	Newspaper. Radio. Television.	Television.	Television. Newspaper.
Has this information influenced your purchasing habits? If so, in what way?	Yes. No longer buy product.	No. Don't use product.	Yes. Follow maker's instructions.	No. Don't use product.
What do you think that the company could do to restore public confidence to former levels?	Not much. Damage already done to reputation. Correct problem.	Depends on whether reports are correct.	Nothing unless reports can be proved to be false.	Run public announcement campaign on TV explaining how to use product safely.

Focus Group Example 2: Representative Comments

The recent hurricane has brought a fair amount of unfavorable publicity to Florida. The real estate industry has become concerned. This concern has led a real estate association to hold a series of focus groups in different regions to determine how much impact the hurricane is likely to have on people's decisions to relocate to Florida.

Question	Responses by Region			
	Southeast	Northeast	Midwest	West
How do you feel about Florida as a possible place to relocate?	No real interest in Florida. Florida's OK.	Would be a nice change. Wouldn't be a bad place to live.	Sounds like a nice place. Wouldn't want to live there.	Never really thought much about Florida, sounds OK though.
What do you find attractive about the state?	Have family there. I like the ocean.	No snow! Florida has great beaches. I like warm places.	Disneyland is there. Warm weather.	You can play a lot of golf. A lot of tourist attractions.
What do you find unattractive about the state?	Too hot. The threat of hurricanes. Too many drug problems.	Too much drug trafficking. Dangerous because of hurricanes and tropical storms.	Would miss the change in seasons. Hurricanes are scary. Might be too hot.	Too far away from friends and family. Wouldn't want to have to worry about hurricanes.
If you relocated here, would you choose to rent or buy?	Would probably buy. Definitely rent.	Buy. Might rent for a while.	Would depend on what was available. Would like to buy.	Would rent first to see how I like Florida, then buy if I decided to stay for a prolonged period.
What kinds of factors would influence this decision?	Finances Market situation. How likely the place could be lost to a hurricane.	How long I planned to stay. If I bought a condo, could keep it even if I moved again.	If I was going to be there for a long time, I would buy. I don't think I'd have the money to buy.	I know I wouldn't want to stay there permanently; so I would just rent. How much it cost.
Some states such as California and southern Atlantic coastal states are prone to damage from natural disasters. Do you believe people pay much attention to the possibility of earthquakes, hurricanes, etc., when they buy property?	People probably don't think about it too much. Think people are more afraid of earthquakes than hurricanes. Crime is more of a problem.	I definitely would not buy in an area where everything could be lost in an earthquake or hurricane, and insurance wouldn't cover it. People forget. People go where jobs are.	I think that hurricanes and earthquakes might influence my decision on whether to move there but would not really affect my decision on whether to buy or rent.	People are concerned about these things, but financial and other aspects seem to be greater influences.

ANALYSIS OF FOCUS GROUP RESULTS

Many analytic tools can be applied to focus group results. These range from simple descriptive summaries to information reduction and complex multivariate analysis techniques. The kinds of content analysis techniques that were discussed in a previous chapter on media analysis can also be applied to understanding focus group results. Content analysis involves creating categories, classifying the information according to these categories, and tabulating the frequencies with which different categories appear. The quantity of data, both verbal and nonverbal, that can be generated in a focus group poses the most serious challenge to the analyst. If you engage in a content analysis of your focus group results, you will require transcripts of the focus group sessions. For a detailed description of how to conduct content analysis, see Chapter 5.

The accompanying charts illustrate how summaries of focus group comments can be presented in a shorthand form for easy consumption. The comments that are included are "typical" of the general tone of the discussions. They are not intended to be comprehensive. Including representative comments in a chart of this nature gives a flavor of the interactions that took place. Further descriptive summaries and analyses of the data are also necessary.

NOTES

1. John Pound, "Beyond Takeovers: Politics Comes to Corporate Control," *Harvard Business Review,* March/April 1992, p. 92.
2. Joan Bryden, "Canadians Using Plebiscite to Vent Anger on Elites," *Ottawa Citizen,* October 10, 1992, p. B2.
3. Ibid.
4. Ibid.
5. Ibid.
6. These terms were used by Dan Nimmo and James E. Combs, *Mediated Political Realities* (New York: Longman, 1990), pp. 166–83, in their discussion of current techniques used to assess public opinion.
7. *The Public Mind: Leading Questions,* VEC/Criterion Video, Toronto, Ontario, 1991.
8. Survey conducted by Sherry Ferguson in Spring 1992, to which 15 Fortune 500 companies responded.
9. Survey conducted by Sherry Ferguson in Spring 1991, to which 24 "top performing" Canadian businesses responded.
10. Earl Babbie, *Survey Research Methods,* 2nd ed. (Belmont, Calif.: Wadsworth, 1990), p. 99.
11. James E. Grunig and Fred C. Repper, "Strategic Management, Publics, and Issues," in *Excellence in Public Relations and Communication Man-*

agement, ed. James E. Grunig (Hillsdale, N.J.: Lawrence Erlbaum Associates, Publishers, 1992), p. 138.

12. Angus Reid, "Public Affairs Research: Quantitative and Qualitative," in *The Canadian Public Affairs Handbook,* eds. W. John Wright and Christopher J. DuVernet (Toronto: Carswell, 1988), p. 124.
13. Ibid.
14. Otis Baskin and Craig Aronoff, *Public Relations: The Profession and the Practice,* 3rd ed. (Dubuque, Iowa: Wm. C. Brown Publishers, 1992), p. 111.
15. David L. Morgan, *Focus Groups as Qualitative Research* (Newbury Park, Calif.: Sage Publications, 1988), pp. 46–47.
16. Barbara Westbrook Eakins and R. Gene Eakins, *Sex Differences in Human Communication* (Boston: Houghton-Mifflin, 1978), p. 66.
17. Ibid. See also Barbara Bate, *Communication and the Sexes* (New York: Harper & Row, 1988), pp. 97–98; and Melanie Booth Butterfield and Steve Booth-Butterfield, "Jock Talk: Cooperation and Competition within a University Women's Basketball Team," in *Women Communicating: Studies of Women's Talk,* eds. Barbara Bate and Anita Taylor (Norwood, N.J.: Ablex Publishing, 1988).
18. Richard A. Krueger, *Focus Groups: A Practical Guide for Applied Research* (Newbury Park, Calif.: Sage Publications, 1988), p. 93.
19. Bate, p. 98.
20. Krueger, p. 93.
21. William G. Zikmund, *Business Research Methods,* 2nd ed. (Chicago: Dryden Press, 1988), p. 80.
22. Floyd J. Fowler, Jr. and Thomas W. Mangione, *Standardized Survey Interviewing: Minimizing Interview-Related Error* (Newbury Park, Calif.: Sage Publications, 1990), p. 92.
23. David Taras, *The Newsmakers: The Media's Influence on Canadian Politics* (Scarborough, Ont.: Nelson Canada, 1990), p. 184.
24. Krueger, p. 97.
25. David W. Stewart and Prem N. Shamdasani, *Focus Groups: Theory and Practice* (Newbury Park, Calif.: Sage Publications, 1990), p. 97.
26. Krueger, p. 91.
27. Ibid, p. 98.
28. Ibid.
29. Morgan, p. 44.
30. Krueger, p. 100.
31. Morgan, pp. 45–46.
32. Ibid.
33. Roger D. Wimmer and Joseph R. Dominick, *Mass Media Research: An Introduction,* 3rd ed. (Belmont, Calif.: Wadsworth, 1992), p. 154.
34. For a more detailed account of the influence of environment on communication, see Sherry Devereaux Ferguson and Stewart Ferguson, *Organi-*

zational Communication, 2nd ed. (New Brunswick, N.J.: Transaction Publishers, 1988), pp. 165–200.

35. Ibid., p. 174.
36. Ibid., 176.
37. Myril D. Axelrod, "Ten Essentials for Good Qualitative Research," *Marketing News,* March 14, 1975, p. 11.
38. Krueger, p. 77.
39. David M. Dozier and Fred C. Repper, "Research Firms and Public Relations Practices," in *Excellence in Public Relations and Communication Management,* ed. James E. Grunig (Hillsdale, N.J.: Lawrence Erlbaum Associates, Publishers, 1992), pp. 191–92.
40. Wimmer and Dominick, p. 154.
41. H. Mariampolski, "The Resurgence of Qualitative Research," *Public Relations Journal,* 40(7), pp. 21–23.
42. Morgan, p. 63.
43. Reid, p. 124.
44. Krueger, p. 59.
45. Reid, pp. 142–43. Also Krueger, pp. 62–63.
46. Axelrod, p. 7.
47. Reid, p. 125.
48. Stewart and Shamdasani, p. 78.
49. The classic study that identified these small group roles was K. Benne and P. Sheats, "Functional Roles of Group Members," *Journal of Social Issues* 4 (1948), pp. 41–49.
50. Dozier and Repper, p. 193.
51. Morgan, p. 40.
52. Reid, p. 123.
53. Morgan, p. 13.

CHAPTER 9

CREATING THE STRATEGIC COMMUNICATION PLAN

Strategic planning serves the function of determining where the organization is headed in the long term. An organization focused on the near term is "sailing a rudderless ship."[1] From a policy perspective, a strategic plan is a navigator's map for change and improvement or "the process of articulating the organization's vision of a strongly desired future that the organization is committed to pursue."[2] Although some researchers have proposed that corporate strategy should begin with analysis of the external business environment,[3] others have argued that such an approach is reactive. They say that during the past 15 years too many businesses have succumbed to this logic.[4] Today, it is more commonly accepted that the starting point for strategic planning is the delineation of organization objectives, which are tied to the mission and mandate of the organization.

RELATIONSHIP BETWEEN MISSION STATEMENT AND STRATEGIC PLAN

The first step in the strategic planning process is to identify the organization's "strategic heartbeat" (that is, the basis of its success), which could be "the most cost-efficient warehousing system" (Wal-Mart); "the best-engineered car" (Daimler-Benz), or "the leader in . . . biochemistry, neurology, immunology, and molecular biology."[5] Visa identified its business "as enabling customers to exchange value for virtually anything, anywhere in the world. AT&T positions itself in the information business rather than in the telephone business (or even the communications business), whereas the 'baby Bells' are still attempting to identify 'visionary' missions that will enable them to capture the full potential of deregulation and divestiture from their parent."[6] At the end of the 1980s, Levi Strauss and Company formalized its mission statement in a document titled "Crusaders of the Golden Needle":

> We seek profitable and responsible commercial success creating and selling jeans and casual clothing. We seek this while offering quality products and service—and

by being a leader in what we do. What we do is important. How we do it is also important. Here's how: By being honest. By being responsible citizens in communities where we operate and in society in general. By having a workplace that's safe and productive, where people work together in teams, where they talk to each other openly, where they're responsible for their actions, and where they can improve their skills.[7]

Four elements common to mission statements are *purpose, strategy, values,* and *behavior standards.*[8] Strategy includes scope of operations, product or service offerings, the market in which the firm intends to operate, and philosophical premises that guide actions.[9]

Bell Atlantic's CEO Raymond Smith involved 1,400 managers in articulating the values of this corporation. At the end of a lengthy process, managers at Bell Atlantic reached consensus on five values: integrity, respect and trust, excellence, individual fulfillment, and profitable growth. They wrote a paragraph describing each value. Using these values as a base, the corporation then moved toward operationalizing the values in the form of concrete behaviors and work practices.[10]

In the same way, British Leyland Motor Corporation, Ltd. recently engaged many of its internal and external stakeholders in reshaping its strategic vision.[11] At Washington Mutual Financial Group, Chairman Lou Pepper formed a committee on values and appointed middle managers to roam the organization "to determine where conflicts exist between rhetoric and reality." Where the two diverge, the managers report back to Pepper, who makes the necessary changes.[12]

DON'T ASK ME TO KILL FOR SOMEONE ELSE'S STRATEGIC VISION

Similar to writing a mission statement, the overall process of strategic planning is a cooperative exercise, which builds teamwork among those involved in decision-making processes. Gaining commitment from the larger membership implies obtaining high levels of participation. Employees throughout the organization should feel a sense of ownership in the corporate strategic plan:

Ownership in the final plan is of paramount importance. The senior executives are responsible for the development of the plan, but a plan to which only a handful of people is committed has little chance of becoming more than a piece of window dressing to which people, at best, will pay little attention and which, at worst, will contribute to the image of the executives as unrealistic, uncommitted, or unable to do what they plan.[13]

Rather than being considered as an area suitable only for the "eyes and ears of CEOs and a few of their most trusted lieutenants . . . the effort to implement strategy must capture the heads, hearts, and hands of the entire organization."[14] At some point, every member of the organization, especially those responsible for communicating the organization's vision, should keep a copy of the company's strategic plan in his or her top desk drawer. Canada Mortgage and Housing Corporation publishes and circulates its strategic plan to employees and the general public. Few employees will feel motivated to work toward a vision about which they can only speculate. As one middle manager of a New Jersey utility company aptly stated, "Don't ask me to kill for somebody else's vision."[15]

The company's corporate plan is a "motherhood" document, which lays out strategic direction in broad, visionary terms; it does not contain the very specific language that goes into operational planning documents. Strategic planning develops a reference point for coherent and unified planning exercises, offering a raison d'être against which organizational decisions can be assessed an justified; it is the "driving force behind operational and work plans."[16]

WHAT IS THE RELATIONSHIP BETWEEN THE CORPORATE STRATEGIC PLAN AND A STRATEGIC COMMUNICATION PLAN?

A growing number of organizations are accepting the principle that every strategic plan should have a communication component that addresses management of the company's critical and emerging issues. A recent Conference Board report found that companies that value the "soft side" of strategic development involve communicators in the strategic planning process.[17] At companies such as Douglas Aircraft, public relations staff play an important role in planning. John Hancock is said to be changing its strategic planning process to include communications strategies. Communicators at New York Telephone Company (and other telecommunications firms) have been contributing, for a long time, to the formulation of company policies. Recent examples at New York Telephone Company include "the rollout of the corporate force reduction plan, creation of the company's five-year business plan, and ongoing cost reduction/revenue generation programs."[18] An issues-management group, operating out of the company's public relations department, identifies critical issues and gives early warnings. With the assistance of company experts who have expertise or work in specific areas, communication specialists project the likely impact of issues on the company, on employees, and on stakeholder groups. Current issues include multilingual service assistance, environmental concerns, and regional economic development.[19] One public relations expert acknowledged the role that communication groups play in this process when he observed, "We help plan the parade, not just carry the shovels afterward."[20]

Firms such as New York Telephone tend to view public relations as a management, rather than as a service, function.[21] They also tend to view communication planning as part of the strategic planning process rather than as a separate and distinct planning exercise. They dispute the view that issues management requires planning from the "outside-in," using the external, rather than the internal, environment as the starting point for selecting priority issues.[22] Planning from the "outside-in" can result in a failure to take organizational objectives into account. In such a situation, it would seem to be easy for the organization to lose sight of its most important issues (i.e., those that can influence the achievement of the organization's mandate and mission) and to take a scattergun approach to dealing with its issues.

This book argues that the communication plan (or the issues-management plan) should be developed as a corollary document to the larger corporate strategic plan. As such, the communication plan uses *corporate objectives,* not the external environment, as the starting point for planning.

The policies that are articulated in the corporate strategic plan will generate much debate—among the general public, with interest groups, and even among stakeholders within the organization. Communication and public affairs directorates are charged with the responsibility of managing this public and intraorganizational debate. In order to plan effective communication strategies, communicators must be able to articulate the *policy issues* that they will confront. They also need to make the distinction between issues that are "owned" by their organization and issues for which they have no responsibility. Therefore, the first step in any communication plan is to extrapolate, from the strategic plan, the issues (owned by the organization) that will become subject to debate.

The communication plan will also examine the *positive and negative factors in the planning environment* that have the potential to influence the organization's ability to address its strategic issues. Some of these influences will be *external* to the organization; others will be *internal.* On the basis of this delineation of issues and factors in the planning environment, the communication planner will frame *communication objectives. Themes and messages* will emerge from the communication objectives, and *initiatives* will follow. The initiatives section of the strategic communication plan serves as a bridge to the operational and work planning stages. The strategic communication plan helps to ensure that communication initiatives support the achievement of corporate priorities. Later requests for funding of communications initiatives, made at the operational stage, will be evaluated on the basis of whether they further the organization's ability to achieve its strategic objectives.

In order to develop the strategic communication document, the communication planner must access the most recent corporate strategic plan and/or consult with planners in policy or business units. It is essential that these two documents, the corporate strategic plan and the strategic plan for communication, complement rather than conflict with each other. Ideally, updates of the corporate plan and the communication plan should take place at the same time.

Issues management is typically the responsibility of those engaged in communication planning. Thus, the communication planner begins by examining the corporate plan. He or she reviews the results of a situation audit (that identifies major demographic, technological, economic, and social variables likely to have an impact on the firm's or government department's operations in the coming year), the organization's priorities, and the organization's objectives. Then the communication planner considers the policies that are being proposed and defended. Out of these policies will emerge the major issues that both external and internal stakeholders will be debating in the coming year(s). This is the point at which strategic communication planning can begin.[23]

In short, the strategic communication plan performs the following functions:

- Uses the corporate plan as a starting point.
- Complements the corporate plan.
- Anticipates public debate.
- Articulates issues that will require management's attention.
- Frames communication objectives.
- Ensures that communication activities and initiatives support corporate objectives.
- Ties back to organization priorities (mission and mandate).
- Establishes criteria by which operational funding requests can be evaluated.
- Requires updating at the same time as the corporate plan.

Strategic plans are highly useful on political as well as other levels. It is common, for example, for heads of communication to receive many requests to perform services and generate communication products related to managers' "pet projects." Without a strategic plan, the communication manager has no basis for refusing the requests. Once a strategic plan is in place, a framework exists for evaluating requests and denying the ones that do not conform to the strategic framework.

WHAT IS THE "IDEAL MODEL" FOR STRATEGIC PLANNING IN COMMUNICATION

The following points should be taken into consideration in attempting to establish strategic communication planning systems:

- Strategic planning should be the responsibility of the executive team, and the head of communication should be a member of this team.

- The head of communication should actively participate in describing the corporate mission and setting corporate goals.
- To function with maximum effectiveness, the head of communication should be recognized as the principal communication adviser.
- Strategic communication planning should be integrated with corporate strategic planning.
- The strategic communication plan should be a product of the executive team's vision; it should be integrated with corporate goals; and it should be "owned" by the most senior managers of the organization.

In some cases, a planning staff assumes responsibility for generating the strategic plan.[24] Even in these cases, however, the commitment of upper management is critical to obtaining broad-based support for the plan. If planning gets shoved to the division level, the result can be a failure to capture the "big picture."[25]

In some organizations, the strategic planning cycle, on both the division and corporate levels, recurs every three to five years. A growing number of companies update their plan each year.[26]

GUIDELINES FOR WRITING AND USING STRATEGIC PLANS

Writing Style
- Be brief. Keep the plan to no more than 5–7 pages.
- Keep the style tight and focused; avoid wordiness.
- Avoid complexity.
- Avoid including more than one point in a statement.

Content
Tie each section of the strategic plan to previous sections of the plan (and, ultimately, to organization objectives that reflect mission and mandate statements, major speeches, and policy announcements).

Procedures
Coordinate the writing of the corporate strategic plan and the strategic communications plan so that both are accomplished simultaneously.

Format
Present the plan in a format that is amenable to updating. Strategic plans should not change dramatically from year to year. They are, by definition, long-range plans.

A format that works well is to organize all sections of the plan so that they adhere to the same progression of ideas followed in "organization objectives." In other words, you should list all issues related to "organization objective A" prior to listing issues related to "organization objective B"; list all issues related to "organization objective B" before listing issues related to "organization objective C," etc.

Similarly, when you articulate the external factors and other sections of the plan (communication objectives, themes and messages, and activities), adhere to the same ordering of points. All external factors that are related to objective A should precede those that relate to objective B; external factors related to objective B should precede those related to objective C, etc.

Remember that the strategic communication plan is the broadest of the communication planning documents. As you move from the strategic to the operational and work plans, you will become increasingly more specific.

Uses

Make the strategic plan available as a basic reference document to all communication officers engaged in operational planning, work planning, and planning for specific activities and initiatives.

WHAT ARE THE COMPONENTS OF A STRATEGIC COMMUNICATION PLAN?[27]

Organization Objectives

The strategic communication plan results in the delineation of communication initiatives that will support corporation or government objectives. The objectives that appear in the strategic communication plan should be derived from the organization's corporate strategic plan, which describes current priorities. These corporate objectives are typically broad and lacking in detail.

As a communication planner, you will use these corporate objectives as a starting point for the strategic communication plan. Transfer the objectives, intact, from the corporate plan to the strategic communication plan. If no corporate strategic plan exists to detail the organization's objectives and priorities, you will need to refer to the same documents that would have been used by the corporate planner in writing a strategic plan (e.g., the annual report, any existing planning documents, executive speeches that outline organization priorities, etc.). You will also need to interview people who are working on policy to learn the plan that exists in their heads, even if it does not exist on paper. Otherwise, your communication planning efforts will be futile.

If the objectives that offer a starting point for the corporate and the communication plan are not the same, the two processes will diverge. Because the communication plan is intended to support the achievement of organization objectives, a separate and independent communication plan does not make sense. Furthermore, where a gap exists between the objectives cited in the corporate plan and the strategic communication plan, it is not possible for the public affairs or communication director to justify requests for funding of communication activities.

Under ideal circumstances, the head of communication will have been part of the executive team that set organizational objectives.

Strategic Issues

The second part of the strategic communication plan involves identification of the organization's strategic issues (e.g., legal suits; bankruptcies; falling productivity; allegations of insider trading; layoffs; charges of fraud, price-fixing, or embezzlement; failure to address environmental problems; and tax evasion).[28] Governments are dealing with issues spawned by a growing national deficit, a shrinking tax base, foreign affairs crises, and intermittent scandals.

Strategic issues are fundamental policy questions "affecting the organization's mandates; mission and values; product or service level and mix, clients, users or payers, cost, financing, management or organizational design."[29] Issues may arise as a consequence of both setting and implementing policies and strategies.[30] An organization, in order to survive and prosper must deal "expeditiously and effectively" with its strategic issues,[31] which are more important than tactical or operational issues.[32] Issues have several characteristics:

1. Issues imply conflicts in values.
2. Issues are debatable, with at least two sides or points of view.
3. Issues are unresolved.

Value conflicts may be over "ends (what); means (how); philosophy (why); location (where); timing (when); and who might be helped or hurt by different ways of resolving the issues (who)."[33]

The strategic-issues section of the communication plan should suggest current and emerging issues of a strategic nature that are likely to confront the firm or the government department in the coming year(s). In reviewing the corporate plan, the communication planner may find the organization's strategic issues articulated in the situation-analysis section of the plan. Alternatively, the planner who is working without benefit of a corporate plan may see that certain policy choices could result in public or intraorganizational debate. This debate will have to be managed. By anticipating the issues that could generate debate, the communication planner contributes to the organization's ability to assume a proactive stance.

Future sections of the plan that deal with communication objectives and priorities will link back to the issue-management needs identified in this section, so you should state these issues as clearly as possible. Organize your statement of issues so that they correspond, in presentation order, to your previous statement of organization objectives. In other words, what issues could undermine or enhance your ability to achieve objective A, objective B, etc.? Some issues may relate to all objectives; others may correspond only to specific objectives.

It can be useful to frame strategic issues in the form of questions. Doing so keeps the planner focused on the *unresolved* nature of strategic issues. Take the example of acid rain. If you wish to write an issues statement on acid rain, you would not list *acid rain* as the issue. Rather, you would focus on the *strategic questions relevant to acid rain. The specific question would depend on your firm's or your department's perspective.* For example, the strategic question for a federal government department concerned with environmental issues might be "How should the federal government exercise leadership with regard to acid rain concerns?" A different strategic question might be "What is the priority that the federal government should give to dealing with the acid rain problem?" An alternative strategic question might be "Should the federal government be pushing industry to enact more effective controls?" Or the strategic question might be "Should the federal government be pushing state governments to enforce, with more consistency, state legislation relevant to the acid rain problem?" These questions also demonstrate that issues are *debatable* (i.e., more than one point of view is represented). Issues also involve *conflict of values* (in this case, economics may be pitted against human health and other environmental concerns).

Alternatively, you may wish to articulate the issue in some other fashion that focuses on the strategic questions in the issue but doesn't state the questions explicitly, for example, "the adequacy of federal efforts to force state actions on acid rain" or "the federal government's role in dealing with acid rain concerns." Either of these phrases could be translated easily into strategic questions.

An inappropriate issues statement would be "elimination of acid rain" or "depletion of natural resources." No one would disagree that acid rain should be eliminated or that our natural resources should be preserved. Many people would argue over "how" and "who should be responsible." In that sense, strategic questions dictate a different wording. In the case of acid rain, that wording could be "how to eliminate acid rain" or "responsible party for eliminating acid rain." Even this wording, however, is probably too vague because you should demonstrate the relevance of a strategic issue to your organization. Strategic issues are, by definition, policy related. Corporations and governments don't deal with issues about which they can do nothing. There are too many pressing issues to consider. Therefore, if concerns related to acid rain do make it a strategic issue for your company or your government department, the policy concerns must be evident in your statement of the issue. In this case, the strategic questions might be "the federal government's role in dealing with the acid rain problem'' or ''adequacy of federal leadership efforts in regard to the acid rain problem'' or ''adequacy of federal government participation in international efforts to deal with acid rain concerns.'' Issue statements will be more specific than other parts of the communication plan.

Different groups will ''own'' different aspects of an issue. For example, consider the Waco stand-off. At one point in the confrontation with cult leader David Koresh, the office of the U.S. attorney general had to make a strategic policy choice regarding whether or not to use force in ending the stand-off. The strategic policy issue was *''Should the attorney general sanction the use of force?''* For local hospitals, the issue from the initiation to the conclusion of the conflict was: *To what extent should hospitals prepare for the worst possible scenario?* Extensive preparations could be costly in financial terms, but inadequate preparations could be costly in human and political terms. Community churches and religious leaders had to decide what position they should take on an issue that had potentially serious ramifications for the constitutional right of people to worship as they please. For these groups and individuals, the strategic questions was: *Should the church approve state and federal actions against the cult group?* For human rights activists who followed the conflict, the question was similar: *Should human rights groups condemn government actions against private citizens who had restricted their activities to private property?* With the unfavorable resolution of the issue (the burning of the compound and the loss of many lives, including children), the strategic issue for President Clinton became: *Should the office of the presidency distance itself from the decision made by the office of the attorney general?* Clinton chose not to do so; instead he spoke out in support of the attorney general's decision.

Within the same organization, different sectors or units may own different aspects of an issue. Consider a well-known case like the Tylenol poisonings. For the CEO and his executive constellation, the strategic policy choice (after learning of the poisonings) was: *Should the company remove all Tylenol products from the shelves?* For research and development, the policy issue evolved into the question: *Should the company replace all capsule products with tablets or ''caplets''?* For the legal team at Johnson & Johnson Company, the issue was: *Should the company accept legal responsibility for the poisonings?*

Chapter 4 discussed the situation at Oka, Quebec, where the Mohawk Indians became engaged in an armed stand-off against first the Quebec provincial police and later the Canadian military. In this case, the strategic issue for the Quebec police was whether to become engaged in active combat with the Mohawks. The question for the federal Department of Indian and Northern Affairs was whether or not to enter the fray and to negotiate with the Mohawks. The Canadian military first faced the issue of whether to assume a role in resolving the conflict and then whether to employ force. Other native organizations and leaders had to decide whether to sanction native actions in what escalated into a violent confrontation between Mohawks and Quebec police. Once the Mohawks surrendered, the question for Justice Canada became: *Should the government prosecute those who had participated in the barricade?* The prime minister had to decide whether to distance himself from the controversy or to assume an active role as negotiator in the conflict.

Low-priority issues must be omitted from the strategic plan. An organization can deal with only so many issues. If its agenda is spread too thin, the organization cannot deal effectively with the most critical issues. Issues that acquire priority (or those of first-order status) will appear in the strategic communication plan. A few emerging issues will fit into this category. Less-important issues will not be addressed. Decisions about addressing an issue on a rhetorical level will be determined by *issue variables* (salience, value potency, maturity, and field of influence), *opposition stakeholder variables* (power capability and credibility), and *organization variables* (the bearing of the issue on the mission and mandate of the organization). See Chapter 3 on prioritizing the organization's issues for a discussion of these variables.

It is true that unexpected events and crises will often create the need for organizations to address issues that are not represented in the strategic plan. A Tylenol poisoning, the eruption of a war in the Persian Gulf, or the meltdown of a nuclear power facility—none of these kinds of situations will be addressed by the long-term strategic plan. However, in such cases, some of the funds allocated to the management of long-term strategic issues will be diverted to managing the crisis situation, and short-term plans will be generated to facilitate the organization's coping with these issues. (See Chapter 12 on crisis management for an in-depth consideration of contingency planning for crises.) Unlike the contingency plan, which is intended to help the organization cope with unexpected developments, the strategic plan is an effort to establish future direction for the organization.

External Planning Environment: Positive and Negative Factors

This section of the strategic communication plan should outline major positive factors (or opportunities) in the external public opinion environment that could influence your choice of communication strategies. It should also outline major negative factors (or threats) in the external opinion environment that you will need to take into account in making strategic communication decisions. In other words, the issue-management decisions that you make will be influenced by the environment in which you are working. These positive and negative factors will directly affect your ability to manage your organization's issues and to contribute to the achievement of corporate objectives. Many strategies fail because of unanticipated changes or instability in the environment. Environment is a "major and sometimes unpredictable force to be reckoned with."[34]

In writing this section of the strategic communication plan, refer back to your statement of strategic issues. Your environmental statement must focus on the factors that could enhance or inhibit your organization's ability to engage successfully in issues management. This environmental statement should also offer a framework for later choices on communication strategies. As with policy issue statements, it is useful to organize your discussion of factors in terms of the overall company or department objectives that you are seeking to achieve. Doing so will remind you that all of your efforts relate back to achievement of organizational objectives. Since some factors are double-edged, having both a positive and negative dimension, you may decide not to separate the factors into positive and negative categories.

1. You will be identifying factors in the opinion environment that are *external* to the organization. In other words, you will be outlining the *opinion climate that exists outside the organization.* Therefore, you will be drawing conclusions based on *data that give a profile of external stakeholders.*

2. You will be drawing your information from sources such as telephone inquiries, consultations, correspondence, formal surveys, evaluations of customers' and clients' opinions and concerns, and print and electronic media analyses.

3. The factors identified in this part of your plan should be based on consistent monitoring of the environment. Your conclusions should be based on *hard data,* not just impressions.

4. Rather than reporting individual surveys or items of data, your statements should be *conclusive* and of an *omnibus nature* (i.e., "Polls suggest that the large majority of Americans will support government efforts to control deficit spending" or "Correspondence suggests that many shareholders will support disinvestment in South Africa").

5. Your environment statements should describe the environment *as it is* and *not necessarily as you would like it to be.* Your statement must be an accurate representation of social reality. An inadequate statement of problem areas or one that "glosses over" potential obstacles could result in the organization's having to respond *reactively,* rather than *proactively,* to its environment at a later date. It is natural to seek out positive elements and elements that are congruent with corporate goals; however, the areas that most often need addressing will come from negative influences.

6. At the same time, *take care to identify positive factors* that offer strategic communications opportunities. Directing excessive energy toward negative factors can sometimes be counterproductive, especially if the source of the negative comment is more "shrill" than representative.

7. In drawing conclusions on the planning environment, it is important to distinguish between comment related to the *merit of policies* and comment on *how the policies are being implemented.*[35] Sometimes a comment will qualify as a positive factor if judged on the first criterion, and it will qualify as a negative factor if judged on the second criterion. For example, public opinion may be in favor of free trade as a concept, but it may be against the specifics of a negotiated agreement. Or public opinion may be in favor of parole as a means of providing a supervised reentry of offenders into society, but it may hold that inadequate administration procedures and inefficient communication in the system allow some parolees an unjustified opportunity to commit unprovoked and brutal new crimes.

Internal Planning Environment: Positive and Negative Factors

In this section of the strategic communication plan, you are describing *internal* organizational influences that could enhance or inhibit your ability to engage in effective and efficient issues management. These are the *strengths and weaknesses* of the company or government department that will make your job easier or harder.

Your ability to contribute to achievement of organizational objectives will be affected by these internal variables. For example, what budget size or other resource constraints are you facing? What intradepartmental or interdepartmental efforts are influencing your efforts to manage the public debate over policy issues? Internal constraints will often result from wide objectives and narrow resources in people and skills. At other times, strategies fail because of "narrow-minded" bureaucrats who are strapped to tradition, "small-minded" ones with limited understanding, "bloody-minded ones" who "prefer to go their own way" or "right-minded" people who understand that some strategies can't or won't succeed.[36] Identifying these latter kinds of factors in a plan, without offending anyone, can pose a serious challenge to the most diplomatic of strategic planners.

Even though the factors identified may be internal to your planning environment (e.g., levels of expertise in the firm or government department and budgetary limitations), these factors can be potent influences in supporting or undermining your attempts to manage the public debate over issues. For example, the amount of money available to a department can be a planning constraint. This constraining factor is capable of generating an internal debate over how the money should be spent, whereby different areas of the department will compete for the limited funds. How such an internal debate is resolved can later have consequences for management of issues in the public sphere. An executive decision on allocation of funding can provoke an even more heated debate outside the organization, as special interest groups argue that insufficient funding is available for their causes. Thus, an internal factor may produce an issue that becomes external. For this reason, factors identified in this section of your plan should be taken into consideration in framing your communication objectives, which come later in the plan.

Internal factors will also influence your choice of communication strategies, which are delineated at a later point in the plan. For example, the choice to communicate the levels of expertise available in your department will depend on whether this is a strength or weakness for your organization.

The communication specialist who is capable of both transcending the boundaries of his or her discipline and understanding the needs of diverse operating and support units will be best able to assume a place at strategy sessions. Much of the information incorporated into the internal environment section of the plan will be drawn from networking within the organization. Herb Schmertz, who formulated Mobil Corporation's communication strategies during the 1970s and early 1980s, is considered exemplary of this type of communicator.[37] Communicators who are widely read in areas affecting both the external and internal environments of the organization have the best chance of making an important contribution to the strategic planning process.[38]

Communication Objectives

Some communication objectives may not stem from issues. With "good news" items, you can sometimes leapfrog from organization objectives to communication objectives in your plan. For the most part, however, the communication objectives section of the strategic communication plan relates directly to the issues you will be managing and to your statement of company or departmental objectives. As with the other sections of the plan, it is useful to organize your discussion so that the presentation order corresponds to your initial ordering of organization objectives.

In a strategic communication plan, statements of communication objectives should be broad in scale and scope. However, your communication objectives will differ from the broader organization objectives because they incorporate a *communication* component (e.g., "to contribute to a public understanding of how the company . . ." or "to increase public awareness of. . . ." Communication objectives must be *clearly relevant to the function of a communicator*. In other words, statements such as "to establish a program for . . ." or "to reduce inequities in access to . . ." are policy and program objectives, *not* communication objectives.

Communication objectives will have both external and internal components. It is essential to remember, however, that the communication plan fits within the larger corporate plan. Therefore, a statement such as "to inform the marketing division of the need to give greater support to sales" would be inappropriate. Even though your objectives will be communication objectives, you will be writing the objectives from the *perspective of the larger organization*. You will not represent the special interests of any one group within the organization. Also, avoid wording such as "to ensure that . . ." or "to guarantee that. . . ." These phrases imply unrealistically high goals.

You have a choice of writing three kinds of communication objectives. These objectives can relate to attempts to:

1. Change or reinforce the level of knowledge of the target audience (*cognitive* influence).

2. Change or reinforce the way the audience feels about the subject (*attitudinal* influence).

3. Change or reinforce existing behaviors of the audience (*behavioral* influence).

In other words, you will be seeking to *inform*, to *persuade*, or to *move to action*.[39] Only after asking yourself "What am I trying to change or to maintain and reinforce?" can you frame your communication objectives. Only after framing your communication objectives can you move to the next stage (the themes and messages part of the plan) by asking "What symbols (message design) can I use to effect this end?"

You should limit your communication objectives to realistic numbers. Plans with too many objectives are unrealistic; no organization should have too broad an agenda. In most cases, budgetary restraints will influence the range and number of your communication objectives. Do not forget that your objectives must be framed in such a way as to direct the company or government department toward a proactive approach to dealing with its issues (i.e., to capitalize on positive factors and to deal with negative components).

An organization may decide to address an issue on a rhetorical level or a pragmatic level (through policy, legislation, etc.). Communication objectives will relate only to the rhetorical level. There may be some issues, however, on which you choose to remain silent. The decision to research and analyze an issue or even the decision to include the issue in a strategic plan does not necessarily imply that you must frame a communication objective for the issue. Some issues are so volatile that you must be knowledgeable about them, but you may decide that a low-key approach to them is preferable. Sometimes, the less communicated about an issue, the better, particularly regarding highly contentious issues that are not owned predominantly by your organization.

If you have decided that an issue is owned by your organization, that it is sufficiently salient and potent to be a potential threat, and that it is important enough to justify an investment in human and financial resources, you may respond to the issue in a direct way. As was previously stated, some communication objectives framed for external publics will relate back to internal environment factors. For example, a high-technology company may consider acknowledged scientific expertise as a positive internal factor. The company may choose to send a message concerning this expertise to external stakeholders. The stated intent of your plan should not become promoting your organization's image, for example, "to depict the company as concerned about environmental issues." Most organizations do have, however, unstated objectives that relate to image. One unstated communication objective is to convey the idea of the organization's being in control, in charge of itself and its issue environment, knowing what to say and why.[40] Communication objectives appear first in the strategic plan, but they resurface in the multiyear or annual operational plan.

Themes and Messages

A theme is a general overriding, often recurring idea that can encompass a variety of related messages. A theme is developed to reflect broad principles of an organization (e.g., customized services, traditional quality, social responsibility, a just society, or constructive internationalism).

A message, on the other hand, is a specific statement of limited scope, usually containing only one main idea. Messages are statements sent out by the organization that someone inside the organization hopes will be picked up outside. Any individual message will be a variation on a particular theme. An organization has many more messages than themes. Several messages, grouped together, may represent a broader theme.

This section of the strategic communication plan should express, in the simplest terms, the themes and messages to be carried in all the organization's communication products. Messages may be transmitted in press releases, in speeches by chief executive officers and other company officials, in conference presentations, in brochures, in slide shows given to community groups, and in media interviews. These messages should relate directly back to communication objectives. They should also respond to the needs and opportunities identified in the planning environment. All messages will be tied to the organization's strategic issues. It is necessary to connect all parts of the plan so that it is a coherent whole.

Formal statement of messages in a communication plan can serve several main purposes:

1. To force the organization to crystallize its thinking by transferring its ideas to paper.
2. To gain the commitment of others in the organization who must approve the content of the messages.
3. To provide a coherent statement that can serve as a reference document for those who write messages for limited-scope communication plans. (Chapter 11 discusses these kinds of communication plans.)
4. To remind the communicator who is charged with producing speeches, brochures, press releases, and other communication products of what messages *should be appearing* in communications to the public.

The messages that appear in the annual or multiyear strategic communication plan will be different from the messages that appear in the limited-scope, or single-purpose, communication plan. Messages appearing in the strategic plan will be much broader and less specific than those that appear in single-purpose plans. For example, an appropriately framed message for a strategic plan might be "The government is pushing industry to find innovative solutions to environmental problems" or "Bank Z is working to make its banking services more user friendly." The message statement is appropriate because it has been written in broad consensual terms.

Priority Activities/Initiatives

An example of a priority activity is a public relations campaign designed to address some organizational concern. Sometimes the management of major policy issues will call for a number of activities. Clusters of associated activities compose an *initiative* (e.g., an environmental green plan, free trade, market expansion plans, or restructuring of the tax system).

Priority activities can be justified only insofar as they relate back to communication needs implied in the communication objectives section of the strategic plan. These objectives, in turn, should reflect the planning environment and issue priorities. The ability of a communication group to justify a proposed operational budget (which comes later at the operational planning stage) will depend on the extent to which the communication priorities tie back to the strategic priorities of the organization. The relationship between major communication activities and overall organization objectives should be easily discernible.

Communication activities may address factors in both the internal and the external planning environments. To establish the capacity to meet its external communications requirements, an organization may need to strengthen its research and analysis functions, improve its communications with shareholders, establish a mechanism for coordinating communications with regional offices, or develop better evaluation methods.

Activities that address internal factors will probably not relate back to specific organization objectives, to specific issues, or to specific communication objectives, but they will have a general and important influence on the organization's capacity to meet its obligations to external publics. An inadequate research and analysis program, for example, can weaken the ability of the organization to understand and respond to public needs or to meet other objectives.

The activities section of the strategic plan will be used as the starting point in the operational planning process, which follows the formulation of a strategic plan. Even if other sections of the strategic plan are not updated each year, it will be necessary to update this part.

Consultation Requirements

To achieve your communication priorities, you may need to consult with officers or employees in other parts of the organization. You should state anticipated requirements for consultation, coordination, or the active cooperation of other individuals or groups in the organization. You may want to designate concerned individuals, units, or areas of departments that should be consulted regarding each major issue. Or you may want to make a more general statement of planned involvement.

Resources

This section identifies the resources available for achieving your communication priorities. The anticipated amount of money that will be devoted to communication activities should include the total budget for the communication unit or the public affairs department and any money allocated to communication by other parts of the organization.

SAMPLE STRATEGIC COMMUNICATION PLAN

The plan that follows illustrates the points made in the preceding discussion. Alphabetical letters are attached to the statement of organization objectives. The ordering of subsequent sections of the plan relates back to this initial ordering of objectives. Therefore, if an issue is labeled as "C," that means the issue relates to objective C. If an external factor (positive or negative) is labeled as "B" and "D," that means the factor is relevant to objectives "B" and "D." If a communication objective is labeled as "A" and "C," that means the communication objective has relevance for organization objectives "A" and "C." The same is true for other sections of the plan. Parts of the plan that relate to internal issues are not labeled because they relate to the achievement of *all* organization objectives.

STRATEGIC COMMUNICATION PLAN
FEDERAL DEPARTMENT OF THE ENVIRONMENT*

Organization Objectives

The objectives of the FDE are as follows:

A   • To encourage increased public knowledge, interest, and involvement in environmental issues.

B   • To give firm leadership and support to domestic efforts to overcome the environmental threat to our country.

---

* This plan was the joint effort of Sherry Ferguson and M. Natalie Lam. The Federal Department of the Environment is a fictitious government department.

C   • To give firm leadership and support to international efforts to overcome the environmental threat to our planet.

D   • To deal effectively with the relationship of environmental concerns to economic issues.

Strategic Issues

A&B   • FDE's role as a leader in defining options for individual action on environmental issues.

B   • Delegation of responsibility for leadership on environmental questions (i.e., conserving and improving water supply, clean-up activities).

B   • Adequacy of current legislation and enforcement in reducing acid rain.

B   • Adequacy of FDE interventions in the case of questions involving transporting, storing, and disposing of toxic waste and locating disposal facilities.

B   • Adequacy of FDE efforts to control toxic contamination of soil, air, and water.

B   • Adequacy of FDE efforts to protect the ozone layer.

B   • Adequacy of FDE efforts to protect parklands, wilderness, and wildlife.

B&C   • Adequacy of FDE efforts to secure international cooperation in solving the acid rain problem.

D   • Extent to which the public should be taxed to pay for environmental protection.

External Planning Environment

Positive Factors or Opportunities

A   • Growing sense of concern in Eastern United States about environment and resource conservation, especially in states like New Jersey.

A   • Perception that individuals can make a difference.

A   • Reported evidence that Americans are taking some limited actions on environmental concerns (e.g., recycling, buying biodegradable products, etc.).

A   • General perception that current personal efforts are inadequate.

A   • Continuing priority of health-related environmental issues (e.g., toxic chemicals, clean water supply, and acid rain) on public agenda.

A   • Trend toward increasing interest in acid rain and atmospheric change factors.

A   • Continuing interest in preservation of parklands, wilderness, and wildlife.

A   • Trend toward seeing environmental issues as "cumulative" and "global."

A   • Increased press coverage of environmental issues.

B   • Belief in FDE as key player on environment issues (e.g., setting national standards, establishing immediate rather than phased-in controls on industrial emissions, etc.).

B   • Tendency for public to assign responsibility for remedial measures to industry violators.

B   • Trend toward more positive perception of FDE performance.

C   • Perceived opportunity for government to show leadership in ongoing negotiations with other countries on acid rain accord.

D   • Perception that environmental and economic well-being go together.

D   • Public willingness to place environmental concerns over economic concerns.

D   • Public willingness to pay to protect the environment.

Negative Factors or Threats

A   • Evidence of discrepancy between rhetoric and action on part of many Americans in regard to environmental issues.

A   • Declining sense of efficacy on part of individual Americans.

A   • Pessimistic view of issues being resolved in near future and perception that situation continues to deteriorate.

A   • Complexity in situation growing out of tendency for environmental issues to interact with many other issues.

A   • Generalized levels of public anxiety not amenable to simple solutions.

A   • Lack of public understanding of toxic chemical issues.

A   • Relatively low level of concern in some southwestern states.

B   • Government perceived as not taking sufficient initiative on environment.

B   • Government perceived as siding with polluting industries and having inadequate regulatory mechanism.

B   • FDE viewed as less-credible information source than environmental interest groups.

B   • Generalized perception of government as anti-environment.

C   • Industry dissatisfaction with government's position on environmental issues that have an international dimension.

D   • Feeling that industry, not government, should pay for problems industry has generated.

Internal Planning Environment

Positive Factors or Strengths

        • Growing recognition by other federal agencies and departments of shared responsibility for environment.

        • Legislative support for many initiatives undertaken by the FDE.

        • High level of scientific expertise, knowledge, and skills within the FDE.

Negative Factors or Weaknesses

        • Lack of a structural mechanism for coordinating federal communications on environmental programs.

        • Unexpected new policies from other federal departments and agencies and events that create ad hoc need to redirect funding to crisis communications.

        • Budgetary restraints within the FDE, and government as a whole, that are having an impact on communication units.

Communication Objectives

In addressing its priority issues, the communication group within FDE will seek:

A   • To assess levels of public knowledge, awareness, and interest in environmental issues and perceptions of government and agency performance in these areas.

A   • To contribute to public understanding of major environmental concerns.

A   • To encourage Americans to take action on environmental concerns.

A   • To reinforce Americans' sense of personal efficacy.

B   • To promote accurate public perceptions of FDE leadership on environmental questions.

B   • To communicate existing legislative support for environmental initiatives.

B   • To encourage partnerships among all levels of government (domestic and international), the private sector, and special interest groups.

B&C   • To increase public awareness of government initiatives on the international front.

B&D   • To reinforce the perception that the environment and the economy share a symbiotic relationship (i.e., they are dependent on each other for growth).

         • To enhance awareness in government departments and agencies of the need to share information and responsibility on environmental questions.

         • To showcase the FDE's scientific knowledge, skills, and expertise.

Themes and Messages

Departmental themes are *personal efficacy, competency, leadership, partnerships,* and *sustainable development.* The messages that relate to these themes are as follows:

A   • Individual efforts can make a difference in preserving and enhancing the quality of the environment.

A   • With adequate effort, the problems of the environment can be solved.

B   • The FDE is setting and enforcing national standards for environmental protection.

B   • The FDE is using its scientific expertise to find solutions to environmental problems.

B   • The FDE is pushing industry to find innovative solutions to industry-generated problems.

B&C   • The FDE is forming partnerships (at home and abroad) with industry, other levels of government, individuals, and groups to enhance and preserve the quality of the environment.

D   • An investment in the environment is an investment in economic growth and jobs.

         • Departments with environmental components to their mandate must accept shared responsibility for environmental issues.

         • Exchange of information between departments and agencies sharing responsibility on environmental questions is essential.

Major Communication Activities/Initiatives

A
- Research into and analysis of the public opinion environment (public consultations, media and correspondence analysis, inquiry tracking, etc.).

A
- Public information campaign on individual options for action.

B
- Advertising campaign on federal efforts to protect and clean up the environment and preserve America's natural heritage.

B
- Public information campaign on existing and proposed environmental legislation and current enforcement measures.

B
- Media relations campaign to educate media and the public on scientific expertise available in the FDE.

R
- Conference to promote cooperation among different levels of government, the private sector, and interest groups *and* to promote concept of sustainable development.

B&C
- Media relations campaign to publicize American involvement in international negotiations on environmental questions.

D
- Public education campaign on concept of environmentally sustainable economic development.

- Internal communications to encourage shared responsibility among government departments and agencies on environmental questions.

Consultation Requirements

Consultation, coordination, and active cooperation with the following departments is required on an ongoing basis: Agriculture; Commerce; Energy; Forestry; Health and Human Services; Industry, Science, and Technology; Justice; Federal Emergency Management Agency; Federal Energy Regulatory Commission; the Interstate Commerce Commission; Department of Transportation; Federal Maritime Commission; the Fish and Wildlife Service; and the Forest Service.

Specific linkages between issues and appropriate departments could also be made in this section of the plan.

Anticipated Financial Resources

It is anticipated that the following resources will be devoted to FDE communications in 1992–1993, based on the 1991–1992 agency communication plan:

1. Total budget for communication unit: $xxx,xxx
2. Total allocations from budgets of other units: $xx,xxx,xxx

CONCLUSIONS

In the past, organizations involved a limited number of individuals in the writing of strategic plans. Once written, these plans were left to gather dust on a bookshelf or in a drawer. Fearful that a competitor might obtain a copy of the strategic plan, company officials would label plans as *top secret*. But as one executive stated, "The problem was that our own employees didn't even know what was to be accomplished, so how could they work toward that goal?"[41] Strategic plans need to be *sold* and *used*.

More and more companies are accepting the view that strategic planning is critical to the success of their enterprises. Governments are coming to the same conclusions. One study found a 20 percent failure rate among small firms that did not engage in strategic planning, compared to an 8 percent failure rate among those that engage in "sophisticated strategic planning."[42] One measure of an organization's commitment to strategic planning is the existence of a mission statement, considered to be prerequisite to a meaningful strategic planning exercise. Yet one researcher found that almost 60 percent of chief executive officers of *Business Week*'s top 1,000 firms run companies without mission statements,[43] and Walker Lewis, head of the Strategic Planning Association, warned that these kinds of deficiencies mean that "Western companies are in for 10 years of competitive hell."[44] Moreover, an organization that fails to transmit its vision (through oral and written communications) to its stakeholders may be assumed to have no vision, and if enough stakeholders (employees, investors, bankers, and others) reach this conclusion, the organization may be unable to contain the rupture of confidence.

NOTES

1. F. Paul Carlson, "The Long and Short of Strategic Planning," *Journal of Business Strategy,* May/June 1990, p. 15.
2. Ole Ingstrup, Commissioner of Correctional Services, Government of Canada, speech, 1990. A similar point is made in Benjamin R. Tregoe and Peter M.Tobia, "Strategy Versus Planning: Bridging the Gap," *Journal of Business Strategy,* November/December 1991, p. 14.
3. Robert E. Brooker, Jr., "Orchestrating the Planning Process," *Journal of Business Strategy,* 1990 p. 5.
4. Michael M. Robert, "Managing Your Competitor's Strategy," *Journal of Business Strategy,* March/April 1990, p. 24.
5. Ibid., p. 25.
6. Ian Wilson, "Realizing the Power of Strategic Vision," *Long Range Planning,* October 1992, p. 23.
7. R. Duane Ireland and Michael A. Hitt, "Mission Statements: Importance,

Challenge, and Recommendations for Development," *Business Horizons*, May/June 1992, p. 35.

8. Andrew Campbell, "The Power of Mission: Aligning Strategy and Culture," *Planning Review*, September/October 1992, p. 10.
9. Ibid.
10. Rosabeth Moss Kanter, "Championing Change: An Interview with Bell Atlantic's CEO Raymond Smith," *Harvard Business Review*, January/February 1991, p. 119–21.
11. Ireland and Hitt, p. 40.
12. Benjamin B. Tregoe and Peter M. Tobia, "An Action-Oriented Approach to Strategy," *Journal of Business Strategy*, January/February 1990, p. 20.
13. Ingstrup, speech.
14. Tregoe and Tobia, "An Action-Oriented Approach to Strategy," p. 20.
15. Ibid.
16. Mary Gusella, Assistant Secretary to Cabinet, Communications, Privy Council Office, Government of Canada, letter to directors generals of communication, 1988.
17. Robert W. Kinkead and Dena Winokur, "How Public Relations Professionals Help CEOs Make the Right Moves," *Public Relations Journal*, October 1992, p. 19.
18. Ibid., p. 23.
19. Ibid.
20. Ibid.
21. As a consequence of a 1988 Communication Policy, this change of focus is now well established in the Canadian government. Authors such as Susan L. Bovet, "Making the Move into Strategic Planning," *Public Relations Journal*, October 1992, p. 4, suggest that more and more U.S. firms are also including public relations executives in the corporate planning process.
22. Fraser P. Sietel, *The Practice of Public Relations*, 2nd ed. (Columbus, Ohio: Charles E. Merrill Publishing, 1984), p. 509.
23. Eleanor White of Employment and Immigration Canada suggested the placement of issues as the starting point for the strategic communication plan.
24. Hans H. Hinterhuber and Wolfgang Popp, "Are You a Strategist or Just a Manager?" *Harvard Business Review*, January/February 1992, p. 109.
25. Alexander Hiam, "Exposing Four Myths of Strategic Planning," *Journal of Business Strategy*, September/October 1990, p. 25.
26. Brooker, Jr., p. 4.
27. This is a modified version of a format developed by a Canadian government working group chaired by a member of the Privy Council Office.
28. Frank Winston Wylie, "Business and Ethics—and Long Term Planning," *Public Relations Quarterly*, Summer 1991, p. 8.

29. John Bryson, "A Strategic Planning Process for Public and Non-profit Organizations," *Long-Range Planning* 21 (1988), p. 76.

30. Tregoe and Tobia, "An Action-Oriented Approach," p. 18.

31. Bryson, p. 76.

32. Jane E. Dutton, Stephen A. Stempf, and David Wagner, "Diagnosing Strategic Issues and Managerial Investment of Resources," in *Advances in Strategic Management,* eds. Paul Shrivastava and Robert Lamb, vol. 6 (Greenwich, Conn.: JAI Press, 1990), p. 144.

33. Ibid.

34. Henry Mintzberg, "The Design School: Reconsidering the Basic Premises of Strategic Management," *Strategic Management Journal,* March/April 1990, p. 185.

35. Angus Reid, "Public Affairs Research: Quantitative and Qualitative," in *The Canadian Public Affairs Handbook: Maximizing Markets, Protecting Bottom Lines,* eds. W. John Wright and Christopher J. DuVernet, (Toronto: Carswell, 1988), pp. 137–38, speaks of a similar kind of distinction that should be made between a policy *issue* and policy *process*.

36. Ibid., p. 186.

37. Ibid.

38. Kinkead and Winokur, p. 19. Because the internal planning factors are not specific to communication, communication planners may wish to make a contribution in this area to the corporate plan rather than include internal factors in the communication plan. The rationale for doing so stems from the fact that some of the factors identified in the internal factors cannot be addressed by the communication unit. Despite the fact that mentioning the factors can result in a heightened awareness, the communication planner will not frame strategies for addressing these factors.

39. These categories were first delineated by Aristotle in *The Rhetoric*.

40. Alan Morgan, Department of External Affairs Canada, interview, spring 1989.

41. An interview with Ingeborg A. Marquardt, "Strategists Confront Planning Challenges," *Journal of Business Strategy,* May/June 1990, p. 7.

42. Ireland and Hitt, p. 37.

43. Ibid., p. 36.

44. Ronald Henkoff, "How to Plan for 1995," *Fortune,* December 31, 1990, pp. 70–79.

CHAPTER 10

IMPLEMENTING STRATEGIC OBJECTIVES THROUGH OPERATIONAL AND WORK PLANNING IN COMMUNICATION

Operational planning follows from the strategic planning process. Whereas strategic planning sets long-term objectives, determining future direction for the organization, operational planning establishes the steps that the organization will take to achieve these objectives. Strategic planning is the "what" in planning, the "driving force behind operational plans"[1]; operational planning is the "how."[2] Three of the "how's" associated with operational communications planning are: "How is the organization planning to put its strategic plan into action?" "How does the organization intend to allocate budgeted financial resources among different activities?" "How does the organization intend to allocate human resources?"[3]

The stand-off with cult leader David Koresh at Waco, Texas, can be used to demonstrate the difference between policy issues and operational questions. For the attorney general of the United States, the overriding strategic issue at Waco was whether or not to sanction the use of force in ending the confrontation. Once the attorney general had made that strategic policy decision, the question for the Federal Bureau of Investigations became operational: *Out of all possible choices available, what type of force should be used to bring the matter to a speedy conclusion (with minimal threat to compound residents and to federal agents)?* The policy issue had been resolved; only the operational question of how best to effect the policy decision remained.

An annual operational plan allows the organization to decide how it intends to implement its strategic objectives in the year to come, to establish ways and means: "The operational plan is both a process and an instrument whereby actual plans, operations and related resources are described and rationalized for the planning period."[4] It is used for the following purposes:

- To merge priorities, policies, and issues from the strategic phase of planning with ongoing activities and services.

- To review and place priorities on activities and services.
- To justify resource requests.
- To give direction to the formulation of work plans.[5]

Compared to strategic planning, operational planning is much more concrete and specific.

As with the strategic plan, the operational communication plan must be a shared product if it is to garner the commitment of organization members. You don't just present a completed operational plan to middle or senior management. You produce the plan during the same time period as the corporate operational plan, and you consult regularly with others in relevant areas of the organization. At some stage, executives at higher levels of the organization will have to approve your plan and accept partial ownership of it.

WHAT IS THE "IDEAL" MODEL FOR OPERATIONAL PLANNING IN COMMUNICATION?

The following steps have been given as the "ideal model" for operational planning:

1. Communication officers are assigned to specific policy or business units (clients) in the company or government department.
2. These communication officers are regular invitees to the management committee of the client area that they serve.
3. These communication officers perform the following tasks:
   a. Give advice.
   b. Act as liaisons, obtaining input from clients and relaying this information to those who produce the communication services and products.
   c. Work with program and operational managers on operational plans.
   d. Do planning at the same time as program and operational managers.
   e. Integrate the functions of the communication planner with the corporate planner (usually a middle manager or division head at the operational planning stage).
   f. Establish credibility.
4. Once completed, the operational plans go to a higher level for approval and acceptance.

The interplay between strategic planning and operational planning at Huntington Banc was described in the following way: "At some point, the strategic planning and the operational planning at Huntington Banc will blend together and you will not be able to determine where one begins and the other ends. We have time lines to evaluate that."[6]

PLANNING CYCLES

The Washington Mutual Financial Group in Seattle, Washington, also follows a planning cycle that allows the integration of the strategic and operational planning phases:[7]

1. Each January, the top team updates its strategy.
2. The board of directors reviews the strategy.
3. In June, the six divisions and the subsidiary companies that compose Washington Mutual generate one-year operational plans, based on the updated strategy.
4. These annual operational plans become the basis for departmental work plans and budgets.
5. The company monitors progress against the operational and work plans on an ongoing basis during the year, using measures such as performance indicators, budget variances, and periodic progress checks.

The same general model is followed by the Canadian government, but with different timelines.

1. Between June and August, the government develops its policy framework, which reflects priorities expressed in major government statements such as:
   a. The Throne Speech (the equivalent of the State of the Union address delivered in the United States).
   b. The budget speech.
   c. Policy statements developed by the Priorities and Planning Committee of Cabinet.
2. In August, the Privy Council Office (a central agency of government) sends out a call letter, along with relevant documentation, requesting that all government departments prepare strategic plans.
3. The Privy Council Office gives guidance to individual departments in preparing their strategic plans.
4. In October, individual government departments submit strategic plans.
5. In November and December, Privy Council Office officials meet with departments to give feedback and to discuss the March request for financial information (which will appear in the operational plan).

6. In January, the Privy Council Office sends out a call letter, requesting that operational plans be prepared.
7. In March, departments submit operational plans to the Privy Council Office.

WHAT ARE THE COMPONENTS OF AN ANNUAL OR MULTIYEAR OPERATIONAL COMMUNICATIONS PLAN?

The operational plan should address the following points: the major planned communication activities/initiatives and the priority placed on each, the linkage of planned communication activities to strategic communication objectives, identification of key client groups (external and internal), identification of complementary activities and services not performed by the communication group but which support communication objectives, and resources allocated to support communication activities and services.

Priority Activities/Initiatives

The starting point for the annual operational communication plan is the priority activities/initiatives section of the strategic plan. The communication planner lifts the communication activities directly from the strategic plan and places them as part I of the operational plan. Thus, these communication activities serve as a link between the two stages of planning: strategic and operational. Priority activities or initiatives often involve clusters of activities centered around some organizational issue or theme: for example, public relations campaigns or information campaigns designed to respond to some organizational issue.

Rank Ordering of Activities/Initiatives

The operational plan should explain the emphasis that is to be placed on different communication activities, giving each a priority ranking. At the same time, the plan should refer to any changes from activities designated in the earlier strategic planning phase. For example, an organization may face a crisis situation between the time that it formulates or updates its strategic plan and the time that it writes or updates its annual or multiyear operational plan. The organization may need to transfer funds from one of the activities that appeared in the strategic plan. This depletion of funds may mean that some priority activities will be dropped from the operational plan. A brief note should indicate any changes from the planned activities that appeared in the strategic plan.

Linkages to Strategic Plan

The relationship between the proposed activities/initiatives and the communication objectives (that appeared earlier in the strategic plan) should be clearly articulated in this section of the annual operational communication plan.

Typically, different individuals are involved in strategic planning from those who are involved in operational planning. Strategic planning is usually carried out at senior levels of the organization, involving top executives and the head of communications; operational planning takes place at middle levels of the organization. Restating the priority activities and objectives forces the tactical planner to link the operational plan to the strategic plan. The origins of the operational plan can be found in the strategic plan, and these connections should be explicit and clear.

Key Client Groups

The term *key client groups* refers to internal and external stakeholders who compose the main client groups for communication products and services. These client groups may be interest groups, specific units or divisions of the company, other government departments, shareholders, the general public, or others.

Complementary Activities/Services

Organizations have ongoing activities and services upon which they can draw when they plan special events or communication activities. For example, policy groups often monitor certain newspapers or television stations on an ongoing basis. Assume that a state health department is engaged in planning an anti-drug campaign. Other government departments also may be involved in producing materials on this same topic (e.g., the Department of Justice and the Attorney General's office). A special bureau set up to deal with the concerns of AIDS victims may have related antidrug materials on hand. The state health department can draw on its own resources and on the resources of these other departments and bureaus.

Resources

The final section of the operational communication plan involves identifying the resources that are necessary to carry out each major communication activity or initiative. The figure presented in the earlier strategic communication plan is broken down into smaller units in the operational plan. A sample operational communication plan follows in Figure 10.1.

FIGURE 10.1

Federal Department of the Environment, Operational Communications Plan, 1991–92*

Activities/Initiatives	Priority Level	Ties to Strategic Communication Objectives	Key Client Groups	Complementary Department Activities/Services	Resources WYs**	$000
Research and analysis of public opinion environment.	I	To assess public knowledge of, interest in, and support for environmental concerns, as well as perceptions of FDE leadership.	Branch executives, policy officers, communication officers, senior management, regional offices, agencies.	Regional reports, correspondence logs, backgrounders generated by policy branches.	X	
Public information campaign on individual options for action.	II	To encourage Americans to take action on environmental concerns and to reinforce their sense of personal efficacy.	General public, media, interest groups, youth groups, community groups, regional offices, agencies, senators, Congress.	Ministerial and executive speeches; special events such as Environment Week, Earth Day; essay writing contests, sustained media strategy including editorial boards.	X	
Advertising campaign on federal efforts to clean up the environment.	I	To promote accurate public perceptions of FDE leadership on environmental questions.	General public, media, interest groups, industry, regional offices, agencies, senators, Congress.	Media interviews, speeches, special events.	X	

Activity	WYs**	Objective	Audience	Products	
Conference on sustainable development.	II	To promote concept of department leadership, to encourage partnerships, and to reinforce belief in the symbiotic relationship of the environment to the economy.	Municipal governments, state governments, federal departments, other national governments, industry, interest groups, scientific community, regional offices, agencies, senators, Congress.	Educational materials generated by program branches, ongoing consultations with private sector and industry.	X
Media relations campaign on international negotiations.	III	To increase public awareness of government leadership in the international arena.	General public, other national governments, interest groups (national and international), regional offices, agencies, senators, Congress.	Interest group profiles, departmental presence on international committees, negotiations with lobby groups, sustained media strategy including editorial boards.	X
Internal audit and network analysis.	II	To encourage better procedures for integrating departmental planning processes.	Corporate and communication planners, government heads, executive committees, regional offices, agencies.	Other audits, employee surveys.	X

* This plan was developed by Sherry Ferguson and M. Natalie Lam. It is a revised version of a format developed by Stewart Ferguson for the Department of the Solicitor General of Canada. The plan is fictitious.

** WYs refers to employee work years. Please note differences, if any, between proposals in the strategic plan and activities in the operational plan.

WHAT IS THE RELATIONSHIP BETWEEN OPERATIONAL PLANNING AND WORK PLANNING?

Work planning is a still more specific level of planning. Annual operational plans are broken down into work plans. These plans detail actions to be taken by the organization in achieving its operational plan. Work plans translate priorities into products and services to be delivered, assign accountabilities, specify goals and milestones, define monitoring and evaluation methods, and identify resource requirements to deliver the products and services. The work plan is said to "constitute an agreement between the supervisor and the responsible employee, which can be appraised."[8]

Work plans are sufficiently concrete that you can monitor and assess the degree to which you have met your goals each year. The importance of this monitoring effort has been described in the following way:

> Monitoring is the function of tracking plans, activities, and expenditure of resources, whether in terms of dollars or time. It collects performance information for reporting and for management decision making. It provides a mechanism to update and adapt work plans. A useful monitoring device is to break down work plans into discrete projects, each with an allocated budget, against which the expenditure of individual time also can be designated and reported. A variety of workload indicators or time measurement systems can be applied to this form of monitoring. The advantage for project leaders is that it furnishes quite precise data on costs. From the standpoint of communication officers, who may be engaged in many distinct projects, time accounting helps guard against overcommitment of resources. Such systems are invaluable to . . . senior management to ensure that resource expenditure accords with priorities.[9]

As one moves from the strategic to the operational to the work-planning level, increased specificity and concreteness result in the statement of measurable objectives. The relationship between the three stages of planning can be depicted visually in the following way. See Figure 10.2.

WHAT ARE THE ELEMENTS IN A COMMUNICATION WORK PLAN?

Priority Activities/Initiatives

This section of the work plan repeats the first part of the operational plan; it is directly tied to the operational plan. The intent is to assure coherency in planning.

FIGURE 10.2*

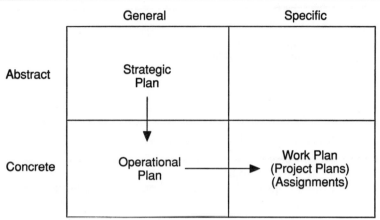

* This figure was contributed by Robert Czerny, Communication Officer, National Archives of Canada. It is used with permission.

Products and Services to Be Delivered

A major communication activity or initiative (e.g., a campaign to inform the public of a company's plans to produce a new type of computer) could generate many potential communication products and services. Examples include brochures publicizing the new computer, press releases that announce when the computers will be on the market, feature articles produced for computer magazines, speeches for the firm's executive officers, and focus groups to determine the best marketing appeals to use in publicizing the new product.

Responsible Party for Delivering Products and Services

Within any firm or government organization, certain designated individuals will assume responsibility for delivering the products and services. This section of the plan allows for a designation of that person(s) or organizational sector (branch, unit, division, or other group). In some instances, the individuals charged with responsibility will generate the product or perform the service themselves. For example, many large firms employ public relations specialists to produce press kits, public service announcements, the text for brochures, and other creative products. Smaller firms and governments often contract out a number of these services. Regardless of whether the task is performed in-house or contracted out, someone within the firm will be asked to assume responsibility for seeing that the task is completed adequately and the product or service is delivered within the required time frame.

Goals

Management specialists disagree on definitions of objectives and goals. Here *goals* are defined as specific ends to be achieved or "milestones along the road to achieving . . . objectives."[10] *Objectives,* by contrast, are more general. The relationship between objectives and goals can be seen in the following examples. If a company objective is "to achieve a better balance between domestic and offshore business," a related goal could be "to have offshore sales account for 30 percent of total sales by 1993." If a company objective is "to develop a preeminent position in customer service," a related goal could be "to attain, by 1995, and maintain the number one position in industry surveys of customer satisfaction with service."[11]

In the operational phase of planning, it may be decided that the best way to achieve a particular communication objective (e.g., "to persuade consumers to purchase multiple watches for different occasions" or "to explain to shareholders why the company is supporting the new tax-reform legislation") is to undertake a national advertising campaign or a public information campaign. Details for these campaigns will be formulated at the work plan stage.

A work plan for an information campaign could include a speaking tour, a conference, and a series of public service announcements. In the case where a company wants to inform its shareholders of its stance on a new tax-reform bill, it could plan a number of different activities, including a survey to find out how much shareholders know about the legislation and the production of a backgrounder, a brochure, and/or a slide presentation for the annual shareholder meeting. Goals for these activities could include "to determine the level of shareholder knowledge or the tax-reform bill" or "to inform shareholders about the costs and benefits of the tax-reform legislation."

Milestones

Milestones specify the deadlines for accomplishing different stages of a project. Typical kinds of deadlines for communication undertakings are the dates by which (1) bids should be requested, received, and evaluated (if the organization decides to obtain the services of an outside firm); (2) the design of a product should be completed; (3) any necessary research should be completed; (4) the product or service should be delivered; (5) product approvals are required; (6) publication should occur, where applicable; and (7) distribution of the product should occur, where applicable.

Evaluation Component

Accountability implies responsibility. In difficult economic times, accountability implies the need for an employee, a company division, or a government group to be able to justify the value of what they are producing. If they cannot justify the worth of their products and services, they will be dismissed or disbanded. Accountability suggests, at the outside limits, the necessity for an individual or group to justify its continuing existence. Manufacturing divisions, marketing, and legal devisions have long been held accountable for their work. If a plant manufactures too many defective parts, an advertising campaign doesn't increase sales, or a legal unit loses all its cases, these organizational units can expect to be replaced. Until recently, however, public affairs groups were held to different standards. Organizations that invested in public relations campaigns and issues-management strategies did not expect the public affairs managers to answer for the effectiveness of their efforts. This situation has changed in recent years. Both private firms and governments are demanding new standards of accountability for all employees, including those who specialize in public relations work. Public affairs and public relations personnel are being asked to document their successes.

Some of the kinds of evaluation instruments and techniques currently being used by communication specialists are expert reviews, pre- and post-testing, internal assessments, focus group testing, readability tests, pull-out inserts requesting user feedback, telephone surveys, mail surveys, intercept surveys, portfolio tests to measure recall, use of a 1–800 telephone line, information audits, theater-type tests to rate communication products, dummy advertising tests, backcasting to identify past performance gaps in planning and decision making, inquiry tracking, usage counts to determine the number of times a message appeared in the media, and interviews of opinion leaders. Still more effort needs to be put into designing creative instruments to measure the effectiveness of public relations efforts.

Resources

Required resources to deliver each product or service are identified in this part of the work plan. Resources may be broken down into work years (the cost of time used by company employees to perform a task) and additional expenses for expertise, materials, and equipment not owned by the firm. A sample communication work plan follows in Figure 10.3.

KEY POINTS

In an ideal model, operational and work planning flow out of the strategic planning process, and each stage of planning produces corollary documents in communication. The intent of this chapter has been to suggest what elements should appear at the second and third stages of planning. To place what is happening at the operational and work-planning stages in context, it is useful to review the strategic planning process (discussed in Chapter 9) and to see

FIGURE 10.3
Federal Department of the Environment, Communication Work Plan, 1991–1992*

Activities/Initiatives	Product/ to be Delivered	Person to Deliver Product/ Service	Goals	Milestones	Evaluation Component	Resources	
						WYs	$000
Research and analysis of public opinion environment.	Media analysis.				Survey of client users.		
	Issue A.	Person 1.	To assess media reaction to environmental policy.	Prepared by: 01-Nov-91. Approved by: 08-Nov-91. Circulated by: 15-Nov-91. Evaluated by: 30-Nov-91. (Milestones as above with appropriate dates)		X	Y
	Issue B.	Person 1.	To assess media reaction to tabled legislation.	(Milestones as above with appropriate dates)		X	Y
	Issue C.	Person 2.	To assess media reaction to government performance at international convention.			X	Y
	Issue D.	Person 2.	To assess media coverage of public information campaign.	(Milestones as above with appropriate dates)		X	Y

Research and analysis of public opinion environment (continued)					X	Y
Public opinion surveys. Issue B.	Person 3.	To assess public knowledge of Issue B.	Bids in by: 15-May-92. Contracted out by: 10-Jun-92. Results by: 15-Sep-92. Distributed by: 25-Sep-92. Evaluated by: 0?-Oct-92. (Milestones as above with appropriate dates)	External expert review.	X	Y
Issue C.	Person 3.	To assess public attitudes toward Issue C.			X	Y
Inquiry tracking reports.	Person 4.	To prioritize public concerns.	Month's end (12 reports).	Internal branch assessment.	X	Y
Issue identification surveys with branch executives.	Person 1.	To identify and prioritize issues likely to impact on department.	Questions prepared by: 05-Jul-92. Approved by: 20-Jul-92. Administered by: 10-Aug-92. Results analyzed by: 01-Sep-92. Report prepared by: 15-Sep-92. Results circulated by: 22-Sep-92. Evaluated by: 0?-Oct-92.	Follow-up user assessment.	X	Y
Monthly issue tracking reports.	Person 2.	To provide updated reports for strategic planning.	Month's end (12 reports).	Executive committee assessment.	X	Y

* This plan was developed by Sherry Ferguson and M. Natalie Lam. It is a revised version of a format developed by Stewart Ferguson for the Department of the Solicitor General of Canada. The plan is fictitious.

FIGURE 10.3 *(concluded)*

Activities/Initiatives	Product/ to be Delivered	Person to Deliver Product/ Service	Goals	Milestones	Evaluation Component	Resources	
						WYs	$000
Public Information campaign on individual options for action.	Brochure.				Readability test.		
	On general environmental issues.	Person 5.	To inform the general public and to encourage action.	Contracted out by: 05-Jun-91. Evaluated by: 04-Jul-91. Prepared by: 18-Jul-91. Approved by: 02-Aug-91. Printed by: 16-Aug-91. Distributed by: 30-Aug-91. (Milestones as above with appropriate dates)		X	Y
	On Issue A.	Person 5.	To urge youth groups to take action.			X	Y
	TV public service announcement. On Issue B.	Person 6.	To inform the general public.	Contracted out by: 05-Sep-91. Prepared by: 06-Nov-91. Content evaluated by: 14-Nov-91. Approved by: 21-Nov-91. Distributed by: 07-Dec-91. Usage evaluated by: 07-March-92. (Milestones as above with appropriate dates)	Focus group testing, usage count.	X	Y
	On Issue C.	Person 6.	To urge the public to take action.			X	Y

Public information campaign on individual options for action. (continued)				Internal review.	X	Y
Feature article for community newspapers. On Issue A.	Person 7.	To encourage community groups to promote individual options for action.	Researched by: 19-Aug-91. Written by: 05-Sep-91. Approved by: 13-Sep-91. Distributed by 20-Sep-91. Evaluated by: 27-Sep-91. (Milestones as above with appropriate dates)		X	Y
On Issue B.	Person 8.	To encourage community groups to promote individual options for action.			X	Y
Press kit.	Person 6.	To inform the general public.	Prepared by: 15-Jan-92. Approved by: 22-Jan-92. Printed by: 08-Feb-92. Evaluated by: 08-Mar-92.	Usage count.	X	Y
Speeches for special events.				User assessment, user count for messages.		
Event 1.	Person 8.	To encourage youth groups to promote environmental concerns.	Prepared by: 18-Jan-92. Approved by: 22-Jan-92. Delivered by: date of event. Evaluated by: 1 week after event. (Milestones as above with appropriate dates)		X	Y
Event 2.	Person 8.	To inform and encourage community groups to take specific action.	(Milestones as above with appropriate dates)		X	Y
Event 3.	Person 7.	To inform special interest groups on government programs related to individual options.			X	Y

* This plan was developed by Sherry Ferguson and M. Natalie Lam. It is a revised version of a format developed by Stewart Ferguson for the Department of the Solicitor General of Canada. The plan is fictitious.

how the three stages relate to each other. At the strategic planning stage, the communication document contains a statement of:

- Organization objectives.
- Strategic issues.
- Positive and negative factors (opportunities and threats) in the external planning environment.
- Positive and negative factors (strengths and weaknesses) in the internal planning environment.
- Communication objectives.
- Themes and messages.
- Priority activities.
- Consultation requirements.
- Budgeted resources.

At the operational planning stage, the communication document contains a statement of:

- Priority activities/initiatives (note the link back to the strategic plan).
- Rank ordering of priority activities/initiatives.
- Linkages to communication objectives in strategic plan (again, note the tie back to the earlier planning stage).
- Key client groups.
- Complementary activities/services.
- Budgeted resources.

At the work planning stage, the communication document contains a statement of:

- Priority activities/initiatives (note the link back to the operational and strategic plans).
- Products/services to be delivered.
- Responsible party for delivering products/services.
- Goals.
- Milestones.
- Evaluation component.
- Budgeted resources.

NOTES

1. Privy Council Office document, Government of Canada, taken from *Strategic Planner's Handbook,* 1988.

2. Benjamin B. Tregoe and Peter M. Tobia, "An Action-Oriented Approach to Strategy," *Journal of Business Strategy*, January/February 1990, p. 17.
3. Mary Gusella, Assistant Secretary to Cabinet, Communications, Privy Council Office, Government of Canada, letter to directors general of communication, February 9, 1989.
4. Privy Council Office document titled "Operational Communication Planning," 1988.
5. Ibid.
6. Tregoe and Tobia, p. 17.
7. Ibid.
8. Privy Council Office document, 1989.
9. Ibid.
10. Ian Wilson, "Realizing the Power of Strategic Vision," *Long Range Planning,* October 1992, p. 23.
11. These examples of objectives and goals are also drawn from Wilson, p. 23.

CHAPTER 11

LIMITED-SCOPE COMMUNICATION PLANNING: PLANNING FOR SPECIAL EVENTS AND ACTIVITIES

An organization that has a well-developed strategic and operational planning culture will also produce a number of single-purpose or limited-scope plans each year. These plans will anticipate upcoming events and activities (e.g., a policy or program announcement, the tabling of a piece of legislation, executive involvement in a major conference or proceedings, a press conference, release of a new publication, or a crisis situation).

A typical organization or government department might produce 20 or 30 different communication plans in the course of a year. If plans already exist, the organization may update the plans on a regular basis. The frequency with which the organization will update a communication plan depends upon many factors, for example, the importance of the event or activity (its potential impact on the organization's survival and well-being), the responsiveness of the issue to influences in the external environment (interaction with other issues or susceptibility to shifts in public opinion or political or economic climate), and the responsiveness of the issue to internal influences (executive priorities, budgetary restraints, or other variables). Diversion of funds to the management of crises, for example, may cause an organization to rework its priorities and rewrite some of its communication plans.

A communication plan that is framed to guide the management of a specific event or activity has both strategic and operational components. Strategic elements in the plan include a statement regarding the public opinion environment, communication objectives, a statement of messages, strategic considerations, and requirements for consultation with internal or external stakeholders or the establishment of coordinating mechanisms. Elements that are common to operational and work plans include an identification of target audiences, tactical considerations, specifics related to announcements, requirements for CEO involvement, requirements for supporting materials, requirements for briefings of press and other groups or individuals, suggested follow-up activities, budgetary needs, and evaluation criteria.[1]

A limited-scope plan will rarely be more than five to seven pages long. For activities of a limited nature (e.g., a press conference or a minor issue) a plan may be very short, no more than a page. On the other hand, a pressing concern or a major event may warrant a longer communication plan. In writing the communication plan, you should use plain everyday language, avoiding bureaucratic jargon. Avoid lengthy sentences and paragraphs; short sentences and bullets are best. Avoid unnecessary detail; make every word count.

The following is a breakdown of what could appear in a limited-scope communication plan, produced in anticipation of some event or activity. Not all categories will appear in every plan.

Event or Issue

Identify the subject of the communication plan (e.g., a policy or program announcement, an upcoming conference, the withdrawal of a controversial product, the tabling of a new legislative bill, a rate increase, an executive resignation, the allocation of new funds to a project, etc).

Opinion Environment

The public opinion environment section may begin with a short summary that details the origins of the issue (i.e., its historical development from perhaps an incipient issue to an issue with more mature status) and recent events relevant to an understanding of the issue.

In the same way as the environment component of the annual or multi-year strategic plan, this section of the limited-scope communication plan seeks to describe influences operating in the public-opinion environment. If a company executive or a government official must make a policy or program announcement, the individual will want to have a clear indication, in advance, of the climate of public opinion on the subject. This section of the plan identifies trends in public opinion, suggesting likely reactions to the announcement or planned activity, as well as current sensitivities related to the topic. It should include anticipated reactions to the issue, either by groups supporting or opposing the organization's point of view (e.g., public debate or demonstrations, lobbying, or other manifestations of pressure-group activities).

When you write this part of the plan which identifies trends in public opinion, consider including the following:

- The findings of any surveys, focus groups, or interviews with opinion leaders.
- The results of electronic or print media analyses, including both national coverage and regional breakdowns, where appropriate.

- Analyses of correspondence from experts, special-interest groups, and/
  or the general public.
- The findings of other special studies.

It is important to note that this section of the plan is limited to a discussion of public *perceptions*. These perceptions may, or may not, correspond to reality. The public may have an accurate or a completely distorted view of the organization's position on any given issue. Whatever the view or the organization's image with the public, the organization should be cognizant of this perception. If the public or special-interest groups are strongly opposed to forthcoming legislation or have a decidedly hostile attitude toward program or personnel cuts, decision makers require advance notice. By the same token, if public opinion favors particular options, decision makers may see opportunities for acceptable resolution of an issue.

In order for the opinion environment section of the communication plan to be useful, the organization must be careful not to punish the messenger who brings bad news. Organizations must encourage a climate wherein bad news can travel, as easily as good news, up the organizational hierarchy. I am familiar with one case in which senior management requested that an analysis of a public-opinion environment be destroyed because certain individuals feared that higher-level executives would react angrily to the negative information. On the other hand, I know of another instance in which an organization actually paid a consultancy firm to give them "bad news." Decision makers recognized that only "good news" was traveling upward within the organization, creating a situation whereby the organization was always unprepared, operating in a reactive mode.

Sample statements on the issue of gun control might be as follows:

- Gun-control lobby groups have become increasingly active during the last six months, indicating that a renewed push for stronger legislation could be in the offing.
- Media coverage of the issue has been variable. Urban newspapers have tended to give more favorable publicity to the pro-gun control groups, and rural newspapers have tended to favor the stance of the Rifle Association and other sports organizations.
- The amount of correspondence received by the Justice Department has increased dramatically since the recent shopping-mall killings; the largest number of writers have called for more rigorous laws and better enforcement.
- Recent values studies indicate that Americans may be more apt today, than in the past, to support the balancing of individual rights with social responsibility. If this trend continues, it is possible that this theme may carry over to the debate over gun control.

Sample statements on the environmental movement might be as follows:

- Greenpeace continues to set the agenda for environmental groups concerned about the seal hunt. Most of its new members are 20 to 30 years old.
- The environmental movement also seems to be gaining momentum in the Southeastern United States, particularly with groups concerned that industrialization may pose a long-term threat to the attractiveness of the region to tourists.
- Analysis of interest-group literature suggests a trend toward the proliferation of many small, single-issue environmental groups rather than increasing numbers of members in the larger groups.

Similar to the strategic plan, the limited-scope plan includes factors related to the internal opinion climate. Support or lack of support within the organization for an activity or initiative can determine its success or failure. Noting the extent to which a planned policy or program has the support of stakeholders within the organization focuses attention on their potential level of influence. The following examples illustrate the type of statements that could appear in a limited-scope plan.[2]

- Support for quality-of-work-life initiatives is stronger with senior managers than with middle managers.
- High levels of participation in recycling initiatives at the company suggest that employees will actively support the company's new environmental policy.
- Analysis of suggestion-box contributions reveals that employees are in favor of work sharing.
- There is a high level of esprit de corps among those who worked on the matrix management team for project X; their enthusiasm will probably translate into positive support for this project.

Some issues are of interest only to internal constituencies. For example, if a company is considering switching from a seniority-based system to a merit-based system, those most strongly affected will be company employees and their families. The following statements could appear in a plan formulated to address the proposed change in pay systems.

- Support for changing from a seniority-based system to a merit-based system is strongest among middle managers.
- In recent newsletters, union members have expressed their strong opposition to a merit-based system.
- The strongest criticism for the proposed changes continues to come from older workers.

Target Audiences

The starting point for any communication process is audience analysis. This is true as much in public or group process as in interpersonal communication. We can communicate with each other only to the extent that we understand the communication needs of our receivers. When we give a speech or write a script for someone else to deliver, we learn as much as possible about the audience before beginning the discourse. We research the setting and the occasion, we acquire demographic information about the audience, and we identify the audience's level of familiarity with our topic. In summary, we try to write a speech that is appropriate to the audience and the occasion. If we prepare an article for a magazine or a script for a television show, we try to anticipate the needs of the readers or viewers, and we adapt our style and content to those who will receive the communication. In the case of organizational communication, we seek to understand the perspective of our target groups (i.e., those we wish to inform, to persuade, or to move to action).

It has been said that we can only communicate with each other to the extent that we have overlapping fields of experience. If we have not acquired common fields by actively experiencing what our audience has experienced, we can at least seek to understand their experiences and their needs. This means that in order to inform an audience, you need to know the members' current level of knowledge on a given subject. In order to persuade or convince listeners or readers, you need to understand their present position on the issue, comprehending why they believe as they do. Otherwise, as a communicator, how can you reach out and make your position known and understood? Communication strategies start and end with a clear understanding of the levels of awareness, the knowledge, the beliefs, the attitudes, and the values of your target group. Values research attempts to take into account the psychographic types that make up audiences (e.g., the psychographic classification of people opposed to expansion of a factory).[3] See the discussion in Chapter 3 for further development of this point.

Thus, in this section of the limited-scope communication plan, you identify the principal audiences that you want to target in your communications. Discuss the groups in order of their importance, or priority. Describe the position and the knowledge level of each target group. These groups will have a special interest or stake in the issue or proposition. They will be the publics most likely to be affected by your policy or program (e.g., Wisconsin dairy producers, Midwest farmers, plant workers, middle managers, finance personnel, or computer software specialists). Your later choice of strategies, and the vehicles you select for reaching these audiences, will depend upon accurate identification of these groups. The audiences for your communications may be national or regional in nature; they may be public, private, or voluntary sector organizations or groups; they may be social, economic, or political in orientation; and they may be internal or external to the organization.

Sample statements identifying target audiences and their stance on issues are as follows:

- Midwestern farm associations and their members closely follow the issue of agricultural subsidies; they will undoubtedly give strong support to the proposed legislation.

- A prominent target group for communications about the new retraining programs will be unions; union leaders have indicated that they will support the programs so long as participating workers agree to job relocation.

- The individuals responsible for processing new employees are in a good position to influence initial attitudes toward the company's sick-leave policies; these members of the personnel department are an important target group for communications on the revised sick-leave policy.

- Women at middle management level can be expected to support the new employment equity policy; however, they may feel that the policy does not go far enough.

- The issue of drugs in the workplace is of concern to company executives (who are aware of the yearly losses in productivity, absenteeism, and insurance costs), employees (especially those with an existing drug-abuse problem), local rehabilitation counsellors (who may be called upon to treat referrals), local church groups, and the community at large. The announcement of the program to identify, counsel, and assist drug abusers will probably secure good community support but may generate criticism from those who claim their right to privacy is being violated.

- All employees affected by job reclassification will be targeted in the initial flurry of communications; those not affected will receive a second wave of information.

As suggested above, the target audiences for some communications are internal (e.g., senior managers, legal staff, union members, company employees, or others).

Communication Objectives

Every communication plan that is written for a specific event or activity should relate back to the elements in the strategic plan. in other words, communication objectives and messages will be more concrete and specific versions of the objectives and messages that appeared in the organization's multi-year or annual strategic plan. An objective appearing in a strategic plan might be "To make the public aware that Murdock Chemicals is a good corporate citizen." A related objective appearing in a communication plan for announcing a new company policy on plant emissions might be "To inform the public that Murdock Chemicals is undertaking serious new initiatives in the area of plant emissions."

Communication objectives should flow out of the environment section of the plan. You should be specific and concrete, stating exactly what you want to accomplish through your communications (e.g., to inform certain interest or lobby groups of initiatives being undertaken by your organization, to garner public support for a new policy or stance, to stimulate public discussion or activity in certain areas, or to respond to criticism). These are all legitimate objectives.

As in the case of the multiyear or annual strategic plan, you may be seeking to inform, to persuade, to convince, or to move your audience to action. Some additional examples of communication objectives are as follows:

- To allay fears that Murdock Chemicals may be downsizing its operations in the Cleveland area.
- To inform environmental interest groups of Murdock Chemicals' research initiatives in the area of biodegradable detergents.
- To stimulate community support for a new baseball league that Murdock Chemicals is sponsoring.
- To urge local businesses to contribute to the building of a community recreation hall that Murdock Chemicals is subsidizing.

Some communication objectives will be directed at internal audiences. Examples follow:

- To explain the new promotion policies to all employees.
- To encourage employees to contribute to the building fund for a new community recreation center.
- To promote networking between the design and planning sectors.
- To generate support among middle managers for the new employment-equity policies.
- To encourage at-risk employees to participate in the "Drugs in the Workplace" rehabilitation program.
- To inform records personnel of the revised approach to managing electronic records of employee files.
- To encourage employees to attend more company functions.

Messages

In this section of the plan, you are identifying the principal message or messages to be conveyed to stakeholders. A message appearing in a communication plan for activities sponsored in association with Environment Week might be "Murdock Chemicals is doing its part to ensure that Americans can breathe clean air." A still more concrete version of this message would be "Murdock Chemicals is making major changes to plants to ensure that emissions conform to national safety standards." The more concrete the message, the better; the more simple and clear the language, the better. You should get at the essence of the idea, avoiding unnecessary detail.

Messages in the limited-scope plan must relate back to the messages that appeared earlier in the organization's strategic plan. The previous examples, for instance, are offshoots of a broader message that could have appeared in a strategic plan for Murdock Chemicals. That message is "Murdock Chemicals is a good corporate citizen that is concerned about the environment." The message that appeared in the strategic plan is broad and consensual in nature. The more specific message that could appear in the limited-scope plan is "Murdock Chemicals is making major changes to plants to ensure that emissions conform to national safety standards."

An executive from Murdock Chemicals who speaks at a conference on the environment could espouse still another version of the broader strategic message, for example, "Murdock Chemicals is doing its part to ensure that the ozone layer is not depleted." A more concrete version of this message would be "Murdock Chemicals is sponsoring university research concerned with solving the ozone problem." Again, the two examples represent increasingly specific incarnations of the strategic message "Murdock Chemicals is a good corporate citizen that is concerned about the environment."

Some additional examples of corporate messages are as follows:

- Wally's Department Store offers high quality goods at low cost.
- Jerald's Furniture is a traditional company with a modern outlook.
- First National Bank offers personalized banking services.
- Bay Optical gives affordable eye care.

Examples of messages directed at internal audiences are the following.

- Job sharing allows employees the opportunity to work flexible hours.
- Drinking in the workplace is not an acceptable practice.
- The enhanced software creates new opportunities for networking with regional representatives.
- A new day-care facility located at the plant will allow working parents to be close to their young children.

The more specific and concrete the message, the easier it will be to evaluate the success of your communication efforts. One of the ways by which an organization evaluates the effectiveness of its efforts to communicate to external audiences is to do a usage count (i.e., to track the extent to which the media has picked up and carried the organization's messages). In doing a usage count, you quantify the number of newspapers, radio stations, and television stations that transmitted the message to the public. Although a usage count cannot tell you the number of people who were persuaded to your organization's point of view, it can tell you whether they received the message. There is no chance of attitude change with an audience that does not hear your message. Usage counts are most appropriate in examining straight news coverage of events and issues (e.g., learning how many newspapers referred to a large corporate donation, tracking the number of times local radio stations broadcast a public service announcement, tabulating the number of times national networks announced a new medical discovery.

Messages in annual strategic plans are typified by statements such as "The government is pushing industry to find innovative solutions to environmental problems" or "Murdock Chemicals is a good corporate citizen that is concerned about the community." Such motherhood statements, which are broad and philosophical in nature, are appropriate for long-term plans but not for communication plans of more-limited scope. A media-monitoring team would find it impossible to track such a message or to do a usage count to determine the frequency with which the message was picked up or carried by the print or broadcast media. It would be difficult to quantify its appearance or to comment on its absence. Media use a different kind of language, one that is more factual and explicit. Messages such as these last two might appear in comments by organization spokespersons or, occasionally, in editorials or newspaper columns, but they would never appear in news stories. To decide whether a message of such a broad nature is being carried by the media would require making an inference, based either on the entire newscast or on the entire article. The task would become much like deciding whether the article is balanced in favor of, or against, the organization's position on the issue.

Unlike the above examples, some messages are explicit, factual, and easily tracked. Consider the following message statements: "The U.S. government will not negotiate until Iraq leaves Kuwait" or "Refugee claimants will not be allowed to work while awaiting status." If you want to be able to track a message at a later date, you must write the message in newspaper language instead of articulating the idea as a bureaucratic memorandum.[4] That is, after all, how the message will appear in print. It has been said that artfully constructed messages that are appropriate for the media should be "uneditable, dramatic, concise, and synoptic."[5]

Strategic and Tactical Considerations

This part of the limited-scope communication plan involves outlining recommended approaches to communication activities. Under strategic and tactical considerations, you will need to take into account the following kinds of points: level of visibility desired (high or low profile); audience to be reached (national, regional, etc.); field of influence of the issue (with what other issues does the issue interact); existing level of public and media interest in the issue; choice of media for carrying messages (television, radio, newspapers); opportunities for "piggybacking"; and whether you will want to rely predominantly on emotional, logical, or credibility appeals in messages sent out by the organization.

Do you want to take a high-, medium-, or low-profile approach? Some issues such as abortion and surrogate motherhood are no-win issues, incapable of generating consensus. Gun-control questions likewise evoke heated debate. The population is so divided on such questions that no politician or government likes to deal with them. In such cases, the organization may choose *no* publicity over *negative* publicity. On the other hand, if a company is building a new child-care facility for working mothers, it may want to give this announcement high-profile billing.

Another relevant question to answer under the topic of strategic and tactical considerations is "What audience(s) are you trying to reach? National? State? Local? Your communication approach will be influenced by the answer to this question. For example, a case of shellfish poisoning can generate a situation that necessitates government involvement to locate the origins of the contamination, to isolate the zone of contamination, and to identify which products need to be removed from the market and for how long. At the earliest stage of the issue's development, the communication approach will need to be national in scope. Every individual, depending upon dietary habits, is potentially at risk. Once the source of the poisoning has been isolated and identified and the situation is under control, a different communication strategy becomes necessary. After the general public has been assured that the health threat no longer exists, the government will probably want to shift to a regional approach in its communications, concentrating its efforts on restoring confidence to shaken coastal fisheries. The issue will have changed from a national focus on health concerns to a regional focus on economic concerns, which are of particular interest to groups that depend upon shellfish harvesting for a living.

You will want to point to the most salient elements of the opinion environment that could facilitate the achievement of your communication objectives (e.g., widespread public and/or media support for your proposal or the support of lobby or interest groups, company employees, senior management, state or local governments, or influential individuals).

In the same way that you will be identifying factors in the opinion environment that present communication opportunities, you will also identify major impediments to the achievement of your objectives such as public apathy or ignorance; media hostility to the organization, its CEO or officials, or the concept that is being advocated; the complexity of the issue; or conflict among stakeholders with competing interests (e.g., local, state, or national governments). This section of the plan will outline suggested strategies for dealing with these impediments.

An issue's field of influence will also have a bearing on communication strategy. For example, if you are dealing with a company's economic issues, you may also need to address the concerns of environmentalists as they relate to the operations of the company. Long-term economic development is now being linked to protection of the environment (i.e., sustainable development). You must take these interactions into account when you design your communication strategies.

In this section of your communication plan, you will need to take into account the existing level of media interest in the topic. Some of the factors that influence media interest are *degree of controversy* attached to the issue (controversial issues are more media worthy), *sensationalism* of the issue (media thrives on the unusual and the bizarre), *celebrity support* for the issue, the *attractiveness* of the issue *to political parties and interest groups,* and the *linkages* of the issue *to central values* of the audience.

Under strategic and tactical considerations, you will choose the appropriate media for carrying your messages. Television is good for reaching national audiences, radio is good for reaching young audiences, and newspapers are good for reaching more politically aware and educated audiences. If you look at events and activities that are ongoing or that are planned to celebrate special occasions, you will find some occasions that can be used as vehicles to carry your message. For example, you may decide to announce a new policy at an anniversary celebration (for which you have an existing budget and agenda). A cross-country executive tour of plants can become a useful vehicle for speaking out on economic or sociopolitical issues that concern the company. You must consider opportunities for "piggybacking" other events and planned activities.

In developing a message, a communicator can use logical, emotional, or credibility appeals. Logical support materials include evidence and reasoning (e.g., the use of statistics, quotations, or facts to back up your position). Emotional appeals involve relating a topic to the audience by tapping into their needs and wants. Using credibility appeals means asking an audience to accept a message on the basis of your reputation or prestige. Most messages are developed by using a combination of the three techniques. If you use only logical appeals, you will probably sound like Mr. Spock on "Star Trek." On the other hand, if you seek to persuade an audience through extreme fear—which is designed to evoke an unthinking, irrational response to an issue—you will probably trespass the boundaries of ethical communication. Asking an audience to accept your message strictly on the basis of your credibility may be expecting a lot, unless you are someone of the stature of Sakharov speaking on world peace or Einstein speaking on physics.

In framing this section of your communication plan, you will take the above kind of points into consideration. The preceding discussion is not, however, intended to be comprehensive.

Examples of statements that you could make in this section of the plan are as follows:

- The anticipated popularity of the new state tax incentives for small business justifies giving a high profile to this policy announcement.
- The difficulties that many small businesses are experiencing in this period of economic recession should guarantee media interest in the announcement, and it is likely that newspapers across the state will produce follow-up stories that explain the policy.
- Because the announcement will have statewide impact, television is the best first-contact medium for reaching these audiences.
- Because there may be some confusion regarding how the new provisions will interact with existing tax legislation, a campaign to inform small business is planned for the six-month period following the announcement. A brochure that explains the specifics of the policy and its applications will be mailed to all small businesses registered in the state.
- Those who have been pushing for increased spending in the public sector may need to be reassured that these new incentives for private business will not adversely affect the state's potential to maintain its commitments in other areas such as education.
- The present state government has a proven track record in regard to supporting small business; it seems appropriate to emphasize this record in communications to the public.
- The employee newsletter is a "friendlier" vehicle for informing rank-and-file employees of sick-leave policies than is the corporate magazine.
- Raising the issue of merit-pay increases for employees will probably generate renewed discussion of promotion criteria; senior managers should be prepared for these questions.
- Reaching street youth with messages on the dangers of AIDS necessitates using alternative media and techniques such as distributing leaflets on streets inhabited by youths.
- Low to moderate fear appeals and reasoned arguments should be used to educate college youth on risks related to AIDS.
- Armistice Day will be a good occasion to announce the restructuring of the military and to stress its new peacekeeping functions.

Requirements for Briefings of Press or Other Groups and Individuals

Details related to any policy or program announcements should appear in this part of the plan. Some specifics that may be addressed are as follows:

- Timing of the announcement (date, time of day, etc.).
- Vehicle for announcement (e.g., statement in a speech to be delivered to the Farmers of America Association meeting, national press conference, local television news briefing, community groundbreaking ceremony, media event in a selected location, etc.).
- The most appropriate audience for the announcement (seniors, business people, media, representatives, teachers, college students, union members).
- Media strategy (regional or national press conferences, key interviews).
- Designated spokespersons for organization, including the role that will be played by the chief executive officer, his or her subordinates, lead government officials, or legislators.
- Role to be played by others in the community, by representatives from business and industry, by voluntary sector groups, etc.
- Any special requirements such as a lock up of journalists before a budget announcement or a briefing of journalists after a press conference.

It is important to take particular care in selecting the vehicle for your announcement: "Often this will involve bypassing standard and routine communications vehicles intended to convey information to the national media in favor of more creative methods such as audiovisual presentations, news conferences held in environments that typify the subject matter, teleconferencing, and regional tours by . . . designated officials."

Government groups will probably want to use this section of the plan to outline their strategy for briefing party members and opposition groups.

Requirements for Supporting Materials

Identify any requirements to produce background or other supporting materials. Some typical requirements are as follow:

- Information kits for media personnel (describe contents and distribution requirements).
- Background information for briefing party members, legislators, opposition or interest groups, and other stakeholders.
- Briefing notes, press lines, and question-and-answer packages for your CEO or other lead officials.
- Materials that legislators may want to pass on to their constituents (e.g., inserts for newsletters, pamphlets, etc.) or materials that organizations may want to pass on to their customers or clients.

Likely Media Reactions

If you believe the media will cover your event (e.g., the announcement of a new policy or program) or issue, you may wish to speculate about the amount of media attention the event or issue could receive. For example, you might say:

> Based on the company's experience two years ago and the current sluggishness of the local economy, the proposed utility rate increases may unleash a tidal wave of protest from interest groups; the media is likely to give extensive coverage to this outcry.

You could anticipate media attention on a Likert scale of 1 to 5, with 1 representing little attention and 5 representing much attention:

Anticipated Media Attention

Much   5   4   3   2   1   Little

You could also speculate about the line up of media for and against your position, as follows:

> It is anticipated that 60 percent of news coverage will be favorable toward the organization's announcement, 30 percent will be unfavorable, and 10 percent will be balanced.

You may want to suggest a best-case and worst-case scenario in terms of media coverage. You could write a headline for each scenario (limit your headline to five or six words), for example, "Parole Laws Give First-Time Offenders Second Chance" or "Parole Laws Turn Hardened Criminals Free." Another example might be "Allergy Medication Safe if Used Properly" or "Company Irresponsible for Not Withdrawing Allergy Medicine." Such headlines serve to focus the organization on how the public opinion debate could evolve.

Budget: How Do You Pay for Project or Communication Components?

Identify the resources, both human and financial, that you will require to carry out the planned activities. Indicate at what stage you will require the funding. Also, if funding has not already been designated in a work plan, indicate the fit with the yearly operational plan, for example:

> Cost for the announcement should be less than $2000.00, which is well within the amount budgeted in the operational plan.

Consultation Requirements: What Partners Should You Involve?

There is a growing recognition, by organizations, of the importance of consulting with clients, customers, and other stakeholders. It has become increasingly difficult for organizations, public or private, to ignore the views of stakeholder groups. Organizations are coming to the conclusion that many confrontational situations can be avoided if an effort is made to meet and talk with advocacy groups and their opinion leaders.

There is, at the same time, a growing cognizance of the need to consult within one's own organization, in order to gain information from people at all levels of the organization. Successful issues management usually depends on securing the involvement of a number of areas of the organization (e.g., administration, marketing, public affairs, etc.).

In this part of the communication plan, you delineate who must be consulted. Who will be responsible for coordinating any joint efforts? What areas of the organization will need to interact? List all departments or units consulted to date, and describe what agreement has been reached regarding the roles that will be played by different parties. Identify other organizations or groups that you must consult. Be specific about how you intend to involve these groups and/or individual opinion leaders. Examples of statements that could appear in this part of the plan are as follows:

- Branch offices in Chicago, Lansing, and Boston have been cooperating in planning the marathon for "Progress Against Poverty." The Austin and San Diego offices also should be consulted.

- Voluntary groups that should be consulted include the Salvation Army, the Good Neighbors Association, and Good Will.

- Concerned departments in government include the Education Department, Social Welfare, and Finance.

- Officials in the United Automobile Workers organization will need to be consulted when we draw up plans for downsizing.

Requirements for Senior Management or Executive Involvement

Examples of statements that could be made under this heading are:

- Senior managers should be brought on board early, to help in communicating the necessity for the revised equity policies.
- Executives will need to be available to act as liaisons with community groups.

Evaluation Criteria

A number of different methods may be used to monitor and evaluate your communication efforts. Polling, focus group testing, media monitoring, analysis of correspondence, inquiry tracking, pull-out inserts in publications, readability assessments, user surveys, and expert assessments are but a few of the techniques that are available to you. In this section of the plan, you note which instruments you intend to use to evaluate your communication activities. Don't be afraid to use unorthodox means: Visit the local pub or the nearest senior citizens' home. Take a cross-state tour; travel first-class one way and coach on your return. You have ready-made focus groups with distinct characteristic in many cases.

Requirements for Follow-up Activities to Sustain the Message

Any longer-term media strategy will be detailed in this part of the communication plan. You may wish to reinforce your message, for example, through "speaking tours, advertising, brochures and booklets, direct-mail campaigns, follow-up media interviews, or radio 'hotline' programs."[6]
You could make the following type of statements:

- Upon proclamation of the new family violence legislation, an article that outlines the major points of the law will be submitted to *Physician's Quarterly* to explain the implications of the law to doctors.
- Videotapes detailing what constitutes elder abuse will be distributed to state seniors' organizations.
- The Christmas newsletter will orient employees to the revised bonus system.
- Feature articles on the new automobile warrantee policy will be posted at all dealerships; a brief description of the revised policies will be included in literature mailed to former customers.

SUMMARY

Limited-scope plans contain the following features: a statement of the event or issue being addressed by the plan, opinion environment, target audiences, communication objectives, messages, strategic and tactical considerations, requirements for briefings of press or other groups and individuals, requirements for supporting materials, likely media reactions, budget allocations, consultation requirements, requirements for senior management and/or executive involvement, and evaluation criteria.

NOTES

1. The Privy Council Office, Government of Canada, format for preparing the communications component of a Memorandum to Cabinet served as a model for this discussion.
2. In an interview with Arnold Wood, communications specialist, National Archives of Canada, August 1992, Wood emphasized the importance of including internal components in the limited-scope plan. Some company units and government departments have a predominantly internal clientele.
3. David M. Dozier and Fred C. Repper, "Research Firms and Public Relations Practices," in *Excellence in Public Relations and Communication Management,* ed. James E. Grunig, (Hillsdale, N.J.: Lawrence Erlbaum Associates, Publishers, 1992), p. 203.
4. Alan Morgan, interview, spring 1989.
5. Kathleen Jamieson Hall and Karlyn Kohrs Campbell, *Interplay of Influence,* 2nd ed. (Belmont, Calif.: Wadsworth, 1988), p. 96.
6. Privy Council Office, Memorandum to Cabinet instructions document.

CHAPTER 12

CONTINGENCY PLANNING FOR CRISIS MANAGEMENT

It has been said that the history of life contains "long periods of boredom and short periods of terror."[1] One type of communication plan that deserves special mention is the *contingency plan,* which is produced in anticipation of possible "terror" or crisis situations. A crisis is distinguished by the elements of surprise and perceived threat, real or imagined, to the survival and well-being of the organization.[2] Other characterizing features include insufficient information, events outpacing the organization's capacity to respond, perceived or actual loss of control, important interests at stake, intense scrutiny from outside the organization, panic and confusion, the development of "a siege mentality," disruption of regular decision-making processes, and a tendency for managers to focus on the short-term.[3]

Poorly managed crises have the potential to affect the company's public image, its ability to carry on normal operations, its bottom line, and even the personal reputations of corporate executives. Much publicized crises faced by modern organizations have included the Tylenol poisonings, Three Mile Island, Chernobyl, the *Challenger* disaster, Exxon Valdez, Bhopal, the Dow Corning breast implant controversy, and problems faced by the makers of Seldane allergy medications and cellular telephone manufacturers. Crises can include anything from "a failed takeover bid to the mishandling of employees in a plant closing to environmental problems."[4] Some people argue that a crisis becomes a crisis when the media, Congress, and/or credible or powerful interest groups define it as a crisis: "A crisis need not pose a serious threat to human life, but it must somehow challenge the public's sense of appropriateness, tradition, values, safety, security, or the integrity of the government."[5]

Few organizations are invulnerable to crises. One survey found that 89 percent of Fortune 500 CEOs agreed that crises in business today are as inevitable as "death and taxes."[6] The general progress of events that define a situation as a crisis have been identified as follows: (1) Something unexpected happens to upset normal operations. (2) Immediate action is required to rectify the situation. (3) Normal operational procedures are not adequate for dealing with the crisis event. (4) The event poses a threat to people, property, or the organization. (5) The event calls for corrective action.[7]

OPERATIONAL VERSUS MISMANAGEMENT CRISES: TRENDS IN PRESS COVERAGE

A crisis may come from inside or outside an organization. A crisis that has its origins *within* the organization typically results from real or perceived errors in judgment on the part of organization officials; this is called a "mismanagement crisis." A crisis from *without* results from events over which the organization has little control such as war or revolution, the collapse of world money markets, famine, earthquakes, or other natural calamities. These events may nonetheless impinge on the organization and even threaten its survival. Many of these crises fall into the "operational" category.

In many regards, it is the media that ultimately defines a situation as a crisis. For that reason, it is useful to note a trend in the type of crises that have received press attention in recent years. An analysis of 31,500 business stories between 1989 and 1991 shows that reporters are giving increasingly more attention to crises caused by "mismanagement" (and its resulting ramifications) than to "operational" crises such as plane crashes, train derailings, and industrial accidents. The Institute for Crisis Management, based in Louisville, Kentucky, found that the focus of newspaper coverage of business crises shifted dramatically in the three-year period leading up to 1991:

> The fastest growing crisis categories involved executive policies and decisions that reflected badly on the quality of business management. Bad press generated by consumer activism increased 196% over the three-year period, followed by sexual harassment (160%), court decisions (125%), whistle-blowing (122%), product recalls (119%), and executive firings (118%).[8]

Close to one third of the 31,500 stories concerned federal, state, and local government investigations of businesses, industries, and nonprofit organizations for questionable management practices. A significant increase in the number of articles on court decisions demonstrates that corporation executives are experiencing the same kinds of pressures with the news media as happened with Supreme Court Justice Clarence Thomas at his confirmation hearings. The introduction of television into courtrooms has given increased visibility to those accused of mismanagement, and the lengthy appeal process means that issues can be kept before the public for years after the surfacing of the original problem.[9]

At the same time that the amount of space given to poor management practices has increased, negative stories about environmental crises have dropped 43 percent between 1989 and 1991. This decline is due, in part, to the fact that environmental protection assumed a higher priority on corporate agendas after the Exxon Valdez affair. The Institute for Crisis Management found, however, that these kinds of trends have not been acknowledged by American companies and nonprofit organizations, who are still preoccupied with planning for operational crises.

It is true that operational crises continue to garner their share of press coverage. In recent years, the largest number of articles on operational crises have focused on the U.S. airline industry, especially U.S. Air, subsequent to two crashes in New York and Los Angeles. Also several large refinery explosions have "kept oil companies in the news—as did AT&T's massive service breakdown in New York and Southern Pacific's train wreck that wiped out a small town in California."[10]

The president of the Institute for Crisis Management predicted the ongoing development of the following trends.[11]

1. Operational crises will continue to decline in importance, relative to crises generated by mismanagement.
2. Greater media and public attention will be focused on top-management practices.
3. Government will take an increasingly aggressive role in communicating its position on business-related issues such as criminal investigations, indictments, product recalls, and large fines levied on companies.
4. Personnel problems will activate the largest number of crises for senior management, with employee charges of discrimination based more on sex, age, and disabilities than on race (*The Americans with Disabilities Act* will give impetus to some of these lawsuits, including court actions launched by victims of AIDS).
6. Consumer groups and other activists (e.g., those supporting animal rights, abortion rights, and workers' rights) will use the media to push their causes.
7. Intent on reversing declines in membership, unions will use strikes and boycotts to force settlements, with resulting media coverage of the conflict situations.
8. Whistle-blowing will become more prevalent.

ORGANIZATIONAL VULNERABILITIES

Some of the many influences that make businesses and industries, governments, and nonprofit organizations more susceptible than ever to crises are:

- Massive restructuring.
- Relocation of organizational boundaries.

- Accelerating technological developments.
- Socioeconomic and regulatory flux.
- Changing patterns of competition.
- Revised public standards for what is acceptable or ethical behavior on the part of government and corporation officials.
- The proliferation of citizen advocacy groups and coalitions.
- Changes in the nature of information, media, and publics.

As a result, organizations now in "the throes of quantum change" include the telecommunications industry, financial services, airline and health care industries, among others.[12] Banks are among the most vulnerable of institutions in terms of their dependency on external economic and political factors; they are also subject to regulatory reforms. Banks are at risk because a mismanaged crisis can result in loss of confidence and withdrawal of funds.[13] A number of professionals, including architectural and engineering firms, have become increasingly aware of the need to prepare for crisis situations. Swanke Hayden Connell Architects said they were hurt in 1990 by rumors that the recession in the building industry was causing financial problems for the firm. According to some rumors, the firm was even going out of business.[14]

For their part, government officials are finding that many of their crises are being generated by changing public perceptions of morality. A recent sting operation in the South Carolina legislature found that 1 out of every 10 legislators accepted a bribe to vote a particular way on a piece of legislation. Members of the U.S. Senate have recently been called to task for accepting gifts from lobbyists. The reality is that legislators at all levels of government have *always* accepted payments from lobbyists, whether in the form of trips to the Caribbean or monetary payments. The practices haven't changed, but public standards for what is moral and acceptable have shifted dramatically. Politicians have always had affairs; more than a few presidents have entertained mistresses and female companions in the White House. The interesting point is that, although standards in society as a whole have continued to become more liberal, there has been a corresponding trend toward more rigorous expectations of our government and corporate leaders. These revised public expectations are confusing to some older politicians and corporate executives, who were reared in an environment that had more flexible standards for "right" and "wrong." Richard Nixon, who rose to political prominence during the years when the CIA and FBI had free reign to operate domestically and abroad, may have been the first to fall victim to these changed norms, but he has been joined in recent years by many distinguished others, drawn from government and corporate boardrooms, educational institutions, and, occasionally, from the highest levels of nonprofit organizations.

CRISIS MANAGEMENT VERSUS ISSUES MANAGEMENT: A MATTER OF TIME AND SCALE

Crisis management can be viewed as a subset of issues management. The difference between the two processes is predominantly a matter of time. In crisis situations, the time available for managing change, or assuming control under unstable conditions, is dramatically reduced. Former chairman of American Motors Gerald C. Meyers noted the similarities in planning for long-term change and for crises: "Both deal with the management of change, their common goal being organizational survival in a competitive world."[15] Similar to planning for issues management, contingency planning for crises prepares organizations to "predict problems, anticipate threats, minimize surprises, and develop coalitions to effect defined goals and implant solutions."[16]

Contingency planning is concerned with managing "discontinuous" change. Continuous change occurs within a system that remains basically unchanged. Discontinuous, or second-order change, has the potential to structure a new reality, transforming "fundamental properties or states of the system," as happened with recent events in eastern Europe and the former Soviet state.[17] Crisis-management theories can be regarded as theories related to managing change of the second order. Planning for crises is equivalent to "thinking the unthinkable." The U.S. Postal Service exemplified this behavior a few years ago when it planned for rerouting of all mail in the event of a nuclear war![18]

IDENTIFYING HIGH-RISK AREAS

A company or government department that is concerned with planning for crises should look carefully at all aspects of its operations. Director of Corporate Communications at Dow Chemical Canada, Inc., Donald Stephenson suggests that the following list can be helpful to identify potentially vulnerable or high-risk areas, for example:[19]

- *Products or services*—their safety, their effects on the environment, the company's use of scarce materials in manufacturing the products, choice of firms for contract awards.
- *Processes*—vulnerabilities in areas such as manufacturing, transportation, or finance.
- *Locales*—potential problems related to where your operations are located, workplace safety, where you ship, how you handle hazardous products, and where you get your materials, for example, from the Baltic states (a politically unstable area), from South Africa (problems with trade sanctions), from Central America (earthquake zones).

- *Officers and executives*—corporate practices, private or company associations, activities and sponsorships.
- *Personnel*—hiring and firing practices, equity policies, benefits, job security, tasks assigned employees, or union-related matters.

In one survey, Fortune 500 CEOs unanimously agreed that the following areas tend to be common sources of crises: industrial accidents, environmental problems, union problems/strikes, product recalls, investor relations, hostile takeovers, proxy fights, rumors/media leaks, government regulatory problems, acts of terrorism, and charges related to fraud and embezzlement.[20]

A company or government must be prepared to respond to all potential threats. Being prepared means having accurate and updated information on all vulnerable products, policies, services, locales, and operations. It requires focusing on your weaknesses. Handling the crisis properly also means devising strategies that build on your strengths. Because crises are open to development along more than one line, contingency plans—developed to respond to crises—must be flexible.

STAGES OF A CRISIS

Precrisis Indicators

Although crises are not (by definition) completely foreseeable, there may be advance indications when a crisis is close, for example, "nonperformance, targets not achieved, budgets exceeded, and prototypes that are not working."[21] Other symptoms are "samples rejected, an unusual number of violations, an upsurge in the number of people reporting sick."[22] A government may see its popularity plummeting in the polls or may see major pieces of legislation being defeated in the House or Senate. These signs of a crisis constitute a *precrisis* phase. During this phase, the organization will often deny the existence of a problem. Fear and expressions of anger follow denial.

Onset of the Crisis

The *acute* phase begins when catastrophe strikes (i.e., deaths, bankruptcy, or a full-blown scandal and resignations). Organizational responses to the acute phase of a crisis include panic, fear, confusion, and infighting. If the organization does not manage to move beyond this point, its very survival will be threatened. If a crisis continues for any length of time, a siege mentality develops among organization staff members. Even though crises can't always be avoided, they can be managed.

The first 24 hours of a crisis are believed to be critical to its containment and control. This 24-hour period is likely to be marked by sensational and often negative press. It is impossible, at this early stage, to assess the long-term impact of the crisis; however, how the organization responds in those early hours can have a critical influence on how the public views later actions.

In the acute phase of a crisis, the spokesperson's job is more to express concern than to offer information. At this stage, when so much is unknown, it is dangerous to be specific, to offer explanations, or to assign blame. The organization can, however, usually confirm that an incident has occurred, the nature of the incident, the location, the immediate effect, what steps the organization is taking to bring events under control, when the situation is likely to improve, whether there are any known injuries or fatalities, and whether there is any known damage to property. Names of victims and specifics related to injuries or damage should be withheld pending verification.

Regaining Control

Regaining control in a crisis requires:

- Acknowledging the threat.
- Engaging in fact finding.
- Diagnosing the nature of the problem.
- Evaluating alternative courses of action.
- Deciding on the best plan of action.
- Implementing the plan.
- Monitoring progress.

It is easiest to devise crisis plans in the days preceding the acute phase of a crisis. Companies such as Uniroyal have learned to reduce rumors, to stave off lowered morale, and to co-opt employees to become ambassadors for the company by communicating openly and honestly with them. At one time, crisis management meant painting over the company's name on a crashed aircraft before photographers arrived.[23] Now, crisis management is part of every manager's job, and openness and frankness characterize the operations of model organizations. When Graham and James (an architectural firm) made the decision to lay off a number of employees, the *Daily Journal* and the *Recorder* (legal trade publications) covered the story. The firm chose to deal directly with the situation by acknowledging that the company was facing difficult economic times; at the same time, they assured stakeholders that they were coping. Muriel Chess, the director of corporate communications at Swanke Hayden Connell Architects, reinforced damaged confidence by holding two large parties to demonstrate that the firm was doing well.[24]

Critical to regaining control is deciding what message the organization wants to disseminate to its stakeholders and finding (or creating) opportunities to state the message.[25]

Postcrisis Recovery

For those organizations that survive the crisis, the *postcrisis* phase leads to attempts to restore public and employee confidence to former levels and to stabilize internal relations, often through the acceptance of radical changes in regulations and procedures, officials, or structures. Full recovery may take months or years, if it occurs at all.

Furthermore, it has been said that crises, "like migraines, often occur in clusters and the people involved seldom have the luxury of dealing with each one separately."[26] As one crisis is being resolved, early warning signs may signal the appearance of other crises that are activated by the first.

DEALING WITH THE MEDIA

Critical to crisis management is media relations. Sometimes there is a conflict between media's requirement to provide information to the public and the organization's need to control information. However, it is important to avoid treating crisis situations as a zero-sum game, with the media and the organization both attempting to win.[27] Organizations should work with, not against, the media.

Media coverage of a crisis is said to be predictable, with early stories focusing on "fatalities, destruction, and proximity to the newsroom."[28] Follow-up reports entail a three-step sequence: "First come the colorful descriptions of personal heroism, grief, and suffering by individuals. . . . Next come discussions of property damage and cost. . . . Finally come the discussions of preparedness and competence of response by authorities."[29] The questions that media ask tend to fall into three categories:[30]

- Who is at fault? When will the party at fault be punished? Fired?
- When did the organization learn about the problem, and what did it do when it discovered the problem existed?
- What is the organization doing now? How can the individuals or groups who are at risk be compensated and/or protected?

In terms of specifics, the media will want to know the number of fatalities and injuries; an estimate of the damage; who or what was destroyed or harmed; the time; the location; the names of dead and injured; their addresses, ages, and length of time with the company; and details about the company such as number of employees and products manufactured.

Technology contributes to the ability of companies to negotiate crises because the tendency in television news is to cover events as a two-day story.[31] Observers have noted that electronic coverage of crises tends to be short lived.[32] By quickly disseminating facts to the media, the organization can collapse the time given to the crisis as a major news story.

Companies should view crisis situations as opportunities to demonstrate concern for the community and their constituencies: "Just as a fire department gets credit for its heroism—and a boost for its next year's budget—by minimizing the damage, so a company can get some benefit in good will by handling itself conspicuously well in a crisis. . . . When a company assumes a defensive position, that is taken by the media and the public as indication of guilt."[33]

Crisis situations demand open information policies. Rumors and cries of alarm will fill any information vacuum. Media will go elsewhere if they don't get information from the concerned organization.[34] In the confusion that accompanies the acute phase of crises, there will be many inaccuracies and misinterpretations of events by media personnel that require rectification. For example, in the 1991 Gainesville, Florida, murders, the national media made many mistakes in their reporting of the incidents. Some of the errors, or "myths," in the coverage included: (1) The university administration had suspended classes. (2) The notorious Ted Bundy killings had also occurred in Gainesville. (3) Suspects in a battery case are frequently held under a $1 million bond. Those involved with handling media relations at Gainesville learned that it is often necessary to educate reporters to the specifics of the story.[35] Chapter 4 discussed other examples of inaccuracies in reporting crisis situations.

Even though openness in communication is advised, some cautions are in order:

- Never offer an opinion on the *cause* of a problem until a thorough investigation has taken place.
- Avoid speculation, at all costs.
- Verify information before communicating it to the media or to the public (some organizations use a spider-web procedure for verifying information); doublecheck all facts.
- Avoid going "off the record"; journalists often ignore such labels.
- Avoid responding with "no comment"; silence will be interpreted as guilt.
- Don't be afraid to say, "I don't know."

If you haven't been briefed, tell media representatives that you will get back to them as soon as you have more information. As soon as you have gathered a sufficient number of facts, give as comprehensive an account as possible of the known extent of damage or injuries; explain who has been hurt; and describe the level of continuing risk to individuals, property, the organization, or the environment.[36]

If you don't know the answer to a question, say so; you have no obligation to the media to manufacture information. Robert Baugnier, president of Berger & Associates, Ltd., and official spokesperson for many companies involved in crisis management situations, warned of the potential dire consequences of speculation: "The implications of naming the wrong manufacturer, of placing blame on the wrong party, of announcing wrong names insofar as victims are concerned are too horrific to consider . . . from both personal and legal standpoints."[37]

The organization must be cognizant of the need to obtain legal advice on the limits of disclosure. If public access to information has to be restricted, explain why. With issues such as land use and development, municipal and private labor negotiations, and political referenda, attorneys will be an indispensable part of the crisis-management team.[38] For that reason, attorneys should be participants in any crisis simulations.[39] A problem sometimes arises, however, because attorneys tend to value silence over disclosure, whereas public relations theorists tend to value openness and public persuasion. Decision makers must weigh carefully the counsel of both parties.[40]

One of the best ways of assuring fair media coverage during a crisis is to develop good media relations prior to the time of the crisis.[41] The quality of media relations will be built on factors such as the extent to which management understands and respects media deadlines, the accuracy of communications, the consistency of efforts to present a balanced account, and whether the organization treats all reporters and news organizations in the same way.

Most companies accept the necessity for spokespersons to receive training in media interviewing techniques, and one of the first actions of any new government is to put its newly elected/appointed officials through media training. Simulations and role plays are popular techniques used in such training exercises. Twice-yearly reviews are regarded as necessary to ensure that organization spokespersons maintain the facility that they acquire during initial training sessions.

The decision of companies like Shell U.K. Exploration and Production, Aberdeen Operations, to invest in contingency planning reflects the grim reality that many organizations face. In the latter case, for example, the company experienced three helicopter craches between 1986 and 1992, an explosion within an accommodation block in 1991, and a number of other life-threatening incidents. Training and crisis simulations are essential to the continuing viability of firms such as Shell.[42]

CREATING THE CONTINGENCY PLAN

What an organization says and does in a crisis situation can permanently affect the organization's image and its policy and program agendas. To many people, crisis communication *is* the most important aspect of managing a crisis, both during and after the crisis. Pan American Airlines, for example, never recovered from its inability or unwillingness to answer the public's questions regarding the crash over Lockerbie, Scotland. Dow Corning suffered immeasurable damage as a consequence of its decision to withhold information on the controversial breast implants. The "fallout" from the crisis and the FDA's actions against Dow Corning cost the company over $300 million.[43] An organization's failure to accept responsibility for the consequences of its actions (or sometimes its inaction) can sometimes be more devastating than the act that generates the crisis.[44] Organizations should be prepared to assume that crises can and will occur. Every organization should have, at the least, a generic contingency plan.

To ensure that the organization remains in control, maintains public confidence, and avoids escalation of the crisis, those in positions of authority often commission the development of contingency plans. Such plans provide crisis managers with a sense of direction and purpose at a time when it is easy to succumb to panic and fear. All of those who are to be involved in the execution of a crisis management plan must be consulted in its development. All participants must understand and be committed to the implementation of the plan. New procedures cannot be introduced at the time that an emergency occurs, except as adaptations are required. Typical categories that appear in a crisis management plan follow.

Type of Crisis

Because no organization can anticipate every possible crisis situation, it is necessary to create typologies (e.g., airplane crash, hostage taking, oil spill, plant shutdowns, worker layoffs, whistle-blowing incident or leak, coverup allegations, or major accident at an industrial facility). Generic plans can be created to help the organization to adjust to and deal with crisis situations.

Probability that Crisis Could Occur and Potential Impact of Crisis

An organization can rank a crisis on the basis of its potential *impact* and the *probability of its occurrence*. The "crisis barometer"[45] was devised to predict impact and probability. This barometer measures impact on a scale of 0 to 10. Five *impact-related* questions concern (1) intensity of the crisis, (2) the likelihood that the organization will come under media and/or government regulatory agency scrutiny, (3) the extent to which the crisis could interfere with the ongoing operations of the organization, (4) the extent to which the organization will be perceived as either a victim or as a culprit, and (5) the extent to which the organization's bottom line could be damaged. It measures *probability* on the basis of (1) the organization's safety record, (2) past crises, and

(3) the experiences of similar organizations. The probability that a crisis will occur is rated on a scale that ranges from 0 to 100 percent. These scores are plotted on a grid; the location of issues on the grid reflects the perceived seriousness of the crisis to the organization. Crises that have a potentially serious impact and a high probability will fall into the red zone. Those with a high impact but a low probability fall into the amber zone. Crises with a low impact but high probability of occurrence fall into a gray zone. Finally, crises with a low impact and low probability of occurrence are placed in the green zone. Plotting all of the organization's issues on the same grid gives an overview of where the organization should place its priorities in terms of contingency planning.[46]

Whether you choose to use the crisis barometer will depend on how you judge the appropriateness of the questions that are asked. If you ask the wrong questions or omit important questions, you may misjudge the impact and/or the probability of occurrence of the crisis, thus placing it in the wrong danger zone. Additional specific questions that you may wish to consider are the following: What is the potential for media involvement? What is the field of influence of the crisis, both in terms of geography and in terms of interaction with other issues? How many stakeholders have expressed an interest in the crisis? What is the intensity of their interest? What is threatened? Community health? Worker safety? The economic viability of the company? What is the potential for adverse reaction by employees? By investors? By unions? Has the organization suffered short-term damage to its reputation? Has it suffered long-term damage?

Jurisdiction(s) and Parties Responsible for Managing Crisis

Management of crises implies the need to agree upon jurisdictions. If too many different parties are simultaneously assuming lead responsibility for dealing with the crisis, inconsistent messages will emerge from the organization. There is a need to agree on responsibilities.

Team Members
It is important to designate a crisis management team and to have complete information regarding where and how to best reach these individuals (name and telephone numbers at work, home, cottage, automobile, and other contact places). A crisis-management team should not exceed 10 members. Roles and responsibilities should be specified.

Common areas represented on crisis management teams are finance, human resources, law, science, medicine, occupational health, risk management, safety and security, international affairs, and communications. The specific makeup of the team will vary according to the nature of the crisis and the perceived needs. It has been said that the people on the team should possess "creativity, knowledge, power, and perspective."[47] They should be able to invent solutions, understand the inner workings of the business, be powerful enough to command resources and authority, and know how and when to communicate to the public. Outside experts can be valuable additions to a team.

Chain of Command

It is necessary to specify the chain of command. Who is in charge? Who is below that individual? Someone must have the authority to delegate responsibility. In critical situations, the team is led by the CEO, and key members are at individual sites. There may be a team coordinator who is someone other than the CEO. Decisions must be made regarding how information is to move during a crisis and who is to control its movement.

Lead Spokesperson(s)

Most experts suggest the designation of a single spokesperson, and some argue that the best spokesperson is the CEO or company chairman. Seventy-one banking firm executives, representing 35 commercial institutions, expressed this point of view.[48] In the Iraqi–U.N. confrontation, the Commander of Allied Forces in the Gulf General H. Normal Schwarzkopf, Secretary of Defense Dick Cheney, and Joint Chiefs Chairman Colin Powell—all high-ranking officials—shared the duties of spokesperson for the armed forces.[49]

Others argue that specialists are best able to answer questions on specific aspects of a crisis. Scientists, for example, are better able to answer technical questions, whereas financial analysts can predict the economic consequences of events. Situations are often too complex for one person to understand everything on the topic. Sometimes, regional spokespersons may be required to answer questions at a local level. Other persons may be required to answer questions directed to a hotline. However experts differ on specifics, they agree on the need to designate a checkpoint for the dissemination of messages.

The more serious the crisis, the more senior the spokesperson(s) should be. To onlookers, the level of the spokesperson will give a good indication of the perceived seriousness of the crisis. If a top executive represents the firm on a matter of moderate crisis dimensions, onlookers may attach more significance to the event than it merits. If, on the other hand, a junior spokesperson represents the company on a more critical issue, the public may see the company as placing little importance on the outcome of the crisis.

Coordinator of Operations

One member of the crisis-management team will be responsible for coordinating operations. This individual takes a position at the center of operations. Other individuals will head up specific areas such as command, security, safety, engineering, personnel, data processing, and communications. These operations link up at a central point, which is occupied by the coordinator. All support functions should report to this individual, who is ideally a senior-level manager with at least some technical knowledge.

Different individuals occupy positions such as head of the crisis-management team (often the CEO), lead spokesperson (often an executive officer with communications training), and coordinator of operations (an individual who has a good idea of the nuts-and-bolts functioning of the organization and its many parts). The coordinator chairs crisis management meetings, and the CEO listens, observes, questions, and reacts to the group's decisions. The coordinator should not be affiliated with any one division or area of the organization. Such an affiliation could bias the person's handling of the crisis situation.

Alternates

There will be occasions when designated spokespersons or coordinators are not accessible or available. For that reason, advance agreement on replacement individuals will facilitate the management of the crises.

Liaison with Victims' Families and Hospitals

A crisis-management plan should specify who will contact the families of victims, who will decide when names can be made public, and how these tasks will be accomplished. Communication plans should also be shared and coordinated with local hospitals. The individual selected to be a liaison to victims' families should be someone with an empathetic manner and strong interpersonal skills. Most experts agree that it is best in crisis situations to keep the media and the victims' families in separate locations. Transportation for victims' families may need to be arranged.

Required Support Systems

Physical Facilities

The contingency plan should designate a crisis-management operations center, bringing it as close as possible to the crisis site[50] without placing it in a restricted area.[51] A typical operations room has been described in the following way: "This is a special room, generally with limited access and equipped with special telephones, maps, computer terminals, and audiovisual equipment. Blackboards, flip charts, and modest kitchen facilities are other essential elements. The room should be close to typing and transmission facilities."[52] There should be backup generators. Food and bedding should be arranged for crisis-management team members. Some required supplies and equipment will have to be transported to the central operations site. Team members may also need to be transported to a site location or to crisis-management headquarters.

Communication Hardware and Software Systems

Some required systems may include telex, telephone, computer, facsimile, and modem. Telephones should also be available to media personnel, "with two or three private numbers for communications between the chief spokesperson, the crisis scene, and other experts."[53]

All plant or company sites require "working crisis-management kits that detail what actions are to be taken in the event of a crisis. Site management may need to take initial action before the crisis-management team arrives on location.

Staff Requirements

Requirements for staff include administrative help, telephone staff, typists, computer specialists, maintenance operators for equipment, and messengers capable of carrying information in the event that telephone service is disrupted.[54] The organization must consider whether there is a need to augment regular staff at the time of a crisis. Reporting requirements must be established for any supplementary staff. Transportation arrangements will need to be considered.

Budgetary Requirements

Budgetary requirements cannot be firmly fixed in advance of a crisis. However, estimates can suggest ballpark figures for carrying out certain kinds of activities; so that if a crisis strikes, the cost of various options can be known. Sometimes the organization has no choice but to make high-cost investments in crisis-management strategies because the price of apathy can be the destruction of the organization.

Information Strategies

Key Messages

The organization should decide upon key messages that it would like to deliver to its publics. It has been said that successful interviews are "message-driven, not question-driven."[55] In the early hours of a crisis, the most important message that the organization can transmit is concern. Neither explanations nor blame are appropriate in the first place.[56] Throughout the crisis, the organization must convey its commitment to the health and well-being of concerned publics. Part of conveying this commitment is demonstrating an active involvement in the search for solutions. Spokespersons must deliver consistent messages in clear lay language, avoiding jargon and "bureaucratese." In some instances (e.g., strike situations), it can be better to hold press conferences off the premises.[57] Television visuals and photographs pose the highest risk to organizations faced with a crisis. To the extent possible, visuals should be controlled. Offering photographs or videotaped materials can be one answer to the media's demand for visual materials.

Inventing a scapegoat is not advisable: "Such action should be taken only if it is a genuine solution; firing somebody or retreating on policy as a quick-and-dirty attempt to abort the crisis will achieve nothing and may create more problems than it will solve."[58]

Mounting a defense of the organization based on its past performance, superior products, or exceptional policies is inappropriate in a time of crisis. Such achievements should be communicated in noncrisis periods; if the organization does, in fact, have a laudable past record, others will no doubt come to the organization's defense and point to these accomplishments.[59]

It is useful for an organization to develop question-and-answer kits that anticipate the questions most likely to be asked in the event of a crisis and to generate appropriate responses. The organization should nonetheless be prepared to modify its answers when the crisis actually strikes. Fact sheets inform the media about the organization's products, operations, services, and management. They ensure that the media has relevant names, dates, and statistics. As the crisis progresses, press releases keep the media informed on how the organization views key issues. It is important to have employee records, as well as safety and labor records, available for quick reference.[60]

Media for Carrying Messages

Decide, in advance, what media will be most appropriate to carry your organization's message. Create a plan for sharing your communication strategy with the media. Identify the organization's spokesperson to the media. Keep the media informed of any changes in personnel, and provide them with telephone numbers and contact locations. Providing reporters and photographers with guidelines and specifying restrictions helps to clarify the organization's position. Identification badges and contact cards, indicating 24-hour availability, should be distributed to media personnel. Security guards, safety personnel, switchboard operators, plant managers, and secretarial staff should know where to direct reporters.[61]

The specification of a backup site gives the organization a second option for a newsroom if conditions deteriorate so that reporters cannot gain entry to the original site.

Establishing a hotline can be important, if you are willing to give open and honest responses to callers. Shareholders may need to be contacted by letter, for example, in the event of an accident involving top-members of management. In the aftermath of a crisis, follow-up letters can reassure employees, community officials, and others affected by the crisis. If the crisis involves a product, management may wish to communicate with customers.[62]

Target Publics for Communications

As with any other communication plan, it is important to identify and prioritize stakeholders in the situation. What publics must you reach first? The board of directors? Senior executives? Shareholders and investors? Customers or consumers? Government? Interest groups? Suppliers? Accountants? The general public? Other concerned organizations? Target publics may be emergency services such as police, fire, hospital, and ambulance; media representatives with the greatest knowledge of the situation; elected officials; community leaders; regulatory officers; and facility neighbors. Partisan supporters should also be among those publics that are provided with information; they can be valuable advocates for the organization.[63]

Contact lists should be prepared and updated regularly. These lists should include names and telephone numbers of all television and radio stations and newspapers, hospitals, fire departments, and other target publics listed above. Plans for communicating with target publics should take into account the need to notify families of victims before notifying the general public of any injuries or deaths resulting from a crisis event.

Minicrises that can be Activated by Crisis

An earthquake or a hurricane can generate minicrises associated with transportation, clean water, bacterial infections, diseases such as typhoid fever, and communications. The resignation of a chief executive officer can bring the viability of the firm into question, thus provoking other resignations, sell off of stocks, or rumors that fraud and corruption charges are in the offing. When someone laced Tylenol capsules with cyanide and several people died, Johnson & Johnson had several crises to manage, including the issues of random poisonings, deaths, and public fear.[64] They also had to contend with the issue of how to package future products. Interest groups use crisis situations as an opportunity to secure media coverage for their own issues. It is useful in this section of the plan to identify minicrises or other issues that could achieve visibility, on the coattails of this crisis.

Sensitivities/Cautions

Opposition forces may use opportunities posed by crisis situations to undermine the organization, particularly in cases where misconduct or mismanagement is alleged. Some interest groups may be sensitive to issues activated by a crisis. For example, police shootings or street riots may provoke outbursts of violence from affected racial or ethnic minorities. Dealing with the crisis means dealing, in a sensitive way, with these groups. In other instances, the organization may need to proceed with caution in changing certain policies or invoking certain procedures, for example, calling out the National Guard or military to deal with a domestic crisis. This part of the plan should point to sensitivities and should detail strategies for dealing with these sensitivities.

Response and Control Mechanisms

Alert System for Activating Crisis-Management Network

The organization should agree upon a sequence of actions to be taken during a crisis. It has been suggested that a "fan-out and callback" system can alert network members to the presence of a crisis component.[65] If an organization has a hotline, callers can activate the crisis-system network by calling to report threatening events.

Daily Operations

A timetable for daily activities of different groups should be created. For example, some individuals will be assigned to monitor media coverage of the crisis. Others will be charged with writing daily strategic communication overviews, based on environmental intelligence. Committee meeting times and places will need to be set, and debriefings will need to be scheduled. Key members will be involved in giving and receiving strategic advice. Recommendations will be passed on to committees.

It is necessary to keep a log of all facts that were disseminated to the media and other groups, along with the times of the communication and telephone numbers of reporters. Accurate recordkeeping preempts the possibility for circulating contradictory information or duplicating information.

System for Deactivating Crisis-Management Network

Just as an alert system activates crisis-management networks, the organization should standardize its procedures for deactivating the networks. Many years after World War II ended, there were still pockets of Japanese soldiers hiding in remote island areas, unaware that the war had ended. Crises are not unlike wars. The organization prepares, does battle, and then dismantles its operations. This section of the plan details the necessary actions that must be taken to facilitate a return to normalcy. The term *normalcy* should not, however, be interpreted to mean that the organization will necessarily ever be the same again. The crisis may have changed, forever and irrevocably, the character and structure of the organization.

Evaluation of Operations

Pretesting of Systems and Procedures

Trial run throughs and simulations allow organizations to practice how they will behave in a crisis. Some of the simulations are based on games theory, which enables the organization to test assumptions, establish norms, and analyze the outcomes of its crisis communications. Hypothetical situations give participants an opportunity to make decisions and negotiate the release of sensitive information. Many of these simulations focus on interaction with the media under crisis conditions.

Postcrisis Debriefing

Postcrisis debriefings allow the organization to judge how its plan worked. Experts may be called into the organization to oversee the evaluation of operations. Those involved in the crisis—including the media, emergency centers, employees, relevant communities affected by the crisis, and corporation executives—should participate in this assessment of organizational performance. To gather additional information for this evaluation, the organization can send out questionnaires to the media, community groups, and management that ask for their evaluation of how the organization dealt with the crisis. Logbooks are other useful sources of information for evaluating performance. You may want to arrange for copies of news stories, transcripts of radio and television broadcasts, and videotapes to be sent to your organization at the conclusion of the crisis. These materials can contribute to a comprehensive evaluation of organizational performance.[66]

Modifications to Crisis-Management Plan

It is necessary to update crisis-communication plans on a regular basis. Some recommend every two years.[67] This necessity arises because *personnel change, situations change,* and the company must *integrate new experiences* into the plan. After evaluating the organization's performance on one crisis situation, planners should revise the existing plan to take this learning experience into account.

Appendixes—Principles and Regulations Governing Crisis Management

- Regulations governing decision-making procedures.
- Regulations governing delegation of authority (when previously designated individuals cannot be reached).
- Regulations governing intelligence-gathering operations.
- Regulations governing dissemination of information (how to interact with media and affected parties, responsibilities of spokesperson, procedures for dealing with families of victims, procedures for verifying information, procedures for clearing press releases, etc.).
- Regulations governing the keeping of a logbook that details the technical aspects of a crisis (what is happening, what damage has been done, who has been injured or killed).
- Regulations governing management decisions (procedures to be followed, role of resource persons, ethics, etc.).

- Regulations governing the keeping of a communications logbook that would include the date and time of information releases, logs of calls in and out (e.g., media and other inquiries and responses to media, community leaders, shareholders, etc.), what was published or aired in the media, and key issues.
- Principles of effective crisis management (openness, integrity, consistency, flexibility, accuracy).
- Procedures for updating lists of those who hold crisis-management manuals and for destroying old copies of crisis management manuals.
- Lists of experts on topic.
- Lists of stakeholders who should be contacted (local police, fire, hospitals, elected officials, key civil servants, newspapers, radio and television stations, key reporters, special interest and advocacy groups, regulatory agencies, employees, union representatives, senior management, specialized functional managers, shareholders, visiting groups, tour companies, etc.)[68]

AVOIDING FUTURE CRISES

Donald Stephenson, director of corporate communications for Dow Chemical Canada, Inc., claims that "tracking and coping with issues that originate outside the organization can mean more to the future of the company than all the other functions. And knowing how to defuse a crisis and turn it into a positive development can be the most beneficial of all."[69] Another crisis management expert defined *crisis* as "a turning point," implying that the impact can be positive or negative, depending on how the crisis is managed.[70] Organizations must learn to see both opportunities and dangers in crisis situations.[71] Crises, for example, can focus attention on matters of vital concern to the organization, allowing the organization to reach audiences that it would not normally reach. Crises provide opportunities to build credibility with the media and the community.

The existence of a crisis-management plan can significantly shorten the duration of a crisis. Some studies have found, for example, that organizations without crisis-management plans experience chronic phases of crises that last two and a half times longer than those experienced by organizations with crisis-management plans. Companies without plans also report longer acute crisis phases. CEOs in one study agreed that the best part about a crisis-management plan is not just knowing "where the flashlights are kept, but knowing as well who is in charge of the flashlights and the batteries."[72]

A growing number of private, public, and voluntary sector organizations are integrating crisis management into their ongoing planning activities. An organization's environmental intelligence system should be capable of sensing emerging crises before they mature. The media, government hearings and investigations, the competition, consumer mail, surveys and polls, and political and economic indicators are useful sources of information. Consultations with stakeholders can alert the organization to problem areas before they deteriorate to crisis proportions.

The likelihood that crises will occur has not diminished in recent years; in fact, statistics indicate that crises due to "mismanagement" are increasing. With this escalation come a number of potential risks, including "long-term damage to the organization's reputation with resulting loss of confidence in its management by investors, customers, and employees; continuing deterioration of employee morale, labor relations problems, and recruitment difficulties; adverse impact on stock prices and investor relations; waste of management time and financial resources by prolonged preoccupation with crises issues; political intervention resulting in excessive government regulation, increased scrutiny of other activities and operations, and punitive actions; costly litigation (even if ultimately successful); involuntary bankruptcy or reorganization; and community relations problems."[73] Contingency planning is one of the most effective ways of ensuring that the organization is prepared when the moment of "terror" arrives.

NOTES

1. Stephen Jay Gould, cited in Alan D. Meyer, Geoffrey R. Brooks, and James B. Goes, "Environmental Jolts and Industry Revolutions: Organizational Responses to Discontinuous Change," *Strategic Management Journal,* Summer 1990, p. 93.
2. Privy Council Office document, Government of Canada, *Proceedings of the Meech Lake Meeting of Communications Managers,* October 8–9, 1987.
3. Ibid., p. 6.
4. Fraser Kelly, cited by Tim Falconer, "Beat the Odds," *Enroute,* March 1992, p. 2.
5. Government of Canada, Privy Council Office, *Crisis Management,* 1989, p. 5.
6. Steven Fink, *Crisis Management: Planning for the Inevitable* (New York: AMACOM, 1986), p. 67.
7. Speech by William Wilton (Niagara Institute) to Institute of Association Executives, cited by Peter Meyboom, "Read the Signs: Manage the Crisis," *Manager's Magazine,* Summer 1989, p. 25.
8. Adam Shell, "Crises Caused by Executive Miscues on Rise," *Public Relations Journal,* October 1992, p. 8.
9. Ibid.

10. Ibid.
11. Robert B. Irvine, "The Crisis Outlook for '92 and Beyond," *Public Relations Journal*, October 1992, p. 8.
12. Meyer, Brooks, and Goes, p. 93.
13. Anne H. Reilly, "Communication in Crisis Situations," in Jerry L. Wall and Lawrence R. Jauch (eds.), *Academy of Management Best Papers, Proceedings 1991*, 51st Annual Meeting, August 11–14, Miami Beach, Florida, p. 251.
14. Gilda Yolles Mintz, "Making Professional Services Grow," *Public Relations Journal*, May 1992, p. 12.
15. Gerald C. Meyers, *When It Hits the Fan: Managing the Nine Crises of Business* (Boston, Mass.: Houghton Mifflin, 1986).
16. Interview with John Scanlon, cited in Fraser Sietel, *The Practice of Public Relations*, 3rd ed. (Columbus, Ohio: Merrill Publishing, 1987), p. 508.
17. Meyer, Brooks, and Goes, pp. 93–94.
18. Sherry Ferguson and Stewart Ferguson, *Organizational Communication*, 2nd ed. (New Brunswick, N.J.: Transaction Books, 1988), p. 46.
19. Donald R. Stephenson, "Are You Making the Most of Your Crises?" *Public Relations Journal*, June 1984, p. 18.
20. Fink, p. 68.
21. Ibid.
22. Ibid.
23. Thomas Pexzinger, Jr., "When Disaster Comes, Public Relations Men Won't Be Far Behind," *The Wall Street Journal*, August 23, 1979, p. 1.
24. Mintz, pp. 12–13.
25. Helio Fred Garcia, "On Strategy and War: Public Relations Lessons from the Gulf," *Public Relations Quarterly*, Summer 1991, p. 30.
26. L. D. Cross, "How the Crisis Was Won," *Ottawa Business Magazine*, November/December 1990, p. 2.
27. Priscilla Murphy, "Using Games as a Model for Crisis Communications," *Public Relations Review*, Winter 1987, pp. 20–21.
28. Stephen Hume, "Reporting Disasters: What's the Media Thinking Of?" *Content*, November/December 1989, p. 19.
29. Ibid.
30. Privy Council Office, *Crisis Management*, pp. 6–7.
31. Charles Tuggle, "Media Relations During Crisis Coverage: The Gainesville Student Murders," *Public Relations Quarterly*, Summer 1991, pp. 23–27.
32. Privy Council Office, *Crisis Management*, p. 5.
33. Stephenson, p. 17.
34. Robert G. Picard, "The Journalist's Role in Coverage of Terrorist Events," in *Media Coverage of Terrorism: Methods of Diffusion*, eds. A. Odasuo Alali and Kenoye Kelvin Eke (Newbury Park, Calif.: Sage Publications, 1991), p. 44.

35. Tuggle, pp. 23–32.
36. Stephenson, p. 18.
37. Robert N. Baugnier, "Crisis Communications Management: Forewarned is Forearmed," *Emergency Planning Digest,* October/December 1984, p. 7.
38. Douglas A. Cooper, "CEO Must Weigh Legal and Public Relations Approaches," *Public Relations Journal,* January 1992, p. 40.
39. Steven B. Goldman, "Drill Legal/PR Crisis," *Public Relations Journal,* April 1992, p. 5.
40. Cooper, p. 40.
41. Michael D. Tabris, "Crisis Management," in Bill Cantor, *Experts in Action: Inside Public Relations,* ed. Chester Burger (New York: Longman, 1984), p. 62.
42. J. K. Dickson, "Contingency Planning for Emergencies," *Long Range Planning,* August 1992, p. 82.
43. Mark T. Rumptz, Robb A. Leland, Sheila A. McFaul, Renee M. Solinski, and Cornelius B. Pratt, "A Public Relations Nightmare: Dow Corning Offers Too Little, Too Late," *Public Relations Quarterly,* Summer 1992, p. 30.
44. Patricia Chisholm, "Anatomy of a Nightmare: Dow Corning Fights a Public Outcry," *Maclean's,* March 9, 1992, pp. 42–43.
45. Fink, pp. 38–45.
46. Ibid.
47. Meyboom, p. 29.
48. Reilly, p. 254.
49. Garcia, p. 30.
50. André Bouchard, "Freak Explosion Jolts Baie des Ha! Ha!" *Public Relations Journal,* October 1992, p. 43.
51. H. Seymour Smith, "How to Plan for Crisis Communication," *Public Relations Journal,* March 1979, p. 17.
52. Meyboom, p. 28.
53. Judith A. Ressler, *Public Relations Quarterly,* Fall 1982, p. 10.
54. Smith, p. 17.
55. Barry McLoughlin, "Who Shapes the Agenda?" *Manager's Magazine,* Summer 1990, p. 38.
56. Privy Council Office, *Crisis Management,* p. 12.
57. Smith, p. 18.
58. Privy Council Office, *Crisis Communications,* p. 13.
59. Ibid., p. 14.
60. Doug Newsom and Alan Scott, *This Is PR: The Realities of Public Relations* (Belmont, Calif.: Wadsworth, 1976), pp. 147–48.
61. Ressler, p. 9.
62. Ibid., p. 10.
63. Privy Council Office, *Crisis Communications,* p. 14.

64. Fink, p. 27.
65. Privy Council Office, *Crisis Communications,* p. 9.
66. Tabris, p. 64.
67. Michael Cooper, "Crisis Public Relations," *Public Relations Journal,* November 1981, p. 57.
68. Bart J. Mindszenthy, "Preparation and Process: Key Factors in Successful Crisis Management," in *The Canadian Public Affairs Handbook: Maximizing Markets, Protecting Bottom Lines,* eds. W. John Wright and Christopher J. DuVernet (Toronto: Carswell, 1988), p. 203.
69. Stephenson, p. 17.
70. Barbara Hunter, "Crisis Public Relations: Communicating in an Emergency," *Public Relations Journal,* June 1974, p. 15.
71. F. Paul Carlson, "The Long and Short of Strategic Planning," *Journal of Business Strategy,* May/June 1990, p. 18.
72. Fink, pp. 69–70.
73. Tabris, p. 59.

CHAPTER 13

MEDIA STRATEGIES FOR CONTROLLING ISSUE DEVELOPMENT

As organizations approach the beginning of a new century, they face a large array of competing issues that sometimes threaten their very survival as institutions. The problems posed by a volatile public opinion are no small part of this challenge. An organization's publics include *all-issue* publics (those concerned about all the issues), *apathetic* publics (those with little, or no, involvement in issues), *single-issue* publics (a subset of the larger population, who actively oppose or espouse a single-issue cause, for example, the slaughter of dolphins or sale of infant formula to developing countries), and *hot-issue* publics (a large part of the population, who are concerned about a single issue that has received extensive media attention, for example, abortion, toxic waste disposal, or escalating gasoline prices).[1] The same kinds of characteristics that establish issues as high priority (salience, value potency, maturity, and field of influence) also contribute to the difficulty that an organization experiences in attempting to manage the issue.

LIMITING FACTORS

Controlling the development of an issue implies the possibility for negotiating changes in people's attitudes and stances on the issues. *Yet the more salient the issue, the more difficult it is for power brokers to negotiate changes.* An issue that receives much media attention will be more difficult to manage because parties with opposing points of view have to make public shifts in order to achieve a point of compromise. In a society that values strength of conviction, those who appear to waver in conviction can suffer long-term damage to image. Rather than appearing flexible, moderate, and open to new points of view, the individual or organization that effects a public shift in position can acquire labels such as "weak-kneed," "wishy-washy," and "indecisive." Also, the more prominent the issue, the greater the number of different viewpoints regarding the issue and the more complex the process of managing the issue or achieving consensus on how it should be managed.

The more central the beliefs housed in the issue, the more difficult it is to control the activity of the issue. Ability to control an issue implies ability to influence public opinion. Central beliefs will be more resistant to change, and attitudes associated with issues that are connected to these central beliefs will tend to resist manipulation.[2]

According to one theory,[3] *Type A* beliefs are within the most central core of the belief system and constitute basic truths about physical reality, social reality, and the nature of the self. Examples are "I am Nancy Jones"; "This is a table"; and "I live in New York." Type A beliefs require 100% consensus. People acquire these beliefs early in life and continue to validate them as they go through life; Type A beliefs are seldom controversial. A person learns the beliefs by direct encounter with the belief object, and unanimous social consensus reinforces faith in them. Because of object constancy, person constancy, and self-constancy, the individual maintains a certain stability. Beliefs that concern existence and identity and the physical world have many connections with the other parts of the belief system. If a belief that is under assault has consensus within the society (which is the case with Type A beliefs), the resistance to change will be great.

Type B beliefs, which form the next layer of the belief structure, also are highly resistant to persuasion efforts. Ego-centered Type B beliefs require zero consensus. A person learns these concepts by direct encounter, but external authority does not necessarily support the concepts. The concepts may be either positive ("I am intelligent") or negative ("I am unattractive"). Phobias, delusions, and hallucinations exemplify negative Type B beliefs ("People hate me"). Negative Type B beliefs are the ones that psychiatrists seek to change. Unshared beliefs (Type B) have fewer connections with other parts of the belief system than do shared beliefs (Type A).

Effecting change in *Type C* beliefs, or authority beliefs, is easier than effecting shifts in Type A and Type B beliefs.[4] People develop authority beliefs to deal with facts of physical and social reality that have alternate explanations. These beliefs, not personally experienced, are often controversial. Reference persons and reference groups help individuals decide which Type C beliefs to accept. Authorities may be "positive" or "negative" (i.e., a person may like or dislike the authority). The individual typically regards statements originating with positive authorities as credible and discredits the views of negative authorities.

Type D beliefs emanate from authority figures: "Believing in the credibility of a particular authority implies an acceptance of other beliefs perceived to emanate from such authority."[5] Type D beliefs have fewer connections with other parts of the belief system than do authority concepts. For example, rejecting the church's views on birth control may result in limited changes in a person's belief system. The individual may still attend church, give financial support to church activities, and participate in rites of baptism and confirmation. On the other hand, rejecting the church itself as an authority may result in far-reaching changes in beliefs, with accompanying changes in lifestyle.

Although belief Types A and B are difficult to manipulate, Types C and D are easier to change because not all persons share these beliefs:

> Beliefs about such issues as birth control and sin, Communism and fascism, Russia and the South, and beliefs about such personages as Hitler and Krushchev, Lincoln and Christ do not seem to be among the most deeply held of man's beliefs. More resistant to change . . . are those taken-for-granted beliefs about identity that are incontrovertible either because they are shared by virtually everyone or because they are not at all dependent on social consensus.[6]

Type E beliefs, which are on the periphery of the belief structure, involve arbitrary and essentially inconsequential matters of taste. The maintenance of these concepts does not require social consensus. These beliefs have the fewest connections with other parts of the belief system; therefore, Type E beliefs respond more readily to attempts at persuasion than do more centrally placed beliefs.[7] Peripheral beliefs may be just as intensely held as more central ones, but because these beliefs have fewer connections with the rest of the belief system, they are more subject to change. The advertiser often achieves a persuasive goal by associating Type E beliefs with more psychologically central beliefs such as A, B, and C. The advertiser who connects a Type E belief with a negative Type B belief may be exploiting a person's primitive fears in order to achieve change in inconsequential beliefs. Mouthwash and deodorant commercials illustrate attempts to appeal by making such connections. Other persuasion attempts may seek to link Type E beliefs to Type C authority concepts to achieve change. Testimonials exemplify this variety of persuasion.[8]

The larger the field of influence, the less controllable the issue. It can be argued that local issues are more controllable than state issues, state issues are more controllable than regional issues, regional issues are more controllable than national issues, and national issues are more controllable than international issues. The reasoning behind this argument assumes that the greater the field of influence, the larger the number of variables. It is further proposed that the extension of an issue's field of influence into other issue zones will complicate the issue-management process, and the larger the array of issues that must be taken into account, the higher the likelihood that the issues will be connected with diverse, and sometimes conflicting, beliefs. The possibility that some of these beliefs will have connections with more centrally placed beliefs also grows in likelihood. A policy issue such as genetic engineering activates a network of associations that include attitudes toward other issues that have a bearing on religion and abortion. Most people have little experience with the euthanasia issue but interpret the issue in relationship to better-known issues such as abortion and the right to life. Thus, the term *field of influence* relates both to geographic and ideological spheres of intelligence.

The greater the number of dimensions to the issue (social, political, technological, economic, legal), the less controllable the issue. Investment issues, for example, may have strong economic and legal dimensions, but unless the investment issues hold a potential threat to our lifestyle, taking on additional social and political dimensions, these issues will not be so difficult to manage as, for example, environmental issues, which activate a plethora of considerations. An investment issue could take on additional dimensions in an instance where foreign ownership of American industry and agricultural land threatened national sovereignty.

The more an issue tends to respond to specific and generally unpredictable events (i.e., to be event driven), the less controllable the issue. Managing an issue implies being able to plan ahead in order to predict the timing and impact of the issue. Yet the events that serve to activate many issues are difficult to foresee. Questions of airport security, for example, will be debated most often in the wake of terrorist acts. Questions related to victims' rights and to the parole and justice system will be discussed most often following the revelation of heinous and sensational crimes. The trials and sentencing of individuals for such crimes will stimulate renewed calls for capital punishment, with groups such as Victims of Crime taking control of the media agenda. Allegations of police brutality evoke heated discussion of multicultural and racial issues. In such cases, although the initial events are not predictable, the follow-up stages are predictable (trial and sentencing of offenders, for example).

Some environmental issues will surface erratically. The revelation of unjustifiably high levels of toxins in certain areas may be ignored until an environmental rights group demonstrates a cause-effect relationship between toxin levels and birth defects or between toxin levels and higher-than-usual occurrences of cancer. The surfacing of this kind of information may be relatively unpredictable and out of the control of industry or government. The recent revelation that some studies have linked the use of cellular telephones to increased risk of brain tumors well exemplifies this point. The most highly erratic issues are tied to health concerns, and these issues will often piggyback highly visible and spectacular events. Mining disasters precipitate debates over safety issues; meltdowns generate animated discussion of nuclear power issues; famine in Africa creates a new round of talks regarding Third-World debt. An instance of mercy killing fuels the ongoing debate over euthanasia.

The greater the number of stakeholders in the issue, the less controllable the issue. When the responsibility for managing an issue becomes a shared responsibility, involving more than one business or government department, the problems in reconciling the interests of the different parties grow in magnitude. The necessity of assigning accountability may bring different organizations or units into conflict. Members of these organizations may interpret the same issue in different ways, depending on their individual perspectives and personal commitments.

The ongoing North American Free Trade negotiations illustrates this point. Although it was possible for the U.S. government, prior to free trade negotiations, to assure individual states with logging or other interests that the government would place their interests first, the administration had to be more discrete in its assurances once the negotiations were in progress. At the same time that the U.S. government has had the ongoing responsibility of convincing its commercial stakeholders that their concerns are high on its agenda, the negotiating team has had to assure Mexicans and Canadians that the U.S. team is negotiating in good faith, placing the mutual concerns of the three countries first on the agenda. Although compromises and sacrifices must be made in the process of negotiating, these points must be downplayed for domestic audiences. For this reason, it is difficult for any side to celebrate what may be perceived as gains in the negotiations when the press in three countries is covering the negotiations. Statements appearing in the U.S. press one day may be carried the same or the next day in the Canadian and Mexican press. If the U.S. negotiating team appears too pleased with a concession by Canada or Mexico, media audiences in the latter countries become skittish, the public and opposition parties react, and further negotiations become more difficult. In the same way, commentaries appearing in the Canadian or Mexican press have the potential of being picked up and carried in the U.S. press. In such cases, the maxim by which the organization operates is "the less coverage, the better." The same is often true for businesses engaged in negotiations with labor.

Regarding high-visibility issues, interest groups become engaged and special-issue publics coalesce around the issue. It is said that much of the present difficulty in issue management grows out of the number of single-issue groups that spring up, often with opposing agendas. These single-issue groups coalesce around whatever party or person adopts their issue.[9]

There are increasing signs that the American political system has indeed broken down into narrowly focused publics. Providing evidence of this trend is the growth of single-issue groups known as *political action committees (PACs)*. Unlike interest groups, which traditionally have been partners in the political system with the political parties, these groups have a narrow focus. Each one is engaged in projecting *its* issue and *its* concern as the most important of the day; the task of the PAC is to mold opinion in its favor. PACs direct their attention to policymakers at all levels of government; in 1985 there were over 14,000 officially registered national PACs. These groups represent not only a major shift of direction *away* from traditional political structures but the projection of an enormous future growth for public opinion polling. Single-issue politics makes the decision maker's job more difficult because the citizens' use of selective perception allows them to choose the "most important" issue without having to compromise, bargain, or negotiate with other groups.[10]

It has been said that "motivation concerning a particular issue or candidate drives the American citizenry much more than a tightly organized belief structure that is grounded in a wide, coherent base of knowledge."[11] The abortion issue, for example, has divided public opinion into two political camps in a way unrivaled since the Viet Nam war.[12]

The more polarized the stakeholders, the less controllable the issue. In instances where large numbers of the population have aligned themselves on opposite ends of a continuum on a specific issue, as has happened with issues related to abortion and capital punishment, the people responsible for managing the issue will find their task a difficult one.

Those who are most susceptible to persuasion are the stakeholders with moderate views, the undecided. It is unlikely that those either strongly for or strongly against a particular stance on an issue will change their attitudes. If information does not fit well within the existing belief, value, and attitude structures, the individual will filter out or distort the information. People selectively expose themselves to information with which they basically agree. The democrat tunes in to political messages from democrats; the republican changes channels when a democrat begins to speak. The term *selective retention* refers to the phenomenon whereby people forget much of what they perceive. The quantity of information that must be processed by the average person each day means that large amounts must be dumped into our subconscious storehouse. What we retain at a conscious level will frequently be the information that we find congruent with our existing beliefs and values.[13] The smoker will fail to recall the specifics of anti-smoking literature; the environmental activist may not note or remember the details of an article that suggests the atmospheric problem is not so severe as depicted by environmentalists. People maintain their equilibrium by filtering out dissonant or uncomfortable information.[14]

Factors that have been found to mediate people's responses to dissonant information are the extent to which people are well informed on the issues, the extent to which they have partisan affiliations, the strength of their political convictions, and their level of education.[15]

The more credible and resource rich the stakeholders that oppose an organizational stance, the less controllable the issue. Arguing against Nader's Raiders or Greenpeace is difficult because the groups have won credibility for their organizations and their causes. They have also become sophisticated users of the media. If organization members stand to gain little personal benefit (or even to lose) from their actions, they will earn additional credibility points with their publics. And just as credibility helps to decide the potential influence of a stakeholder, so do resources. Large bureaucratic organizations have the financial capability to produce usable press material on a regular basis. They also employ media relations personnel to cultivate relationships with reporters. Even if small, less wealthy groups gain the favor of reporters, they must still have the capability to generate usable press copy, to set professional standards, to document their claims, and to meet the press on the press's terms.

COPING STRATEGIES

Because no organization can afford to ignore all of its high-impact issues, judging these issues to be fundamentally uncontrollable serves little purpose. It is perhaps more appropriate to classify issues according to the level of investment that the organization must make if it is to influence the development of the issues. For example, some issues will require the organization to make a greater financial investment. More funds will need to be committed to tracking the issue, to changing the situation or policy that created the issue, and/or to influencing advocacy group or general public perceptions related to the organization's performance on the issue. To make a difference with the most contentious of these issues, the organization must be rich in resources and be highly credible. The organization must also have judged these issues to be high-priority issues. These points were discussed in Chapter 3 on prioritizing the organization's issues.

Chapter 3 also discussed general strategic approaches to issues management, in which the approach is governed by a consideration of *issue variables, stakeholder variables,* and *organization variables.* Avoidance or clarification strategies would be adopted for issues that are not owned by the organization. In cases of shared ownership, the organization would opt for clarification of jurisdiction. For emerging issues, the organization would limit its activities to scanning. For higher-priority issues, the organization would escalate its investment to monitoring the issue. In a situation of limited resources or diminished credibility, the organization might select low-profile, low-cost media strategies. A resource-rich, highly credible organization might choose to adopt more high-profile, high-cost strategies, including the potential for a basic policy shift.

To decide upon more specific media strategies, the organization must construct a profile of its priority issues and adjust its strategies to take specific issue characteristics into account. For example, the organization will choose not to act on some issues, regardless of cost or credibility factors:

> A successful communication campaign begins by being part of effective strategic planning to consider which policy issues will yield to communication efforts and which ones will not. Because of the hostility and rigidity of opinions surrounding some issues, some communication efforts will not succeed and therefore are not cost effective. Taking a stand on some issues is not politically or tactically expedient. The planning process must consider when it is better to change company mission, philosophy, or operations than to wage a communication campaign. Public relations, public affairs, or any other corporate communication department cannot buffer an irresponsible company from its critics. Survival demands that com-

panies recognize the reality that hostile stakeholders can discredit their statements and severely constrain their operations. Strategic planners should look at the short- and long-range public opinion, public policy picture to determine what must be said and what should be said, to whom, and with what potential effect. This stance is motivated by the conviction that communication must be judged, at least in part, by standards of cost effectiveness and good will.[16]

Communication will also be judged by ethical considerations. Before an issue is "rejected as strategically uncontrollable, the firm should consider whether there are other stakeholders (suppliers, customers, or potential sources of new products) whose mutual interest and participation could make an issue controllable."[17] Inflation may not be in the controllable range, but issues related to the impact of inflation may be controllable (e.g., housing subsidies and rent controls).

To better understand an issue, the organization can generate an issue profile, using the following questions as a guide:

Typology and Character of the Issue

Does the issue have social, political, legal, economic, technological, ecological, or other dimensions?

Is it local, state, regional, national, or international?

What social values are at the heart of the issue (belief in the individual, collective responsibility, etc.)?

Is this a first-order or second-order issue? If not a first-order issue (e.g., abortion is a first-order issue linked directly to the value of right to life), does the issue have indirect links to a first-order issue (any issue pertaining to women in conflict with the law is linked to women's rights, which, in turn, is linked to the value of equality of opportunity)?

Genealogy of the Issue

What is the history of the issue?

Its roots?

What is its relationship to other issues?

Behavioral Characteristics

What kinds of events or incidents tend to activate the issue? Is it self-sustaining and ongoing?

Does it ride piggyback on other issues (e.g., immigration issues piggyback unemployment issues and unemployment issues piggyback other economic issues)?

Is the issue controllable? Semicontrollable? Uncontrollable?

Is the issue erratic or predictable in its behavior?

How does the issue interact with other issues (e.g., free trade with investment issues, CEO resignation with relocation of plant)?

Influence

How prominent is the issue? What is its place on the public/media agenda?

Is the issue critical or noncritical to the organization?

Will the issue have a direct or indirect impact on the organization (e.g., direct impact of environmental policies on bottom line; indirect impact on long-term development of firm)?

Will the issue have limited or far-reaching consequences (local, state, regional, national, global)?

Is it likely to spawn other issues (e.g., deregulation of airlines generating issues related to air safety)?

Advocates/Adversaries

Once the issue is activated, what groups and/or individuals will become engaged?

What is their level of influence? Their credibility? Their potential access to resources? Their access to people who can make a difference?

Is the interest group institutionalized (has a large relatively stable membership and long-standing informal access to government), quasi-institutionalized (has a shorter collective history and a more formal relationship to government), or emergent (has membership coalescing around an issue but lacks a coherent articulated structure and has no well-defined political influence)?

Through what media do these groups make their opinions known? Meetings? Demonstrations? Petitions? Advertising campaigns? Circulars? Letters to the editor? Talk shows? Write-in campaigns? Lobbying legislators?

Does the issue divide people along lines such as language or culture, region, socioeconomic class, age, occupation (e.g., AIDS-related issues dividing the business, the religious, and government communities)?

Have single-issue groups formed especially for this issue? (Groups such as Greenpeace started as single-issue groups but expanded the focus of their concern, whereas Students Against Drunk Driving and Mothers Against Drunk Driving remain single-issue groups.)

Life Span of the Issue

At what stage of development is the issue? Emergent? Administrative or legislative phase? Other?

At what future date is the issue likely to reach maturity? In the near term? Medium term? Long term?

What environmental factors could encourage its development?

What factors could inhibit its development?

Is there any event that could cause the issue to reach maturity at an earlier date than anticipated? Could the issue reach crisis dimensions?

On the basis of answers to the previous questions, an organization can best choose the appropriate strategic response to its issue. Constructing an events calendar for purposes of predicting issue behavior is another technique used in issues management. Consider, for example, the issue of economic sanctions against South Africa. This issue can be charted on an events calendar. Occasions such as the anniversary of the Soweto uprising, Nelson Mandela's birthday, and the anniversary of Mandela's release from prison will precipitate increased coverage of South African issues, as well as calls by interests groups and the media for stepped-up sanctions. There will be increased media coverage of South African issues at the time of Commonwealth meetings. The interaction between different issues will also be taken into account in drawing up events calendars. Plotting relevant events connected with related issues helps the analyst graph the behavior of a given issue.

CRITERIA FOR MEDIA STRATEGIES

The success or lack of success that an organization experiences when it attempts to control and manage its issues will depend, in large part, on the nature of its interaction with the media. Some organizations manage this interaction better than others. An understanding of how media organizations operate is critical for an organization that seeks to persuade its publics, or even for a organization that wishes to avoid unwanted media coverage of its issues. Some of the factors that should be taken into consideration are described in the following sections.

Meeting Media Deadlines

Every media establishment faces deadlines; every reporter and editor and producer adheres to these deadlines. Organizations and individuals that recognize these time limitations will be better able to manage their issues. For example, media are biased toward early release of information: Stale news is no news. Therefore, if an organization releases controversial information shortly before media deadlines, there is a high likelihood that initial coverage of the event or issue will be uncritical. Media will not have time to react; they will print a hard news version of what they receive. Editorial coverage or commentaries will follow later, *if* the item maintains its newsworthiness and *if* it is not bumped from the media agenda by a more current event. Organizations are often willing to wager that the news item will lose some of its appeal or impact, given an adequate lapse of time between the event and the analysis of the event.[18] At other times, organizations withhold unfavorable news releases until the "current edition is on the street." A late Sunday morning release is a favorite time for those who don't want the news to reach the public before Monday evening. When Ford announced Nixon's pardon, he did so on a Sunday morning, hoping that fewer newspapers would carry the story.[19] A weekend press conference will draw fewer reporters than one called on a weekday.

The reverse of this situation occurs when an organization releases news at a time when numerous people are available to receive the information. Many groups plan their events for times when the events can be easily covered by the media (for example, near prime time for live television coverage). Political parties plan their conventions so that chosen leaders make their acceptance speeches at peak viewing times. Information released in the opening week of the fall television season will reach optimum numbers of the viewing public.

Providing prepackaged materials to the media also increases the chance that the organization's viewpoint will be aired. Many reporters working on tight deadlines make only minor changes to materials received in press kits. Similarly, layout editors often fill last-minute news holes with materials prepared by public relations personnel.

Meeting the Commercial Requirements of the Media

Television is answerable to its sponsors, and news programming is an important source of its revenues. For that reason, this medium is vulnerable to manipulation by those who understand its requirements. The following news values are reflected in media coverage:

- News tends to stress the highly visual.
- News tends to stress the sensational, which is often the unusual and the bizarre.
- News tends to stress the negative.
- News tends to stress the controversial.
- News tends to stress the simple over the complex.
- News tends to stress the immediate.
- News tends to stress elite personalities.
- News tends to stress the views of opinion leaders.

Highly visual material attracts media audiences, as does the sensational and the bizarre. If pro-lifers position themselves before an abortion clinic and thrust baby gifts at women entering the clinic, the event will almost surely be televised. The picture of a young widow, at the graveside of her husband killed in military action, will receive preference over a less-emotional depiction. Images of starving children in Somalia and the bleeding victims of an airline crash have the stark dramatic quality that television demands. Visually interesting settings will be preferred over uninteresting or inappropriate settings.[20]

As the watchdogs of society, the media also tend to be drawn to stories that expose scandal, fraud, and corruption (i.e., weaknesses over strengths). In the same way, news stresses the controversial; it thrives on public debate over opposing points of view. Today's news is preferred over yesterday's news.

There is a tendency in the press to prefer issues that are simple, easy to verify, and nontechnical. There is also a tendency to avoid issues that require interpretation and analysis, leading some groups to complain that their causes are overlooked because the media is unwilling to deal with the historical elements of the issues. Those who write speeches for executive officers and politicians understand the function of "press lines," lines intended to grab the reader and to ensure media coverage. The media looks for statements that are "uneditable, dramatic, concise, and synoptic . . . capable of being delivered in under 35 seconds by a skilled speaker."[21] Obtuse wording, jargon, bureaucratese, vague and rambling statements are not acceptable to the media. The concrete and the picturesque sell.

Organizations that want to *minimize* the chances that they will receive coverage sometimes use unclear and abstract language. In a report titled "Politics and the Oval Office," the Institute for Contemporary Studies suggested that President Reagan had suffered from too much uncontrolled news coverage. To limit future coverage, the Institute recommended that Reagan should "overwhelm media representatives with technical data,"[22] thus circumventing the possibility that the media could complain about lack of access to information. Dry news, the report stated, was unpalatable to the media.

The presence of a celebrity increases the chances that media will cover an event or issue. Exclusive interviews with influential figures guarantee media attention. Incumbents in office have an advantage over those who only aspire to office. Information leaked from high places will be media worthy. Because news organizations require ongoing good relations with people in positions of power, they are likely to accommodate these individuals and groups, in return for continued access.[23]

Much has been written on the phenomenon of pack journalism, a practice that evolved largely because of pressures that media organizations put on their reporters.[24] If an event is listed in a United Press International or an Associated Press (wire service) calendar, the media will be afraid *not* to cover the event. If a respected journalist or an elite medium covers an issue, other media will follow. Reporters traveling in packs borrow quotations from each other and compare perceptions prior to writing their stories. They check with pack leaders to learn what is likely to be the lead story for the day. In the same way, if a story appears in the *New York Times,* local newspapers will soon follow this precedent.

Meeting the Technical Requirements of the Media

Photographers and television camera crews have needs of a technical nature. They require adequate light, adequate facilities for accommodating sound and video equipment, and a good vantage point for filming or witnessing events. An organization that wants live media coverage plans its event so that daytime conditions guarantee optimum light levels. Ensuring the presence of these conditions contributes to the likelihood that a media organization will choose to cover the organization's event.

The tendency of television to prefer close-up shots to distance shots means that organizations should anticipate and plan for personal and intimate encounters rather than public encounters. Speech delivery, dress, and language style should be geared to the proxemics of television. Television reaches into the most intimate of settings—bedrooms and living rooms. "Shouting in public" is not an appropriate way to deliver a television message to these audiences.[25]

WHY ORGANIZATIONS SEEK TO CONTROL THE MEDIA

Understanding the nature of media deadlines, the commercial pressures, and technical requirements equips an issue-management specialist to work with the media rather than against it. The common belief is that if you don't get the media to work for you, they will work against you. Media respond well to those who are familiar with media's needs, which explains why so many organizations have traditionally hired ex-journalists to act as media relations specialists. Those who plan strategically to control their issues take these basic operating principles into account.

Television, in particular, has certain characteristics that make it a threatening medium to corporate executives and government leaders. Television has the potential to transfer unedited and uncensored information. The *visual nature* of television makes it more threatening than other communication media such as radio. Radio necessitates the translation of ideas into the local or national language, and this translation brings with it a certain level of control. Television, on the other hand, has visual properties; in fact, its visual content is its dominant characteristic. Language is not required to mediate the content of television. Even without knowledge of the language, people can access television, making it difficult for authority figures to control this medium.

The *immediacy* of television means that the public can receive information at the same time as authorities. Information was traditionally controlled by those at the top of the authority pyramid, whether in business or government. The people at the bottom were prisoners of the lack of information. In modern technological society, information flows in such a way that those at the bottom of the pyramid have direct access at the same time as those at the top of the pyramid, sometimes sooner. A different information-flow model applies, one that could be termed a *simultaneous access* model. It is much more difficult to control issues or govern groups in situations where competing parties have equally high levels of access to alternative information. In East Germany, Romania, the former Soviet Union, and other Eastern bloc countries, the ruling elites suffered the consequences of uncontrolled information flow within and between countries. In a world characterized by massive information exchanges among corporations, political systems, groups, and individuals, decision making becomes incredibly complicated. Debates over mergers, for example, may move into the public arena before decisions are finalized in the corporate boardrooms. It is expected that companies will be open in their communication policies, but shareholders and top management often fear the effects of imprudent disclosures. Public companies that appear too profitable, for example, may open themselves up to the potential of take-overs if they reveal the extent of their assets,[26] whereas revelations of difficulties can trigger panic sell offs of stocks.

When the public responds to this kind of information in unexpected ways, policy makers must react quickly to accommodate public opinion. New communication technologies reduce the information "float time" between the occurrence of an event and the circulation of information about the event.[27] Ideally, a business or government would like to have time to formulate strategies for implementing official policy and to manage the issues placed before the public. But the mass media detect incipient issues and disseminate discourse on the issues, so that media-public interaction sets the agendas. Much of the determination and control of issues has passed from business and government institutions to media organizations. Although this state of affairs is supposed to be the democratic ideal, it puts corporations and governments in a follower role, not always the best position. As a result, many administrations spend a great deal of their time attempting to second guess public opinion. Even the most authoritarian of societies must reckon with these same forces of public opinion, and the love-hate relationships that many government and corporate leaders have with the media result from the feeling that the forces influencing public opinion are outside the control of either traditional institution. Editors, producers, station managers, and owners of communication media are the new gatekeepers, and government and corporations often perceive themselves to be in conflict with these organizations.[28]

A third characteristic of television which makes it threatening to authority institutions is its *subjective camera*. Television has a reputation for being the most objective and egalitarian of the media, yet there is a high degree of subjectivity and selectivity to this medium. Television demystifies authority figures and brings them down to earth for us. In the same way that a political cartoonist concentrates on some characteristics and builds an image that is a caricature, the media, especially television, can concentrate on one or another characteristic of a prominent figure and build an image of the person. The image will not always be flattering or true. Television portrayed former President Gerald Ford as bumbling and inept, forever falling down airplane steps or tripping over his own feet. Yet Ford was a trained athlete, a former college football player. Former Canadian Prime Minister Joe Clark was similarly depicted, shown losing his luggage when traveling abroad and having a near miss with an bayonet, which was unsheathed for a military welcoming ceremony. "Saturday Night Live" has caricatured more than one presidential hopeful. Corporation executives are also not exempt from the critical eye of television. Some studies have concluded that television shows tend to depict characters in business corporations as behaving in evil ways.[29] The subjective camera of television, combined with its ability to be an eyewitness to events, can quickly diminish the credibility of authority figures and institutions.

The *perceived selling power* of television causes those in positions of influence to see it as a threat. Legislators, for example, know they will be seen by those back home and evaluated on the basis of this performance; they believe that the standards by which they will be judged will be set by television.[30] Because television gives leaders the impression that they are constantly being evaluated, it is not unusual for their first priority to be to look good, rather than to do their jobs well. Such responses are a reaction to the perceived power of public opinion and the perceived ability of television to sell images just as it sells soap, toothpaste, and deodorant.[31]

Another characteristic of television that influences people's perceptions of the medium is its *tendency to be drawn to the bizarre and the outrageous*. The driving forces behind media are economic: Media organizations operate for a profit. Making that profit means being competitive, that is, selling newspapers and garnering radio and television audiences. The formula for what constitutes news is clearcut: The unusual and the sensational sell newspapers and television news programs. As previously observed, television also has a *tendency to focus on celebrities and the elite* elements of society. Causes that can claim the active support of celebrities such as Elizabeth Taylor, Glenn Close, and Robert Redford have a better chance of being covered, and scandals that involve personalities such as Princess Diana or the CEO of a major North American company will almost certainly receive publicity. This particular characteristic of the media to focus on celebrities and society elites strikes fear into the hearts of many corporate executives and government leaders.

The *interpretative function* of television (as well as that of other media) is viewed with suspicion by groups in positions of authority. In the same way that the media tend to set agendas and to exert pressures on governments and corporations, they also act as opinion packagers. They interpret the debate over public and corporate issues. It is now standard practice for media comment to follow statements made by public figures. Immediately following campaign debates, messages to the nation, or major policy statements by corporate leaders, media analysts assess the performance of the spokespersons and draw conclusions on what the statement means. The process can be depicted as follows: organizational spokesperson → interpreter → public.

Other stages may intervene, in which elite opinion leaders discuss ideas with their followers. There may be a two-step or a multistep process involving these elite opinion leaders, for example: organizational spokesperson → interpreter → opinion leaders → public.[32] The inability of corporate and government executives to have a direct influence on their publics can be a source of frustration. They believe that everything they say is restated, reworded, analyzed, and dissected by those who mediate and package public opinion. They complain that what remains of their words, in the end, is the journalist's or the elite opinion leader's interpretation. Much of the public, they say, never hears or gives proper consideration to their original words. Their complaints are made more real by the tendency of television to use voice overs in order to fit excerpts within time restraints and to compensate for technical problems such as poor audio content.

The *watchdog function* of the media makes authority figures uneasy. The media champions the public's right to know, whereas corporations argue the right to guard trade secrets and to protect the ability of the organization to be competitive. Government claims the right to withhold information for the public good. The resulting situation is that the establishment and the media often see themselves as being in conflict.

Finally, the *interactive potential in new media* generates a certain level of discomfort among authority figures. The possibility for instantaneous referenda and a new dimension of participatory democracy emerged with cable technology. Those who have little faith in the wisdom of the masses say that collective ignorance could come to govern the daily workings of government and the decisions of business and industry.

Managing an organization's issues requires understanding how best to respond to the requirements and demands of media. The influence of the media is powerful; it is not to be taken lightly by any organization.

CONCLUSION

Satisfying the expectations of diverse publics with often-conflicting interests, while at the same time fulfilling one's mission and mandate as an organization, can be draining on morale and exhausting on resources. The additional challenges posed by trends toward globalization, the relocation of organizational boundaries, rapid technological change, and an evolving information environment contribute to the complexity of the task. In response, organizations are developing cultures that place a greater value on partnering and sharing. They are forming alliances with suppliers, customers and clients, employees, franchisees, all levels of government, universities, and even competitors. Cross-sector partnerships are becoming increasingly common, and a trend toward technological fusion is driving many of these partnerships. Organizations are also stressing the importance of continuous learning, emphasizing the role of research and analysis in decision making. Strategic and operational planning have assumed a new importance, flowing naturally out of these information-acquisition processes. At the foundation of the learning organization is consultation (i.e., taking the views of all the organization's stakeholders into account).

Organizational survival in the 21st century will require, above all else, a new mindset that includes an appreciation for democratic process and a political approach to governance. Such an approach implies an adherence to the belief that people at all levels of the organization can contribute and make a difference, a willingness to consult, a belief in the importance of continuous learning, a conviction that sharing is the better alternative to competing, and a willingness to translate knowledge into strategic direction and operational process.

NOTES

1. James E. Grunig and Fred C. Repper, "Strategic Management, Publics, and Issues," in *Excellence in Public Relations and Communication Management,* ed. James E. Grunig (Hillsdale, N.J.: Lawrence Erlbaum Associates, Publishers, 1992), p. 139.
2. Milton Rokeach, *Beliefs, Attitudes, and Values* (San Francisco: Jossey-Bass, 1968).
3. Ibid.
4. Ibid., p. 181.
5. Ibid., p. 10.
6. Ibid., p. 57.
7. Ibid., p. 182.
8. Ibid., p. 181.
9. Claire Badaracco, "Religion Lobbyists in the Public Square," *Public Relations Quarterly,* Spring 1992, p. 32.
10. Jerry L. Yeric and John R. Todd, *Public Opinion: The Visible Politics,* 2nd ed. (Itasca, Ill.: F. E. Peacock Publishers, 1989).
11. Yeric and Todd, p. 116. See also pp. 110–15 for a discussion of the decline in party identification.
12. Badaracco, p. 31.
13. Classic studies illustrating this point include P. Kendall and K. Wolf, *The Personification of Prejudice as a Device in Educational Propaganda* (New York: Bureau of Applied Social Research, Columbia University, 1946); Eunice Cooper and Marie Jahoda, "The Evasion of Propaganda," *Journal of Psychology* 23 (1947), pp. 15–25; Paul F. Lazarsfeld, Bernard Berelson,

and Hazel Gaudet, *The People's Choice* (New York: Columbia University Press, 1948); and Bernard Berelson, Paul F. Lazarsfeld, and William N. McPhee, *Voting* (Chicago: University of Chicago Press, 1954). A summary of some of the early works on selective perception, selective exposure, and selective retention appears in Joseph T. Klapper, *The Effects of Mass Communication* (New York: Free Press, 1960). Examples of more recent studies with similar findings include Fred W. Grupp, Jr., "The Magazine Reading Habits of Political Activists," *Public Opinion Quarterly,* 38 (1974), pp. 264–70; David O. Sears and Steven H. Chaffee, "Uses and Effects of the 1976 Debates: An Overview of Empirical Studies," in *The Great Debates: Carter vs. Ford,* ed. Sidney Kraus (Bloomington: Indiana University Press, 1979); Thomas E. Patterson, *The Mass Media Election* (New York: Praeger Publishers, 1980); and C. Cannell and J. MacDonald, "The Impact of Health News on Attitudes and Behavior," *Journalism Quarterly,* 36 (1956), pp. 315–23.

14. Leon Festinger, *A Theory of Cognitive Dissonance* (Stanford, Calif.: Stanford University Press, 1962).

15. Numerous studies in political communication have confirmed these variables as influential factors.

16. Robert L. Heath, "Communication Campaigns for Influencing Key Audiences," in *Strategic Issues Management,* ed. Robert L. Heath and Associates (San Francisco: Jossey-Bass, 1988), p. 171.

17. John Stoffels, "Environmental Scanning for Future Success," *Managerial Planning,* November/December 1982, p. 11.

18. Kathleen Hall Jamieson and Karlyn Kohrs Campbell, *The Interplay of Influence,* 2nd ed. (Belmont, Calif.: Wadsworth, 1988), pp. 89–91.

19. Ibid., p. 89.

20. Interview with Craig Oliver, Ottawa, Ontario, April 17, 1989, reported in David Taras, *The Newsmakers: The Media's Influence on Canadian Politics* (Scarborough, Ont.: Nelson Canada, 1990), p. 156. The concept of the pseudo-event was first developed in Daniel Boorstin's *The Image: A Guide to Pseudo-Events in America* (New York: Atheneum Publishers, 1962).

21. Jamieson and Campbell, p. 96.

22. Ibid., pp. 99–100.

23. This point is discussed in Robert G. Picard, "News Coverage of the Contagion of Terrorism," in A. Odasuo Alali and Kenoye Kelvin Eke, *Media and Terrorism* (Newbury Park, Calif.: Sage Publications, 1991), p. 60.

24. "History on the Run: Media and the '79 Election," National Film Board, Canada, 1979. Also Dan Nimmo and James E. Combs, *Mediated Political Realities,* 2nd ed. (New York: Longman, 1990), pp. 168–74, and Taras, pp. 89–91.

25. Stewart Ferguson and Sherry Ferguson, "The Proxemics of Television: the Politician's Dilemma," *Canadian Journal of Communication,* Spring 1978, pp. 26–35.

26. Joseph J. Penbera and Charles Bonner, "The Director's Role in a Take-over Bid," *Journal of Business Strategy,* May/June 1990, pp. 39–42.
27. Peter G. W. Keen, "Redesigning the Organization through Information Technology," *Planning Review,* May/June 1991, pp. 4–15.
28. Some argue the opposite point of view, saying that traditional political and economic interests control the media; this viewpoint is not espoused by most corporate and government leaders, who perceive themselves to be in conflict with the media.
29. Sari Thomas, "Bad Business? A Reexamination of Television's Portrayal of Businesspersons," *Journal of Communication,* Winter 1992, pp. 95–105. Thomas argues against the results of some of these studies.
30. Shanto Iyengar and Donald Kinder, *News that Matters* (Chicago: University of Chicago Press, 1987), pp. 116–18.
31. Taras, pp. 95–112.
32. The classic literature on this topic is embodied in the following two studies: Paul F. Lazarsfeld, Bernard Berelson, and Hazel Gaudet, *The People's Choice* (New York: Columbia University Press, 1948) and Elihu Katz and Paul F. Lazarsfeld, *Personal Influence: The Part Played by People in the Flow of Mass Communication* (Glencoe, Ill.: Free Press, 1955).

INDEX

Other excellent resources available from Irwin Professional Publishing . . .

THE CORPORATE COMMUNICATOR'S QUICK REFERENCE

Peter Lichtgarn

ISBN: 1-55623-892-4 (192 pages)

This essential guide explains the duties, responsibilities, and functions of today's corporate communicator by anticipating the challenges and answering the questions communicators face daily.

POWER VISION

How to Unlock the Six Dimensions of Executive Potential

George W. Watts

ISBN: 1-55623-808-8 (206 pages)

Shows how managers can exceed their career and life goals by viewing themselves honestly, capitalizing on their strengths, and overcoming their weaknesses. Also tells how to become a more effective manager, one who makes profitable and positive contributions to your company.

GETTING THE WORD OUT

How Managers Can Create Value with Communications

Frank Corrado

ISBN:1-55623-785-5 (212 pages)

Shows how to relate communications to the bottom line—and increase profits. You'll discover how to communicate effectively with employees, customers, the media, and your community.

Available at fine bookstores and libraries everywhere.